EXPLORING CULTURES
A Prentice Hall Series in Anthropology

This volume is dedicated
to
PROFESSOR DOUGLAS L. OLIVER,
Dean of Pacific Studies,
University of Hawaii

CONTEMPORARY PACIFIC SOCIETIES
Studies in Development and Change

edited by
Victoria S. Lockwood
Southern Methodist University

Thomas G. Harding
University of California, Santa Barbara

Ben J. Wallace
Southern Methodist University

preface by
Douglas L. Oliver
Professor Emeritus
University of Hawaii and Harvard University

PRENTICE HALL, *Englewood Cliffs, New Jersey 07632*

Library of Congress Cataloging-in-Publication Data

Contemporary Pacific societies : studies in development and change /
   edited by Victoria S. Lockwood, Thomas G. Harding, Ben J. Wallace :
   preface by Douglas L. Oliver.
      p.   cm. -- (Exploring cultures)
   includes bibliographical references (p.) and index.
   ISBN   0-13-174723-1
   1. Oceania--History. 2. Oceania--Social conditions.
   3. Acculturation--Oceania.   I. Lockwood, Victoria S., (date)
   II. Harding, Thomas G. III. Wallace, Ben J., (date) . IV. Series.
   DU28.3.C66 1993
   995--dc20   91-32354
                                    CIP

Acquisitions Editor: Nancy Roberts
Copy Editor: Kathryn Beck
Editorial/production supervision and
   interior design: Elizabeth Best
Cover Designer: Karen Salzbach
Prepress Buyer: Kelly Behr
Manufacturing Buyer: Mary Ann Gloriande

©1993 by Prentice Hall, Inc.
A Simon & Schuster Company
Englewood Cliffs, New Jersey 07632

Excerpts adapted from *Samoan Planters: Tradition
and Economic Development in Polynesia* by Tim O'Meara,
copyright ©1990 by Holt, Rinehart and Winston, Inc.,
reprinted by permission of the publisher.

Printed in the United States of America

10 9 8 7 6 5 4 3 2 1

0-13-174723-1

Prentice-Hall International (UK) Limited, *London*
Prentice-Hall of Australia Pty. Limited, *Sydney*
Prentice-Hall Canada Inc., *Toronto*
Prentice-Hall Hispanoamericana, S.A., *Mexico*
Prentice-Hall of India Private Limited, *New Delhi*
Prentice-Hall of Japan, Inc., *Tokyo*
Simon & Schuster Asia Pte. Ltd., *Singapore*
Editora Prentice-Hall do Brasil, Ltda., *Rio de Janeiro*

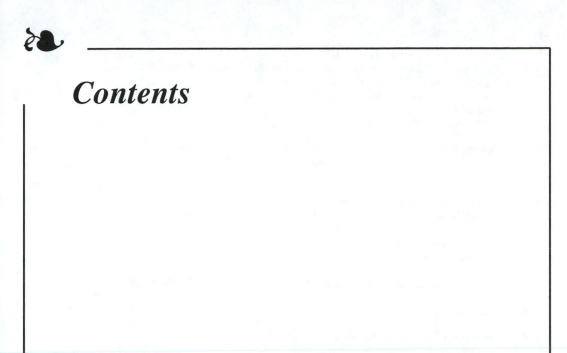

Contents

Section I: The Colonial Legacy and Nation Building

Section II: Markets, Development, and Capitalism

List of Tables
and Numbered Figures

Preface

Douglas L. Oliver

In another preface—the one to a survey of Oceania's pre-European native cultures (Oliver 1989b)—I expressed disagreement with the implications contained in the currently fashionable slogan, "The Pacific Way," and added that, although that slogan may be evocative and euphoric, the modicum of reality it reflects is the product, not of similarities among all those *indigenous* cultures, but rather of the homogenizing effects of colonialism. However, after reading the chapters in the present collection, I am led to question whether "colonization" has in fact produced any region-wide homogenization beyond, say, the adoption of metal tools and European garments, or a wider use of multi-purpose money—or a nearly universal taste for alcohol.

Compare, for example, the Tubuaians (as described by Victoria Lockwood) with the Pohnpeians (as described by Glenn Petersen): the former accepting and reveling in their economic dependency upon their colonial masters, the latter rejecting—with creative deliberateness—the comfortable dependency offered to them by theirs. Or, for another example, contrast the eager and successful adoption of "capitalism" by some Pacific Islanders (for example, some New Guinea Highlanders, male and female), with the negative and defeatist responses of many others, in the Highlands and elsewhere, to alien influences of similar kinds.

Clearly, the widely dissimilar responses to colonialism exemplified in the chapters in this book serve to confirm the wide range of cultural differences that prevailed in the Islands before they were colonized. But they also bear witness to the wide differences obtained among the colonizing powers as well.

Acknowledgments

The editors would like to express their appreciation to the many people and institutions whose support have made this volume possible. First, and most importantly, we would like to acknowledge the scholars who have contributed chapters to this volume. Their hard work and dedication is reflected in the quality of the analyses presented here. We would also like to thank the contributors for their patient willingness to make revisions in their chapters, always with the needs of the volume as a whole foremost in their minds.

We would also like to thank the Center for Pacific Islands Studies, Robert C. Kiste, Director, for giving us permission to use their regional maps in this volume. The maps were created by Manoa Map Works of Hawaii.

We are grateful to the University of California Press for permission to reprint a shortened version of Lorraine Sexton's article on the Wok Meri Movement; it was originally published in Denise O'Brien and Sharon Tiffany, editors, *Rethinking Women's Roles: Perspectives from the Pacific* (1984). We would also like to thank Holt, Rinehart, and Winston for their permission to use material originally published in Tim O'Meara's *Samoan Planters* (1990) in sections of his chapter in this volume.

In the preparation of this volume, we have benefited greatly from the contributions made by a number of graduate students of the Department of Anthropology, Southern Methodist University. Darlene Evans and Katherine Browne worked long hours assisting with editing and proofing. Jesse Ephraim handled much of the computer processing of the final manuscript. Their help was instrumental and much appreciated. We would also like to thank the Department of Anthropology at SMU for its support in making this student assistance available to us.

1

An Introduction to Contemporary Pacific Societies

Victoria S. Lockwood
Southern Methodist University

Scattered like confetti across an ocean covering more than one-eighth of the earth's surface, the thousands of islands and coral atolls of the Pacific basin (see Map 1–1 on page 2) are inhabited today by over eight million people.[1] The Pacific campaigns of World War II brought the islands to the world's attention, and ended their relative isolation. Since that time, the region has modernized rapidly, and the islands' Melanesian, Polynesian, and Micronesian societies have entered a new era of accelerated political, economic, and social change.

Our goal in this volume is to document the major themes in the recent sociocultural evolution of Pacific Islands societies. In so doing, we hope to make a contribution towards answering the following questions: What kinds of people are Pacific islanders today? What kinds of societies are they fashioning for the future? How are Pacific societies tackling the myriad political, economic, and social challenges they face in the 1990s and beyond? Appreciating the great social diversity that characterizes the region is the first step in a greater understanding of the nature and impact of change in contemporary Pacific societies.

PACIFIC ISLANDS DIVERSITY: A HISTORICAL OVERVIEW

Pacific Islands societies are highly diverse not only in their sociocultural organization, but also in their strategies and responses for confronting change over time. This diversity is partly rooted in important cultural differences which emerged among island societies in the precontact era. It also has its roots in the variable physical characteristics and resource endowments of the region's atolls, volcanic islands, and continental islands. But perhaps the most significant influence from which this modern social diversity has flowed

1

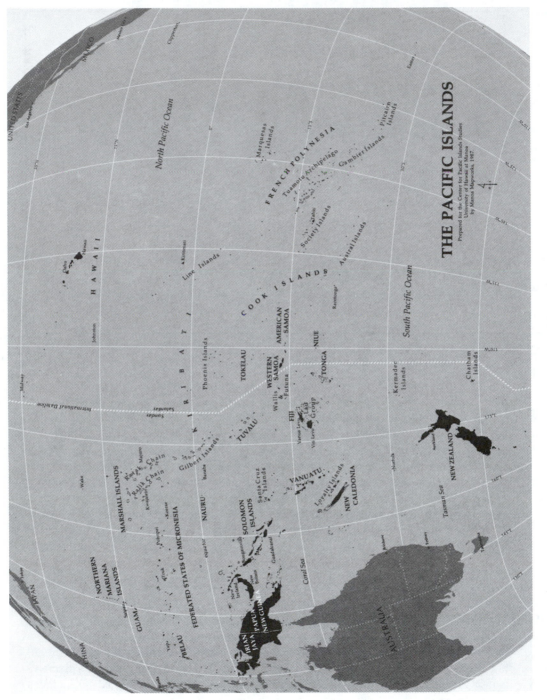

MAP 1-1 The Pacific Islands

has been the variety of historical experiences with foreign colonialism and intervention. Thus, the unique character of each contemporary island society reflects the interplay of culture, habitat, and history.

Cultural and Environmental Variability

The islands of the Pacific, the last area of the world to be occupied by humans, were settled by people whose ancestral origins were in Southeast Asia. About forty thousand years ago or more, the first migrants settled New Guinea and a few of the nearby islands (Oliver 1989a; Shutler and Shutler 1975: see Map 1–1). These groups were speakers of Papuan, or non-Austronesian, languages and their descendants today inhabit areas of coastal and highlands New Guinea, parts of the Solomon Islands, and Vanuatu.

Archaeologists hypothesize that subsequent migrations into the region did not take place until many thousands of years later, at about six thousand years ago (see Oliver 1989a). These peoples differed culturally and linguistically from the earlier migrants, and they are known today as the ancestral stock of the Austronesian-speaking Melanesians. These peoples settled islands in Melanesia, finally reaching Samoa, Tonga, and Fiji by about 1500 B.C. (thirty-five hundred years ago).

Scholars believe that the peoples of Samoa, Tonga, and Fiji evolved along their own distinctive cultural paths after 1500 B.C., gradually forging the traditions which would become the foundations of Polynesian culture and society. Migrant groups from these particular islands (proto-Polynesians) then went on to settle the islands of the eastern half of the Pacific, taking their cultural system with them. Archaeological evidence suggests that the Marquesas were first populated by about 400 A.D., and that by 800 A.D. all of the major Polynesian islands, including Tahiti, Hawaii, Easter Island, and New Zealand had been settled (see Campbell 1989; Bellwood 1987).

There is less clear information on the settlement of the Micronesian islands of the northern Pacific. Some anthropologists believe that Belau, Yap, and the Marianas were colonized by Austronesian speakers who migrated in a predominantly eastward direction from the Philippines and northern Moluccas at about the same time the proto-Polynesians were settling Samoa, Tonga, and Fiji, about 1500 B.C. The other Micronesian islands—Kiribati, the Marshalls, Kosrae, Pohnpei, Chuuk (Truk), and so on—were probably settled in the later part of the first millenium B.C. by a northern flow of migrants from Vanuatu and the eastern Solomons.

There has been much debate about the forces which caused these extensive population movements. While certainly a few island discoveries were accidental—fishermen or seafarers lost at sea—anthropologists now believe that most islands were settled by groups who had purposefully left their home islands in search of new islands to colonize. Population growth, scarce resources, and warfare probably caused groups to search for new lands. Setting out in outrigger canoes laden with the essentials they would need to survive in a new home, including root crops and pigs, early migrants utilized their extensive seafaring expertise to travel the long distances between islands.

In the process of adapting to the particular environmental conditions they encountered, Pacific peoples diverged along their own cultural paths. Nevertheless, they shared basic features of their way of life, including agricultural and fishing economies; social systems organized around lineage, clan, and village and community units; and a strong seagoing orientation (with the exception of the inland populations of the large continental islands of New Guinea, New Caledonia, New Zealand, and of some of the larger volcanic islands) (Oliver 1989a). The smaller island populations shared the various problems associated with adaptation to island environments, including those arising from small land areas, limited resources, and, in some cases, geographic isolation.

Three broadly defined cultural "configurations" can be identified in island Oceania: Melanesian, Polynesian, and Micronesian.[2] Polynesian peoples inhabit the eastern part of the Pacific basin, Micronesian peoples the northwestern part, and Melanesian peoples the southwestern part. However, there are a number of Polynesian outlier societies located in the Melanesian and Micronesian culture areas. The three major culture areas of the Pacific are shown in Map 1–2 on page 5.

One can generalize about the constellation of cultural traits that characterized each of the precontact, regional cultural configurations. It is important to remember, however, that such generalizations, by definition, disregard the intracultural variation characteristic of Melanesian, Micronesian, and Polynesian cultural groups (see Thomas 1989). For example, while it was generally true that the precontact social structures of Polynesian societies were stratified and those of Melanesian societies were more egalitarian, it was also true that some of the island Melanesian societies were probably as stratified (and possessed "chiefs") as some of the smaller Polynesian atoll societies (who were much more egalitarian than their Polynesian cousins on the high volcanic islands). Bearing in mind the limitations of overly broad generalizations, I offer the following summary profiles of Pacific island cultural systems.

Most indigenous Polynesian societies—those occupying the predominantly high volcanic islands of the southeastern region of the Pacific within the triangle formed by Hawaii, New Zealand, and Easter Island (encompassing Tahiti, Samoa, Tonga, and other smaller islands)—developed stratified chiefdoms. In the most sociopolitically complex chiefdoms (Hawaii and Tahiti, for example), there were well-developed class structures, an administrative bureaucracy (usually the close kin of the chief), and craft specialization. Polynesian religion centered around the supplication of a pantheon of gods and goddesses. Two concepts that were central to Polynesian religious world view were *mana* (sacred power or efficacy) and *tapu* (forbidden by sacred sanctions). The gods and high-ranking chiefs possessed the most *mana*. Polynesian economies were based on intensive taro cultivation, tree-crop plantations (coconuts, breadfruit), and fishing.

Most Micronesian societies—those occupying the Marshall, Marianas, Caroline, and Gilbert (now Kiribati) Islands—struggled to prosper on low-lying atolls. With the exception of the region's few high islands (such as Belau and Pohnpei), these societies were notably less politically and economically stratified than those of Polynesia, although many were organized into chiefdoms. Islanders made their living by cultivating swamp taro and breadfruit, but because agricultural lands were limited, Micronesians depended heavily on the sea for their subsistence. Micronesian religions centered around a small pantheon of gods (relative to Polynesia), as well as beliefs in spirits and ghosts. The concepts of *mana* and *tapu* were also important in Micronesian religious ideology.

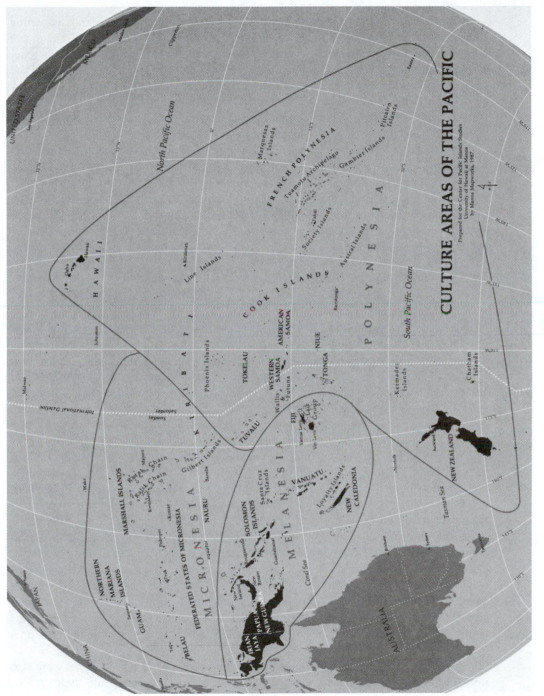

MAP 1–2 Culture Areas of the Pacific

Melanesian societies—the populations of New Guinea and of the islands extending southeastward to Fiji (including New Britain, New Ireland, the Solomons, Vanuatu, and New Caledonia)—were generally more egalitarian than those of Polynesia and Micronesia. Communities were smaller and structured along lines of kin-group affiliation and village networks. In many areas informal, yet influential, leaders known as "Big Men" organized activities involved in gardening (horticulture: mostly root crops) and pig raising, warfare, cult activities, and ceremonial exchange systems. Melanesian religion was concerned with beliefs in spirits and ghosts, as well as the practice of magic and sorcery.

As this description of Pacific societies suggests, some of the precontact cultural diversity found in the region can be linked to the ways in which different peoples adapted to the particular opportunities and constraints offered by their island habitats. For example, the region's more structurally complex and populous societies tended to develop on the resource-rich, volcanic islands. In contrast, atolls offered a more limited resource base and usually supported smaller and structurally less complex societies (see Sahlins 1958).

Variability in the Islands' Historical Experience with Colonialism

Like other areas of the non-Western world, the indigenous societies of the Pacific islands were "discovered" by the West during the era of European exploration and imperialist expansion. Following discovery, traders and merchants moved into the region looking for sandalwood, trepang (sea cucumbers), and other items to exchange for Chinese spices and tea in the flourishing trans-Pacific trade (see Wolf 1982; Oliver 1989a). Whalers came to the islands seeking oil and other whale products for the European and American markets. Not long after, Europeans seeking to establish plantations (sugar, copra, coffee, cocoa, and cotton) and missionaries bent on converting the native populations to Christianity arrived in significant numbers.

While particular islands' contact experiences varied greatly, "the usual marks of contact" were "disease, bloodshed, depopulation, land-grabbing, commercial exploitation, and disruption of native life..." (Keesing 1941:6). Islanders were exposed to Western diseases to which they had no immunity and many islanders died as a result. In a few of the most extreme cases, as much as 90 percent of an island's population was lost.

The Europeans also brought with them their own institutions, values, and material goods. To peoples whose economies were based on reciprocity, redistribution by chiefs, and ceremonial exchange, Westerners introduced market exchange and capitalist relations of production. In order to acquire the Western material goods islanders had learned to covet, they began to participate in the commercial production of cash crops and other commodities sought by the Europeans. They were also induced to sign on as wage laborers on the plantations or in the mines of the foreigners. Island socioeconomic life took on a new theme: the search for money.

Western political institutions, legal codes, and systems of property rights were also introduced (or imposed) as the Europeans incorporated the islands into their various colonial empires. At the same time, missionaries began proselytizing, introducing a foreign god and legislating what they considered to be appropriate forms of family life, male-female relations, personal attire, and behavior. In most Pacific societies, missionary influence permeated virtually every aspect of island life, becoming a major force in the transformation and Westernization of indigenous society.

Although all Pacific societies were significantly altered by their contacts with the West, the changes that have been described were not imposed or felt uniformly across all island societies. Indigenous society was transformed most markedly on those islands that attracted large numbers of European settlers, such as New Caledonia, Hawaii, and New Zealand. On New Caledonia, the French settlers took land they intended for plantations away from the native Melanesians and put them on "reservations." The Maori of New Zealand and the Hawaiians also lost much of their land to white settlers and, as a result, their societies fell into disarray and came close to extinction.

In other cases, the European presence was less destructive of indigenous society. Instead of taking land for plantations from Kosrae Islanders in Micronesia, the Germans, for example, were content to obtain the copra they sought by encouraging islanders to produce it themselves on their own coconut plantations (see Peoples 1985). As a result, the disruption of native life was of lesser magnitude than that experienced by the islands which became settler colonies.

The islands that were of little interest to the Europeans were the least touched and altered. These islands included those that were not suitable for plantations, those that possessed few attractive resources, and those that were geographically isolated. In these cases, basic features of islanders' precontact way of life, including some of their indigenous institutions, were left more intact.

The intensity of the Western presence was not, however, the only factor responsible for the islands' various degrees of transformation. Perhaps the more significant factor was the manner in which the different European powers in the region restructured the island societies they subjected to their colonial control (see Lingenfelter 1977; Hanson 1973).

The two major colonial powers in the Pacific were the British and the French. The British, who governed most of the western South Pacific, followed a practice of indirect colonial rule in some areas under their control, including Fiji, Tonga, the Cook Islands, and the northern Gilbert and Ellice Islands (today Kiribati and Tuvalu, respectively). In these cases, native institutions were somewhat preserved and protected, and local affairs were left largely in native hands. As a result, Fiji is today still governed by its chiefs, and Tonga is ruled by a king, the descendant of traditional chiefs. In both Fiji and Tonga, however, the rights, duties, and prerogatives of contemporary leaders, as well as the political institutions associated with them, differ significantly from the precontact patterns. In other areas under British control, most notably the central and southern Solomons and Papua (southeastern New Guinea), colonial intervention was more direct and thus more disruptive of indigenous institutions. Administrative responsibility for Papua was transferred to Australia in 1906.

The French intervened directly in most of the Pacific societies they colonized, believing it to be their prerogative, as well as their duty, to implant French civilization in the region. Accordingly, they worked to undermine and destroy indigenous institutions, and ultimately to replace them with French institutions. Indigenous populations could then be more readily assimilated into the French colonial empire.

In French Polynesia no vestige of the indigenous chiefly system or political structure remains today, having been replaced by the French civil code, an elected assembly, and local island mayors. In addition to French Polynesia (the Society Islands, Austral Islands, the Marquesas, Tuamotus, and Gambiers), France followed this policy in its other colonies: Wallis, Futuna, New Caledonia, and the Loyalties. The New Hebrides (Vanuatu) were administered as a joint colonial condominium of both the French and the British.

The other islands of the Pacific came under the control of other nations whose colonial policies varied greatly. Spain claimed many of the Micronesian islands in the early 1500s, but only exerted influence of any significant degree over Guam and Saipan. Spain lost its holdings as a result of its defeat in the Spanish American War in 1898. The United States took control of the Hawaiian Islands and American Samoa, and was ceded Guam by Spain in 1898. From their colonial base in Indonesia, the Dutch controlled the western half of New Guinea (today, Irian Jaya), while Chile extended its dominion over Easter Island. The Germans acquired Western Samoa and northeastern New Guinea, and were ceded the Marshall, Caroline, and northern Marianas Islands of Micronesia by Spain in 1898.

Germany lost its Pacific possessions following its defeat in World War I. The Micronesian islands went to Japan, Western Samoa to New Zealand, and the northeastern half of New Guinea and the northern Solomons to Australia (as a League of Nations—mandated territory; after World War II, they became a United Nations Trusteeship). Following World War II and the ultimate Allied victory, Japan lost its holdings in Micronesia and the islands became the United Nations Trust Territory of the Pacific Islands, administered by the United States.

As this summary of colonial history in the Pacific Islands suggests, the various islands of the Pacific experienced foreign intervention in many different ways. Each colonial power left its own particular imprint on its island possessions. A few of the islands, like those of Micronesia, experienced a succession of colonial regimes—first the Spanish, then the Germans, the Japanese, and, finally, the Americans. In general, the highly diverse characters of contemporary Pacific island societies—their various social institutions and organizations, forms of government, and degrees of Westernization—are largely the product of their respective colonial encounters.

RECENT TRENDS IN PACIFIC ISLANDS' DEVELOPMENT

Although contemporary Pacific Islands societies are different in many ways, it is nevertheless possible to isolate major themes in their recent sociocultural evolution. Generally speaking, patterns in that evolution can be identified within the broad categories of political, economic, social, and religious change.

Political Development

The decolonization of many Pacific Islands societies has been one of the most important transformations sweeping the region in recent decades. Starting in the early 1960s, a number of Pacific societies achieved their independence (or were granted effective self-government) from the various Western states which had either colonized them in the eighteenth and nineteenth centuries or assumed their administration at the end of World Wars I or II. These new nations include Papua New Guinea (1975), Vanuatu (1980), the Solomon Islands (1978), the Cook Islands (1965; self-governing in association with New Zealand), Fiji (1970), Tonga (1970), Kiribati (1979), Nauru (1968), Tuvalu (1978), Niue (1974; self-governing in free association with New Zealand), and Western Samoa (1962). Within the former U.S. Trust Territory, the Federated States of Micronesia, the Republic of the Marshall Islands, and the Republic of Belau have recently achieved self-government in association with the United States.

Most of the islands still governed by foreign nations have achieved a measure of local political autonomy. This is true of the Pacific colonies France has retained: French Polynesia, New Caledonia, and Wallis/Futuna (now French Overseas Territories), as well as of American Samoa (administered by the U.S. Department of the Interior), Guam (a territory of the U.S.), the Northern Marianas (a commonwealth of the U.S.), Easter Island (Chile), and Tokelau (New Zealand). In contrast, Irian Jaya (West New Guinea) remains firmly under the direct colonial control of Indonesia, the legacy of its previous status as a Dutch colony. Hawaii became one of the fifty United States in 1959. The political entities of the Pacific are shown in Map 1–3 on page 10.

Political development in the contemporary, postcolonial Pacific has focused on the fashioning of new political, legal, and judicial structures. This process has proven to be complex, for the political institutions in place at the time of independence were those left by the former colonizers. In some cases islanders have found that their new societies are well served by these introduced institutions. In others, islanders' perceive them to be vestiges of a colonial past incompatible with their vision of the future.

For virtually all Pacific Islands societies, political development has also involved the careful negotiation of affiliations and relatively close relationships with various Western nations. In particular, Australia, New Zealand, the United States, and France possess entrenched political and strategic interests in the region, and they have sought to preserve a significant degree of influence over island affairs.

To the West today, the significance of the islands is mainly linked to their strategic location in the expanse of Pacific ocean that separates the economic and military powers of the West (U.S. and Europe) from those of the East (Japan, China, and the Soviet Union). At various times some of the islands have been used as sites for military installations and bases by foreign nations (the U.S., France, and Britain; until World War II, Japan). At the present time, France operates a nuclear weapons testing facility and military bases in French Polynesia, and the United States maintains a number of major military bases and missile test ranges in the islands of Micronesia (on Guam and in the Marshall Islands in particular) and, of course, in Hawaii. One can only speculate about how these Western nations' strategic interests might change in the "post" Cold War era.

Although they do not keep military bases in the islands, Australia's and New Zealand's interests are somewhat parallel to those of the other Western nations. They consider the western Pacific to be their "backyard" and thus central to their security. They also consider it to be a natural area for expansion of their export markets. Overall, they believe the islands of the western Pacific to be their particular strategic, political, and economic sphere of influence.

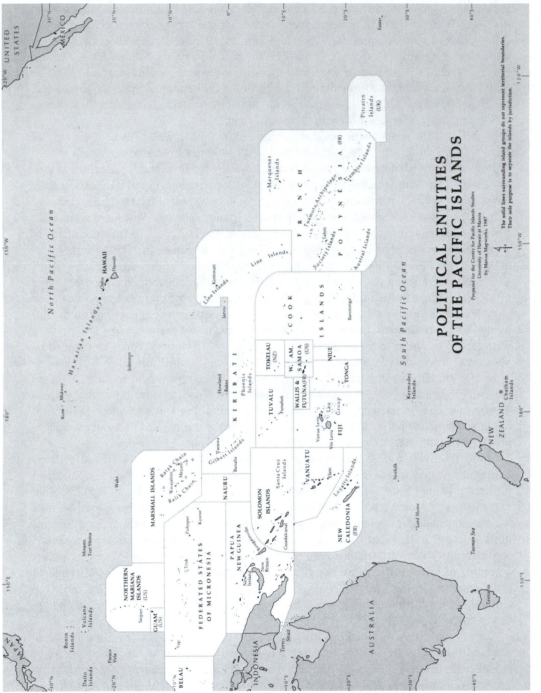

POLITICAL ENTITIES
OF THE PACIFIC ISLANDS

Prepared for the Center for Pacific Islands Studies
University of Hawaii at Manoa
by Manoa Mapworks, 1987

The solid lines surrounding inland island groups do not represent territorial boundaries.
Their sole purpose is to separate the islands by jurisdiction.

MAP 1–3   Political Entities of the Pacific Islands

Specific islands are also of interest to the Western industrialized nations because they possess valuable resources, although the vast majority are notably poor in this regard. New Guinea has extensive oil, timber, copper, gold, and other mineral deposits, and New Caledonia produces much of the world's nickel. The tiny island nation of Nauru was a major phosphate producer, although its mines are now largely exhausted.

There is also growing Western and Japanese interest in the possible exploitation of the Pacific's rich marine resources, including fish and seabed minerals. Those marine resources found within the 200-mile zone that surrounds each island nation are legally owned by it, as stipulated by the Law of the Sea Convention. The 200-mile Exclusive Economic Zones of Pacific Islands nations are shown in Map 1–4 on page 12.

For their part, many of the Pacific Islands have become financially dependent on the substantial foreign aid that many Western nations offer in exchange for their ongoing military and political presence in the region. (In recent years, Japan has also become a major aid donor.) Not surprisingly, the islands have chosen to maintain a close political affiliation with these nations. Examples of this phenomenon are numerous. The Cook Islands are independent "in free association" with New Zealand; Cook Islanders are citizens of both the Cooks and New Zealand, and many Cook Islanders now reside and work in New Zealand. The people of the Northern Marianas have agreed (under substantial pressure from the United States) to retain their affiliation with the United States in a commonwealth status (instead of voting for independence) and to house U.S. military bases; in exchange they receive extensive financial supports from the U.S. French Polynesians, when given the opportunity to vote in referendum on independence, chose to remain a territory of France and thereby to be largely supported by it. In general, Western nations remain an ever-present and, one might argue, neocolonial force shaping the political development of both the independent and nonindependent Pacific nations.

Another factor that makes the political development of a small number of Pacific Islands nations more complex is their ethnic pluralism. Unfortunately in these particular cases, ethnic pluralism has fostered internal divisiveness. The foundations for internal strife were laid during the colonial era when communities were arbitrarily grouped into administrative units (for example, Papua New Guinea, the Solomon Islands, some of the Micronesian states) with complete disregard for tribal and interisland cultural differences. Ethnic pluralism was also generated on some islands (notably Fiji, Tahiti, and Hawaii) when white settlers imported Asian laborers (mainly Chinese and East Indians) to work their plantations or mines. On these islands today there are large Asian populations. On Hawaii and Tahiti, Asians are relatively well integrated with other segments of the population. This, however, is not true of Fiji, where there is open conflict between indigenous Fijians and Fiji Indians.

Economic Development and Migration

Since the end of World War War II, Pacific Islands societies have become increasingly integrated into regional and international markets. For many islanders, this major economic transition has involved a shift from subsistence agricultural production to cash-earning activities. More specifically, islanders have adopted cash cropping (commercial agriculture) or other forms of commodity production (crafts and so on), or have

200 MILE EXCLUSIVE ECONOMIC
ZONES OF THE PACIFIC ISLANDS

Prepared for the Center for Pacific Islands Studies
University of Hawaii at Manoa
by Manoa Mapworks, 1987

Lines depicting the 200 mile Exclusive Economic Zones are generalized and should NOT be used for any legal purpose.

MAP 1–4   200 Mile Exclusive Economic Zones of the Pacific Islands

become wage earners. Their greater integration into the market system has also involved their ever-increasing consumption of manufactured goods and consumer items from the industrialized countries. Today, indigenous technologies, crafts, and material culture have largely been replaced by imports.

Structural changes in some island societies have accompanied this transition, including a shift from familial kin-group ownership of land and other property to Western-style individual ownership. In general, where capitalist enterprise has been adopted by islanders, capitalist relations of production have largely replaced indigenous systems of exchange and production.

In recent decades, many Pacific Islands societies have sought to develop and diversify their largely agrarian economies and to raise their standard of living. As they strive for economic development, many of the region's smaller islands and atolls find that their economic options are limited. Most are poor in resources (oil and other sources of energy, minerals, and so on), and they depend on the export of one or two primary commodities, usually copra (the dried meat of the coconut from which oils are extracted) or fruits; a few islands export fish, shell, or sugar (Fiji). Distances from markets, transportation inefficiencies, and limited labor power contribute to these islands' economic marginality and unsuitableness for industrialization even on a small scale. A number of islands are working to develop tourism as one source of income, although this option is itself fraught with problems of various sorts (see Wu 1982; Finney and Watson 1977). To ensure their economic security, people in some of these economically marginal island societies have retained their subsistence-oriented production of staple food crops, as well as their "traditional" systems of exchange and distribution, usually alongside market production and market institutions.

While economic opportunities on some islands are limited, many islanders nevertheless aspire to the material standard of living of the rich West introduced during the colonial era. Imports of manufactured items (radios, automobiles, electronics, and even food) have increased sharply in recent decades, creating huge trade deficits in many island nations and promoting their ever-greater dependency on foreign aid.

The larger volcanic islands, and especially the continental islands, are in a much more favorable economic situation than the smaller islands and atolls. Papua New Guinea, for example, possesses abundant natural resources, rich agricultural lands, and a large population (approaching four million). It has pursued a course of fast-paced, capitalist development over the last decade. For this nation's peoples, many of whom still live in relatively "traditional" rural communities, the local-level growth of capitalism has set in motion a fundamental socioeconomic transformation of their way of life.

The widening economic differential between less-developed rural areas and urban areas, between the small, marginal islands and the larger, richer islands, and between the islands in general and rich, Western nations has promoted widespread population movements since the end of World War II. Many Pacific Islanders are abandoning rural areas and seeking the greater employment opportunities, higher earning potentials, and the more Western lifestyle found in towns and cities. Several decades ago, for example, Papeete, Tahiti, was a struggling port town of several thousand people. Today it is a bustling, overcrowded city where the vast majority of the Tahitian population, about one hundred thousand people, is concentrated; the entire territory's population is today about

one hundred and eighty thousand. Other islanders have emigrated to international metro-
politan centers like Los Angeles, Honolulu, or Auckland. About one hundred thousand
Pacific Islanders, for example, now live in Auckland, while Los Angeles and San
Francisco possess growing populations of Samoans and Tongans.

Such massive population shifts have exacerbated the problems of rural underdevelopment in Pacific Islands societies and generated new problems linked to overly
rapid growth and urbanization of the region's port towns. International emigration
from some of the smaller islands (for example, Niue—population 2,800; the Cook
Islands—population 19,000; and Tuvalu—population 8,200) has generated a situation
in which a larger proportion of the islands' populations now reside in foreign countries
than at home. The at-home population has become increasingly dependent on remittances sent home from family and kin for their major source of income.

Social and Religious Change

In addition to the many political and economic changes which have swept the
region, pervasive social changes have also taken place. Many of these changes are directly
linked to the more direct and sustained contacts between island societies and Western
culture that have characterized the last several decades. Improved communication (satel-
lites, television, and other media) and transportation networks (shipping, airlines), as well
as the expansion of regional tourism and islanders' international migration, have greatly
accelerated the pace of Western acculturation.

For many islanders, greater immersion in particular aspects of Western culture
has resulted in an intensified clash between their own indigenous cultural values,
lifestyle, and world view and those of the West. Young people can barely remember
the "traditional" lifestyles of their grandparents, and their values and aspirations now
differ significantly not only from those of their grandparents, but also those of their
parents. The Western media (television, magazines, and movies), for example, present
compelling views of life in the rich industrialized nations, creating aspirations among
young people that are not only financially beyond reach, but frequently at odds with
local values and customs. Moreover, as islanders become more enmeshed in Western
culture, they cannot remain immune to many of its negative aspects which appear to
be a part of the cultural package. These include drug and alcohol abuse, juvenile
delinquency, and urban gangs.

Moreover, as island societies modernize, the "traditional" roles and statuses once
occupied by various categories of people—men, women, young people, elders—are
changing rapidly. The structure of gender relations is in flux as women have new
opportunities for formal education, to obtain jobs, or to practice family planning. Young
people no longer want to bend to the authority of their extended family or kin group elders,
but to pursue more individualistic courses. In general, new patterns of community and
interpersonal relations, including gender relations, are emerging. And finally, money and
material wealth are increasingly taking the place of traditional criteria linked to kinship
and community service for achieving social prominence in Pacific Islands communities.

As Western institutions, values, and consumer goods are increasingly incorporated
into the cultural systems of Pacific Islanders, they must somehow be reconciled with

islanders' own values and understandings of the world. As this reconciliation process proceeds, Pacific Islanders are ultimately negotiating new cultural identities and world views.

As the pace of change escalates, religious activity has become a dynamic forum for social and political expression in many contemporary Pacific Islands communities. This is not surprising considering the central role the Christian church plays in these communities; it is the ideological and social cornerstone of islanders' lives. Religious activity—ritual, socioreligious movements, cults—has become a vehicle through which islanders are negotiating new social identities and world views. In addition, in some communities religious activity has provided the framework for political activism—sometimes antiwhite and anticolonial. Such activism can be seen in the cargo cult activity of a number of Melanesian societies, as well as in the contemporary nationalistic, "resistance" movements of the New Zealand Maori and native Hawaiians.

As one considers the dynamic role the Christian church plays in contemporary Pacific societies, it is important to remember that Pacific Christianity, like the Christianity of so many other non-Western regions, typically embodies elements of indigenous belief and world view. Moreover, since islanders were converted by missionaries representing a large number of different denominations, some mainstream and some fundamentalist, there are presently many different forms of Pacific Christianity.

THE GOALS AND SCOPE OF THE VOLUME

Most of the chapters in the volume are ethnographic case studies of particular island societies or communities, and each examines a particular issue related to that group's contemporary situation. In no instance, however, are the issues described unique to those single islands or communities. Instead, these issues are relevant to, and representative of, either island societies at large, or of particular subsections of island societies. In addition to the case studies, the volume includes several chapters that specifically examine regional or subregion-wide processes—cult activity in Melanesian societies, patterns of drug and alcohol use across Pacific Islands societies, and evolving political statuses in the Micronesian islands.

We have sought to include a representative cross-section of the types of societies found in the three culture areas: Melanesia, Micronesia, and Polynesia. The reader will note, however, that a larger number of studies (eleven of the volume's seventeen case studies) deal specifically with Melanesian societies. This bias reflects the fact that Melanesians are today over 75 percent of the total population of island Oceania (Polynesians: 20 percent; Micronesians: 5 percent—see Crocombe 1987). It also reflects the fact that Melanesian populations have been the subjects of the largest proportion of recent anthropological research in the region.

The reader will also find that the chapters in the volume reflect a number of different theoretical and methodological approaches to the study of sociocultural change. Indeed, they represent something of a cross-section of the types of anthropological research being conducted in the region. We believe this theoretical and methodological diversity offers the reader an opportunity to gain some insight into the many different ways anthropologists go about investigating problems and finding meaningful explanations of cultural phenomena.

Finally, these studies are by no means an exhaustive discussion of the many changes taking place in contemporary Pacific societies or of the status of all islands. As discussed earlier, Pacific Islands societies are a diverse group and their particular situations vary greatly. No one volume can do justice to that diversity. Moreover, the sheer number of important change-related topics itself precludes consideration of all of them in one volume. Omissions from this volume include discussions of the impact of tourism on Pacific Islands societies and of environmental concerns related to the economic development of fragile island ecosystems. In general, our aim has been to outline, in a broad and representative way, some (if not all) of the major trends of economic, political, social, and religious change in the region.

The Importance of Studying Contemporary Pacific Societies

Identifying the major trends in the evolution of contemporary Pacific Islands societies is an important and timely endeavor for several reasons. First, it expands our knowledge of some of the world's non-Western peoples whose ways of life are being rapidly transformed. Second, documenting change in Pacific societies generates a descriptive foundation for more broadly analyzing the general processes of sociocultural change, specifically *Westernization*. Under conditions of Western-style modernization, why do societies change as they do? Why are some elements of Western culture accepted and incorporated, while others are rejected? How do external forces for change—colonial administrators, missionaries, merchants, the Western media, and so on—intervene in non-Western, "traditional" societies and change them? In what ways do non-Western peoples selectively participate (or not participate) in their own transformation? In what ways have islanders inititated change? How do they perceive and assess the changes transforming their societies?

Describing change and development in the contemporary Pacific is also important for another reason: the challenges islanders are confronting today are in many ways similar to those faced by the other developing nations and peoples of the Third World. Those challenges include postcolonial nation building, underdevelopment and poverty, rapid urbanization, massive population migration (rural to urban and local to international) and dislocation, and severe cultural dislocation. How Pacific Islanders have experienced and dealt with these problems, whether successfully or not, is directly relevant to the experiences and strategies of other Third World peoples. The studies in this volume, then, are useful for both intraregional and cross-cultural comparisons of Third World social change and development.

Finally, by labeling Pacific Islands societies as "Third World" nations, we hope to encourage substantial revision of their overly romanticized popular image. Many Westerners visualize the islands as the lush tropical paradises of swaying coconut trees and carefree natives described in novels and depicted on travel posters. Not only is this image inaccurate, but it does a great disservice to the region's peoples by diverting attention away from the hard realities many island societies face today, and from islanders' efforts to confront those realities and build new societies.

Acknowledgments: In the preparation of this introduction, I have benefited greatly from the comments and suggestions of Tim O'Meara, Mac Marshall, Tom Harding, Darlene Evans, Jane Albritton, and Katherine Browne. Responsibility for any errors or omissions, however, is my own.

NOTES

1. The term "confetti" was first used by Jean-Claude Guillebaud (*Les Confettis de l'Empire*, Paris: Seuil, 1976) to describe the far-flung island outposts that make up France's world-wide colonial network.
2. Excellent discussions of precontact Melanesian, Polynesian, and Micronesian cultural systems can be found in Oliver (1989a and 1989b).

The Colonial Legacy and Nation Building

INTRODUCTION

The major themes that dominate recent political development in Pacific Islands societies are (1) the consolidation of nation states and building new political structures, and (2) the negotiation of political affiliations with various Western nations. As islanders work to achieve their goals in these areas, they confront at every turn the ever-present legacy of the colonial era: foreign institutions and bureaucratic structures, foreign values, and pressure from foreign powers to devise policies amenable to their strategic interests in the region (neocolonialism). The chapters in this section of the volume consider various dimensions of these processes in the newly independent nation states of Tonga, Fiji, and Vanuatu, and in the nonindependent island societies of French Polynesia and the Micronesian Islands (whose present political statuses are quite diverse).

George Marcus (Chapter 2) provides some insights into the "global" strategies the tiny and resource-poor kingdom of Tonga has developed since independence in 1970 to put itself "on the world map." One of these strategies has involved the establishment of international family networks through emigration. Tongan elites, in particular, have capitalized on these international connections to enhance their position at home. Marcus also describes how, in this increasingly outward-looking, internationalizing society, Tonga's King has sought to create a strong nation-state base at home. His efforts have involved other types of "global strategies" aimed at securing a niche for Tonga in the world economy and promoting its development through foreign investment and other schemes.

Martha Kaplan (Chapter 3) describes the efforts of Fijians to consolidate their new nation state (independent in 1970) in the problematic context of extreme internal ethnic conflict. She presents a charged picture of the volatile relations between native Fijians and Fijian Indians whose ancestors were brought to the islands as contract laborers. Kaplan proposes that institutionalized inequality and hostility between the two groups is the modern legacy of short-sighted British colonial policies. She then discusses several recent political coups in the context of Fijian political instability.

William Rodman (Chapter 4) describes some of the difficulties the new nation of Vanuatu has encountered in its effort to bring its seventy-plus inhabited, dispersed islands under one legal system. He argues that in the "administrative vacuum" generated by the Anglo-French colonial condominum government, the populations of many of the far-flung islands were largely able to ignore colonial efforts to control them, maintaining their own autonomous legal systems under the auspices of chiefs. Following independence, Vanuatu Islanders in peripheral areas (outer islands) steadfastly maintained their legal "semiautonomy," undermining efforts to consolidate the new Vanuatu state.

Robert Kiste (Chapter 5) examines some of the characteristics of American neocolonialism in the various new political entities of Micronesia. Although agreeing to grant independence to the islands, the United States has sought to retain its military installations and bases in the islands. To do this, Kiste discusses how the U.S. has created various financial and administrative ties to the islands, and directly promoted the new nations' economic dependency. Kiste suggests that the United States will continue to be a major neocolonial force shaping the political development of this region.

Victoria Lockwood (Chapter 6) examines neocolonialism in France's Overseas Territory of French Polynesia. France has sought to generate positive sentiment on the part of the Tahitian population regarding its ongoing control of the islands, as well as regarding the presence of French military bases and nuclear installations in the territory. To do this, France has implemented "welfare state colonialism," a neocolonial strategy not unlike that pursued by the United States in Micronesia. Lockwood describes how this strategy has been implemented on the rural island of Tubuai, and how islanders have become financially dependent on France. She then describes how Tubuai Islanders perceive their dependency and how they feel about French control of their islands.

2

Tonga's Contemporary Globalizing Strategies:
Trading on Sovereignty amidst International Migration

George E. Marcus
Rice University

The Kingdom of Tonga,[1] a western Polynesian archipelago with a total land area of 269 square miles and a population of over one hundred thousand, is one of the last monarchies in the world where the King rules as well as reigns. The relative stability of the monarchy, founded in 1875 by George Tupou I, has rested on early, resourceful accommodation to Christianity and a Western form of government, as well as on vigilance against foreign influence (including a constitutional prohibition on the sale of land and the strict control of leasing).

Since independence (1970), Tonga's King, Tupou IV, has presided over an increasingly "international" society, one which has created world wide family networks through international migration. In addition, the King has actively pursued international "schemes and strategies" to create a meaningful niche for his impoverished island nation in world affairs. The major actors in both of these "global" strategies are Tonga's contemporary aristocratic elite (nobles of ancient chiefly lines), as well as a newly emerging "modern" elite of church families, government bureaucrats, and Tongan merchants descended from early European traders. Following a brief discussion of Tonga's early history and its contemporary social organization, I discuss the nature of these global strategies and their implications for Tonga's future.

Early History

Tupou I's declaration of a constitutional monarchy for Tonga in 1875 was a conscious adaptation to increasing European colonization of Polynesia. The declaration was preceded by Tupou's treaty making with foreign powers to secure formal recognition of Tonga's political independence, as well as by his growing suspicions concerning the ambitions of the Australian-controlled Wesleyan mission. The Wesleyans had implanted a strong church organization in Tonga, through which much of the early Westernization occurred. Their support was significant in Tupou's ability to consolidate his own power among the major chiefly factions.

During the scandal-ridden reign of Tupou II (1893–1917), Tonga reluctantly became a British protectorate. Under the ensuing long and stabilizing rule of Queen Sālote (1917–1965), British protection came to be appreciated and nurtured by the monarch as an asset to her culturally conservative reign. The British shielded Tonga from the turbulence of world politics and economics and also provided the funnel through which the introduction of external influences could be closely controlled by the kingship (except for the massive Allied presence during World War II). The social reforms of Tupou I, especially his land policies and his mode of selectively assimilating Western institutions, took shape in the everyday lives of Tongans during the reigns of his successors, and Tonga experienced an insulated development typical of monarchies preserved and protected by the British (Marcus 1978).

During the past century, Tonga has remained principally an agrarian economy. However, that economy has become increasingly dependent on cash-crop production and money (see Bollard 1974). Most recently, the islands' fragile economy has also come to depend on external injections of aid from patron states, on remittances from the large numbers of Tongans working overseas, and on direct investment by overseas church organizations seeking to develop their Tongan missions.

THE CONTEMPORARY STRUCTURE OF TONGAN SOCIETY

At the top of this highly stratified society, a powerful centralized kingship oversees the operations of a weak state bureaucracy and of largely autonomous church hierarchies whose influence permeates all villages and towns of the kingdom. A class of nobles composed of some of the most powerful chiefly lines of the old order holds hereditary privileges and estates; however, they are considerably constrained in their formal powers and in the degree to which they are able to exploit the land and people of their estates. At the base of society is a small-holding, rural peasantry which, although possessing secure tenure to hereditary plots of land, has fluctuated in its participation in commercial agriculture.

In the past century, a commoner elite has gradually developed in the new social order. This group is composed of prominent families in the church hierarchies (often the children or siblings of leading clergymen) and of individuals who have distinguished themselves in the local educational system and have been rewarded with bureaucratic positions. Distant or forgotten kinship linkages between these commoners and chiefly lines have been renewed and elaborated, but only subsequent to the commoners validating their status through achievements in the new institutions. The commoner elite is thus truly a new elite group created by the processes of Westernization; it is not an old-style elite in new form.

Local commerce has been in the hands of a segment of the Tongan elite who are the descendants of European traders who earlier settled in Tonga. These so-called half-caste families, of German, English, and Scandanavian heritage, have occupied an ambiguous position in the kingdom—on the surface integrated into a homogenous culture, but with specialized functions as merchants. These Tonganized Europeans have also acted at various times as close advisors and representatives of the King, especially in managing relations with overseas Europeans. Large portions of their wealth acquired in Tonga have been spent and invested abroad, thus making them among the first Tongans, along with the royal family itself and their close aristocratic kin, to create family networks and resource bases abroad.

The first overseas university degree was earned by the present monarch in the early 1940s, although a number of prominent noble and commoner families had already been educating their children in overseas, church-affiliated schools. Permanent residence, purchase of land overseas, and the exploitation of other opportunities have often followed the sending of children overseas (principally to New Zealand) to be educated. In much the same way, education is the oft-stated impetus for current internal migrations within the kingdom from the outer islands to the capital.

During the first three reigns of Tupou monarchs (1875–1965), then, Tongan elite formation has largely been an internal process. Because it is a highly centralized kingdom, the economic infrastructure of the society has most heavily developed on the main island of Tongatapu, and particularly in and around the port capital of Nuku'alofa (Sevele 1973). In recent decades, the drift of population has been from outer regions to Tongatapu, thus artificially accentuating already overcrowded conditions in the kingdom. This phenomenon mimics earlier migration patterns among the elite who, while never losing their regional and village associations, clustered as residents of the capital during the reigns of Tupou II and Queen Sālote. At present, the old commoner and noble elite (including the part European families) compose thirty to forty families based in Nuku'alofa, with continuing linkages both to their outer island regions of origin (mainly through their holding of hereditary plots of land) and to the newer overseas concentrations of Tongans.

These families, conceived in their dispersed form, constitute the contemporary focus of an elite subculture in Tonga. As noted, they have become elites, not through entrepreneurship (with the exception of the part-Europeans), but by making niches for themselves in new institutions controlled by the kingship and church organizations. Economically, the Tongan elite should be seen collectively as accumulators and redistributors of the local resources of Tongan society, both through family networks and through positions they control within government and church hierarchies. Here, resources should be understood broadly as land, jobs, privileged statuses, and the establishing of preferences among clients and kin for distributing controlled values and goods of all kinds.[2]

Carol Smith (1976) has emphasized the importance of elites as controllers of modes of exchange and distribution in agrarian societies, and noted that when dendritic market systems organize peripheral economies, local political and economic elite subcultures, clustered in market centers such as port towns, assume wide-ranging control of the distribution of "goods" of all kinds to their respective populations. Their elite status rests not so much on the direct ownership control of productive resources such as land, as on the control of a population's consumption habits.

Even during the long period of Tonga's insulated development as a monarchy, there was a collective level of awareness and sensitivity among Tongans to their regional and international position among other states. This kind of awareness is by now a cultural ideology, supported by Tonga's central historic achievement of preserving both its independence and its kingship. In relative terms, this "world" view has been most sophisticatedly and consciously developed among Tongan elite families, and of course most notably among the royal family and its aristocratic kinsmen, who for so long under Sālote monopolized the management of Tonga's postion in relation to its British protector and others. However, consistent with the general cultural pattern of emulating those of the highest status, the old commoner elite under Sālote also achieved a sophistication about Tonga's leverage in a world of more powerful states, especially about how they might use their position at home to build part of their futures abroad, at first in New Zealand, but then as is true most recently under Tupou IV, in the United States as well.

THE INTERNATIONALIZATION OF TONGAN SOCIETY: 1965 TO THE PRESENT

In 1965, King Tupou IV ascended the throne, and not long after, in 1970, Tonga achieved full independence. Only since 1970 has this nation become fully responsible for its own development. This contemporary period of Tongan history and development can be seen in terms of two "internationalizing" trends: (1) the new monarch's search for foreign capital to fund Tongan development, in part accomplished by his "trading on sovereignty" as a nation state; and (2) the extensive emigration of Tongans overseas and the establishment of international family networks. Both internationalizing processes have opened the Tongan state and people to multiple linkages with particular larger and richer societies, most of which border on the Pacific. Tongan elites, in particular, have been able to manipulate, exploit, and expand new international family networks to gain position and personal power in the nation-state framework at home.

Trading on Sovereignty

Both as Crown Prince and as King, Tupou IV has sought opportunities to overcome Tonga's economic limitations and transform it into a prosperous small state like Brunei or Nauru, each rich in a strategic natural resource. Tonga, however, has no such resource. Constraints on its economy include monocrop commerical agriculture, overpopulation, fluctuating remittance flows from overseas migrants, dependence on paternalistic sources of development aid, and the largely autonomous economic activity of churches. The impact of the churches has been likened to that of multinational corporations, where decisions crucially affecting local economic conditions are made abroad and with nonlocal agendas in mind.

To promote local development, the King has conducted negotiations with private and government parties in the United States, Australia, New Zealand, Japan, India, Saudi Arabia, the Soviet Union, and the former state of West Germany. Several of these negotiations have apparently ended without clear result; others have been mutually sustained as long-term personal friendships; others have resulted in suspect deals and losses for Tonga; while others have given the kingdom leverage in aid requests to regional patrons (for example, the courting in the early 1970s of the Russians, which, intended or not, attracted New Zealand's concern). The negotiations have seemed aimed at finding one large investor to subsidize Tongan development, which has been conceptualized in various ways over the years in terms of specific schemes.

The King's moves to improve dramatically Tonga's position as a "mini-state" in the overall community of nations is a bold game with considerable risks. Finding a backer for Tongan development could replace the diffuse dependency and economically stagnant conditions characteristic of most peripheral states with a very narrow kind of clientage.

After promoting a number of ambitious, small-industry projects during the 1970s with unsatisfactory results, the King came to view luxury tourism, necessitating an international airport and perhaps a Tongan airline, as the most appropriate solution to economic stagnation. In a series of costly state visits and receptions for dignitaries and businessmen, the King has entertained potential investors from Japan, Germany, Australia, and the United States. Yet, the real hope was that Tonga might generate its own investment capital for such a project—the remaining question being from what resource, natural or otherwise?

Events of the last decade have indicated that such a resource might be found in the rights accruing to the status of state sovereignty. These have drawn Tonga into the schemes of particular businessmen who need the use of the sovereign status of a state as a competitive advantage in the pursuit of seemingly futuristic enterprises. This trend was first imagined, appropriately enough, in science fiction. A story by the science fiction writer Jerry Pournelle (1977), "A Matter of Sovereignty," tells of a company, Nuclear General (NG), which, attracted by Tonga's lack of regulation and taxation, leased atolls for the production of protein and plutonium. NG pays off Tonga with electric power, fresh water, fish, fertilizer, and advice on population control. Inadequately protected by the laws of the United States, NG requires the status of a sovereign state to defend its transport from seizure by other small nations. A company envoy proposes that Tonga nationalize NG's ships and lease them back to the firm; NG would then arm the ships and become Tonga's new protector. NG personnel would act as Tonga's honorary consuls worldwide, looking after Tonga's increasing migrant population, and the company would subsidize the Tongan domestic economy.

In real life, as in fantasy, Tonga may well come to interest multinationals. Tupou IV's dealings with private overseas investors interested in ocean resources have, in fact, sometimes resembled Pournelle's scenario. Foreigners have served as honorary consuls abroad, and the King offers a tax- and regulation-free environment for private investment. For now, however, the King is more likely to attract individual businessmen of varying reputations, rather than multinationals, to support speculative, high-risk projects.

In 1977 and 1978, "the Meier affair" was reported in the *Wall Street Journal* of November 17, 1978, and other international newspapers. Reporter Barry Newman of the *Journal* recounted the tale of John Meier, a former employee of Howard Hughes with a history of arrests for swindling and tax evasion. Meier created the Bank of the South Pacific, and in June 1977, Tonga granted it a ninety-nine year monopoly on merchant banking and extraordinary freedom from government regulation. In May 1978, Meier and the King opened a site for the construction of an airport and industrial park, and Tonga issued Meier a diplomatic passport so that he could sell airport bonds. But Meier was wanted on criminal charges abroad and was arrested in Vancouver in October 1978. He was later extradited to the United States. The net result for Tonga was a bulldozed industrial site. When asked in July 1978 if he had any reservations about Meier's background, the King replied, "His background is, of course, unfortunate. The point is he is in a position, and is willing, to help Tonga in a way nobody else is willing to help Tonga."

Such "help," however, brings high risks. Each deal, whatever the outcome, requires considerable expenditures on Tonga's part, and the King's projects divert limited available resources from more practical possibilities for growth. Scandal resulting from the King's efforts draws undesirable publicity to Tonga, and the Western press continues to view the Kingdom as a quaint anachronism.

More promising, and more evocative of the futuristic use of Tonga's sovereign status as an economic resource, is a current venture in satellite communication. Under the article title, "Tiny Tonga Seeks Satellite Empire in Space," *New York Times* reporter Edmund L. Andrews writes (1990):

> Spurred by an ambitious American entrepreneur, a tiny South Pacific Kingdom has started what amounts to a turf battle that could affect future control of satellite communications between Asia and the United States.
>
> The island nation of Tonga has seized on a loophole in international law to lay claim to the last 16 desirable unoccupied orbital parking spaces for satellites that can link Asia, the Pacific and the United States. Control of the spaces, called "slots," determines who can provide satellite communications to a given part of the world. The number of these spaces above the earth is sharply limited by international law to prevent interference between satellites, but they can be reserved at no cost by nearly any nation on an essentially first-come, first-served basis.
>
> Before Tonga's move caught it by surprise, the 119-nation consortium that provides most international satellite service, known as Intelsat, pretty much thought it had a lock on the slots.
>
> Intelsat officials now contend that Tonga, with an economy based largely on fishing, coconuts and foreign aid, is merely a front for financial speculation by a slick American operator, Matt C. Nilson. Intelsat, of which the United States is a member, contends Mr. Nilson's goal is to make a quick profit by leasing the orbital slots to the highest bidders...
>
> ...Tonga's venture into satellite communications began in 1987 when Mr. Nilson, who had been in the satellite business, persuaded King Taufa'ahau Tupou 4th to sponsor an ambitious satellite system over the Pacific.
>
> A government-sponsored company, Tongasat, was formed to join foreign partners to launch a fleet of satellites capable of reaching from the Middle East to Hawaii. Mr. Nilson is Tongasat's managing director and has a 20 percent take in the venture.
>
> Tongan officials concede that they can put up none of the money for the satellites they are proposing, and that Tongasat has only six employees. But the princess who is Tongasat's chairman seemed offended by accusations that the satellite positions are being hoarded to make a quick profit. "Countries in Asia and the Pacific region have a need for better communication," said the princess, Salote Pilolevu Tuita. "They make it sound as if we are only interested in financial gain."
>
> ...Mr. Nilson said in a recent interview that $2 million a year for each slot might be reasonable. That would be $26 million annually for all 13 positions. If Tonga retained about half of that amount after Mr. Nilson and others got their cuts, it would still increase the Government's budget by about 20 percent....

One can argue that a spectacular success such as Tongasat, on which the King's long-term strategy of unholy alliances with lone operators depends, would make the game worth its costs; and one can admire the King's refusal to accept the negligible place that the paternalistic larger states allow Tonga in the world system. Yet, in such schemes, the King relaxes the traditional caution of Tongan rulers in dealing with outside interests and offers concessions that evoke Pournelle's futurist parable. Sovereign status and its rights and privileges in diverse arenas of commerce, as well as the power to tax and regulate business, are bargaining tools with which small states such as Tonga can attract otherwise indifferent private investors for special development projects. When those states compromise sovereignty itself, however, they may jeopardize the very rationale for national development.

Other than obvious financial gain, we might now ask what else might be at stake in the King's repeated and risky trading on Tonga's sovereignty.

The Center Might Not Hold: Emigration, International Family Networks, and the Predicament of the Local Elite

The King's development ambitions for Tonga should be understood not merely in the context of a conventional nation-state model of Tongan society as a mini-state among major states, but more critically in the context of the international dimension of contemporary Tongan social organization. This dimension is itself a consequence of Tonga's subordinate integration into the world-wide political and economic system, which has stimulated a flow of emigration.

Tongan elite formation, in particular, is one by-product of this trend of emigration and has depended on the development of international family networks, yielding a kind of parasitic access to resources and opportunities in richer locales. These networks represent diversified economic activity, which increases the degree of autonomy and flexibility of groups of individuals in relation to both local and overseas poltical and economic institutions. This is a "boot-straps" kind of development of family groups in the interstices of states, which some Tongans (by definition, the elites) are able to convert into position and personal power within the nation-state framework at home. Such overseas development of family networks is a phenomenon that occurs throughout the contemporary world, but it is Tonga's relative smallness of scale as a nation-state entity that makes the effects of diffuse international development of families so much greater on local nation-state development.

Shortage of land, increasing population, and Tongan fascination with the sources of the influence that changed their society have led during the past three decades to large concentrations of Tongans living in certain overseas locales. It is difficult to know how many thousands of Tongans are living abroad, since there are no reliable census figures concerning them. Based on my own rough estimates,[3] there are nearly one hundred thousand Tongans permanently residing abroad, a number that nearly equals the current population of Tonga. The largest concentrations are in New Zealand (particularly, Auckland), Australia, Fiji, the United States (particularly, Hawaii, California, and Utah, although there is a sprinkling of Tongans throughout the United States), and much less so in Great Britain. The numbers as well as the wealth of overseas Tongans are increasing

relative to the home population. Intermarriage, church and private sponsorship, overstaying temporary visas and, primarily, education have been the footholds that have led to the
permanence of migration.

Migrants' rootedness abroad is now apparent, and linkages of variable intensity and
content with home kin have important effects on the Tongan economy and social structure.
In the short term, and particularly since 1970, there have been great fluctuations in flows
of temporary migration between Tonga and New Zealand, and these have been governed
largely by conditions in the New Zealand economy. Unpredictable remittance flows back
to Tonga, accompanied by a steadily increasing demand for imports, have had an overall
destabilizing effect on the Tongan home economy. Temporary migration has also been a
potentially new source of elite formation in Tonga or, at least, a source for the appearance
of a broader-based Tongan middle class (a middle class that possesses the locally
interpreted symbols and attributes of modernity, so long available only to a much more
restricted noble and commoner elite).

Important for understanding this kind of Tongan development are the characteristics
of the networks that are maintained between permanent overseas Tongans and Tongans
at home, how long network configurations last, and what kinds of relationships and
transactions compose them. Consideration of these issues is still somewhat academic
since overseas concentrations are relatively very recent and the long-term characteristics
of family networks barely established. Even the old elite overseas networks have been
developed only since World War II, and most have not yet been challenged by factors that
could be expected to weaken them, including a decline in involvement of second-generation overseas Tongans with their relatives in Tonga.

These permanent overseas concentrations of Tongans are to be distinguished con-
ceptually from the flows of temporary migrant labor during the 1970s, since only rarely
do the temporary migrants lay down roots abroad, at least not without the assistance of
permanent Tongan residents. How family networks with permanent migrant branches
control this flow of temporary migrants (as one of their resources or fields of enterprise)
is a tantalizing question on which I have little systematic evidence.

In referring to Tongans overseas, I use the word *concentration*, rather than
community. On the basis of the elite networks which I have studied, it appears that
although Tongans do associate with one another abroad and there are organizations that
bring them together (for example, overseas branches of Tongan churches), they are far
more dispersed and isolated from one another in host societies, than are, for example, the
Samoans (see Chapter 10, "The Samoan Exodus," by Paul Shankman in this volume).
Samoans seem to have more of a community identity than Tongans when living abroad,
identifying each other and themselves by village of origin in Samoa. As in Albert Wendt's
novel, *Sons for the Return Home* (1974b), even Samoans who spend decades abroad
retain aspirations that they or their children will eventually make a triumphal, permanent return home and will use what they have achieved abroad to enhance their
positions in their villages of origin. In contrast, permanent Tongan migrants seem
much more culturally self-sufficient abroad, while maintaining their strongest ties of
support with specific kin, rather than villages, at home. If this is in fact a real
difference, it might have something to do with the extension abroad of fundamentally
different kinds of local organization at home in Tonga and Samoa—that is, the

importance of village and community organization in Samoa characterizes overseas Samoans; its relative unimportance in Tonga characterizes overseas Tongans.[4]

While international ties of cooperation permeate the entire Tongan home population, their strength, regularity, and durability are highly variable and of unknown patterning.[5] It is clear that such networks are most strongly developed and anchored among the old and new elite families, clustered in the capital. During the preindependence period of British rule, elite status for these families had depended on the accumulation and coordinated sharing of resources in dispersed networks within the kingdom, and this feature of elite formation has merely expanded in space with the internationalizing dimension of Tongan social organization.

As noted, segments of the old elite were the first to establish their interests as families abroad, and more recently, they have been in the most favored position to travel and spend long periods overseas. The internationalizing of elite networks characterizes to a lesser degree even the most traditional segment of the old elite—the nobility—with their most important inherent advantages closely tied to the nation-state model of Tonga as a society (Marcus 1980).

There is also a small, but growing new elite or middle class joining the slow circulation of elites at the center of Tongan society. These are families catapulted to prominence by the extraordinary achievements of one or more of their members usually in education overseas, who return to Tonga and are co-opted into the local system of church and state offices. The advantage to the kingship of such an arrangement is that it provides an increasingly larger pool of previously unrecognized talent to draw back to Tonga, thus giving Tonga an alternative to the sole dependence on domestically established noble and commoner elite families.

These old and new elites represent the extreme end of a diverse continuum. They are distinguished by features that make their networks appear more consistently "structured"—a coordinated mix of resources and an internal authority structure, anchored by an unambiguous elite identity in Nuku'alofa society, even though their overseas branches may be anonymous as members of a diffuse Polynesian minority. In contrast, there are many other Tongans who have achieved wealth and distinctions abroad, but who have no anchorage in Tonga by which to convert these resources into elite status; they are merely the pride of their undistinguished kinsmen at home. Such successful overseas Tongans tend to cut most substantive ties with their networks. However, there are anomalous cases where they fund and support relatives at home, who thus become economically well off in Tonga, but who, ironically, are unable to trade on this acquired relative wealth to improve their local personal status. These cases index the formation of a stunted middle class in Tonga as a product of receiving overseas advantages combined with limited possibilities for local social mobility. The increasing occurrence of such cases epitomizes a contradiction in the alternative diaspora and homeland models of Tongan social structure.

Possibilities in the context of an internationally dispersed population are thus the crucial framework for assessing the life chances even for people who will remain lifelong residents of Tonga. To be able to migrate is not essential in order to economically enhance a family's position in Tonga. Rather, the capacity to call on international resources, continually or on important occasions, has become a crucial factor in influencing a family's local economic conditions. The lowest stratum in contemporary Tonga are those totally dependent on the nation-state framework and the limited resources it embodies without any overseas options at all. Elites and an emergent middle class, in contrast, are those not only with the greatest potential options abroad, realized through family connections, but also those who successfully organize to capitalize on them.

Forgoing here a discussion of the dynamics of relationships within elite family groups, it might be useful merely to list resources that have been shared through active exchanges within geographically dispersed elite kin networks. Property, businesses, positions, jobs, reputation, and influence with local authorities are typical kinds of resources developed by old and new elite families with footholds abroad. The following are resource listings for one old commoner elite family and one new commoner elite family:

OLD ELITE FAMILY

In Tonga:

1 high church office
1 school principal
3 in executive bureaucratic
   positions
1 airline clerk
Ownership of garage/gas station
Taxi business
Mild chiefly associations/
   longtime reputation as elite
1 retail business/shop
Hereditary interest in 6
   agricultural allotments
   (4 around Nuku'alofa)
Hereditary interest in 5
   town allotments
   (residential property in
   Nuku'alofa)

In Hawaii:

Handicraft business and
   importer
Yard-cleaning business
5 wage earners (3 skilled;
   2 unskilled)
3 individuals seeking
   university degrees

NEW ELITE FAMILY

In Tonga:

Strong influence in
   a minority church
1 high-level bureaucratic
   position
3 middle-level civil
   servants
1 executive at radio
   station
Hereditary interest in 3
   agricultural allotments
   (leasing of 5 others);
   considerable commercial
   agriculture
2 Nuku'alofa town
   allotments
2 retail businesses
1 Ph. D. employed in Tonga
3 teachers

In California:

1 gas station operator
   and owner
2 residential properties
2 employed at San
   Francisco airport

OLD ELITE FAMILY	**NEW ELITE FAMILY** (*cont'd*)
In New Zealand:	In Utah:

Residential property
    Secondary school education
      of children
	3 employed at unskilled
	      jobs (1 permanent; 2
	      temporary residents)
	    1 teacher

In Fiji:	New Zealand:

University instructor	1 person in transport work
	    1 rental property
	    1 residence
	    2 in secondary school
	    1 at university

Both families can be seen as anchored in Nuku'alofa with various kinds of options that are being exploited in different overseas locales. An interesting question is under what conditions the center of gravity of these families would change from a focus in Tonga to a focus abroad, while not yielding any options completely, paricularly those in Tonga. It is the possibility of such shifts within dispersed family networks that might eventually change the central position of the Tongan nation-state relative to the international distribution of the Tongan population. At present, the focus of these cooperating, but dispersed, families is still in the homeland. There is a tendency for particularly well-off families overseas to grow apart from their home networks, rather than to build their positions within them, or for particular individuals residing abroad to contemplate an eventual return home. For example, young, highly educated Tongans whose university degrees would bring deference in Tonga could originate overseas branches of their families, but they would then probably prefer to trade on their educational qualifications at home, if the opportunity to move into a place in the Tongan institutional order arose.

The fact that commoner elite families must mediate high prestige roles at home and a relatively low or marginal status as minorities abroad does not generate the kind of cognitive dissonance that Westerners might anticipate. Social contexts in which options occur are kept quite separate in the activities of dispersed family networks, and thus there is no conceptual bar to developing any new options in separate contexts. Janitors in New Zealand are as much a part of the family network as are bureaucrats at home (and some bureaucrats even work as janitors when they reside temporarily abroad). This capacity to integrate all kinds of resources that are geographically separated is one of the key elements of economic strength and flexibility in elite family networks.

It is worth offering a speculative scenario to suggest where the present internationalizing trend of Tongan culture might lead. A fully internationalized Tongan culture would result from an international scale of family operations, still tied to kin at home, which would equal or exceed in economic value the Tongan national product. While the homeland might never lose its symbolic and emotional importance for emigrants as a means to retain a Tongan cultural identity, it might become decentered as the political and economic focus of the Tongan people. Tonga might remain merely a struggling nation-state in the face of flourishing overseas concentrations in places such as Hawaii and California, and residents of these outposts would continue to affect the overall conditions of Tongans at home by their selective participation in and contributions to persisting family networks.

IMPLICATIONS

The King's effort to trade on sovereignty to find a strong base for Tonga's development, even at the risk of its becoming a narrowly defined client-state, can be understood, on one hand, as the kingship's continuing assertive orientation to a world of more powerful states, on which the historic pride and popular image of the Tupou monarchs in Tongan society have been based. On the other hand, it can be understood as an effort to preserve Tonga's position as *both* the economic and symbolic center of an internationalizing culture. Migrant dispersion generates an alternative model of Tongan development as an international population that challenges the model of Tongan development as a nation-state. This alternative model of development, against which the King's must be vigorously played, involves the appearance of family networks, most prominently among the established elite subculture, which is also a pervasive feature of the Tongan home population at large. Most Tongans have instrumental linkages of some sort with overseas concentrations. The development aims of the King are thus in part an effort to retain the Tongan state as the center of a society in centrifugal motion.

More practically and realistically at present, this clash of development contexts should be seen narrowly as an affair of elites. All of the Tongan national elite families now have an international dimension, and thus see their fields of activity as a strategic mix of options in the framework of dispersed family networks that span different places, each with different kinds of opportunities; and one such place is Tonga itself. Those who invest in the nation-state/homeland option most strongly and see it as a markedly more important option than others include the royal family, certain of the noble families, and old commoner elite families with a greater vested interest in the running of Tongan bureaucratic institutions. In one sense, the monarch represents those who see Tongan resources as more important than others, and he has perhaps expectedly been most involved in the aggressive and innovative development plans for Tonga itself.

For the rest of the elite, the nation-state option remains important, but in comparison to the high bureaucratic and aristocratic elite, it now takes a more modest place among other possibilities which can be pursued opportunistically. Members of the elite classes see themselves flexibly as participants in both contexts of development, but are not overly committed to either one. Their development as families still anchored in Tonga aids Tonga's development as a nation-state, an option controlled by and heavily invested in by the kingship-focused subset of families. Yet, this conventional nation-state model of development is simultaneously challenged by the possibility of such families decisively transferring abroad their tentative and relative commitments among options in the present general trend of migration. The development moves of those investing heavily in the nation-state option can be seen as an attempt to improve Tonga's position, not so much as an extreme peripheral state involved in a world system of states, but as the core of its own migrant periphery.

NOTES

1. This paper is based on my fieldwork in Tonga during the summer months of 1972, a full year in 1973–74, and a brief visit in 1975. In addition, between 1974 and 1978, I attempted to track specific family networks, during brief visits to Auckland, Suva, Honolulu, Salt Lake City, and San Francisco.

2. These are the well-recorded traditional functions of chiefship in Polynesia and there is some justification for claiming that new elites function in a manner similar to traditional chiefs. This is particularly so in the institutionalized patterns of collection and distribution of money, goods, and services to and from the population at large, as they are mediated by the clergy in the hierarchical organization of church congregations. However, historically and culturally, the functions of the Tupou-era elites have their own specific manifestation that accords more realistically with the integration of periphery elites and markets into an international economic system, controlled by more powerful core states.

3. During my research, I could find no official or unofficial numbers of temporary and permanent Tongan residents in the various overseas locales I visited. I did have the opportunity to discuss the size of concentrations of Tongans with Tongans who were permanent residents in each locale I visited, and in some places, I had access to church lists. From these discussions and lists, I derived the estimate of one hundred thousand, which, regrettably is rough.

4. The longstanding adaptive mimicry by Tongans of Europeans as well as the traditional Tongan use of kinship and genealogical categories to locate themselves culturally in space and time, in preference to village and place orientations, might in part account for the salience among Tongan migrants of family networks across international spaces, in the absence of strong, insulating overseas communities.

5. Since the tracing of ties for the entire internationalized Tongan population would be difficult, given the diffuseness of the phenomenon, my claims here are based specifically on readings of my data on elite families, which show very clearly the importance of international networks in their formation as elites, and of my earlier, sketchy, but suggestive data on one island community (Marcus 1974).

3

Imagining a Nation:
Race, Politics, and Crisis
in Postcolonial Fiji

Martha Kaplan
Vassar College

The legacy of the colonial British to the new nation of Fiji is one of "racial" division and political contradiction.[1] ("Race" is the term used locally for ethnic groups.) In 1987 these contradictions came to a head in the overthrow of Fiji's elected government by military coup. This chapter analyzes both culture and history to address the question: Why has it become difficult, perhaps even impossible, for the diverse peoples of Fiji to "imagine a community" together?

Unlike many other Pacific nations whose colonial history is primarily the story of encounters between Pacific indigenes and colonizing Westerners, Fiji's is a story of a tripartite encounter. In addition to the descendants of indigenous Fijian Pacific Islanders, Fiji is home to the Fiji Indians, descendants of South Asian indentured laborers who came to Fiji at the turn of the century. There are almost equal numbers of Fijians and Fiji Indians living in Fiji.[2] The colonial British ruled the indigenous Fijians through a paternalist system of indirect rule based on their chiefly system and preserved Fijian land ownership. At independence in 1970, Fijian chiefs were Fiji's highest national leaders, and Fiji's constitution was written to ensure indigenous Fijian political paramountcy and landholding rights. In contrast, the Fiji Indians came to colonial Fiji as indentured laborers. Exploited to create an economic base for the colony, the Fiji Indians have been the economic backbone of the nation.

Since independence, Fiji's economy has been based on sugar cane (the colonial staple), tourism, and foreign aid. Fiji Indians continue to grow most of Fiji's sugar cane. They have also entered a diverse field of new occupations, including "white-collar" as well as "blue-collar" work. Indigenous Fijians have also entered the work force in increasing numbers. But unlike the Fiji Indians who depend on cash incomes, many

Market, Suva, Fiji, 1985 (Photo by M. Kaplan)

indigenous Fijians still gain their livelihood partly or wholly from subsistence economic activities undertaken on the land they own communally. In postcolonial Fiji, although a significant expatriate community represents multinational corporate interests, Fijians and Fiji Indians have largely replaced Europeans in the public and private positions of authority in the former colony. Fiji Indians predominate in many areas of business, and indigenous Fijians predominate in government.

Politically, the Fiji Indians seemed fated to be the perpetual opposition party within the Fijian-dominated national parliament. From independence in 1970 to 1987, Fiji's parliamentary government was headed by the Alliance party, a chiefly led, predominantly indigenous Fijian party. The National Federation party, a primarily Indian party, was the opposition party. But in 1987, Fiji Indians for the first time elected a majority government, a coalition betweeen the National Federation party and a new party, the Fiji Labour party, headed by a nonchiefly Fijian. This newly elected government was overthrown in a series of military coups led by a Fijian army colonel who claimed to act on behalf of the paramountcy and political interests of indigenous Fijians, and who returned to leadership the chiefly Fijian politicians of the Alliance party. In 1990, Fijian high chiefs approved a new constitution, which denies Fiji Indians representation proportionate to their percentage in the population of Fiji, and provides that only Fijians can serve as President and Prime Minister, the highest officials of the nation.

What is the cultural and historical context of the 1987 military coups? And why has it become difficult, perhaps impossible, for all Fijians and all Fiji Indians to "imagine a community" together? In the decades after World War II, many political leaders and social

Market, Suva, Fiji, 1985 (Photo by M. Kaplan)

scientists around the world believed that development and decolonization could lead—unproblematically—to modernization and the creation of new nations. Instead, it has become clear that these very categories require re-examination. Benedict Anderson's (1983) evocative phrase "imagined communities" reminds us that the "nation" is but one culturally and historically constituted social form among many, and not an ideal or inevitable one.

Consequently, this Chapter takes a cultural approach to Fiji's political history. (On this history see also Gillion 1977; Lal 1986, 1988; Macnaught 1982; Mamak 1978; Norton 1977; and Scarr 1984.) In this chapter I seek to show how the recent crisis reveals competing cultural visions of the order of a "national" polity. One view, as expressed by those who perpetrated the coups, is based on a rural Fijian, anticapitalist ethic and seeks a chiefly led, Christian polity. A contrasting view, that of the overthrown coalition government, envisions a democratic system, stressing common interests of Fijian and Indian workers, in which the nation belongs to those who labored to build it. These different views of Fiji were formed in a complex and unequal British colonial history, in which "racial" divisions between Fijians and Fiji Indians were established by the colonial British and have been fostered and manipulated to the advantage of ruling elites, from the colonial period to the present.

Further, these competing visions of Fiji are not a simple matter of a Fijian versus an Indian political stance. Neither group is monolithic and both groups are cross-cut by emerging class relations and other interests. Among Fijians, divisions between confederacies and regions (some of which are indigenously constituted and longstanding and some more recently formed) motivate political conflict. Indian factionalism emerges out of religious, communal, and historical differences. Finally, class relations are critical in the understanding of the recent crisis, although they must be understood as class relations of a particular sort, emergent within pre-existing indigenous and colonially generated hierarchical relations.

To interpret the coups in the context of Fiji's colonial and postcolonial political history and to analyze the actors, parties, forces, and conditions that are now shaping Fiji's future, I will focus on four important moments. I begin with a historical overview of the shaping of Fiji as colony, and the differing relationships between the British and indigenous Fijians and Fiji Indians. Then I turn to examine recent political relationships: the "Deed of Cession" debate following World War II, the establishment of Fiji's constitution at independence in 1970, and the military coups and the founding of the Republic of Fiji in 1987.

COLONIALLY CONSTITUTED RELATIONSHIPS

When the British brought Fiji Indians to Fiji they created a contradiction. They wanted to shield the indigenous Fijians from exploitation and to extend to them the "benefits of civilization." But colonial imperatives required the exploitation of someone's labor, and therefore the Indians were imported as, in the words of one colonial Governor, "a working population and nothing more" (Scarr 1980:88) and were exploited in the Fijians' stead. These contradictory British goals of civilizing and exploiting—and the ways in which the Fijians and the Indians accommodated or resisted them—set the framework for the different colonial experiences of Fijians and Fiji Indians.

The British and the Fijians

Fiji's "national" boundaries were fixed in the colonial encounter when, in 1874, a group of high chiefs ceded the islands to Queen Victoria. Indigenously there had been no single, united Kingdom of Fiji. Instead, a number of expanding chiefly led kingdoms or confederacies, on the two large islands of Viti Levu and Vanua Levu and on a series of smaller island groups to the east (the latter with close ties to Tonga), competed with one another within the island group. In Fiji, as in other cases in the Pacific, European incursion began with ships and their crews, and came to include planters, missionaries, and then colonial administration. Critical in the changing Fijian social field were the Wesleyan missionaries who came to the islands in the 1830s. Conversion proceeded kingdom by kingdom, as it fit into the strategies of high chiefs. When chiefs converted, their people followed them en masse. Thus, when the influential high chief Cakobau converted in 1854, the majority of the islands' people were converted. Resistance to Wesleyan Christianity persisted largely in those areas of interior, northern, and western Viti Levu island that had never acknowledged Cakobau's claims to rule them. Increasing European settlement by cotton planters in the 1860s engendered conflict, especially with the unconverted peoples of the interior. These and other conflicts brought Fiji to the attention of Great Britain. In 1874, Cakobau and twelve other chiefs (recognized by Europeans—but not by all Fijians—as Fiji's rulers) ceded the islands to Queen Victoria.

"Cession" is a founding myth in Fiji, interpreted and reinterpreted throughout the past century to serve as a charter for different British and Fijian projects and political stances. Here I concentrate on the ways in which it was interpreted by Fiji's first colonial governor and the way it articulated with indigenous Fijian cultural understandings of the relation between ruler and ruled.

Like the imperial British more generally, Fiji's founding colonial governor Sir Arthur Gordon (1879) viewed the relation of British and Fijians within a nineteenth-century social evolutionary racial framework (see France 1969), a hierarchy in which the British conceived themselves to be the historical and racial pinnacle. Paternalistically concerned about the survival of the Fijians, whose population and birth rate had dropped significantly because of European-introduced diseases, Gordon was also impressed by Fijian Christian conversion, and by Fijian chiefs. He found them worth saving and civilizing.

In Gordon's estimation, Fijians needed to be protected from the exploitation planned by resident white planters. He therefore set in motion regulations that reserved 83 percent of Fiji's land for indigenous Fijians, inalienably registered to kin groups. He further instituted a paternalist system of indirect rule. Indigenous Fijian society was constituted as a polity within the colonial polity, with its own administration, under a Minister (later Secretary) of Native Affairs. This Fijian polity was subdivided into provinces and districts (continuous with indigenous divisions) under chiefs chosen by the British, often men who held hereditary rank in their province or district. Well into the twentieth century, Fijians remained rural subsistence farmers, tied to their land and districts, under the direction of their chiefs (see Macnaught 1982).

From the indigenous Fijian perspective, Cession established a relationship between foreign chiefly rulers and indigenous people of the land. In the nineteenth-century Fijian ritual-political system, chiefs (*turaga*) were conceived of as foreigners. People of the land (*itaukei*) welcomed the foreigners and ritually installed them as "divine kings" (see Hocart 1929; Sahlins 1985:73–103). The divinity of the chief is created when he is reborn as a local god. The relation of chiefs and people is hierarchical, but based on mutual and reciprocal responsibilities and obligations. Chiefs held the rule (*lewa*) while the people of the land owned the land, installed the chief, and supported him in his ritual and political endeavors.

This Fijian cultural logic of the relation of chiefs and people has oriented solidary Fijian polities, in which chiefs have exercised prerogatives that outsiders have seen as "tyrannical." It has also oriented movements of resistance, in which people of the land asserted their prerogatives in the face of chiefs whom they did not acknowledge as their own. Not all Fijians acknowledged the right of Cakobau and the other signators of the Deed of Cession to cede Fiji, and significant resistance movements arose throughout the colonial period, particularly in the northern and western areas of Viti Levu Island (Macnaught 1982:75–111; Kaplan 1988a, 1990). However, for most Fijians, the colonial experience has been conceived of as a relation of people of the land and chiefs, in which the people of the land ceded the rule, but not their land, to a divine (Christian) Queen and her representative. In consequence, Fijians as a whole have never "agitated" for independence, nor have they ever collectively opposed the idea of chiefly rule.

Fijian kava ceremony, Ra, Fiji, 1985 (Photo by M. Kaplan)

The congruence of British paternalism and the Fijian cultural logic of foreign chiefs and indigenous people has shaped the Fijian colonial experience. Although chiefs in Fiji are commonly referred to as "traditional leaders," the British also "invented tradition" in Fiji, especially in relation to Fijian chiefs as political figures. In England, the relationship between the aristocracy and the populace was top-down and hierarchical, rather than complementary. In indirect rule, a political class of chiefs was created, authorized and legitimated, not by local people of the land, but from the top down, by colonial authority. Colonial authority as well as traditional right created the "Great Council of Chiefs" established by governor Gordon to advise the colonial government as the voice of Fijian opinion. Colonial authority designated Fijians as government chiefs (officials) at all levels of indirect rule. In the postcolonial era as well, "chiefs" are a class within a colonially established and bequeathed political order, rather than simply traditional rulers, empowered by local people of the land.

Few Fijians, however, regard their chiefs as colonially constructed figures. Instead, they see them as "traditional" figures of authority, just as today they consider it Fijian tradition to be Christian and to idealize an ethos of generalized reciprocity (Sahlins 1972:193–194) in opposition to the "life in the way of money" of Europeans and Indians. The identification of Christianity and generalized reciprocity is expressed in the important Fijian concept of "*loloma*" (kindly love), which can be used to refer to gifts, to the ethos of generalized reciprocity, and is also a term used to translate Christ's "grace," all now linked as aspects of "Fijian custom." This vision of Fijian custom further motivates Fijians' political expectations; they strongly be-

Sugar cane harvesting, Ra, Fiji, 1985 (Photo by M. Kaplan)

lieve that Fiji should be ruled by chiefs, on behalf of the people of the land. Relationships between chiefs and people are seen as mutually obligatory and "customary." Chiefs, even those who are economically interested members of a national elite, are seen by the people as preservers of Fijian tradition, including Christianity, who mediate between Fijians and "the world of money."

The British and the Fiji Indians

Colonial governor Gordon had previously been governor of Mauritius. From that colony he brought to Fiji the idea of temporary, indentured South Asian "coolies" who could provide the labor to grow sugar cane, a crop that could form the basis of the colony's economy. In their desire to protect the Fijians, Gordon and his successors enabled the creation of a brutal and degrading plantation system run by the Australia-based Colonial Sugar Refining Corporation. Thus, the Fiji Indian colonial experience was different from that of the indigenous Fijians in many dimensions. Where Fijians had been viewed as a primitive community to be protected from the depredations of the market, the Fiji Indians were treated as free individuals who could be exploited as labor in it. Rather than privileged indigenes, subject to constant colonial scrutiny, the focus of an elaborate system of indirect rule, the Fiji Indians were expected to be, and were long conceived as, marginal figures in the Fijian social landscape (Kelly 1989). When they began to organize, their anticolonial "challenge to European dominance" (Gillion 1977) made them dangerous figures in British eyes.

A Fiji Indian woman worships at home during the Hindu festival of Diwali, Suva, Fiji, 1985 (photo by John D. Kelly)

Between 1878 and 1919, over sixty thousand Indians came to Fiji as *girmityas* (from the word "*girmit*" meaning contract) and nearly two-thirds stayed on when their contracts expired. The Fiji Indians came from a range of castes and locales in India; many were seeking work, on pilgrimage, or already separated from village roots and families (Lal 1983). They were recruited individually and sent on to Fiji, through depots in Calcutta and Madras.

The Fiji Indian colonial experience was one of oppression and resistance to oppression. Narratives by indentured laborers make it clear that they believed they had been tricked by deceitful recruiters and by the colonial system more generally. In the depots and in the lines (the living quarters for laborers on the plantations) they were stripped of markers of caste relationship and identity and were forced to eat and live across caste lines. Thus polluted, many found themselves unable to return to India or were unwelcome there when their contracts expired. Fiji Indians have conceived of their indenture experience as parallel to the "sorrowful story of Ram," a Hindu god and king forced by circumstance into poverty and exile (Kelly 1988b; Mishra 1979; and Sanadhya, in press).

While the British thought of the Fijians as communal, to be represented politically and ruled through their chiefs, they saw the Indians, not as a community, but as a collection of individuals. The planter's newspaper the *Fiji Times* explicitly referred to them as "labor units" (Kelly 1988a). In Fiji, the Fiji Indians were stripped of their caste-practices and thereby their own forms of decision making and hierarchies. The colonial government made no effort to create any system of indirect rule for Fiji Indians, since they were regarded simply as a temporary labor pool; political organization among the Fiji Indians was discouraged and labeled "agitation." When the Fiji Indians began to organize politically, their first struggles were in the "economic" arena and were manifested as strikes against the Colonial Sugar Refining Corporation and other European employers (Gillion 1977; Moynagh 1981).

Indenture in Fiji and elsewhere was ended as a part of India's wider anticolonial struggle. Gandhi and others argued that as long as Indians were slaves anywhere in the British Empire, India itself could not be free (Tinker 1974). With the end of indenture, Indians became small-scale independent sugar cane growers on land leased from Fijians, or moved into the cities, where they began to establish themselves in various commercial sectors. From 1920 on, Fiji Indians organized to fight for fair payments for the cane they grew and then increasingly, for political representation in the colony. They went on strike to achieve economic goals and "agitated" to achieve the vote, but they never gained substantive power in Fiji's colonial Legislative Council. In contrast, their cane growers' unions succeeded in changing the terms and relations of cane growing to the growers' interest, finally resulting in Colonial Sugar Refining leaving Fiji altogether in 1973, when the sugar industry was nationalized.

In some ways, the relationship between Fiji Indians and the British was a colonial backwater version of the political, economic, and devotional struggle of nationalism in India. As in India, some political leaders were also religious leaders, especially leaders of early cane growers' strikes. And, several of the Fiji Indian leaders were actually sent by Gandhi to assist in the anti-indenture and anticolonial struggle. (Other leaders have emerged from the ranks of the cane growers' unions and political parties.) As in India, internal disputes and factionalism in the Fiji Indian community were always present, whether between Hindus and Muslims, between North and South Indians, or between the small minority of so-called "*Gujeratis*" (high-profile, duty-free retailers, and large-scale entrepreneurs who came to Fiji not as indentured laborers but to trade) and the *girmitya*-descended majority of Fiji's Indians.

But unlike the nationalists in India, the Fiji Indians were not "indigenes" in Fiji. Consequently, unlike the Fijian community (also sometimes the scene of intense internal, especially regional, factionalism) the Fiji Indians have not had the powerful political and rhetorical tool of a colonially defined and idealized, common "indigenous identity" as a bond of union. Instead, as we shall see, their lack of an established, colonially legitimated customary leadership and "customary identity" has hampered effective political action whether in the colonial Legislative Council or in the postcolonial national political arena, in which Fijian chiefly leadership has been reified and privileged.

Instead, the Fiji Indians have more successfully organized their social movements as "economic" projects devised to challenge European exploitation, or as "communal uplift" projects focused around the concept of religious devotionalism. Communal uplift, typified in India by Gandhi's *sarvodaya* (literally "communal uplift" or "welfare for all"), stressed the simultaneously moral, educational, economic, and social goals of anti-colonial struggle (see Fox 1989; Kelly 1991). Among Fiji Indians, religious practice and social organization have long been linked, whether in the rural Ramayan Mandalis (groups meeting weekly to read the Hindu text the *Ramayan*) or in the later, broadly organized and anticolonial organizations for communal uplift, which brought in Hindu and Muslim missionaries, teachers, and political leaders from India. The Fiji Indians have viewed their economic successes as a part of this wider project of moral, social, and religious uplift, begun in the anticolonial struggle. In the postcolonial years, however, Fiji Indians have had to develop a new political rhetoric, as their political stance could no longer be framed in opposition to British colonial exploitation, and their economic successes were viewed as suspect by Fijians (Kelly 1988b).

Thus, as many observers have noted, Fijian and Fiji Indian colonial history was largely constituted in relation to the British, not to each other. Separated spatially and occupationally and governed differently, the Fijian and Fiji Indian colonial experiences were separate and unequal. Intermarriage between Fijians and Fiji Indians has been uncommon, and the two groups retained separate religious and cultural identities. It would not be until the twentieth century, indeed until World War II, that Fijians and Fiji Indians would face each other in political debate, and not until independence that they would face each other with the task of building an independent Fijian nation together.

THE DEED OF CESSION DEBATE

In retrospect, World War II signaled the end of the British imperial era. As Dower (1986) has argued, the war exposed the contradictions of Western imperial racial ideologies throughout the world. In Fiji, the war brought into sharp focus the differing colonial pasts and the differing visions of the future of Fijians and Fiji Indians. The Fijians eagerly fought on behalf of the British during the war. The Fiji Indians, in contrast, offered to serve in the army and auxiliary services on the condition that they have equal status and the equal pay as that of white British citizens. Denied parity, they followed Gandhi in refusing to fight for a nation which classed them as inferior. Faced with the Indian challenge, British political rhetoric forged an ever stronger alliance with Fijians, drawing upon Fijian fears of Indian population growth, and denigrated Indian anticolonial resistance.

In 1946, European, Fijian and Indian representatives sat on Fiji's Legislative Council. However, the majority of representatives were European and were appointed by the Governor. Indians elected their representatives, while Fijian representatives were appointed (see Norton 1977:8). In that year, the Legislative Council debated a motion made by a European representative, a motion proposing that

> In view of the great increase in the non-Fijian inhabitants [and] their political development it was time to emphasize the terms of the Deed of Cession to assure that the interests of the Fijian race are safeguarded and that Fiji is preserved and kept as a Fijian country for all time. (Legislative Council of Fiji 1946:1)

Ostensibly, the debate was about the 1874 Deed of Cession, the document in which the high Fijian chiefs ceded Fiji to Queen Victoria and her heirs. But as Indian Legislative Council member A.D. Patel shrewdly noted, the debate had little to do with the actual principles of the Deed. Instead, it concerned interpretations of the relationship between Europeans and Fijians in the new context of the Indian presence. As Patel and other Indian

speakers argued, in the debate the colonial British were reconstituting their relationship to Fijians and were asserting Fijian sovereignty in order to resist Fiji Indian
claims for equality.

Both Fijians and Europeans began to develop a political rhetoric of "native rights"
and autochthony. The British argued that the Fijians had needed the civilizing mission
that the colonial enterprise provided. The European members of the Council took their
own presence in the islands for granted. As Patel pointed out, they did not include
themselves among the "non-Fijian" population who "threatened" the Fijian way of life.

Indian representative Patel tried to convince Fijians that Indian gains against the
British empowered them as well. Arguing against the rhetoric of indigenous priority as
propounded by the colonial Europeans, he sought public recognition of the Indian
contribution to the making of Fiji:

> [It should be] well understood and well appreciated that we came here to play our part in turning
> this country into a paradise. Indians came here and worked here for those people who gobbled
> up half a million acres of free-hold land from the Fijian owners. We came and worked, under a
> semi-servile state, and thank God, saved the Fijian race from the infamy of coming under the
> same system. As a matter of fact, if anything the coming of my people to this country gave the
> Fijians their honour, their prestige, nay indeed their very soul. Otherwise I have no hesitation
> in saying that the Fijians of this Colony would have met with the same fate that some other
> indigenous races in parts of Africa met with. (Legislative Council of Fiji 1946:48)

But the argument that workers had the right to political representation, and that
the country itself was no "natural" paradise, but a product of the labor of its people,
was never truly acceptable to the hierarchical British, nor to the Fijians. For Fijians,
the Fijian cultural relationship of *itaukei* (people of the land) and *turaga* (chiefly ruler)
had indeed been established with the British sovereign, and no such relationship
obtained with the Indians. With some notable exceptions, Fijians did not seek "equality" within their own community or with Europeans. They were uneasy about Indian
population growth, political representation, and economic success. Not long after the
Deed of Cession debate, the Fijian Affairs Board passed a resolution calling on the
government to "adopt a firm attitude towards the Indians in order that the interests of
the Fijian race remain preeminent in the Colony" (cited in Gillion 1977:196). The
contradictions of Fiji's politics remained unresolved.

In the decades that followed, Fiji's independence was a peculiarly contested matter
in which Indians sought independence and Fijians delayed. In the end, it was the world
trend toward decolonization and a British Labour government's agenda that tipped the
balance toward an independent Fiji. Fiji's two major political parties were shaped in the
political traditions and colonial experiences of Indians and Fijians and in the negotiations
leading to independence.

The largely Indian National Federation party was founded by leaders of cane-
growers' unions and other unions in 1964. The largely Fijian Alliance party developed
out of the Fijian Association, founded in 1956 by heads of the colonial Fijian Administration, in alliance with European businessmen, the disaffected head of an Indian cane-
growers' union, and the colonial government itself (Alley 1986; Norton 1977). Because

of constitutional requirements, since independence each party had mixed "racial" membership and fielded candidates of all three electoral categories (Fijian, Indian, and "other,"; see below). Further, each party at times espoused more or less pluralistic ideals. Notably, the early Alliance party under Ratu Sir Kamisese Mara proposed a multiracial party ideal, which attenuated in the 1980s. But at the beginning, a major difference concerning the constitution of independent Fiji separated the two parties. The National Federation party would have preferred a common roll democracy (no racial subdivisions of the electoral rolls). Instead, the form of government sought by the Alliance party, a constitution based on "racially" defined communal representation (defining voters by "race" and reserving percentages of parliamentary seats for Fijians, Indians, and others) was adopted.

RACE AND POLITICS IN INDEPENDENT FIJI

At independence in 1970, the "imagined community" of the nation of Fiji was to be ordered through this carefully developed constitution, set in place by the departing British administration. The constitution reified the unequal political relations formed in the colonial era in favor of the Fijians, and it reinforced and further routinized "race" as a category in Fijian social and political life.

Independent Fiji (the "Commonwealth Dominion of Fiji") had both a Governor General representing the Queen and an elected government consisting of a bicameral legislature on the Westminster model. The members of the House of Representatives were elected through a complicated system of racial or communal representation. Voters registered themselves on the communal rolls according to "race" as Fijians, Indians, or General Electors (all others).

The House had two types of seats. First, there were twenty-seven Communal seats in which candidates ran to represent people in their district of a particular "race." Thus, Fijians elected twelve representatives, Indians twelve, and General Electors elected three. Second, there were also twenty-five National seats. Here the candidates themselves were defined by their own "racial" heritage, required to run as Fijian, or Indian, or General Elector candidates, but were elected by all registered voters of all "races" in their district (Fiji Constitution 1970:388). As Lal (1986:76) described the situation prior to 1987:

> Each voter has four votes, one for his or her ethnic constituency and one each for the three national seats. Vote splitting does not occur on a significant scale; in fact electorally thus far, ethnic loyalties appear to supersede all other considerations.

Thus, while intended to create party affiliations cross-cutting racial bounds and to interest voters both in candidates of their own racial group and of others, the constitution nonetheless institutionalized race as a defining social and political characteristic.

Further, Fiji's constitution created a privileged political representation for indigenous Fijians. When the constitution was written, Indians were the majority population of Fiji (50.2 percent to 42.4 percent, according to the 1966 census), but Fiji Indians and

Fijians were nonetheless allotted equal numbers of seats. Moreover, the General Electors at 7.1 percent of the population had a disproportionately high representation, and had historically voted in concert with the Fijian-dominated Alliance party.

Most important for Fijian political hegemony—and the privileged place of Fijian chiefs—was the composition of the twenty-two member Senate. The Prime Minister (leader of the party with the majority of seats) nominated seven senators, and the Leader of the Opposition nominated six. But fully eight more Senators were Fijians nominated by the (colonially constituted) repository of "traditional" Fijian authority, the Great Council of Chiefs (Fiji Constitution 1970:395). The Great Council of Chiefs' nominees guaranteed a Fijian majority within the Senate. Furthermore, they had special powers of veto over all legislation regarding "Fijian land, custom and customary rights," which could not be passed by the Senate unless "supported at the final vote thereon in the house by no less than six of the Great Council of Chiefs Nominees" (Fiji Constitution 1970:404–406, cited in Lal 1986:77).[3]

Under this constitution from 1970 to 1988, the Alliance party held the parliamentary majority, with Ratu Sir Kamisese Mara as Prime Minister. In this period, the National Federation party was wracked by several internal factional disputes (see Lal 1986) which prevented them from mounting a serious challenge to Alliance hegemony. Under Alliance governance, contradictory trends developed. On the one hand, increasingly multiracial education and the entrance of growing numbers of Fijians into cane growing seemed to herald new cross-cutting ties between "racial" groups. But simultaneously, established politicians and newly emerging political parties made use of increasingly heightened appeals to "racial" and communal interests. Within this period, several new political parties emerged, notably the Fijian Nationalist party, the Western United Front, and the Fiji Labour party. The first reinforced the "racial" premises underlying Fiji's national politics, while the second two, in different ways, challenged "racial" politics in Fiji with new formulations of the relationships important to the nation.

The Fijian Nationalist party espoused a radically pro-Fijian, anti-Indian position, arguing that the Indians should be "repatriated to India." The party found significant support among rural Fijians and among the growing number of Fijians who had left their villages to come to the cities, where they were often unemployed. Its leader's rhetoric stressed the bewilderment of the *itaukei* (indigenes, or Fijian landowners) in the face of ostensible Indian prosperity.[4]

In the 1977 elections, the Fijian Nationalist party attracted enough Fijian votes away from the Alliance party to give the National Federation party a parliamentary majority. Although the National Federation party consequently had the right to form a government, the party leaders were unable to do so. Internal disputes delayed their decision making, as did their fear that Fijians would not accept an Indian as Prime Minister. While the Federation leaders discussed, the Governor General acted, perpetrating what has been called a "coup from above." Citing his constitutional prerogative to name as Prime Minister "the person best able to command the support of the majority of the House," the Governor General, himself a high Fijian chief, invited the Alliance party leader, Ratu Mara, to form a government (see Norton 1977; Lal 1986). Once formed, the parliament voted "no confidence" and new elections were held in which the Alliance party won an overwhelming majority of Fijian votes and returned to power. The legacy of the experience was to turn the Alliance party's attention and political stance away from multiracialism, and toward a position more similar to that of the Fijian Nationalist party, insistent upon Fijian political paramountcy.

The Fijian Nationalist party briefly posed a challenge from within the Fijian community to the authority of high chiefs as representatives of Fijians. In particular, it raised the charge that the Alliance party favored the eastern kingdoms or confederacies of Fiji. In 1981, another Fijian party was formed that took these issues further, the Western United Front, which was based in the western provinces of Viti Levu island. The immediate impetus for the formation of the party was dissatisfaction with contracts for pine harvesting in the area (Lal 1986:98). But more importantly, long before colonial days the Fijian "western side" peoples have had grievances against the expansionism of eastern coastal kingdoms. These grievances extended into the colonial and postcolonial eras as eastern chiefs became the backbone of the colonial system of indirect rule, dominated postcolonial politics, and controlled development resources. The northern and western provinces have been the sites of anticolonial Fijian political-religious movements (Kaplan 1988a, 1990; Macnaught 1982). Historically, therefore, some Fijians of the western side have been less firmly attached to the vision of colonial and postcolonial Fiji that was constituted in the British system of indirect rule.

Perhaps for this reason, in 1982 an unprecedented Fijian-Indian coalition was formed between the Western United Front and the National Federation party. Representing a new possibility of multiracial politics, it was "widely seen as a milestone in Fijian politics" (Lal 1986:100). This short-lived coalition was actually an arrangement of convenience and did not arise out of a unity of political vision. Nonetheless, it presaged a far more important multiracial coalition: the Labour party—National Federation party Coalition.

In 1985, the Fiji Labour party was founded. Two years later, in coalition with the National Federation party, the Labour party won the national election. Thus, in 1987, Labour party leader Dr. Timoci Bavadra became Fiji's new Prime Minister. The Fiji Labour party explicitly proposed to replace racial politics with a political-economic interpretation of groups and relationships within Fiji. Formed in the context of economic difficulties in Fiji, including a 1984 wage freeze imposed by the Alliance government (Cameron 1987), the platform of the Labour party stressed the mutual interest of all Fiji citizens in economic and social improvement and called for a major reorganization of social policy to promote a more equitable distribution of wealth. The Labour party domestic platform called for increased attention to welfare and education, aid to women with dependent children, provision of a minimum wage, legislation strengthening unionization, redistribution of profits from Fijian land rents to more Fijians, possible nationalization of transportation, development of gold mining and tourist industries, support for health and family planning issues, and creation of a national youth corps. It also stressed anticorruption and freedom of information. In foreign affairs, the Labour party called for political nonalignment, a nuclear-free Pacific, and solidarity with Pacific peoples resisting French colonial domination (Fiji Labour party Manifesto, in Lal 1986:148–155). Most unusual for Fiji was Dr. Bavadra's proposal that the time had come to use the term "Fijian" to refer to all Fiji citizens.

Though similar in aims to other Labour parties, many aspects of the party were more particularly rooted in the specifics of Fiji's history and culture. Dr. Bavadra, an indigenous Fijian medical doctor, was chosen as head of the party, and later of the coalition government, in deference to Fijian sentiments about the office of Prime Minister. Dr. Bavadra was a significant choice as a Fijian political leader because he was a commoner from the western side of Viti Levu island. As a professional he appealed to urban, educated, "middle class," indigenous Fijians. Moreover, although it may initially have seemed puzzling that Fiji's Indian middle class would join forces with a Labour party, there were significant similarities between the positions of the National Federation and the Labour parties, given the roots of the National Federation party in the Indian cane-growers' unions and Gandhian anticolonial resistance.

THE COALITION VICTORY AND THE MILITARY COUPS

The National Federation party–Fiji Labour party Coalition won the election of April 1987.[5] Attracting 9 percent total of the Fijian vote and the vast majority of the Indian vote, twenty-eight Coalition parliamentary representatives were elected. Explicit deference was shown to Fijian apprehensions and sentiments in the formation of leadership and cabinet. Dr. Bavadra became Prime Minister and the leader of the National Federation Party became his deputy. The initial cabinet included six Fijians, seven Indians, and one General Elector. Soon after the election, however, a new group, calling itself the "Taukei Movement" (indigenes' or landowners' movement) held protests and marches against the new Coalition government.

On May 14, 1987 Colonel Sitiveni Rabuka led a coup against the Coalition government. Rabuka was third in command of Fiji's Royal Military Forces, an army manned almost completely by indigenous Fijians; he is also a *bati* (hereditary warrior ally) of the high Fijian chief who was Fiji's Governor General. He and a party of armed, masked men invaded Parliament and took Dr. Bavadra and the members of the cabinet prisoner. Rabuka claimed that he had no wish to rule Fiji and promised a return to civilian government, after a revised constitution was adopted that would preserve "the chiefly system, Fijian land, and religion."

Ratu Sir Penaia Ganilau, the Governor General of Fiji, became a central actor in ensuing events acting upon and constructing his authority as representative of the British crown. He negotiated the release of Dr. Bavadra and his cabinet. On May 23, Colonel Rabuka turned the government over to the Governor General, who appointed an interim government which included both Alliance and Coalition leaders. Rabuka was to head a committee to write a new constitution. Seeking to restore stability in Fiji, the Governor General led negotiations toward a bipartisan Government of National Unity.

Throughout this period of several months, there was an intense popular debate on the respective rights and privileges of the different "races" inhabiting the islands. The debate was carried out in letters to the editor in English, Hindi, and Fijian newspapers and in public activity, including violence and threats of violence directed against Coalition supporters and Indians more generally. The debate focused on the very nature of Fiji as a "nation."

At the political level, the Governor General sought to normalize the situation by arguing that he had dissolved parliament and held authority within the crisis period. Dr. Bavadra sought through the courts to be restored to his elected position, and also sought aid abroad. Without condemning the coup, former Alliance Prime Minister Ratu Mara returned to accept a post in the new interim government. The Great Council of Chiefs met to debate, supporting Rabuka's actions wholeheartedly. Various grass-roots movements were formed to express opinions and to contribute to the decisions being made by the Governor General and other leaders.

As plans for a Government of National Unity solidified, however, members of the Taukei Movement increased their agitation. They threatened further violence against Indians and Labour supporters by building a *lovo* (in nineteenth-century Fiji, an oven in which human bodies were baked before being eaten) in front of the government buildings in the capital. A spokesman for the Taukei Movement said, "We just want to show the judges and Dr. Bavadra that this *lovo* is going to be the ultimate end" (*Fiji Times,* September 5, 1987), an explicit threat of violence against the Coalition supporters. On September 23, the Governor General installed the "Government of National Unity," a balanced council of Alliance and Coalition representatives.

But two days later, Colonel Rabuka led a second coup. He announced that he did not recognize the Governor General's authority to establish a Government of National Unity and that he intended to rule by decree until a new constitution was established. He met with the Governor General, Ratu Mara, and Dr. Bavadra and presented them with the goals and demands of the Taukei Movement, including guaranteed Fijian political leadership and a Christian polity. While Ratu Mara acceded to the terms, Dr. Bavadra would not. On October 7, Rabuka declared Fiji a Republic, breaking ties with Great Britain.

Rabuka ruled temporarily through a governing council made up of representatives from the Alliance party, the Taukei Movement, the Fijian Great Council of Chiefs, and the Fijian Nationalist party, with one token Indian member. To express their disapproval, Fiji's judiciary resigned. The army controlled the country by setting up road blocks and checkpoints and applying population-control tactics learned while participating in the United Nations multinational peace-keeping forces in the Middle East. Army recruitment of Fijian youths increased substantially. Newspapers were shut down and radio broadcasts were supervised by the government.

When Rabuka again began negotiations with the Governor General, Ratu Mara, and Dr. Bavadra, the Taukei movement split, as a result of some of its members refusing to support the proposed compromises. Nonetheless, on December 6, 1987, Rabuka turned the government over to the former Governor General, now designated as President, and to Ratu Mara (former Alliance Prime Minister) the new "Prime Minister." As "Prime Minister," Ratu Mara created a new judiciary and a cabinet composed of Alliance politicians, Taukei Movement representatives, and military officers. He complied with Rabuka's condition that no members of the Labour–National Federation party Coalition be included in the cabinet of this interim government, thus abandoning the attempt to create a government of national unity.

Despite the initial apparent restoration of Ratu Mara, leadership in postcoups Fiji has been divided among different powerful figures and interests. Ratu Mara and the former Governor General sought to refocus national attention on economic rebuilding. Mara has led negotiations with other nations, working toward resumption of aid from former donors and negotiation of new aid relationships with countries such as France. Within the domestic realm, however, Rabuka's powers were expanded enormously. As

Home Affairs Minister, he was empowered to order arrests and hold suspects indefinitely without charge or trial. Security forces were authorized to search premises and vehicles without warrant, to shoot to kill anyone found in any place declared a security area, to impose curfews, and to seize land or buildings. No inquests were to be held into any killings under the decree powers (Kamm 1988). Moreover, Rabuka's public statements concerning Fiji's future continued to advocate a vision of a nation defined by indigenous Fijian leadership and culture. Arguing that Fiji is a "Christian nation," his decrees prohibited recreation and commerce on the Christian sabbath. Far from eccentricity on Rabuka's part, this insistence on a Christian nation reflected his vision of an ideal polity based on the colonial, Christian, and chiefly model of Fijian "tradition."

After two years of debate over a series of draft constitutions, a new Fiji Constitution was approved by the Great Council of Chiefs on July 25, 1990, in a tightly guarded meeting at Queen Elizabeth Army Barracks in Suva. Later on that day, Ratu Sir Penaia Ganilau made a radio broadcast saying that the constitution would immediately take effect as supreme law of the land. The new constitution envisioned and institutionalized restricted Indian representation and pre-eminent Fijian control over the central offices of government. The Presidency and Prime Ministership may be held by Fijians only. Amongst seventy elected representatives, thirty-seven are to be Fijians, twenty-seven Fiji Indians, five Chinese and part Europeans, and one a Rotuman (to represent the island of Rotuma, which is culturally distinct but included in the nation of Fiji). The elaborate system of cross-voting of the 1970 constitution, which was intended to create cross-cutting racial ties, was abandoned. Fijians elect Fijian representatives, Indians elect Indian representatives. Taking upon itself the power to ratify this new constitution, the Great Council of Chiefs institutionalized its role as a central voice of Fijian authority. Indeed, the chiefs institutionalized their claim to *national* political authority as well; the ratification of the constitution was by the Great Council alone, there was no consideration of subjecting the document to any form of popular referendum. The new constitution thus institutionalizes the Fijian political paramountcy claimed by the coup leaders and beneficiaries, and rejects a theory of national leadership based on popular consensus or referendum.

Throughout the deliberations over the new constitution, leaders of the Labour–National Federation party Coalition continued to call for restoration of the Coalition government. They sharply criticized draft versions of the 1990 constitutions as "authoritarian, undemocratic, militaristic, racist and feudalistic," and, in June 1989, Dr. Bavadra stated that his group "[would] not accept an apartheid solution" (*Fiji Times*, 26 June 1989, cited in Lal 1990:9). But on November 4, 1989, Dr. Bavadra died of cancer. His wife, Adi Kuini Bavadra, temporarily assumed leadership of the Coalition. She and other Coalition spokespersons denounced the new constitution on the day it was ratified by the Great Council of Chiefs.

In the framing of the new 1990 constitution, internal power struggles among Fijians continue to mold wider political events. In 1988, the Great Council of Chiefs itself was reduced from over 150 members to 53 members and restructured to reinforce the influence of the three major indigenous Fijian chiefly kingdoms or confederacies (*Overseas Fiji Times*, 1988). Ratu Mara (former Alliance Prime Minister) and his wife, also a high chief, head two of those three confederacies. Other disputes among Fijians concern the rights to the title of "*Tui Viti*" (King of Fiji), and whether the Fijians of the "western side" provinces ought to organize a "fourth confederacy" to ensure their adequate representation. Others have argued that the new constitution overrepresents rural Fijians, the traditional power base of chiefly rule, to the detriment of urban Fijians. What is most interesting is that these Fijian intramural disputes have been held to be of "national" significance, even though they involve offices, titles, and social units in which 49 percent of Fiji's population, the Indians, can have no participation. No one has proposed, for example, that Indians might constitute a "confederacy."

The leaders who have established the new constitution also have to cope with postcoup Fiji's wider social crises. Fiji's economic mainstays, tourism and sugar production, were both severely affected by the coups. Over twenty thousand Fiji Indians (and a number of Fijians and Europeans as well) have chosen to leave the islands. As a result, in the first two years following the coups, Fiji lost over one-third of its doctors, one-half of its lawyers, and a large number of nurses and teachers. However, some departing professional people have been replaced by overseas personnel, including American Peace Corps volunteers, and new donors of aid have stepped in to support the postcoups government. In particular, France has extended its support, thus ensuring that Fiji's current leaders will not take the side of anticolonial movements in various French Pacific territories.

In Fiji and overseas, there has been persistent speculation concerning the possible involvement of covert operatives from other countries in the coups. The coups ousted a government that sought to make Fiji a nuclear-free zone, a policy the Reagan and Thatcher governments of the time found inconvenient. Certainly, overseas training in military tactics, ostensibly at least for use in the Middle Eastern peace-keeping forces, contributed to the effectiveness of Rabuka's military takeover. But whether or not other countries are eventually shown to have been directly involved, to understand Fiji's coups we must look to their basis in Fiji's colonial history and the interests and contradictions that have prevented a unified vision of a Fijian nation.

IMAGINING FIJI

For over a century, Indians and Fijians had lived together in Fiji without major communal violence. During that time, individuals and local groups sometimes worked together for mutual advantage and created bonds of respect and affection that crossed "racial" boundaries. There is a history of understanding, coexistence, and accommodation. Unfortunately, as recent events have shown, Fiji's history has also been shaped by racial intolerance and separations. Why has it been impossible for Fijians and Fiji Indians to imagine a nation together?

In creating the colonial polity, the British defined themselves, indigenous Fijians, and Fiji Indians, in nineteenth-century social-evolutionary terms. For over a century, indigenous Fijians and Fiji Indians lived in that colonial polity, sometimes accommodating, sometimes resisting those British "racial" classifications. Within the colonial period, Fijian and Fiji Indian "imagined communities" were communities imagined in relation to the British. In very different circumstances, both Fijians and Indians created new communal identities, through which they asserted distinctive characteristics as peoples and as communities.

In colonial days, the Fiji Indians imagined a nation in which they had equal political rights with Fiji's Europeans. The Fiji Indians organized their own community in an anticolonial struggle largely modeled on Indian nationalism. But the Fiji Indians have not been able to articulate a vision of Fiji as a nation that could include and satisfy indigenous Fijians as well. Just as many Fijians placed Indians in the stereotyping cultural category of *kaisi* (slaves) of the British, many Fiji Indians viewed Fijians as "low people" of little culture and either did not seek, or were not able, to enlist them in the anticolonial struggle. Further, Fiji Indian resistance to colonial dominance was largely organized through forms of Hindu nationalism that celebrated Indian religious and cultural difference and was unlikely to engage Christian Fijians. Indian communal uplift thus focused on Indian successes; whether educational advancement, religious devotionalism, or economic prosperity. In relation to the British, Indian success in any sphere was resistance to oppression. But in relation to the Fijians, Indians remained a separate, largely Hindu community, more successful in its own uplift than in establishing cross-cutting ties. In the 1940s, during the Deed of Cession debate, A.D. Patel envisioned Fiji as a nation formed through the common cause of indigenous Fijians and Fiji Indians in opposition to the colonial British. But this stance was rejected by Fijians. In independent Fiji, the National Federation party advocated pluralism and development, but failed even more dramatically to propose any vision of Fiji that could appease indigenous Fijians fearful of Fiji Indian advance.

In contrast, the coup leader has "imagined" a Fiji that is simply the colonial system of indirect rule (the old "Fijian Administration") expanded to become the nation itself. In this transformation of the paternalist colonial vision, Fijians are privileged and Indians are negligible figures in the Fijian social landscape. Drafts of the new constitution began, "Fiji shall be a sovereign Republic and shall uphold the teachings of the Lord Jesus Christ"; the new constitution itself proposes that Christian Fijian chiefs should control government and define Fiji as a nation. This vision sees the chiefs of Fiji, and the political position they assumed in the colonial era, as guarantors of Fijian cultural continuity, religion, and noncapitalist ethos. It mobilizes the powerful rhetoric of indigenous rights and the preservation of cultural difference, on behalf of Fijians, and Fijian chiefs. It makes subordinate the interests of the Indians, 49 percent of Fiji's citizens, who have no chiefs, who are Hindu and Muslim, and who from their beginnings in Fiji have had to participate in the marketplace to survive. This Fijian vision of the nation has little place in it for Fiji Indians as citizens; and, indeed, Rabuka has said publicly that Fiji will know peace only if all the Indians convert to Christianity or leave (Kamm 1988:2).

In contrast to both these visions of Fiji, the Fiji Labour party proposed an "imagined community" that might engage and include both indigenous Fijians and Fiji Indians as one people. Appealing to both Fijians and Indians as working people with equal rights in, and commitments to, the nation, the Labour party sought to redefine all Fiji citizens as "Fijians." In so doing, the party challenged the interests of the ruling Fijian elites. At the same time it contested the discourse of "race" and "racial division" in which so much of Fiji's politics was couched. A fragile "imagined community" of great potential, this vision of the nation based on the concerns of common citizenship was denied in the military coups. The project of building a new "nation" was replaced by a new constitution founded in and committed to upholding divisions of race and power set into place in the colonial era.

The ironies of Fiji's situation are all the more explicit in the context of the ongoing anticolonial struggles of other Pacific peoples. In Fiji, the coup leaders and supporters argue that they represent the rights of indigenous peoples in the face of colonial and postcolonial domination. They have won the support of certain New Zealand Maori activists (see Chapter 21, "The Maori Tradition of Prophecy: Religion, History, and Politics in New Zealand," by Karen Sinclair, in this volume), who, in several highly publicized events, strongly supported the coups. Yet ironically, following the coups, the leaders of Fiji have also accepted increasing amounts of monetary aid from France, a well-entrenched colonial power in the Pacific (see Chapter 6, "Welfare State Colonialism in Rural French Polynesia," by Victoria S. Lockwood, in this volume). It is most ironic of all that the coups on behalf of the colonially empowered chiefs of Fiji have engendered an anticolonial rhetoric on the part of many Fijians, a rhetoric which many once rejected when voiced in the anticolonial protest of the Gandhi-inspired Fiji Indians. In Fiji, and elsewhere in the Pacific, independence from colonial rule has not always dispelled colonial systems of classification and divisiveness. Nor does nationalist struggle necessarily engender a unified vision of a new nation.

Acknowledgments: I thank the Government of Fiji for permission to pursue research in 1984–85 and 1986, during which time my research focus was on the *Tuka* movement, a Fijian political-religious movement. I warmly thank friends in Fiji for their insights and hospitality. I also thank S.T. Tuinaceva, Archivist, National Archives of Fiji, for permission to use the Colonial Secretary's Office Series and other records. I thank Henry Rutz for the use of his copies of the *Fiji Times* and Donald Brenneis for the use of his copies of the *Overseas Fiji Times*. I acknowledge funding for research in Fiji from the Department of Education Fulbright-Hays Dissertation Fellowship Program and from the National Science Foundation. I owe special thanks to John D. Kelly for his comments on this chapter in its various stages.

NOTES

1. The locally used terms are "Fijian" for descendants of the indigenous Fijians, "Indian" for descendants of the South Asian indentured laborers, and "European" for descendants of British colonizers and other Westerners. It should be noted that almost all Fiji Indians were born in Fiji, as were most of their parents. As will be seen, one political party has recently sought to redefine "Fijian" to refer to all Fiji citizens.

2. In 1881, Fiji's total population was 127,486. Of this total, 114,748 were Fijians, 588 were Indians and 12,150 were "Others," mainly Europeans. Between 1881 and 1921, the Fijian population declined to 84,475 and the Indian population increased to 60,634, of a total of 157,266. After 1921, the Fijian population has risen steadily, while the Indian population rose and then leveled off. In 1946, Fijians numbered 118,070, Indians 120,414, and "Others" 21,154, out of 259,638 total (Moynagh 1981:2). In 1986, Fijians were 46.2 percent and Indians 48.6 percent of Fiji's population of 715,375 (Fiji Ministry of Information, 1986 census figures cited in the *Fiji Times*, 1987).

3. The twenty-second member of the Senate was a representative from the island of Rotuma, which was administered by the British from Fiji and remained administratively connected to Fiji at independence.

4. While Indians are typically viewed as wealthy by Fijians, the mean average income of Fijian and "other" Pacific Islander taxpayers in Fiji was F$2,841 in 1976, and the mean average income of Indian taxpayers was only F$217 higher, F$3,058. However, there were many more Indian taxpayers (56.9 percent of the total taxpayers) than Fijian taxpayers (together with "other" Pacific Islanders in Fiji, 34.5 percent of the total taxpayers). For

this reason, the total taxable income of the Indians was almost F$96 million, while the total taxable income of Fijians and "other" Islanders in Fiji was just over F$54 million (Bureau of Statistics 1979:115–120). Individual Indians were earning little more, on average, than individual Fijians who were participating in the cash economy. There were and are at least as many poor Fiji Indians as poor indigenous Fijians. However, in terms of total spending power, Indians significantly outweighed indigenous Fijians and "other" Islanders together. Additionally, the two groups on the whole clearly use money in different ways. Fijians spend large amounts of money on collective ritual and other social events, while Indians buy more durable goods.

5. Much of this section is based on daily reports in the *Fiji Times* from May to December 1987 (the newspaper was shut down twice, for six days following the first coup and for about a month following the second).

4

The Law of the State and the State of the Law in Vanuatu

William L. Rodman
McMaster University

Anthropologists with a specific interest in law have studied very few of the thirty thousand islands in the Pacific. Yet in Oceania as everywhere else in the world, conflict is an inevitable part of community life—perhaps not everyday community life, but over time, disputes emerge. They are as certain as sleep, as inescapable as restless nights. People in groups can and *do* live together in perfect harmony, but not very often and not for very long.

Ways of resolving conflict are as universal as disputes themselves. That is, the methods themselves are not universal, but people everywhere have developed systematic ways of resolving their differences. In industrialized nations such as those of North America, the state sets rules and procedures for settling conflict and punishing wrongdoers. The legal system depends for its existence upon codified laws, a complex court system, police who enforce the laws of the state, and prisons for those who fail to obey the laws.

The Pacific Islands today consist of a few old colonies, mostly French, and many new states. Local communities in both colonial and postcolonial societies in Oceania are encapsulated within broader governmental and legal frameworks. This means that—in theory—local communities have only limited autonomy in matters of law. A state may institute local courts and grant local leaders the right to resolve certain kinds of disputes. However, under state law, communities have no mandate to set their own independent laws or create their own courts.

There is a criminal code in Tonga and Western Samoa, just as there is a criminal code in the U.S. and Canada. If you break someone's jaw, or steal a pig, or rape a woman on any of the seventy inhabited islands of Vanuatu, you become liable to prosecution under the laws of the state just as surely as if you committed the same offenses in Memphis or Montreal or Moscow. In theory, the law of *all* states is uniform and all-encompassing; in practice, law in new Pacific states differs considerably from the law as established in Western societies.

I have two goals in this Chapter, one ethnographic, and one theoretical. My first aim is to provide a fresh perspective on the law of the state in relation to the state of the law in many Pacific Islands communities. What role do Pacific Islands states play in local-level law? Should we assume that a state, like King Kong, can pretty much do what it wants, whenever it wants? I focus on the Republic of Vanuatu, and discuss two contrasting views of the relationship between the state and the people. One view assumes the existence of a relatively strong central government and a passive rural populace. The other view, one I believe is more accurate, holds that the reverse is true; that is, Vanuatu is best viewed as a weak state with a local people who have responded to the challenges of the colonial and postcolonial era by actively seeking control over their own destiny.

The case study of Vanuatu raises some questions about the way in which many scholars conceptualize relations between the state and peripheral areas, especially with regard to law. My second goal is to reassess the utility of a key concept in legal anthropology: Moore's notion of a "semiautonomous social field." Moore defines a semiautonomous field as one that exists within a broader social field yet is able to "generate rules and coerce or induce compliance with them" (Moore 1978:57). Her concept has two aspects: first, that the smaller or less-powerful field is linked to some larger or more powerful grouping; and, second, that the field has a degree of detachment from the grouping to which it belongs. Implicitly, *semiautonomy* means that the encapsulated, less-powerful group exists in "some sort of active relationship with some exported form of European law, at the very least in the form of their nation's official law" (Greenhouse 1985:94).

The idea of semiautonomy was attractive to scholars seeking to move away from the structural-functionalist paradigm. Structural-functionalists portrayed islands and peoples as existing in cultural, as well as physical, isolation from each other. The concept of semiautonomy brought anthropology closer to the real world as anthropologists in the 1970s and 1980s experienced it, a world of political superstructures and encapsulated peoples, of powerlessness and degrees of resistance, of creative local responses to national policy initiatives. Today, the use of Moore's concept is pervasive in the anthropology of law; it has become unproblematic, something we tend to assume, a basic conceptual building block. The extent to which semiautonomy has entered the mainstream of ideas in legal anthropology is apparent in Starr and Collier's (1987:371) assertion that "societies may be characterized as having dual or multiple legal systems, *but these systems are never autonomous*" (italics added).

However, there is increasing evidence in the ethnographic literature that some "encapsulated" societies *are* autonomous in the conduct of their legal affairs—perhaps not permanently, but certainly for extended periods of time. Before discussing the evidence, it is necessary to define "legal autonomy" so that readers can judge for themselves the extent to which the island discussed in this case study can be said to be autonomous in the conduct of its legal affairs. An encapsulated group may be regarded as autonomous, from a legal standpoint, when its members process their own disputes and maintain social order without reference to a central government.

This definition implies a continuum of conditions of relative autonomy. The more disputes concerning members of a local community that state officials process, the less independence the local community can be said to have in matters of law; conversely, the less initiative a state exercises in dispute processing in a community, the more a community can be said to control its own legal affairs. No state involvement in local law, for whatever reason, equals *de facto* local-level legal autonomy.

The notion of semiautonomy may oversimplify and misrepresent the true nature of law in some peripheral areas. However, semiautonomy *is* a useful descriptive label for a specific relationship existing between a state and an encapsulated people at a particular point in time. The argument here is simply that scholars have been too ready to *assume* relations of legal dependency and semiautonomy in rural areas of the South Pacific and elsewhere in the world. A better approach would be to view relations between a state and its encapsulated populations as dynamic, variable, and subject to continuous readjustment and change. Further, it should be recognized that conditions of relative autonomy are not uniform within a state. Especially in new states (such as exist in the South Pacific), some encapsulated groups are much more independent in the conduct of their legal affairs than other peoples in the same state.

This approach returns a problematic quality to relations in the domain of law between states and local communities. It opens up a host of interesting questions: Under what conditions might an encapsulated people achieve maximal self-reliance in matters of law? What are the advantages and disadvantages of legal autonomy for a local people? How do local leaders who lack access to the coercive sanctions of the state maintain order? What initiatives might a people take to try to ensure a peaceful way of life for themselves without the state?

REPRESSIVE STATE OR PATCHWORK POLITY?:THE NEW HEBRIDES UNDER COLONIAL RULE

When I first conducted research in the Anglo-French Condominium of the New Hebrides in 1969, the country had two police forces, three codes of law (British, French, and Native) and no political parties. The Condominium was a unique experiment in colonial rule, the only place in the world where two colonial powers ruled jointly on the basis of strict equality over an inhabited territory that was not already a legally organized polity (O'Connell 1969:78). What was the state of the law in rural areas of the New Hebrides during the time of colonial rule?

In a series of recent articles, the political scientist Ralph Premdas presents a bleak view of life in the Condominium. He asserts that "internal autonomy was lost" in local communities in the New Hebrides; "imposed were alien institutions" (Premdas 1986:10). Native New Hebrideans had "no other choice [than to accept colonial rule, for] the modern European state…was superimposed, like a scaffold, on the indigenous system creating a new if abhorrent political reality" (Premdas 1987a:147). He observes that "in the critical sphere of dispute settlement…new Western judicial processes have been introduced" (Premdas 1987a:154; 1987b:122); "the new juridical entities were designed to maximize alien control and exploitation. The instrument of imperial domination was the state" (Premdas 1985:1).

Premdas's description of the Condominium as repressive, expansive, exploitative, nonconsultative, and alien makes the New Hebrides sound like South Africa or perhaps the Belgian Congo. What I observed in the islands did not resemble that description at all. During the twenty-eight months I conducted field work in the New Hebrides at the time of the Condominium, I saw evidence of a minimal state, a patchwork polity, an abortive experiment in joint rule that rural folk found easy to ignore or resist.

An island world presents certain distinctive problems of government control, communication, information gathering, allocation of resources, and mobility. In the New Hebrides, the central government lacked the funding, manpower, and infrastructure necessary to govern efficiently.

Consider the fact that there are eighty-two islands in the archipelago, seventy of which are populated, and these extend over thirteen hundred kilometers of ocean. The population of the country is approximately one hundred twenty-eight thousand (Stanley 1986:413). The cultural diversity of the region is very great. There are 115 local languages, most with several dialects, the highest number of languages per capita of any country in the world (Stanley 1986:414). On most islands, people live in small villages or hamlets. The average size of a hamlet on Ambae, the island on which I conducted my field work, is only 25.3 persons (Republic of Vanuatu 1983:ix). Paths or rough dirt roads join hamlets to each other, but communication links between hamlets are erratic. Sometimes people hike for hours to attend a meeting that has been rescheduled or a feast that has been cancelled.

The Anglo-French government divided the country into four districts for purposes of administration. In each district, there were two district agents, one British and one French. These colonial officials had numerous responsibilities, one of which was to act as magistrates in Native Court. They held court when they toured the islands; most district agents spent less than one-third of their time on tour. Although the formal judicial structure of the New Hebrides included various kinds of courts with different functions, Native Court was the only colonial legal forum with which most islanders ever came in contact.[1]

Eight colonial officials processing disputes part-time on seventy islands do not pose much of a threat to the internal autonomy of most local communities. Indeed, anthropologists who conducted field work in the New Hebrides mention nothing in their published articles even remotely resembling a "politico-administrative structure…superimposed on ni-Vanuatu life to enforce law and order…" (Premdas 1986:10). To the contrary, researchers emphasize the weakness of the state and the autonomy of local people. Police were not stationed on most islands in the group (Jupp 1982:148). Rubinstein (1981:146) writes of the "power vacuum and governmental disorder" he observed on the island of Malo; Allen (1969:14) found that "European administration [was] almost wholly absent in West Aoba" during the time of the Condominium; in his survey of research in Vanuatu, Valjavec (1986:618) concludes that "the impact of the government was negligible" on island politics during the colonial era.

We are left with a puzzle. If the representatives of the Condominium government were out of sight and out of mind in most places most of the time, then who was taking care of the business of law on those seventy inhabited islands in the group? How was order being maintained out on the periphery? The section that follows offers a close look at one locale, the island then called Aoba that is now known as Ambae.[2]

THE OUTER LIMITS OF SEMI-AUTONOMY: AOBA UNDER COLONIAL RULE

Ambae is one of the largest and most populous islands in the northern sector of the archipelago. Today, the total population of the island is close to eight thousand. People engage in subsistence agriculture, but they also raise coconuts, which they process into copra. They derive a cash income from the sale of the smoke-dried coconut meat to ships that visit the island on a regular basis. No Europeans own land or maintain permanent residence on Ambae.

The people of Ambae have no quarrel with much of Western culture. According to the last census, 53 percent of the population over ten years old has a sixth-grade education. The census also documents the fact that only one non-Christian remains on the island. Everyone else is an Anglican, a Roman Catholic, or a member of some other Christian denomination. Every hamlet has at least one radio, and people are interested in affairs in the world beyond the island.

Despite cultural change and the increasing monetization of the economy, customary beliefs and practices play an important role in island life. A grizzled old chief once pointed out to me in an amicable tone of voice that it is much harder to kill pigs than men on Ambae. "If I want to kill you today, I could," he told me mildly, "but there's just *no way* I could kill pigs." What he meant was that killing a man takes no special skill. All one needs is a victim and a blunt instrument of sufficient heft. By comparison, killing pigs in a ceremonial context on Ambae can be an act of formidable difficulty, the culmination of years of planning and plotting, and a sure test of a man's abilities as an economic and political entrepreneur.

Today, as in the past, leaders on East Ambae tend to be men of high rank in an organization known in anthropological literature as "the graded society." In the graded society, there are fifteen major ranks. A person must take each rank in sequence, and each new grade requires the individual to kill (or exchange with a trading partner) boars with more developed tusks than those used in previous grades. The closer the tusks to a full circle, the higher the rank achieved.

Pigs are a kind of investment; literally, live stocks. Individuals own these animals, but allow them to roam free in the bush. Capturing a tusked boar alive so that it can be used in a ceremony is a somewhat risky sport. Rank cannot be inherited, and a man cannot "buy" a rank with pigs purchased for cash or raised in a fence. The only way to achieve rank is by making successful investments in other men's ranktaking endeavours. A rank candidate also must convince potential investors, men who owe him nothing, of his own excellent prospects as a player in the game of pigs and politics.

Why are pigs a passion for most adult men on East Ambae? What does a man gain by taking rank? He gains a few tangibles: a new title (the name of the rank), a new name (my adopted father is "Rock-of-the-Shark"), a ceremonial pandanus loincloth, and also the right to use ceremonial regalia appropriate to the rank taken—things like armbands, a legband, a thick bustle or skirt, and, for the very highest rank, an impressive headpiece made of hummingbird feathers and tiny shells woven into fabric. The real rewards, however, are intangible. If a man makes wise investments and kills his pigs well, and if he speaks at ceremonies with flair and intelligence, then he is accorded respect. People listen carefully to what he has to say, not just at ranktakings but also at meetings and at hearings to resolve conflict. High rank legitimizes leadership on East Ambae, and this makes Ambaean chiefs quite different from most Melanesian Big Men. Unlike stereotypical Big Men, Ambaean men of high rank possess a source of legitimacy that no one can revoke or even question. In addition, the rank hierarchy stabilizes relations between leaders and followers. Everyone knows where everyone stands relative to everyone else.

Throughout the colonial era, the graded society provided a proving ground for chiefs on Aoba. As men climbed the rank hierarchy, step by step, year after year, they learned many of the skills necessary for the exercise of political leadership. Only a few islands in the New Hebrides had a graded society similar to that of Aoba, so was Aoba a unique case in state and local legal relations in the Condominium? Almost certainly not. The specific criteria for becoming a leader differs from island to island, but respect for chiefs was (and still is) a key value in local cultures throughout the archipelago. Ghai (1985:70) is correct in generalizing that the "thinness of the administration on the ground ensured an influential role for (chiefs) up to independence."

Chiefs used their influence to mediate an end to minor disputes in their own villages. They processed more serious cases in unofficial local courts. These courts were bastards of Condominium law, tolerated but unacknowledged, without rights or legal status, but bearing more than a passing resemblance to their two European parents. For the Joint Government, unofficial courts were both a political embarrassment and a practical necessity, a constant reminder of the essential weakness of the state and an efficient solution to the problem of keeping the peace without police.

"Court" is a European concept, not an indigenous one, but unofficial court on Aoba was not especially European in appearance or in operation. A hearing most often resembled a North American town meeting more than a Western court of law. Both men and women attended court as interested observers or as witnesses. Rules of procedure were few: everyone was expected to show respect for other people in attendance, especially the chiefs and elders, but anyone could voice an opinion or present evidence, so long as no one else was speaking.

Two men of high rank "presided" at hearings, but the role they played varied according to the nature of the case. People in conflict with each other, (say, neighbors in disagreement over property boundaries), could use unofficial court as a public forum in which to air their differences. In such cases, the men of rank who led the meeting acted more as mediators than as judges; they sought common ground between the disputants, a compromise that everyone would accept.

At other times, especially in cases involving lawbreaking, the two leaders would act in a sharp, authoritarian manner. For example, I have seen them tongue-lash a village gossip, shame an adulterous couple, and threaten a rowdy young man with exile from the island. Many times, I saw them order an offender to pay compensation to a complainant and also a stiff fine "to restore peace" to the local chiefs. Once or twice, I even saw them resort to force in order to compel obedience with the decisions they made in court.

Some have argued that this kind of behavior is European in origin, an imitation of the demeanor of colonial magistrates. Premdas (1986:5; 1987a:113; 1987b:146) thinks that indigenous decision making in Vanuatu was democratic and consultative. In his view, the colonial order violated this tradition.

The historical and ethnographic record suggests otherwise. Indeed, before intensive contact, chiefs tended to consult local opinion, but often they were more autocratic than democratic in their behavior. Especially in the northern islands, high-ranking chiefs had as much legitimate power as any British or French judge; they possessed the ultimate sanction, the legitimate right to order an offender's execution (Codrington 1891:47; M. Rodman 1983). Chiefs no longer consider themselves to have the power of life or death over their followers, but the past—embodied in myth and tradition—still lives in the present on Ambae, and the current generation of leaders on the island identify more strongly with their own political ancestors than with any colonial role models. Their occasional high-handedness is not necessarily evidence of the occupation of their psyches by colonial oppressors, as Premdas (1987a:152) seems to believe. In historical and cultural terms, they come by their courtroom behavior honestly.

During the colonial era, homicide was the *only* category of offense that chiefs on Aoba automatically ceded to the state. They were willing and able to process all other types of disputes and offenses locally. Chiefs viewed themselves as having an option: they could settle a case themselves, or they could pass it along to the government for resolution. They managed the flow of information to the state in such a way as to maximize their own power and interests. If, for example, they failed to reform a troublemaker, they would report that person to the government. A district agent then would come to the island and convene Native Court. Under Condominium law, the magistrate was obligated to consult with local assessors. Most often, the same chiefs who tried and failed to correct the offender's behavior would act as the district agent's official assessors. District agents did for the chiefs the one thing that chiefs could not do for themselves in unofficial court—sentence troublemakers to jail on another island.

There were some kinds of cases that chiefs *never* passed to the government. Local people were well aware that most district agents scoffed at beliefs in witchcraft, so chiefs withheld from them any information about cases arising from accusations of sorcery. In a similar manner, chiefs placed no faith in Europeans' understanding of local culture, so they simply did not inform the government of cases involving breaches of traditional marriage regulations and contested land rights.

To summarize, the evidence is clear that local leaders, for their own purposes, engaged in a kind of dialogue with the state: they helped the state maintain an illusion of control in return for occasional access to the state's coercive sanctions. This might be viewed as "semiautonomy," but the emphasis should be placed more on "autonomy" than on an implied connection with a centralized government. Local leaders co-opted legal middleman positions, manipulated colonial officials, tapped the state's coercive sanctions, and controlled access to the channels of information that determined the nature and extent of the state's involvement in local law. This, clearly, is the outer fringe of legal semiautonomy.

BEYOND THE FRINGE: AMBAE IN THE POST-COLONIAL ERA

In 1980, colonial rule ended in the New Hebrides and the Republic of Vanuatu was born. It was not an easy transition to independence. On the eve of independence, just as Great Britain and France were preparing to withdraw, armed rebels seized control of the largest island in the country, Espiritu Santo. They shut all the police in their own jail and renamed the island "Vemarana." The newly elected government of Vanuatu requested military assistance from Papua New Guinea. Papua New Guinea responded by airlifting 450 troops to Espiritu Santo. The rebellion soon ended, the troops returned home, and the government of Vanuatu was left to face the task of building a new nation from the ruins of a hodgepodge colonial state.

The colonial legal order melted away with the coming of independence, but the new government had nothing to put in its place so far as law in rural areas was concerned. Government leaders rejected the colonial approach to local law, but they had no alternative vision, no clear plans for local courts, no training program for legal middlemen, no money for local-level police. Only three ni-Vanuatu had university training in law at the time of independence.

The links in the chain of law that bound the periphery to the center soon became undone and whole islands achieved *de facto* autonomy overnight. For some communities, years would pass before the state made any attempt to reassert even minimal control over local legal affairs.

The postindependence period in rural Vanuatu was a time when local leaders consolidated the autonomy they had gained. Between 1978 and 1982, people on Ambae developed a complex legal system that efficiently maintained social order.[3] The system had four levels: the hamlet, the hamlet alliance, the district, and the island itself. On the island level, a Council of Chiefs legislated laws relating to matters of common concern. For example, it banned the sale of liquor on the island, decided on the proper amount of compensation to be paid in cases of homicide, and changed the name of the island from "Aoba", a name the chiefs associated with colonialism, to "Ambae" (Rodman and Rodman 1985).

At the other end of the legal spectrum, local leaders continued to mediate disputes informally in their own hamlets. If a mediator was unable to resolve a dispute, he would pass the case to leaders of the hamlet alliance in which he resided. Hamlet alliance leaders processed cases in courts modeled on the "unofficial courts" of the colonial era. But what if a case involved residents of different networks of allied hamlets? To handle interalliance disputes, leaders innovated a new legal level called "district court." The latter also functioned on occasion as a court of appeal regarding decisions that leaders made in the hamlet alliance courts.

One of the more unusual aspects of the new autonomous legal system on Ambae was that people on the island codified their laws and then used their written codes in dispute processing. There are few examples of legal code-making in anthropological literature concerning non-Western societies, especially in societies encapsulated within a state.[4] However, on Ambae, a number of hamlet alliances formulated their own written codes of law. Leaders were not concerned to codify *kastom* law—indeed, there are customary elements in the alliance laws, but pragmatism was the guiding spirit behind the development of the laws. The codifiers of the laws worked with two questions in mind: what are the most common causes of conflict in everyday life, and what penalties should be imposed for particular offenses? With the laws, they set fines, to be paid either in the national currency (*vatu*, abbreviated VT) or, alternatively, in traditional valuables—specifically, pigs or woven pandanus mats.

The laws in the codes cover a broad range of offenses, from minor ones to the most serious. If, for example, someone steals a single chicken's egg in the district of Longana, the court can order that person to give the egg's owner VT20 (the worth of an egg, as determined locally) and also pay a fine of VT50. One hundred *vatu* equal approximately $1 (U.S.), so the total payment for the theft of the egg would be roughly 70 cents (U.S.). If, however, someone steals a pig, this could be cause for a serious penalty. The Longana code sets the fair value of a good-sized tusker at VT30,000 and the fine for stealing such an animal at VT5,000. That adds up to the equivalent of about $350 (U.S.), enough to make most people think twice before attempting to pig-rustle.

Ambae was not the only island in Vanuatu to codify its laws. Ethnomusicologist Peter Crowe, who conducted field work on the island of Maevo in the late 1970s, reports that the Council of Chiefs on Maevo codified a number of their laws in 1977 (Crowe 1986). Like some of the Ambae codes, the Maevo code included laws against homicide, assault, theft, and damage to property, and also dealt with a number of offenses against *kastom* and local moral standards (Crowe 1986). It appears that the Maevo code was an independent effort, entirely the product of local initiative, a similar response to that of Ambae to conditions of local legal autonomy.

For eight years, peoples' courts were the *only* courts to exist on Ambae. Even though local leaders lost their access to the state's coercive sanctions with the end of colonial rule, they still were able to attract disputes for processing, resolve conflict on a regular basis, and maintain social control in their communities.

Why did the system work? That is, why would anyone pay a fine to a court on an island where there is no jail and no police? The answers are complex, rooted deep in the culture of the place and in psychological factors, and also in other factors as well, such as the possibility of physical coercion. Even the remoteness and social-boundedness of the island play a role in shaping the spirit of the legal system. What follows are some of the reasons why disputants generally are willing to settle their differences and, if a case involves commission of a criminal offense, accept their punishment.

First, we must take into account the culture of politics and law on Ambae. There is a long tradition of respect for law and authority on the island, a tradition children still learn and which the graded society continues to reinforce. When Ambaeans accept without question or complaint the decisions in court of men of high rank, most often they act in accord with a number of deeply ingrained values. It is *right* to show respect for rank; it is *proper* to acknowledge the wisdom of the elders; it is *good* to show fidelity to *kastom*; and it is *ethical* to accept responsibility for one's own actions. All these social virtues predispose most people to conform to the courts' judgments. Most people want to be regarded as good citizens, regardless of the presence or absence of state controls. An adulterer does not view himself as a rebel against the social order. More likely, when he comes before the court, he is an embarrassed man, a man shamed deeply by exposure, anxious to pay his fine, set things right, and get on with his life.

Then, too, it is important to recognize that chiefs reach their decisions in an open hearing after full consultation with the concerned parties. Leaders rarely reach unpopular decisions that go against the community grain. They are sensitive to public opinion, well aware that too many bad calls will leave them with a blemished reputation and reduced authority. A punishment such as a fine may be viewed as representing the will of a community-in-council, not the whim of one or two powerful individuals.

Another factor to take into account is that ties between people on Ambae (or on any similar island) tend to be *multiplex*, a term that anthropologists use to denote relations between people who interact with each other as performers of many different roles. That is, from the perspective of any given disputant, a chief presiding in court is not just a chief. He is also likely to be a next-door neighbor, a mother's brother, a sponsor in a previous ranktaking venture and, perhaps, the storekeeper on whom the disputant depends for tinned corned beef and cigarettes. The individual standing before the court knows that, whatever the outcome of the hearing, he will continue to interact with the chief and also with his adversaries in the dispute for the rest of his life, every day, with no time off for good behavior. Under the circumstances, it is in a disputant's own best interests to accept a compromise and settle the conflict. He might even agree to pay a fine he does not think he entirely deserves. It is hard to remain in conflict with people he cannot avoid in everyday life. If the community thinks he is wrong, then his best chance at a peaceful, happy life is to make amends.

Finally, there is the chiefs' final option, vigilante justice. Vigilantism occurs when a person (or group) who views himself as lawful uses illegal physical coercion to modify the behavior of someone who commits unlawful acts. When chiefs on Ambae fail repeatedly in their attempts to reform a wrongdoer, they may resort to the extraordinary measure of using strong-arm tactics to achieve their ends. This is not surprising. If one lives in a community where state law is weak or nonexistent, one gains a sense of the vulnerability of such communities to violent and antisocial individuals. How can the community defend itself against such people? One way is to engage them on their own turf, outside the law. What is remarkable about Ambae is how rarely chiefs resort to the threat or use of physical coercion. Most of the time, when order is disrupted, chiefs are able to use peaceful means to re-establish a peaceful community. They gather their strong young men around them only as a last resort, as a blunt instrument to get the attention of the most recalcitrant.

In 1983, the government decentralized legal and judicial services, but today many rural areas in Vanuatu still lack access to state law. On Ambae, people have mixed feelings about the government's moves to decentralize law. They welcome the government's Island Court as an adjunct to their own legal system, that is, as a court of appeal from decisions made in hamlet alliance and district courts. But they dislike the fact that Island Court procedures derive from English Common Law rather than from local custom. Also, local justices feel uncomfortable with the minimal training in state law that they have received.

In 1985, I talked with all four chiefs that the government had appointed from the district of Longana to serve as justices in Island Court. They felt strongly that all cases, of whatever nature, must be processed in the people's own courts. Only cases that chiefs failed to resolve in "unofficial" court would then be passed to "official" Island Court. On the basis of their previous record, it seems clear that chiefs will remain in full control of their legal system. They will, in effect, regulate the amount of autonomy they have in the conduct of their legal affairs. Even as the chiefs negotiate with the central government the terms of decentralization of legal and judicial services, they continue to refine their own codes of law. They realize that the initiative in matters of law lies with them, not with the central government. It always has; and, most probably, it always will. They are well aware that they have "an exit option"; that is, they can "withdraw from, or ignore, demands placed on them by the officials" (Hyden 1980:25–26). They know, too, that they have a second alternative—a re-entry option—that can be a mighty tool in shaping the tenor of their relationship with the state. Just as they can disengage at will from discourse with the government, so can they re-establish lines of communication with the state when conditions best suit them.

CONCLUSIONS: THE POWER OF THE PERIPHERY IN THE SOUTH PACIFIC

A visitor to Port Vila, the capital of Vanuatu, might gain the impression that the legal arm of the central government is strong. There are police there, and court buildings, and all the trappings of a postcolonial legal establishment. When you leave the capital, however, your perspective changes. If you live for a while in a rural sector of the archipelago, on an island far away from the air-conditioned offices of Port Vila, it is quite obvious that Vanuatu's periphery is too vast for the small and weak center to control.

This is probably true of many countries in the South Pacific. The term "probably" is more appropriate than "certainly," because good recent information is lacking from most parts of the Pacific Islands concerning the state of the law in local communities in relation to the law of the state. What, then, is the best guess? If the government of Vanuatu has little control over law on most of the seventy inhabited islands in the group, then what are the government of Fiji's prospects of administering state law throughout the 322 islands that make up the Fiji Group? What about Kiribati, a Pacific republic with 33 islands scattered over a sea area larger than the size of the entire Caribbean? It seems likely that people on many islands in different parts of Oceania have a fair degree of autonomy in the conduct of their legal affairs. The true extent and nature of local self-reliance in matters of law will remain poorly understood until anthropologists undertake additional long-term research on law in many communities far removed from the capital cities and port towns of the New Pacific.

Throughout the colonial era, and now in the present day, Ambae has remained semiautonomous from an economic standpoint (see Chapter 11, "Keeping Options Open: Copra and Fish in Rural Vanuatu," by Margaret Rodman, in this volume). This raises an additional question: does economic dependence always create conditions of legal dependence? The evidence of Ambae's economic dependence on the state is plentiful, but there is no evidence *from the local level* in support of a view of legal dependency in the postcolonial era on Ambae or elsewhere in rural Vanuatu. In Vanuatu, most local legal orders are not 'subordinate' to the state, and the total configuration of local legal orders does not constitute a "dominant" legal system.

Over a decade ago, Goran Hyden concluded that "it is perhaps our gravest analytical mistake in the study of Africa to assume *a priori* that the peasants are already caught in…relations of dependence" (1980:32). The same could be said of other parts of the world, and with specific regard to law. In this chapter, I have tried to show some of the reasons why we should not assume that local law is tied to the state in new nations, even in places in which relations of economic dependency exist. Further, we should not assume that new states can create conditions of legal dependency easily; in a "weak" state, the rhetoric of control often bears only a casual resemblance to the exercise of power.

During the last few years, there have been an increasing number of studies of societies in which segments of the population effectively disengage from the state.[5] The main focus of the literature on disengagement has been on resistance: what J. Scott (1986) calls "the weapons of the weak"; what Guha (1983) has termed "elementary forms of peasant insurgency." A tradition of resistance to state control exists in some parts of the Pacific Islands; however, in other places, local people achieve legal autonomy without active resistance or even everyday rebellion. In Vanuatu today, the condition of semiautonomy is variable, true of some places at some times, applicable to some spheres of life but not others.

We are used to thinking of the center as "strong" and of peripheral areas as "weak." I suggest that we need to rethink our old formulas in the context of the New Pacific. What the case study of Vanuatu shows is that there exist places where peripherality—rather than signifying weakness—can be a people's greatest strength.

NOTES

1. In the New Hebrides, there were two basic kinds of courts, National Courts and Condominium Courts. National Courts exclusively processed cases involving British and French subjects. Condominium Courts were of three types. A Joint Court, based in Port Vila, functioned as a kind of Supreme Court: it heard appeals from other courts. The Joint Court also had civil jurisdiction over all claims to land and criminal jurisdiction in cases that involved Europeans and native New Hebrideans. A Court of the First Instance was based in each of the four administrative districts. In theory, its jurisdiction encompassed (with certain exceptions) all breaches of the Anglo-French Convention of 1906 and all Joint Regulations. In practice, the Court of the First Instance mainly processed traffic violations in the two main towns in the New Hebrides. Finally, there were Native Courts, charged with processing violations of the Native Criminal Code.

2. A few years ago, my wife and I published a paper discussing some of the reasons why the island where we conduct field work came to be known by at least eight different names (see Rodman and Rodman 1985). To avoid confusion over place names in this chapter, I will use only two names for our field site. When I discuss events that occur *before* independence in 1980, I will refer to the island as Aoba, which is the name for the island that appears on most post–World War II maps of the archipelago. After independence in 1980, the New Hebrides was reborn as the Republic of Vanuatu. Around the time of independence, the Council of Chiefs on Aoba renamed their island Ambae. Although Aoba continues to appear on many maps of Vanuatu, the people of the island much prefer Ambae, so that is how I will refer to the island in those parts of the chapter that discuss events after 1980.

3. For a full discussion of the legal system that people on Ambae developed when they became "a law unto themselves," see W. Rodman 1985. For a similar case elsewhere in Melanesia (and a good comparative discussion of points of view concerning state and local law in Pacific societies) see Scaglion 1990a.

4. The few local-level legal codes that anthropologists discuss tend to be minimal, unwritten, or else inoperable. Pospisil writes of "mental legal codification" among the "unacculturated and 'uncontrolled'" Kapauku Papuans (1978:70, see also Pospisil 1958 and 1969). Keesing (1978, 1980, 1982) has discussed in detail an innovative but ultimately unsuccessful attempt on the part a Solomon Islands people to write down their customary laws. In Rodman (1985:620), I compare the Solomon Islands case with that of Ambae and try to draw out some of the reasons why the former instance of codification failed in its aims whereas the latter example proved to be successful.

5. Some of the studies I have in mind here include Azarya and Chazan (1987); J. Scott (1985, 1986); Wade (1988); and Westermark (1986).

5

New Political Statuses in American Micronesia

Robert C. Kiste
Center for Pacific Islands Studies
University of Hawaii at Manoa

This chapter examines a number of issues. The focus is on America's involvement in Micronesia, but when appropriate, American Samoa and Hawaii are touched upon. First examined are commonly held myths that obscure American thinking and understanding of the island region. American interests in the Pacific Islands have primarily always been of a strategic nature, and these are explored from the turn of the century until the present day. The history of the American administration of the U.S. Trust Territory of the Pacific Islands is analyzed in some detail, including the implementation of new political entities and statuses in the last decade. Lastly, the nature of those new statuses and the problems inherent in them are evaluated. In part, the chapter is a review of American colonial history in the Pacific Islands.

PACIFIC MYTHS

Much of what Americans think about the Pacific Islands is based on myth, and there are two dominant ones. First, there is the commonly held Western idea that the Pacific region is a paradise, a notion that developed soon after European explorers visited the islands, particularly Polynesia. The myth embodies a vision of high volcanic islands with swaying palm trees, lovely maidens, free love, white sand beaches, blue lagoons, and a life of ease where problems are nonexistent. The myth projects a homogeneity about the islands and never hints at the great diversity of the region and the serious problems that confront Pacific Islands peoples. Such a view is promoted by and is valuable to the travel industry, but it hampers an understanding of the island world. The image of an unspoiled paradise is so pervasive that even after watching television's Jack Lord (and more recently Tom Selleck) chase the "bad guys" around the streets of Honolulu, many first-time tourists are surprised at the city's high-rise skyline and absence of thatched houses. Over two decades of "Hawaii Five-O" have not altered the myth.

The second myth involves an image that most Americans have about themselves and their country, and it involves their perceptions about American history and their nation's relations with other countries and peoples. Assuming that colonialism refers to "control by one power over a dependent area or people" (Webster's Ninth New Collegiate Dictionary, 1986), it cannot be denied that the U.S. has been and is a colonial power in the Pacific Islands and elsewhere in the world. Most Americans, however, have never thought of their country as being a colonial power. In fact, they firmly believe the opposite. The prevailing view is that the U.S. has only fought wars in defense of freedom and democracy. Colonialism is a label for something that other nations do or have done (the experience of American Indians never seems to come to mind), and the suggestion that the U.S. has also "played the game" sometimes generates real anger. At a conference a few years ago at the Australian National University, the American ambassador in charge of negotiating the compacts of free association with the Micronesian states during the Carter administration argued with strong conviction that the U.S. had never been a colonial power because it always gave its territories the option of independence (the Philippines) or integration with the U.S. (Alaska and Hawaii). The recognition that the nation had "territories" would seem a tacit admission of a colonial record. The denial of being a colonial power appears to be rooted in America's own revolutionary war against the British in the 1770s and the American educational system. As understandable as this may be, the myth prevents most Americans from understanding their nation's role in the Pacific Islands (assuming they know something of the region's history).

It is interesting to speculate upon some of the consequences of this denial of a colonial heritage. In contrast to Great Britain at the zenith of its empire, a nation that does not perceive of itself as a colonial power will neither create a colonial service nor develop colonial policies.

STRATEGIC CONCERNS

While the U.S. had economic interests in the Pacific Islands during the heyday of the whaling era during the two decades of the 1830s and 1840s, its primary interest in the region since around the turn of the century has been strategic. In 1898, the U.S. acquired the Micronesian island of Guam (the southernmost island of the Mariana Islands) and the Polynesian islands of Hawaii as territories. Both are located north of the equator. Hawaii is strategically located in the eastern Pacific, while Guam occupies a strategically important position in the far western Pacific. Between 1900 and 1903, two treaties secured for the U.S. a third Pacific Islands territory, American Samoa, also located in Polynesia, but south of the equator. There was some economic motivation behind the annexation of Hawaii (mainly the sugar industry), but the significance of Pearl Harbor had long been recognized. Quite clearly, American Samoa and Guam were coveted because their natural harbors provided coaling stations for the U.S. Navy. All three territories were considered as outright possessions of America, and they were recognized as such by the international community. American Samoa and Guam had naval officers as governors, and the governor of Hawaii was appointed by the American president.

Between the turn of the century and World War II, the three territories fulfilled the strategic interests of the U.S. in the region, and it had few other interests there. The outbreak of the war found the U.S. largely unprepared and lacking basic knowledge (including adequate maps) of much of the Pacific. The U.S. Navy hurried to identify those few Americans who had some expertise on the islands. For the most part, these were a handful of anthropologists, geographers, and linguists, and they were recruited to prepare area handbooks, train servicemen in survival skills useful in the island world, and prepare naval officers to serve as administrators in occupied areas.

After World War II, as would be expected after the devastating and massive conflict in the islands, the primary interests of the U.S. in the region continued to be strategic in nature. The U.S. had regained possession of Guam (it had been lost to the Japanese in 1942), and American forces were in occupation of the majority of the other islands of Micronesia. They had been held by Japan as a mandated territory under the old and by then defunct League of Nations. The islands were initially placed under the control of a U.S. naval administration, and a lively debate about the future of the area ensued in Washington, D.C. Sentiment ran strong that "American boys died for those islands and they should be ours" (the "blood on the sands" argument). The Department of War (later Defense) and many members of the U.S. Congress favored outright annexation (Kiste 1986:127).

The American myth about colonialism was evident when the Secretary of War, Henry L. Stimson, argued: "Acquisition of (Micronesia) by the United States does not represent an attempt at colonialism or exploitation. Instead, it is merely the acquisition by the United States of the necessary bases for the defense of the security of the Pacific for the future world. To serve such a purpose they must belong to the United States with absolute power to rule and fortify them. They are not colonies; they are outposts" (quoted from Goodman and Moos 1981:68).

Strenuous objections were raised by the Department of State. It argued that in the new postwar era, it was no longer acceptable in the international community to acquire new territories. In 1947, the status of a strategic trust within the framework of the United Nations (U.N.) provided a compromise solution. The former Japanese-mandated islands could be used as deemed necessary for American defense and strategic interests, and outright acquisition of new territory was avoided. However, the Departments of War, Interior, and State squabbled over which would administer the islands. The final decision was made by President Harry S. Truman. In 1951, the administration of the U.S. Trust Territory of the Pacific Islands (T.T.P.I.) was made the responsibility of the Department of Interior (Richards 1957).

For administrative purposes and closely following former Japanese partitions, the T.T.P.I. was divided into six administrative districts: from east to west, the Marshall Islands, Pohnpei (then known as Ponape), Truk, the Northern Marianas, Yap, and Belau (formerly Palau). Much later, the island of Kosrae (formerly Kosaie) separated from Pohnpei District and became a district of its own (see Map 1-3 on page 10). The areas of

Micronesia not included in the T.T.P.I. were three in number: Guam, the Gilbert Islands (now the major part of the independent nation of Kiribati), and the island of Nauru (now an independent nation).

The T.T.P.I. was the only strategic trust of the eleven trusteeships created under the authority of the U.N. Nonetheless, and like the other ten, the terms of the trust obligated the U.S. "to foster the development of such political institutions as are suited to the trust territory and shall promote the development of the inhabitants in the trust territory toward self-government or independence, as may be appropriate to the particular circumstance of the trust territory and its peoples concerned...to promote the social advancement of the inhabitants, and...to promote the educational advancement of the inhabitants" (McHenry 1975:33).

TERRITORIAL HISTORY

The history of the American administration of the T.T.P.I. may be divided into three eras. The first began with the end of World War II and ended in the early 1960s. The second began during the administration of John F. Kennedy and ended in the late 1970s with the onset of internal self-government; self-government signaled the beginning of the third and current era.

While the history of American rule may be divided into three eras, two themes cut across the time frames and have shaped events in all of them. First, the primary U.S. interest in the territory has been, and for the foreseeable future will be, strategic. Second, American values and assumptions have consistently been imposed upon Micronesian societies. While the two themes have provided the overall thrust in shaping events, they were never integrated into or employed to develop an overall coherent plan for the T.T.P.I.'s future.

Era 1

The initial era has sometimes been described as one of "benign neglect," and it is suggested that the U.S. attempted to maintain an "ethnographic zoo" (Heine 1974). Supposedly, there was an overriding American concern to protect island cultures from undue outside influence. In reality, there was no explicit policy or grand design, and, in any event, Micronesian societies had already been altered by three previous colonial administrations: Spanish (beginning in the Marianas as early as 1665 and extending east to Pohnpei by the late nineteenth-century), German (late 19th century to 1914), and Japanese (1914 to World War II). Decisions were made thousands of miles away in Washington, D.C. by an officialdom with little or no knowledge of the islands. The concern was not with the preservation of traditional cultures, but it was strategic and jealously guarded by the Department of Defense. Other federal agencies were little interested in an area so remote from the American mainland. Most Americans were unaware that the territory's administration was the responsibility of the U.S., and thus there was no concerned group in the nation that served as a watchdog for Micronesian interests (Kiste 1986:128).

During this era, the islands were cordoned off, and even U.S. citizens needed security clearance to enter the territory (a fact the "ethnographic zoo" theorists advance on behalf of their argument). With few exceptions, Americans in the islands were members of the administration, anthropologists and other scientific researchers, and individuals connected with the defense and intelligence communities. In eastern Micronesia, the Marshall Islands were the focal point of interest. Between 1946 and 1956, nuclear tests were conducted at Bikini (Kiste 1974) and Enewetak Atolls (Kiste 1976). Kwajalein Atoll was initially developed as a support base for the nuclear test program, and gradually it evolved into today's missile test site, and preparations are now being made to have the atoll play a significant role in the Strategic Defense Initiative (Star Wars) research effort. In western Micronesia, the northern Marianas were returned to Navy rule until the early 1960s, and Saipan was used for the training of Nationalist Chinese troops by the Central Intelligence Agency. Thus, early in the American administration, strategic interests became focused on the eastern and western perimeters of the territory, a fact that was to shape later events (Kiste 1976).

Developments elsewhere were minimal. Most war-devastated areas were not rehabilitated and no serious efforts were launched to promote economic development or political independence. Budgets for the T.T.P.I. were meager; the U.S. Congress placed a ceiling of $7.5 million on annual territorial appropriations. However, and beginning in the early days of the naval administration, initiatives that were quite modest in scale clearly reflected American values and eventually were to have far-reaching consequences. Without questioning their appropriateness for the small scale and isolated Micronesian communities, it was assumed that the islanders needed universal education, universal medical care, and democratic institutions—all patterned after American models. Schoolteachers and health aides were given minimal training to establish elementary schools and dispensaries in even the most remote communities; U.S. Navy officers, and later their Department of Interior successors, preached the value of electing magistrates (mayors) and governing councils for local communities. The territory's chief executive officer, the High Commissioner, was appointed by the American president, and he in turn appointed executive officers, District Administrators, for the six districts. In the early 1950s, legislatures with limited powers (initially mainly advisory) were created in the districts.

Era 2

In the early 1960s, a number of events brought major changes in the T.T.P.I. In a speech to the U.N. General Assembly in 1961, President Kennedy denounced colonialism in general, but the timing proved to be awkward. In the same year, a U.N. visiting mission to the T.T.P.I. was extremely critical of the American administration. Chagrined at the criticism, the Kennedy administration launched the beginnings of what was to evolve into a massive array of budget increases and programs for the territory. Within two years, the annual budget was doubled to $15 million. By fiscal 1984, the territory's budget was over $114 million, and about another $35 million was available for federal programs. These represent incredible sums for a small Pacific Islands territory with a population of less than one hundred sixty thousand individuals at the time.

In 1962, Kennedy appointed economist Anthony Solomon to head a mission to visit, report on, and make recommendations about the islands. Solomon's team began their work with the assumption that Micronesia was vital to America's strategic well being. The Solomon report appeared early the following year, and, like the U.N. visiting mission assessment, it was very critical of the absence of progress and development in most areas. Solomon concluded that if the Micronesians were to be persuaded to remain under the American umbrella, a number of improvements were necessary. It was recommended that progress had to be made in economic development, with an emphasis on agriculture, along with improved education and health programs and a variety of capital improvements.

The Solomon report was received with much enthusiasm by administrators in the T.T.P.I. They believed that something was finally going to get done in the territory. However, recommendations concerning the future political status of the islands were classified, and the report gained the reputation of being a covert plan to manipulate Micronesians into a permanent attachment to the U.S. In reality, the Solomon report gave little direction to future events. The recommendations on economic development, particularly agriculture, were never implemented. President Lyndon B. Johnson's administration became preoccupied with other matters. The U.S. became more involved in Vietnam, and Johnson's "Great Society" agenda was launched.

What had begun under Kennedy escalated during the Johnson years, and, in a very real sense, events in the T.T.P.I. ran amok. In 1966, Johnson sent large numbers of Peace Corps volunteers to the territory. Assuming that Great Society social welfare measures designed for the American poor and disadvantaged were also appropriate in Micronesia, well-intentioned but poorly informed members of the U.S. Congress amended legislation to make residents of American overseas territories eligible for a multitude of programs. By the late 1970s, the $35 million federal welfare dollars resulted in 166 separate programs in Micronesia. There was no coordination among them, and they included such culturally inappropriate measures as large-scale food subsidies for the impoverished (with a subsistence economy, most islanders fall below the dollar income-level that defines the American poor); financial, food, and housing aid for the elderly (in societies that traditionally honor and provide for the aged); and employment training programs designed for urban America.

The programs were culturally and socially destructive, and, along with the enormous territorial budget, Micronesians became hopelessly dependent on the U.S. Education became the largest industry in the T.T.P.I. A large number of expatriates were involved, and a huge bureaucracy became the largest employer of islanders. Most everywhere, Micronesians flocked to administrative centers of the seven districts with the hope of obtaining jobs, education, and the benefits of the federal programs. A massive welfare state had been created.

By the 1960s, the district legislatures had been given considerably more responsibility and power. They had become bodies with some law-making capacities, and Micronesians clearly enjoyed the process of self-determination. In 1965, the Congress of Micronesia (C.O.M.) was established. Micronesians quickly declared an interest in determining their political futures, and in 1967, the C.O.M. established its own Micronesian Political Status Commission. It examined political arrangements elsewhere in the Pacific and the Caribbean and considered four possible options for the future: free association, independence, integration with the U.S., and remaining a Trust Territory. The first option was suggested by the new political status that had been established between the Cook Islands and New Zealand in 1965. The commission opted for free association as the best alternative at that time in the history of the territory.

Negotiations with the U.S. began in 1969, and in the following year, the U.S. rejected the notion of free association and instead proposed commonwealth status (integration with the U.S.). A long stalemate and numerous rounds of talks that would span over a decade began.

It was initially assumed that the T.T.P.I. would achieve a new political status as a single unit, but there were factors that soon shattered such a notion. The territory was a political entity only because it was a product of the way the European colonial powers had partitioned the Pacific. In reality, it was an amalgamation of people of at least six major cultural groupings who speak eleven, and some linguists would say thirteen, mutually unintelligible languages. Further, there were differences in the colonial experiences and histories in various parts of Micronesia.

When difficulties in the negotiations over future political status were encountered, any hope of Micronesian unity soon collapsed. The Chamorros of the Northern Marianas and Guam had the longest colonial history of all Micronesian peoples, and, as a consequence, they were the most Westernized and felt a sense of superiority over the others. Further, during the CIA's occupation of Saipan in the 1950s, the Chamorros had enjoyed employment opportunities and other advantages and had greater interaction with Americans than other islanders. They wanted a permanent relationship with America, and they requested and were granted separate negotiations with the U.S.

During 1971 and 1972, the U.S. revised its position and agreed to discuss free association as a potentially viable option. Also in 1972, further momentum for fragmentation occurred when the Department of Defense indicated that it wished to retain land and/or harbor rights in Belau, the Marshall Islands, and the Northern Marianas. As before, U.S. strategic interests remained focused on the eastern and western perimeters of the territory, and the military interests in their districts gave Belau and the Marshalls new leverage. Like the Northern Marianas, they requested and received separate negotiations.

In a sense, the territory had been divided into the "haves" and "have nots." The three districts just mentioned had special strategic value, and the other four districts, Kosrae, Pohnpei, Truk, and Yap, did not. With the exception of Yap in the west, the "have nots" are located between the eastern and western ends of the T.T.P.I.

Within the ranks of the four "have nots" there were strong sentiments for further fragmentation. It appears that the fragmentation that had already occurred served U.S. interests. Further divisions would have no particular value and would only create difficulties, that is, more entities with which the U.S. would have to deal. The U.S. rejected other requests for separate negotiations. The "have nots" had no alternative but to remain together, and eventually they formed the Federated States of Micronesia (F.S.M.).

In 1975, the people of the Northern Marianas voted in favor of a Covenant that would make their islands the Commonwealth of the Northern Mariana Islands (C.N.M.I.). In the following year, the U.S. Congress ratified the treaty and President Gerald Ford gave executive approval. The people of the C.N.M.I. became American citizens and their islands became part of the U.S.

In 1979, the Republic of the Marshall Islands and the F.S.M. formed their own constitutional governments and assumed major responsibilities for internal self-government. Belau followed suit two years later, becoming the Republic of Belau. The three were committed to free association, and each was negotiating a Compact of Free Association that would achieve that status. (The compact documents are much the same for each of the three entities; however, each entity has its own set of separate subsidiary agreements that deal with the particulars of its own case).

Each compact is a long, legalistic, and complex document. Only certain highlights may be considered here, and the following paragraphs are adapted from an earlier summary (Kiste 1983:22–23). Essentially, the compact defines an arrangement in which the island states grant the U.S. a number of strategic prerogatives in exchange for financial subsidies, the provision of certain services, and free access to the U.S. With regard to the latter, islanders are citizens of their own freely associated state, and they have the status of "habitual resident" that allows them to enter freely and work in the U.S. and its territories without visas or green cards.

The prerogatives of the U.S. are carefully defined. With regard to defense, the U.S. has "full authority and responsibility for security and defense matters in or relating to" the island states. This includes: (1) the obligation to defend the islands, (2) "the option to foreclose access of use" of the islands "by military personnel or for the military purposes of any third country," and (3) "the option to establish and use military areas and facilities in" the islands subject to the terms contained in the subsidiary agreement. Further, the U.S. "may conduct within the lands, waters and airspace of" the islands "the activities and operations necessary for exercise of its authority under" the title defining defense relations.

The U.S. ultimately decides what constitutes a defense matter. It is stipulated that the island states "shall refrain from actions which the Government of the United States determines after appropriate consultations with those governments, to be incompatible with its authority and responsibility for security and defense matters." The U.S. also has the right to "invite members of the armed forces of other countries to use military areas and facilities."

As for other prerogatives, the island states "shall permit the Government of the United States to operate telecommunications" in the area, and the U.S. "shall provide and maintain fixed and floating aids to navigation."

With regard to foreign relations, the island states "shall consult, in the conduct of their foreign affairs," with the U.S. In turn, the U.S. in the conduct of its own foreign affairs, shall consult with the island states only on matters that it decides are relevant to their interests.

Such provisions clearly give the U.S. great latitude with regard to its activities in, and future relations with, the island states. An examination of some of the services and subsidies to be rendered by the U.S. also reveals that they guarantee even further American influence in the islands.

With regard to services, it is specified that the U.S. shall make available the services and related programs of the U.S. Weather Service, the U.S. Federal Emergency Management Agency, the U.S. Post Reorganization Act, the U.S. Federal Aviation Administration, and the U.S. Civil Aeronautic Board. The last three have regulatory as well as service functions, and their continued operation in the islands will guarantee the U.S. considerable control over international mail and transport services. Under the

Emergency Management Agency, each of the island states is the equivalent of one of the fifty states of the union and is eligible for disaster relief upon presidential decree.

Once implemented, the compacts have a duration of fifteen years, at which time renegotiations will occur. The financial subsidies and support services provided under the compact agreements are the envy of some other island nations. However, and perhaps because the costs of the services to be rendered by U.S. agencies cannot be precisely calculated, it is difficult to determine the exact amount of U.S. financial support over the period of the compact. The figure commonly quoted for the F.S.M. and the Marshalls together is $2.5 billion. The sum of $1 billion is reported for Belau (Washington Pacific Report 1986).

A recent source discussing the Marshalls alone has indicated that the compact "...will provide approximately $750 million for government operations and development projects over 15 years (in addition to special nuclear testing compensation valued at $270 million).... Through the compact, the Marshalls also has access to a host of U.S. government loan and financing agencies, further escalating the value of the fifteen-year agreement" (G. Johnson 1990).

In 1983, plebiscites on the compacts were held in the three Micronesian states. In each case, a majority of the voters favored the compacts. In the cases of the F.S.M. and the Marshalls, the legislative and executive branches of the governments gave their approval, and the compact agreements were forwarded to the U.S. Congress. Congressional approval came in late 1985. In early 1986, President Ronald Reagan signed the necessary legislation to make the F.S.M. and the Marshalls states in free association with the U.S. In November 1986, Reagan decreed that the compact agreements were in effect and ordered their implementation (*South Seas Digest* 1986).

The history of Belau has been quite different. As in the case of the F.S.M. and the Marshalls, the compact itself requires approval by only a simple majority. However, certain provisions in Belau's constitution are in conflict with the strategic portions of the compact. The compact would allow, even require, the presence of nuclear weapons in Belau or the overflight of such weapons in times of emergency or war. In contrast, Belau's constitution prohibits all nuclear, chemical, gas, or biological weapons without "the express approval of three-fourths of the votes cast in a referendum submitted on this specific question" (Ranney and Penniman 1985:28).

Since the initial vote in 1983, there have been a total of seven plebiscites and several court rulings on the Belau compact. The rulings have been consistent. The citizens of Belau must alter their constitution or approve the compact agreement by an affirmative vote of 75 percent of those who cast their ballots. All seven plebiscites on the compact have received majority approvals, but all have fallen short of the necessary three-quarters. The Republic of Belau remains in limbo and the last remnant of the T.T.P.I.

THE NEW POLITICAL STATUSES

In an era when decolonization is occurring throughout the Pacific Islands, it is ironic that the U.S. acquired a new island possession, the C.N.M.I. This has occurred, however, without comment or criticism in the region, and it is well known that the Chamorro people were overwhelmingly in favor of commonwealth status.

The population of Chamorros is small, only about sixteen thousand people. The C.N.M.I. has a thriving tourist industry, and large numbers of outside laborers (mainly from the Philippines) must be recruited for construction work and service occupations. The C.N.M.I. could be economically self-sufficient, but nonetheless, it receives about $56 million each year from the federal government.

Commonwealth status has not come without its disappointments, however. At least among political leaders, there is widespread feeling that the federal bureaucracy is "colonialist in its basic mentality to the Commonwealth," is insensitive to island needs, is inflexible, and "insists that the Commonwealth is nothing more than another territory" (Tenorio 1989:2). The U.S. government is seen as far too interfering in the affairs of the C.N.M.I. In contrast to the independent and self-governing states of the region, the C.N.M.I. does not control a 200-mile Exclusive Economic Zone of its own, and it is subject to other federal regulations that are viewed as unnecessarily restrictive. Some federal agencies were slow to recognize the citizenship of the islanders, and there has been a recent problem as to precisely who is eligible for citizenship. In perceived contrast to practices elsewhere, a federal judge was recently appointed without any consultation with the local bar association of political officials (Tenorio 1989:9). There are other grievances, and there is some sentiment that the terms of the commonwealth should be renegotiated.

At the same time, the commonwealth agreement has caused some resentment among the Chamorros and other citizens of Guam. The island's population is estimated at one hundred thirty thousand, of which some twenty-five thousand are military personnel and dependents. Guam also enjoys a booming tourist industry, and its military establishment makes a sizable contribution to the local economy. In contrast to the C.N.M.I., Guam does not automatically receive a substantial federal subsidy, and a majority of Guamanians would like to revise their current political relationship with the U.S. A Guam Commonwealth Act has been drafted by the territory's legislature and approved by the voters. The terms of commonwealth would have to be negotiated with the U.S., and they would not have to be the same as those of the C.N.M.I. Essentially, Guam wants more control over its own affairs, and, to date, the U.S. government has not been favorable. Guam is already a possession of the U.S.; the latter is not compelled to negotiate with its own citizens (Rogers 1988).

The governors of both the C.N.M.I. and Guam believe that they should be treated as equals to, and be accorded the same status as, the governors of the fifty states of the Union. It is their perception that this is indeed not the case. Their relations with officials in Washington, D.C. are becoming increasing strained, and the issue is an emotional and highly charged one (they are joined in these sentiments by the governor of American Samoa).

Turning to the two self-governing states in free association with the U.S., the new status is not well understood in the international community, and the issue of sovereignty is at stake. In the Pacific Islands region, Western Samoa was the first to become an independent nation in 1962, and the number has now grown to nine. Their sovereignty is generally accepted, and Western Samoans are fiercely proud of and sensitive that their new status be recognized and unquestioned.

As noted, the notion of free association in Micronesia was originally inspired by the example that was set by New Zealand and the Cook Islands, and later Niue. Some Cook Islanders and Niueans are of the opinion that their self-governing nations are also sovereign entities. When the South Pacific Forum, the organization of independent states, was formed in 1971, the Cook Islands was one of the cofounders, and Niue was later invited to join when it too became freely associated with New Zealand (Kiste 1989). However, there are some observers of international relations who hold the opinion that entities in free association with an independent state are not in themselves sovereign (Firth 1989). The constitutions of both the Cooks and Niue have provisions that indicate that the British monarch, through New Zealand, has continued responsibilities for the external affairs and defense of the two island countries. Further, it has been observed that the Cook Islands is denied some assistance programs because the European Community believes that it is not independent and "is not acknowledged by the United Nations as an independent state or acceptable as a Member of the United Nations" (Aikman 1982:93, quoted in Firth 1989:78). The same applies to Niue.

The Cook Islands and Niue can terminate their relationships with New Zealand unilaterally by amending their constitutions. "They are at liberty to leave. Free association in this case, then, can be seen as genuinely free, a step on the way to sovereign independence if that is what the Cook Islanders and the Niueans should ever want" (Firth 1989:78). Niue's legislature is considering constitutional separation from New Zealand (Frazer 1989:3).

While the New Zealand arrangement with its two former dependencies suggested free association to the Micronesians, there are very important differences in the outcomes. The strategic provisions of the arrangement between the Micronesians and the United States are without parallel in the relationship of New Zealand and its former colonies, and if the sovereignty of the Cooks and Niue is questioned in some quarters, the F.S.M. and the Marshalls, and perhaps eventually Belau, can also anticipate similar difficulties.

There are several threats to the sovereignty of both states. First, the degree of financial dependency is staggering. All islands in the Marshalls and the majority of islands in the F.S.M. are low-lying coral atolls (the exceptions in the F.S.M. are Kosrae, Pohnpei, a few smaller volcanic islands in the almost atoll of Truk, and the islands of Yap proper). The atolls are resource-poor, and the population of the F.S.M. is now estimated at one hundred thousand, while Marshallese number about forty-five thousand. Local resources could never provide more than a small fragment of the sums available under the compact agreements. In the Marshalls, 92 percent of all food is imported. Second, the many and far-ranging strategic provisions of the compacts speak for themselves. They certainly represent potential limits to sovereignty, and they are without real parallel in the New Zealand cases.

There is another potential pitfall. The financial subsidies are "front-loaded." The sums are the largest in the initial years and decline over the course of the fifteen-year agreement. The underlying assumption is that investments in capital improvements and economic development plans will provide for greater economic self-sufficiency in the long run. Such an assumption is questionable at best. The large sums previously invested in the islands have produced little, and hopes for better performance in the future may well be misguided.

There are other reasons for concern about the future. The populations of the F.S.M. and the Marshalls are among the fastest-growing in the world (the number of Marshallese has quadrupled since World War II). There is little in the way of family planning, and the number of islanders may be expected to double in the next two decades. Thus, increased population pressures will occur as the compact subsidies decline.

There is already concern about the financial packages. In both countries, there is growing fear that the sums are not adequate. The Marshalls has recently petitioned the U.S. Congress for about $60 million in additional funding, but for what length of time is not certain. Most federal programs were terminated with the implementation of free association. Both countries would like some to be restored, and the federal government was recently convinced to reinstitute Pell grants for the tertiary education of the financially disadvantaged. Requesting what are essentially domestic programs for American citizens can have potentially damaging consequences for Micronesian claims of sovereignty. One Marshallese recently quipped that the Republic of the Marshall Islands is the only sovereign state with a U.S. postal service zip code (actually, the F.S.M. also has zip codes).

Until quite recently, there was a further complication about the political status of the states freely associated with the U.S. The procedures about the termination of the U.N. trusteeship were contested. The other ten trusteeships that were created after World War II were ended with the approval of the U.N. Trusteeship Council. As indicated, the American T.T.P.I. was the only strategic trust of the eleven. It came under the scrutiny of both the U.N. Security Council as well as the Trusteeship Council, and because of its uniqueness, there was no precedent for the termination of a strategic trust. For reasons of its own, the U.S. held a minority position concerning what was required for termination.

In May 1986, with the support of other metropolitan powers in the Pacific, the U.S. overcame a negative vote by the Soviet Union and obtained the Trusteeship Council's approval of the proposed changes in the statuses of the four entities into which the T.T.P.I. had become divided.

Most observers, however, believed that the approval of the Security Council was also required. Indeed, Article 83 of the U.N. Charter reads: "All functions of the United Nations relating to strategic areas, including the approval of the terms of the trusteeship agreement and of their alteration or amendment, shall be exercised by the Security Council." The Soviet Union, as well as each of the council's other four permanent members, has veto power, and the U.S., fearing a veto, did not bring its proposed changes before the council. The official Soviet view of the time held that free association was nothing less than a thinly disguised form of neocolonialism which gave the U.S. military continued control of the islands. The U.S. countered that it and the Micronesian entities could act on their own and jointly agree to bring an end to the trusteeship. President Reagan's decree of November 1986 was an attempt to accomplish that very goal (Kiste 1989).

By the late 1980s, however, and without fanfare, the Soviet Union reversed its position. Concerned with improving its international image and relations, pursuing its own agenda of reform, and confronting serious internal problems, the Soviet Union no longer considered Micronesia an issue worthy of contention. The Soviets were ready to agree to what had in fact already been arranged.

Therefore, in late 1990, the U.S. took its case to the Security Council. On December 22, and with the exception of Belau, the Council approved the termination of the forty-three-year-old trusteeship (*Honolulu Star-Bulletin & Advertiser* 1990). Because of the defense agreements in the Compacts of Free Association, however, there remains some question about the sovereignty of the two new freely associated states (Firth 1989).

Given the uncertainties involved, the F.S.M. and the Marshalls have achieved considerable success on the international scene. Even though there was hesitation on the part of some members, the South Pacific Forum, which includes the metropolitan states of Australia and New Zealand, recognized both as self-governing states like the Cooks and Niue and invited them to membership in 1987. Nine other countries, including Japan, the Philippines, and the U.S., have recognized them as self-governing states. The U.S. has opened diplomatic missions in the capitals of the F.S.M. and the Marshalls. The missions' representatives hold rank equivalent to ambassadors, and they may soon have the actual title of ambassador as well. Both of the Micronesian states have resident ambassadors in Washington, D.C. The official position of all three parties is that the F.S.M. and the Marshalls are independent and sovereign nations.

One former American official has commented that the freely associated states of Micronesia are sovereign, but not independent. This seems somewhat ambiguous, but the line of reasoning may be as follows: as sovereign entities, the F.S.M. and the Marshalls exercised their sovereignty in deciding to relinquish independence in certain areas (those of strategic interest to the U.S.) in exchange for large financial packages and the provision of certain services. One may wonder what choice they really had. The case of Belau is the case in point. It has been unwilling to accommodate U.S. strategic demands in that island group, and its status remains that of a U.S. strategic Trust Territory.

CONCLUSIONS

The conclusions to be drawn from these considerations seem very clear and straightforward. American interests in the Pacific Islands, and, more particularly, Micronesia, have always been strategic. The involvement in the region around the turn of the century, the acquisition of the T.T.P.I. at the end of World War II, the subsequent history of the T.T.P.I., and the current political arrangements in the territory have been primarily shaped by strategic concerns. At the same time, America's denial that the U.S. has been a colonial power and its fanciful notions about the Pacific Islands as the world's small examples of paradise have clouded American thinking about the region.

The negotiations pertaining to new political statuses for Micronesian countries have been the most tormented and drawn out in the entire history of decolonization in the Pacific. The tenacity of American strategic concerns, the Micronesian desire to maintain the flow of American dollars and services, and the fragmentation of the T.T.P.I have all contributed to the length and legalistic process of negotiations. It can be argued that the result is a trade-off. American defense interests have been served, and the islanders have the levels of support to which they have become accustomed.

There is no evidence to support the notion that the U.S. has ever had a well-formulated and coherent policy concerning Micronesia. During the enthusiasm for social progress during the presidencies of John F. Kennedy and Lyndon B. Johnson, often well-intentioned programs helped create dependency on a massive scale. The bottom line, however, is that U.S. strategic interests have most always been served. While there was no overall plan except to protect defense interests, many observers in Washington, D.C.

and elsewhere had to realize that a drift to greater dependency was occurring and that this was not incompatible with American strategic interests. With a few exceptions, no one cared to blow the whistle.

The entities of the former T.T.P.I. and even Guam face uncertain futures. Many problems loom in the not too distant future, and Micronesian leaders will not find an easy path ahead. And, while it is unpopular to suggest as much, increased pressures on limited resources, along with Micronesians' rising aspirations, could lead in the direction of their even greater dependency and loss of control over their own lives.

6

Welfare State Colonialism in Rural French Polynesia

Victoria S. Lockwood
Southern Methodist University

Despite cultural and historical differences, the small island societies of the eastern South Pacific share a common set of economic and political constraints. Geographical isolation, limited resources, and a legacy of centuries of foreign intervention narrow the options available to these microsocieties for attaining true political autonomy and local economic development. A number of these islands are now politically independent, while others still tied to colonial powers have been granted greater internal self-government. Nevertheless, most continue to rely heavily on foreign aid received from former or current colonial powers to sustain their fragile economies (Bertram and Watters 1985). Through this aid and other ongoing involvements, Western nations maintain a strategic political presence in those island societies linked to them. It is only with difficulty, then, that one can truly speak of a "legacy" of colonialism. Instead, ongoing neocolonial relations of economic and political dependency remain active and potent forces shaping contemporary Pacific Islands societies.

Not only the product of colonial domination, dependency has also been promoted by the relatively dismal prospects for self-sustaining economic development and growth in these resource-poor microsocieties (Bertram 1986). Island economies are primarily based on agriculture and focused on the export of one or two primary commodities, mainly copra. Following post–World War II declines in the world market for this commodity, people in rural areas became seriously demoralized. Stagnant rural economies could not provide the income levels islanders sought to meet their ever-rising consumption standards and expectations. As a result, many islanders abandoned rural areas and migrated to urban centers in search of work. In some cases, families remaining on home islands, particularly Samoa, Niue, and Tokelau, have come to depend on remittances sent from kin employed in New Zealand, Hawaii, or the mainland U.S. for their very livelihoods (see Chapter 10, "The Samoan Exodus," by Paul Shankman, in this volume, and Shankman 1976; Walsh and Trlin 1973; Hooper and Huntsman 1973; Connell 1980). Frequently, foreign aid monies comprise a significant component of island governments' revenues and are central to the provision of local services.

Relative to other areas of the Third World, the islands of the South Pacific have been described as "conspicuously successful" in attracting foreign aid. This success can be attributed to the enduring geopolitical interests of the major powers in the region: Australia, New Zealand, France, the United States, and Great Britain (Bertram and Watters 1985:513). While interests are diverse, Western nations have mainly sought the strategic use of islands for military installations and port facilities. However, in recent years the Pacific region has also garnered greater attention as commercial interests have investigated the exploitation of the basin's potentially rich maritime resources.

The foreign aid monies received by Pacific Islands nations have become an integral part of local funding for social services such as education, health care, communication, and basic infrastructure (for example, roads). In addition to the obvious social welfare benefits, this infusion of capital generates a significant number of salaried jobs for islanders in the public sector. As these relatively secure and well-paying jobs become available, islanders' participation in primary productive activities (agriculture, fishing, and crafts) declines, and island economies stagnate further. Production for export plummets, and islanders begin to rely heavily on imports to fulfill their basic needs. Government salaries become the major source of income and are used to finance a lifestyle in which imported Western foods and consumer items have supplanted local products. In sum, islanders become dependent on external foreign funds for their jobs, social services, and an inflated standard of living which they would be unable to achieve on their own. This form of neocolonial dependency and the artificial "prosperity" associated with it has been called "welfare state colonialism" (Bertram and Watters 1985:508).

An important application of this general phenomenon can be found in France's Overseas Territory of French Polynesia, whose large Tahitian population (approximately one hundred eighty thousand) now possesses one of the highest standards of living in the Pacific. Made up of five major island groups (the Societies, Gambiers, Australs, Marquesas, and Tuamotus), the over one hundred twenty islands of the territory are scattered across 1,600 square miles of ocean between the Cook Islands and Easter Island.

France's Pacific territories, which include New Caledonia and Wallis/Futuna as well as French Polynesia, are but three of its total of ten overseas departments and territories, "the only surviving colonial empire of worldwide dimensions" (Chesneaux 1986).[1] Remnants of a once much grander colonial empire and mostly of little economic value, these scattered outposts are situated around the world. By virtue of their locations, they give France its much-sought global military and strategic presence, an aspiration that has been described as unique among the world's mid-sized international powers (Chesneaux 1986:76). This global network includes a missile base and space station in French Guiana (South America) and a nuclear weapons testing facility in French Polynesia.

In an era when most Western nations have worked towards decolonization, France has actively sought to retain its overseas possessions (Aldrich and Connell 1988). To this end it has assimilated indigenous societies both politically and culturally, granting local populations French citizenship and exporting the French educational system to instill in the natives an appreciation of French civilization. In recent years, France has also granted greater political autonomy and sovereignty over local matters to locally elected island assemblies, retaining control over external affairs, defense, and other critical areas such as higher education and justice. Ultimate political power in each territory is held by a High Commissioner appointed in France.

Most importantly, France keeps tight rein on its possessions through the dependency relationship created by welfare state colonialism (see Aldrich and Connell 1988). To its overseas territories France gives substantial aid, funds which support a large government bureaucracy (and thus jobs) and heavily subsidize local government operations and services. Islanders could sever these ties only at great financial cost to themselves and to an inflated standard of living made possible by government salaries, subsidies, and welfare payments. Thus, it is perhaps not surprising that while other colonized populations strive for independence, the peoples of France's territories (with the exception of New Caledonia) typically vote to continue their political affiliation with France.

What is of particular interest to the anthropologist is how this form of neocolonialism has affected the lives and societies of the island populations subsumed under it. In this chapter I will examine the impact of French policies on one rural island in French Polynesia, describing the mechanisms through which welfare state colonialism has become a major force shaping this rural Tahitian society. Specifically, I describe how French policies have been implemented on the island of Tubuai, an outer-island of approximately eighteen hundred people (three hundred households) located in the Austral chain 700 kilometers due south of Tahiti. I will then look at how islanders themselves perceive their "dependency" and political status as a French territory, as well as how they assess the many changes which have taken place in island society.

WELFARE STATE COLONIALISM IN FRENCH POLYNESIA

Seeking a Pacific port for its mercantile shipping between South America and Asia, France had by 1897 fully consolidated its colonial control over the Tahitian islands. True to the pattern established in its other colonies, France implemented a policy of direct colonial intervention in native affairs (see Hanson 1973). Its ultimate goal was to replace the existing social system of Tahitian chiefdoms with French political institutions and cultural values. This effort, in conjunction with missionaries' conversion of the Tahitian population to Christianity and the decimation of the Tahitian population by Western diseases, ultimately altered "Tahitian society out of all recognition" (Hanson 1973:5). A syncretic, "Neo-Tahitian" society emerged, one which integrated Christianity and French sociopolitical institutions with Tahitian worldview.

Throughout the 1800s and early 1900s, a French governor and a small contingent of expatriate officials administered the far-flung territory from the growing port town of Papeete on Tahiti (see Thompson and Adloff 1971). As the islands possessed little of economic interest to outsiders, Tahitians were able to hold on to their lands and to maintain a rural domestic economy based on agriculture and fishing. While continuing to fulfill household subsistence needs by cultivating taro and tree crops on collectively owned, familial lands, islanders became increasingly integrated into the regional and world capitalist economies as producers of copra, vanilla, and shell for export (Newbury 1980). Social life centered on the family and the activities of various Christian churches. Although communities were officially governed by a resident French *gendarme*, missionaries exerted a strong and ever-present hand in regulating island affairs.

The French administration throughout this time exhibited little interest in the outer-islands, the home of the vast majority of the Tahitian population, and a general situation of "benevolent neglect" prevailed (Cook 1976). Even as late as the 1940s on Tubuai, for example, modern amenities and social services consisted only of a primary school, the *gendarmerie*, and a piped drinking water system. Islanders made their living as predominantly subsistence-based taro farmers and fishermen. The typical residence was of the traditional *fare ni'au* style (woven pandanus and coconut fronds), while canoes and horses were the major modes of transportation. Islanders eagerly awaited the infrequent visits of schooners from Tahiti; at that time, copra and other products were sold or bartered for cloth, kerosene, nails, sugar, and canned foods (see Aitken 1930).[2]

World War II brought many changes to the territory. An American airbase operated on the island of Bora Bora and the Papeete port began to expand significantly in shipping, commercial activities, and light industry. Rural islanders began to converge on Papeete in search of wage work and other opportunities absent on their home islands. Rural society had entered a period of serious socioeconomic decline, while Papeete was experiencing the social problems associated with overly rapid urban growth and high rates of unemployment.

In the years immediately following the war, France found that it was increasingly required to subsidize the operation of the territory financially. Copra and other exports had declined significantly, undermining the territory's major source of revenues: customs duties. Gradually France also assumed financial responsibility for various and much-needed modernization programs. By 1959, "there were no further illusions as to the country's ability to finance any appreciable part of its own development program. The funds from France [previously loans] became outright subsidies..." (Thompson and Adloff 1971:83).

It was to a group of French Polynesian Territorial delegates seeking more financial aid in the early 1960s that France's President, General DeGaulle, announced his decision to relocate France's nuclear testing facility (Le Centre d'Expérimentation du Pacifique; hereafter, CEP) to French Polynesia (Thompson and Adloff 1971). This decision, one which would have an immense impact on the territory and the lives of all its residents, followed the independence of the former French colony of Algeria and the loss of France's testing installations there (see Tagupa 1976). In order "to make the CEP more acceptable to the islanders, the general agreed not only to meet the budgetary deficit and take over the cost of the territory's secondary schools and communications services, but also to finance the expanded public works programs" (Thompson and Adloff 1971:84).

Both the Tahitian population's overwhelmingly negative response to the CEP and a movement for Tahitian independence which had gained impetus in the 1950s were diffused by the economic boom that accompanied the massive investment of capital and technology required to construct the testing and support facilities. These included several military bases, a new international airport, an expanded port facility, a major hospital, and modern transportation and communication networks. Thousands of new jobs were created and rural migrants swarmed into Papeete. The CEP had instigated what would be a decade of unprecedented economic growth and prosperity in the territory.

Simultaneously, the French government formulated plans for regional development that would touch even the most distant outer-islands (Thompson and Adloff 1971). In addition to promoting industry and tourism, the plan set out specifically to revitalize the stagnant rural economy, particularly by developing cash-crop agriculture and by subsidizing copra production. It was hoped that by increasing rural food production, high rates of food importation could be curtailed. It was also hoped that by creating jobs and other cash-earning economic opportunities in rural areas, the flow of outer-islanders into Papeete would subside, and perhaps even reverse. Substantial funds were set aside to promote rural economic development and to help families who had left outer-islands to return and re-establish themselves there. Improvements were also to be made in education and health services, and islanders were integrated into various social welfare programs, including the French family welfare system.

The approach France has taken in French Polynesia—or, in other words, the form of welfare state colonialism it has implemented—differs from that of other Western nations in the region in the degree to which it has promoted (and funded) rural development (see Connell 1985), and in its incorporation of islanders into the extensive system of French entitlement programs. As a result, rural Tahitian Islanders have been offered vast new economic opportunities and provided with incomes that would have boggled the imaginations of islanders thirty or forty years ago. This particular strategy makes sense when one considers that there is little evidence to date to suggest that France ever intends to divest itself of its overseas possessions (see Aldrich and Connell 1988); and that to hold on to them and safeguard its substantial investments, it must foster the goodwill of local populations.

Funding for modernization in French Polynesia comes predominantly from French taxpayers. Islanders themselves pay no income taxes and the territorial budget is funded mainly through French aid, military payments and import duties. In 1981, for example, France gave approximately $400 million (U.S.) of aid (about 40,000 million Polynesian francs) to the territory (*Europa World Yearbook* 1985).[3] By 1986, that amount had risen to $500 million or $2,250 per capita (U.S.) (Crocombe 1987:238), one of the highest per capita levels of aid to any developing nation. The CEP, itself, accounts for 30 percent of territorial revenues (Breeze 1981:31). While only a small proportion of the total French national budget (less than 1 percent; Aldrich and Connell 1988), these funds and the development programs associated with them have played a central role in catalyzing the emergence of a new type of "modern," welfare-dependent Tahitian society.

TUBUAI MODERNIZATION

Tubuaians' transformation from relatively "traditional" taro cultivators and fishermen to prosperous commercial farmers and wage earners began in the early 1960s. At that time, the island was designated as a new regional administrative center and special

Author with Tubuai friends, 1981, Tubuai, French Polynesia (Photo by Victoria S. Lockwood)

target for agricultural development. In conjunction with the new Austral Islands administrative offices and newly installed government service agencies (Public Works, Agricultural Service, and so on), a large number of public sector jobs were created. Agricultural projects were introduced and island farmers were given technical and financial aids to produce European vegetables—first, green vegetables, followed by potatoes—for the burgeoning Papeete market. Because of its designated role in both regional administration and agricultural development, Tubuai has experienced, perhaps more than other outer-islands, the full impact of welfare state colonialism.

In the wake of over twenty-five years of induced modernization, this once little-known backwater today possesses a territory-wide reputation as the "wealthy" island in the remote Australs which produces the rather anomalous potatoes stocked in Papeete markets. Many of the stands of coconut trees so characteristic of the picturesque islands of the South Pacific have been bulldozed and replaced by potato fields. A large number of islanders are employed by the government and, with their relatively high incomes, have replaced pandanus and coconut frond houses with cement houses, furnishing them with Western accoutrements and television sets. A small Nissan or Peugeot truck is typically parked in the front yard. Island children attend (free of charge) what are basically French schools, which are, at the high school level, staffed exclusively by teachers from France. A French doctor and a modern clinic are at the disposal of islanders (also free of charge) for medical care.

Potato field, 1987, Tubuai, French Polynesia (Photo by Victoria S. Lockwood)

As the government had hoped, a number of Tubuai families who had earlier abandoned the island for opportunities available in Papeete have started to return (Lockwood 1990). Return migration to revitalized outer-islands in French Polynesia (see also Pollock 1978) stands out as a unique phenomenon among Pacific Islands nations long characterized by rampant rural out-migration to regional port towns and cities in New Zealand, Australia, and the United States (see Chapter 10, "The Samoan Exodus," by Paul Shankman, and Chapter 2, "Tonga's Contemporary Globalizing Strategies: Trading on Sovereignty amidst International Migration," by George Marcus, in this volume). Between 1981 and 1987, about thirty-five families returned home to Tubuai from Papeete and Noumea. These migrants believed that the employment and cash-cropping opportunities Tubuai could now offer would provide a secure and relatively high standard of living for their families.

Although French development programs have had a pervasive impact on this rapidly Westernizing Tahitian society, the island is today a striking hybrid of things Western (and French) and things Tahitian. Various "traditional" practices, institutions, and beliefs serve the modern Tubuaian well and are important, well-integrated elements of contemporary rural society (see Joralemon 1986; Lockwood 1988). For example, cash-crop agriculture and wage employment have not replaced traditional subsistence gardening and fishing; they have simply been added into the diversified set of economic activities pursued by each family to make its living. A traditionally derived land-tenure system in which kin own land as a collective group continues to function today in the context of commercial agriculture (Joralemon 1983b). Islanders still practice the time-proven techniques of traditional Tahitian cultivation, while simultaneously making use of Western inputs such as chemical fertilizers and insecticides. Islanders, for instance, time planting and harvesting to the phases of the moon and forbid menstruating women to enter gardens lest plants

Newly married couples often build traditional style houses while waiting to accumulate money to build a modern cement house, Tubuai, French Polynesia, 1987 (Photo by Victoria S. Lockwood)

wither and die. And while islanders are highly individualistic, profit-motivated economic actors and avid Western-style consumers, they also highly value the kin-based communal spirit, generosity, and hospitality esteemed by their ancestors before the arrival of Westerners and capitalism.

THE STRUCTURE OF ARTIFICIAL PROSPERITY AND SUBSIDIZED DEVELOPMENT

Compared to other islands of the south Pacific, Tubuai stands out as an affluent society and as a notable development "success story." The foundation upon which this deceptive veneer of prosperity rests, however, is an artificial, externally subsidized economy whose recent productivity was not self-generated, nor is it self-sustaining. By examining the areas of employment, income, productivity, and consumption it is possible to gain some insights into the highly dependent structure of the Tubuai economy and to assess to what extent the island is truly "developing" within the framework of welfare state colonialism.

Income and Employment

The average Tubuai family earns about $12,000 (U.S.) per year. The poorest earn about $2,000 to $3,000 per year, while a small group of the wealthiest earn as much as $35,000 per year (see Table 6–1).[4] Because the typical household is highly diversified in the economic activities it pursues, income is acquired from a range of sources. Families earn money from government employment, pensions, and family welfare allocations, as well as from the sale of the potatoes, fish, green vegetables, taro, and crafts they produce. At the same time, they fulfill the bulk of their subsistence needs by subsistence-oriented farming (taro and tree crops) and fishing.

TABLE 6–1   Tubuai Household Income Levels: Distribution of Income (1987)

Income Level	Number of Households	Percent of all Households
Low: average		
$2,000-$4,000/year	46	16%
Low/Middle: average		
$3,000–$16,000/year	58	20%
Middle: average		
$4,500–$16,000/year	99	35%
High: average		
$16,000–$35,000/year	81	29%
Totals	284	100%

Government employment is virtually the only type of employment on the island. In 1987, there were about 190 jobs, 92 percent of which were government jobs, and about half (54 percent) of all island households included an employed member. Islanders work for the Tubuai municipality, the Public Works and Agricultural Services, the schools, the clinic, and other government agencies, mainly providing social services to themselves. The majority of jobs are unskilled and the employed work at maintaining the island's road, bridges, and government buildings, as cooks for the school and clinic, as janitors, or in agricultural services. Minimum wage levels are set by the government, and the average worker earned $700 to $800 per month in 1987.

The general absence of small businesses and other private enterprises on the island is responsible for the lack of private-sector employment. The only exceptions are two Chinese, family-operated general stores (which have long held a monopoly on retail sales and commercial services) and the island's branches of Air Tahiti and a Tahiti bank each of which employs one or two islanders. A few Tahitian women sporadically operate small, roadside stands, selling a few canned foods, snacks, and sometimes fresh vegetables to passers-by.

For almost half (49 percent) of all island families, government salaries are the major source of income; that is, they comprise approximately 70 to 80 percent of total income (see Table 6–2). For those families that include an employed member, the salary is by far the largest component of total income. It is only rarely that earnings from other economic pursuits on the island can even approach the level of income supplied by a job. For this reason, most islanders prefer wage employment and would give up other activities to take a job should one become available.

TABLE 6–2   Major Source of Tubuai Household Income (1987)

Source of Income	Number of Households	Percent of All Households
Government Sector (75%)		
Employment	137	49%
Pensions	58	21%
Family allocations	14	5%
Private Sector (25%)		
Fish sales	21	8%
Potato sales	19	7%
Vegetable sales	15	5%
Craft sales	4	1%
Sales of indigenous crops (taro, etc.)	3	1%
Small commerce (roadside stands, etc.)	4	1%
Sales of fresh meats (beef and pork)	3	1%
Vegetable exporting	2	1%
Totals	280	100%

The few islanders who are able to achieve incomes commensurate with the employed are those who specialize in the production and sale of fish, vegetables, or crafts. Not only do employed islanders purchase these products from other families, but the schools (which supply daily meals) and clinic buy them in bulk. Moreover, since 1985 a small group of local entrepreneurs has become increasingly successful at exporting Tubuai vegetables (mainly carrots) to Papeete, selling them to restaurants and hotels there. While it is common for island families to market small quantities of their surplus vegetable and fish production, such sales are the major source of income for only thirty-six (13 percent) households.

After government salaries, government pensions are the next most significant source of income on the island (21 percent of all households; see Table 6–2). Upon reaching the retirement age of sixty, those islanders who have been employed receive a pension. In addition, starting in the early 1980s, islanders who declared themselves as employed in agriculture, fishing, or crafts (subsistence or market-oriented) could also receive a retirement pension at age sixty. In 1987, the majority of pensions, which range between $300 and $1,000 a month, were of this last type.

With all of the government's efforts at agricultural development, specifically the successful potato cultivation project, one might wonder to what extent islanders' incomes have been boosted by earnings from this source. Although the majority of Tubuai families (192, or 68 percent of all households in 1987) now plant potatoes (even relatively wealthy wage earners), potatoes supply a relatively miniscule proportion of total family income. Because the average scale of cultivation is small (0.5 hectare) and the cost of imported seed potatoes and other inputs high, the average family's profit from a three-month season is only about $1,000 to $1,500. It is only in low-income, nonemployed families that potato earnings represent a significant component of total income. Potatoes are the major source of income for only 7 percent of all Tubuai households.

One must also question whether or not potato cultivation truly represents "development." Although production levels and yields have increased steadily, the project is heavily subsidized by the government. Islanders pay only 60 percent of the actual cost of the seed potatoes, fertilizers and insecticides they use; transport to Papeete is similarly subsidized, and the Agricultural Service arranges marketing in Papeete. If required to pay the actual costs of cultivation, farmers' "profits" would be reduced to almost nothing. As a component of income, then, profits earned from potatoes are largely a gift from the government. While agricultural officials hope that the program will eventually become self-supporting, rising costs of inputs, as well as competition from more efficient foreign producers, suggest little cause for optimism. Nevertheless, Tubuai's agricultural officials promote expansion of the program every year.

The other government-related source of income for island families is family welfare payments. Irrespective of income, each family receives a monthly allocation for each child in the household. These funds are aimed at promoting child welfare. In 1987, each child was allocated about $55 per month; the typical Tubuai family that has four to six children receives about $275 per month. For nonemployed families that do not produce marketable surpluses of fish or vegetables, family allocations can become the major source of cash income. This is true for 5 percent of all families.

As the summary in Table 6–2 shows, about 75 percent of Tubuai households, then, rely on government salaries or transfer payments for their livelihoods. Only 25 percent could be considered to participate at a significant level in "productive" sectors of the island economy. The data clearly demonstrate the extreme degree to which island families' inflated standard of living is dependent on government expenditures (salaries, pensions, and welfare payments).

Subsistence Affluence and Consumption

While in terms of absolute income Tubuaians are among the world's more well-to-do, islanders' "subsistence affluence" causes their actual standard of living to be even higher than their incomes would suggest. As is true for many Pacific Islanders, all Tubuaians have access to garden lands, tree-crop plantations and to the lagoon, and are able to fulfill their subsistence needs with minimal investments of labor and capital (Joralemon 1983a). Because islanders own their lands, and most families cultivate much of their own food, cash acquired from jobs or vegetable sales is largely "discretionary" income (that is, not required to fulfill basic subsistence). I have argued elsewhere that one of the islanders' motives for maintaining subsistence-oriented production is to minimize their cash expenditures on expensive imported foods so that they can instead purchase coveted consumer luxuries (televisions, motorcycles, cassette players, liquor, cigarettes, and so on) (Lockwood 1988).

Islanders are indeed good consumers of Western imports and save little of their income. The first installation of electricity on the island in the early 1980s has led Tubuaians to purchase electrical appliances in abundance. About 35 percent of all island families own small trucks and washing machines; closer to 65 percent own refrigerator-freezers and television sets. While middle-aged and elderly islanders remember how to produce many household items from locally-available products (wood, coconut, pandanus, and so on), the young no longer possess such knowledge and depend entirely on

Wedding feast, Tubuai, French Polynesia, 1987 (Photo by Victoria S. Lockwood)

manufactured imports. Young people today scoff at the lifestyle they assume their parents and grandparents endured (and which they describe as "sauvage"; literally, "savage") before the coming of electricity and television to the island.

TUBUAI WITHOUT FRANCE?

Envisioning what Tubuai society would be like without French financial largesse is difficult because the impact of these funds permeates all aspects of daily life. One can, however, look at other Pacific Islands societies that have not experienced French influence to gain some insight into what contemporary Tubuai might otherwise be like.

In the absence of government service sector employment and agricultural subsidies, the island economy would in all likelihood be predominantly subsistence-based (taro and fishing). Because Tubuai possesses little potential for the development of industry or tourism, agriculture would be the mainstay of islanders' livelihoods.

The growing market for European vegetables in Papeete and the island's temperate climate would encourage islanders to cultivate vegetables, the only forseeable economic niche they might fill in the larger regional economy, and thus the only source of cash income for island families. However, without government subsidies, price supports, and an infrastructure (marketing, transportation to distant markets, and so on) which reduce many of the production risks for farmers, vegetable cash-cropping would be an expensive, risky, and probably economically marginal endeavor for islanders. Vast tracks of land now cultivated would be covered with brush and coconut trees. Islanders might try to return again to small-scale copra processing, but the island's southerly, temperate climate has never promoted abundant coconut production. Basic subsistence would be secured from the land and sea, but access to cash, and thus to the many consumer luxuries islanders now possess, would be extremely limited. One can estimate that the typical family's annual income (if earned primarily from nonsubsidized cash-cropping, and assuming that such activity would actually prove economically feasible) would probably be cut by at least 75 percent, to about $2,000 to $3,000 per year.

The majority of islanders, particularly young people, would choose to forgo the subsistence-based lifestyle and lack of opportunity on Tubuai and emigrate to an over-crowded Papeete. The island's population would decline steadily (as it did until the early 1960s). Islanders would lack access to secondary schooling, Western-style medical care, and electricity. Those few young people who, without schooling or experience, were able to find jobs in Papeete would send remittances home to families on Tubuai. Many of the latter would depend on these small sums as their only source of cash income.

In short, the island would be a rural backwater with a declining population made up largely of the elderly. Modern social services would be absent, and the social security mechanisms intrinsic to the integrated extended family severely disrupted by out-migration. While islanders' access to the land and sea would preclude the extreme poverty characteristic of many areas of the Third World, their overall standard of living would be quite low.

THE COSTS AND BENEFITS OF WELFARE STATE COLONIALISM

The preceding discussion of what life on Tubuai might be like without welfare state colonialism suggests some of the many ways islanders have benefited from this process. Tubuaians today possess a standard of living and social welfare (education, medical care, and so on) not far removed from that of Western nations. Moreover, islanders have been given opportunities to participate in development programs that may one day generate (at least in theory) a viable, commercial agricultural sector on the island.

Another important benefit of the welfare state approach (one that rarely accompanies other models of Third World development) is that Tubuai's prosperity is not concentrated in the hands of a few wealthy families, but is spread broadly throughout the population (see Table 6–1). Extensive social programs, universal participation in entitlement programs, and provisions that facilitate a broad base of participation in agricultural projects have minimized social inequalities and the gap between the rich and the poor. Indeed, one can truly say there is no poverty on Tubuai.

The drawbacks to welfare state colonialism are as obvious as the apparent benefits. In exchange for their inflated standard of living, islanders have traded their rights of self-determination and agreed to remain French "colonials." Policies that have the capacity to transform Tahitian lives and communities are not formulated by Tahitians, but by a French government (and populace) that has its own regional and world agendas. In short, Tahitians have given up their right to self-determination and their right to shape their own modern society.

ISLANDERS' ATTITUDES

How do islanders themselves perceive their situation? While it is always dangerous to generalize, it is possible to describe a "Tubuaian perspective" on the particular path to development they have been propelled along, on the socioeconomic changes they have experienced in the course of their lives, and on France in general.

It is important to note first, however, that because most adult islanders (middle-aged and elderly) have little formal schooling, they have only a sketchy understanding of the historical and political events which have created and now shape the French territory. Few know much about France or even where it is (islanders consider the distance from one end of the island to the other, about 5 miles, to be "far") and are familiar with it only through its representatives: the island's administrators, schoolteachers, and doctor. Few are familiar with the concept of "colony" or would consider themselves to be a colony of France. That Tubuai is indeed a part of France is, however, reinforced several times a year when the territory's French High Commissioner comes to the island to raise the French flag in a formal military ceremony, and island school children are lined up to sing the French national anthem.

For the most part, islanders consider the changes that have taken place to be good and to have benefited island society. They have enthusiastically participated in new programs, first cultivating green vegetables in the 1960s (this program failed—but not because of islanders' lack of interest) and then rapidly adopting and expanding potato cultivation. Because earning money is one of the dominant preoccupations of most island families, as is "economizing" (islanders' own word) so that desired purchases of consumer luxuries may be made, any and all opportunities for making money are actively pursued.

Do islanders believe that by adopting new ways they are having to abandon aspects of "traditional" culture or of a cherished lifestyle? For example, does the coconut tree's potential disappearance from the island in the next few years concern Tubuaians? Apparently, the answer is no. The young value what is modern (Western) and perceive the preferred economic opportunities of the future (that is, jobs and commercial agriculture) to be open and unlimited. The past and "tradition" (that is, pre-1960s and modernization) live only in the memories of old people.

While I have argued that the operating principle of welfare state colonialism, and certainly the predominant feature of the Tubuai economy, is dependency, islanders do not perceive themselves as dependent on France; instead they describe themselves as both independent and self-sufficient. Tubuaians frequently say that their wealth lies in the land and the sea and that no islander need ever be poor, because with hard work all families can provide for themselves. They display the abundance of their gardens and ridicule those who might be needy and go to others to ask for favors. The ability to be self-sufficient and provide for oneself and one's family is intrinsic to the Tahitian assessment of a person of worth and is highly valued.

That there may be an inconsistency here (in the eyes of the outsider) when these same families rely on welfare payments and subsidies to meet a significant portion of their needs does not occur to islanders. In general, they feel that if France wants to give them money they will take it, although not as a gift, but as their due. Why this should be the case has never been clear to me, although it is certainly not because islanders see

Ceremony to raise the French flag on Bastille Day, July 14, 1987, Tubai, French Polynesia. (Photo by Victoria S. Lockwood)

themselves as having entered into an economic transaction with France, bartering their sovereignty for financial subsidies. Such an idea would be loathsome and spark angry denials.

Islanders' views on potato subsidies further illuminate their general perspective. Indeed, island farmers do not acknowledge the existence of the subsidies through which they are asked to pay only 60 percent of their actual production costs. Instead, they complain at length about just how high those costs are, specifically the prices of seed potatoes and fertilizers. They also complain vociferiously about the "low" price (set by the government) they receive for their potatoes at harvest. In their assessment, the government is made up of "bandits" who are stealing their money (that is, keeping part of their rightful potato profits).

While on a day-to-day basis islanders present a demeanor of independence and self-sufficiency, when the occasional subject of Tahitian national independence comes up, they become concerned and nervous. Most project a "worst case" scenario in which independence would entail the termination of all transfer payments and social services (welfare, pensions, free medical care and education, and so on). And, after centuries of political domination, cultural indoctrination, and financial subsidies, islanders are unable to imagine a future (indeed, they do not even try) in which the Tahitian community could provide these things for itself or exist as an entity apart from France. It is not surprising that islanders spend little time pondering the political vicissitudes of their status as a French territory.

Rural islanders are, as one might guess, extremely politically conservative on the issue of the French presence. Instead of voting in the 1981 French national election for François Mitterand, the candidate whose socialist platform promised reforms and greater local political autonomy for France's possessions, islanders voted for the conservative Giscard d'Estaing and thus a maintenance of entrenched French control. One political analyst (Daniellson 1983:216), who presumes that islanders would see the socialist candidate and greater political autonomy as desirable, has proposed that Tahitians must have been misled by their local leaders to have voted so incorrectly for the conservative. Another possible explanation is that islanders knew exactly what they were doing. As one Tahitian government official noted, "Our education is French. We are used to French development. Our money is backed by France. If we have a piece of land, a home and a job that is more important than independence" (Francis Sanford, quoted in *Pacific Islands Monthly* 1980).

CONCLUSION

In the previous discussion I have examined the motives behind France's entrenched presence in the Pacific Islands and its desire to control the island societies it has engulfed within its world-wide, neocolonial network. I have also proposed that the mechanisms inherent in welfare state colonialism generate dependency and thus insure a virtually unbreakable bond between France and its overseas possessions. The elements intrinsic to this dependency relationship include providing rural islanders with a high (and "modern") standard of living and social welfare as well as economic opportunities, which they themselves would be unable to generate. Another strategic element in the welfare state colonialism process is denial (or, at least, failure to acknowledge) on the part of the subsumed population that dependency exists; this itself plays a central role in maintaining the relationship.

The conclusion that one must draw is that Tahitian society has been, and will continue to be, shaped in the interests and image of France. What also stands out clearly from the example of Tubuai and of French Polynesia in general is that welfare state colonialism, particularly the French version of it, is a highly successful form of modern-day neocolonialism.

Moreover, as Crocombe (1987:197) notes:

"Nobody is independent today, and the critical issue is what extent of dependence is considered acceptable, or inevitable, in what area of life, at what costs, weighed against what benefits."

Acknowledgments: Research on development-induced socioeconomic change was conducted on Tubuai in 1980–1981, 1985, and 1987. Field work in 1980–1981 was supported by a University of California Regents Travel Grant and by the Department of Anthropology, UCLA. Research in 1985 and 1987 was funded by a gratefully acknowledged grant from the National Science Foundation (#BNS 8507861); supplementary support was provided by the Institute for the Study of Earth and Man, Southern Methodist University. I would like to express my appreciation to the Haut-Commissaire de la République en Polynésie Française for permission to pursue the research, and to the staff of the Office de la Recherche Scientifique et Technique Outre-Mer (Papeete) for their support and guidance.

NOTES

1. France's Overseas Departments and Territories are French Polynesia, New Caledonia, and Wallis/Futuna in the Pacific; French Guiana (Guyane) in South America; Martinique and Guadaloupe and its Dependencies in the Caribbean; Reunion and Mayotte in the Indian Ocean, and Saint-Pierre and Miquelon off the coast of Newfoundland (see Aldrich and Connell 1988).

2. Other ethnographic sources that provide information on Tahitian village life before 1960 include Danielsson 1955, Finney 1973, Oliver 1981, and D. Marshall 1961.

3. Bertram and Watters (1985:507) note that France gave A$944 in aid per capita to French Polynesia in 1980.

4. In both 1981 and 1987, detailed socioeconomic censuses of all island households were conducted. The quantitative data presented for Tubuai families is derived from those censuses, as well as from extensive interviewing and observation.

Markets, Development, and Capitalism

INTRODUCTION

Two of the major themes in the Pacific Islands' contemporary economic evolution is the impact of capitalism and islanders' variable responses to it. At one end of a continuum are those societies in which capitalism has been embraced wholeheartedly, as in the resource-rich Highlands of Papua New Guinea. These communities are experiencing a local-level florescence of capitalist entrepreneurship, economic growth, and substantial associated social and institutional change. At the other end of the continuum are the resource-poor, smaller island societies like Western Samoa, Vanuatu, Pohnpei, and Mandok Island (Papua New Guinea). These societies appear to have, at best, only marginal development potential, and capitalism has been greeted with ambivalence. In these cases, some islanders have chosen out-migration in search of wage work or education (for wage employment), and thus to participate in the capitalist system elsewhere. Other islanders have chosen to maintain their indigenous (noncapitalist) economic institutions as a strategy for ensuring their economic security and increasing their economic options.

Ben Finney (Chapter 7) looks at the florescence of capitalism in the highlands of Papua New Guinea (PNG) through the eyes of its own native "big businessmen" and entrepreneurs. Since PNG independence in 1975 and the ensuing withdrawal of expatriate businessmen and plantation owners (mostly Australians), Papua New Guineans have moved into their roles with zest and financial acumen, and they are now creating their own multi-million-dollar corporations and enterprises. Finney proposes that Highlands New Guinea society was culturally "pre-adapted" to capitalism (in its values and social institutions), including a "psychological orientation" towards wealth and achievement. He concludes the chapter with a brief consideration of the capitalist class structures that are emerging in PNG society.

In contrast to Finney's focus on "big business," which is dominated by Papua New Guinea men, Lorraine Sexton (Chapter 8) examines how village women have created their own unique niche in the budding capitalist system. She argues that as new cash-earning economic opportunities have become available in the region, an area known for its patterns of male domination, men have achieved almost unilateral control over major productive resources and cash income. Women have responded to their relatively deteriorating economic position by developing the *Wok Meri* movement, a highly ritualized, collective savings and exchange system. Through Wok Meri activities, women are themselves investing in capitalist enterprises and making money, a phenomenon that will undoubtedly have important implications for the evolving structure of gender relations in the Highlands.

Tim O'Meara (Chapter 9) explains that in Western Samoa, an island nation characterized by low per-capita income, aid dependency, and extensive out-migration, "the word on the lips of government officials, city merchants, and village farmers is 'development'" (pp. 136). He describes how in this outwardly conservative island society, the search for money permeates, modifies, and simultaneously supports traditional institutions such as the chiefly *matai* system, extended family, and ceremonial exchange and prestige systems.

Paul Shankman (Chapter 10) describes the situation of the many Western Samoans who have chosen the out-migration option, abandoning their home islands for American Samoa, New Zealand, and elsewhere. He notes that even though Samoans encounter many hardships at their international destinations, they rarely choose to return home. Shankman goes on to discuss some of the economic consequences of rampant out-migration for Western Samoan society: remittance dependency, increasing importation and declining exports, growing inflation, and rural underdevelopment.

Margaret Rodman (Chapter 11) describes how in Vanuatu islanders have avoided incorporation into the capitalist *mode* of production, while participating in capitalist *markets* as copra producers or commercial fishermen. They work only intermittently producing copra or fishing, spending much of their time in subsistence gardens and fulfilling social obligations. Rodman explains that in this economy, incentives promoting production (particularly strong prices for commodities) are weak, and options to diversify economic activities limited. In response, islanders maintain an "exit option," retiring from market production to ensure their security through subsistence production.

Glenn Petersen (Chapter 12) examines a case similar to Vanuatu's, that of Pohnpei in the Caroline Islands (Federated States of Micronesia). Petersen argues that on Pohnpei, islanders have actively maintained their traditional political economy based on chiefly prerogatives and ceremonial redistribution, minimizing the impact of the expanding capitalist system on their lives. The purposeful bankruptcies of island tradestores is described as a strategy in which men seeking prestige "redistribute" imported goods instead of selling them to accumulate profits. This phenomenon is linked to a wider social context in which islanders are pushing for their political independence from the U.S. by rejecting their growing dependence on American spending in the islands (and thus on salaries and imports).

In the last contribution to this section, Alice Pomponio (Chapter 13) discusses the case of the tiny island of Mandok (coastal Papua New Guinea). Lacking cash-earning opportunities, Mandok islanders devised their own "development" strategy: financing their children's off-island secondary education so that they could find jobs on the mainland and remit money home. However, when changing educational policies and a glutted job market meant that Mandok children could no longer fulfill these expectations, parents judged education to be of little value and a "losing investment." They then stopped sending their children to school altogether. Pomponio argues that national educational aims must be compatible with the more immediate pragmatic goals of parents and children in order for long-term progress towards national development to take place.

7

From the Stone Age to the Age of Corporate Takeovers

Ben Finney
University of Hawaii

The colonial frontier was late in coming to the densely populated valleys of the Highlands of Papua New Guinea. Effective contact with the outside world did not commence until the early 1930s, and the Highlands people did not really begin to be linked with the world economic system until after World War II. Some of these Highlanders have, however, made up for lost time by seizing opportunities in the new economy and developing major commercial enterprises including, most recently, multi-million-dollar companies involved in coffee growing, processing, and sales, and in a variety of other commercial activities. This chapter, based on field research conducted in 1967–1968 and again in 1986, briefly describes and analyzes this remarkable example of indigenous Papua New Guinean enterprise.

BACKGROUND

In 1966, I was invited to be the first Fulbright scholar to Papua New Guinea, then administered by Australia. The host institution, the New Guinea Research Unit of the Australian National University, was interested in an anthropological study of how Papua New Guineans were responding to opportunities in the market economy. They offered the choice of investigating either indigenous cooperative societies or private enterprises owned and operated by Papua New Guineans. Unhesitatingly, I chose to study the latter, for whereas the scanty literature on indigenous economic development in Papua New Guinea indicated that cooperative societies were at best problematic solutions to the economic needs of Papua New Guineans, there were a few hints that entrepreneurship was beginning to blossom in some parts of the country.

Yet, at that time, this nascent indigenous entrepreneurship was not formally recognized either by the Australian administration or the international agencies then becoming interested in Papua New Guinea—perhaps because it was too new, or because it was contrary to European stereotypes of indigenous capabilities, or both. For example, the 1965 World Bank report on Papua New Guinea largely ignored the possibility of indigenous entrepreneurship and focused instead on the necessity for Australian and other expatriates to continue operating their plantations and businesses in Papua New Guinea and to develop still more enterprises there in order to build up the economic base of the country (World Bank 1965). Nonetheless, from a few short items that appeared in newspapers and periodicals, and from what fellow anthropologists recently returned from Papua New Guinea had told me, it was apparent that some Papua New Guineans—notably the inhabitants of remote highland valleys who were hardly a generation removed from the stone age—were enthusiastically trying their hand at cash cropping and were investing their profits in a variety of business ventures. Why this should be so was an intriguing question, and so I set out to conduct field research on Highlands entrepreneurs.

Most economists writing about economic development in the 1960s stressed the demand side of entrepreneurship. They assumed that entrepreneurs—those people who start new enterprises and industries—will naturally arise when economic conditions are favorable for such initiatives, and were not concerned with individual, class or cultural differences that might affect entrepreneurial response (Kilby 1969). It seemed obvious, however, from an examination of actual cases of economic development that individual, social, and cultural factors affected the "supply" of entrepreneurs. In my own work conducted in French Polynesia in the early 1960s, for example, I had found Tahitians to be notably unentrepreneurial in comparison to the Europeans and Chinese living there, a fact the Tahitians recognized and explained by saying, essentially, that they were unsuited to starting and running businesses because of their cultural values favoring sharing and equality (Finney 1973a).

In contrast, a cursory examination of the anthropological literature on the people of the Highlands of Papua New Guinea indicated that their stress on individual wealth accumulation and exchange, and the translation of success in the economic sphere into social status seemed to be ready-made for entrepreneurship. Therefore, my working hypothesis was that Highlanders were culturally pre-adapted to entrepreneurship, and that, once they became linked with the world capitalist economy, their values encouraged them to plunge directly into that economy by starting their own enterprises.

WEALTH AND STATUS IN THE HIGHLANDS

Among the many tribal groups living scattered across the Highlands, there were no hereditary chiefs or fixed social classes. Leadership was exercised by men who had earned the name of "big man," or "man with a name," through their deeds. Big men gained repute through war, oratory, and, above all, through economic success. The ambitious Highlander strove to become wealthy and to use that wealth to gain prominence in the ceremonial exchange system.

To begin a career based on wealth and its exchange, a young Highlander first had to amass pigs, the basic, locally produced wealth item in the exchange system. This was done through a combination of "home production" and "finance." Home production normally came first. For this a young man needed at least one sow, land for growing sweet potatoes (the main pig fodder), and female labor for tending the gardens and pigs (which is considered to be women's work). Although he might be able to prevail upon his mother or sisters to help him for a time, a man on the way up had to marry to assure himself the requisite female labor. Building up a pig herd in this way took time because, among other things, some of the pigs produced had to be repaid to those who had initially loaned the breeding stock and those who had donated pigs and other exchange items needed to secure a bride. Furthermore, as an ambitious man's pig herd grew and, particularly, as he acquired more wives to feed and care for the growing herd, his obligations increased, both in the form of repayments and in the donations for marriages and other ceremonial occasions that he was supposed to make as an aspiring big man.

Once he had demonstrated that he could successfully breed pigs, repay his debts, and manage other obligations, the ambitous man was in a position to expand his wealth by "financial" means. Pigs could be advantageously traded for shells and other valuables with those who needed them for ceremonies. Pigs also could be profitably loaned to younger men anxious to start their own careers or farmed out among relatives, in return for "interest" in the form of piglets or other valuables.

Fellow Highlanders were attracted to a man who was successful in pig breeding and such "financial" manipulations, and he, in turn, could further enhance his reputation by weaving a network of political supporters composed of his trade partners and those indebted to him. The aspiring big man could further add to his reputation and following by making major contributions of pigs, shells, and other valuables on the occasion of marriages and other events requiring the exchange of wealth, and also by organizing the pooling of his clansmen's contributions to these exchanges and the distribution of the valuables they received in return. This arena of valuables exchange shows how individual and group ambitions were complementary. The clan needed the contributions and organizing skill of the big man to further its reputation, while the big man needed a socially sanctioned context in which he could further enhance his prestige. Followers did not, therefore, begrudge the support they gave to a powerful big man, for his success was also the group's success.

The resultant status system was competitive and fluid. At any one time several men in a clan, or group of associated clans, might compete for leadership. Even if one man became pre-eminent, his position was tenuous in that it depended upon his ability to manage his assets and the complex web of obligations he had constructed. If a man lost economic ground through mismanagement or physical disability, he lost repute and his following dwindled. Wealth and leadership were not hereditary. When a man died, his fortune would be redistributed among his clansmen and exchange partners, not just to his children. Furthermore, although the son of a living big man might have an edge because of his access to pigs and other valuables, ultimately he would have to prove himself through hard work and perseverance to gain big-man status.

GOROKA

I chose the Goroka valley, the center of the coffee industry in what is now the Eastern Highlands Province, as a site for intensive field research. At the time of European contact in the early 1930s, some sixty thousand people lived along the floor of this well-watered valley, mostly at elevations around 5,000 feet, and on the lower slopes of the hills and mountains surrounding the valley. Although the people of this valley shared the common Highlander orientation toward wealth and status, they were divided into five main linguistic groups and many more tribal ones, and were not politically unified until the Australians imposed military control in the 1930s.

In the late 1940s, a number of Australians, mostly former gold miners and administration patrol officers, began experimenting with growing arabica coffee in the rich, well-watered soil of the valley. Lack of a road connection to the coast, however, partially restricted development of the crop, as all coffee produced had to be flown down to the port of Madang on the north coast of the island, and all supplies and equipment had to be flown in. Completion in the mid-1960s of the Highlands Highway linking Goroka and other highland centers with the coastal port of Lae provided the needed surface linkage with the external world economy, and from then the coffee industry began to take off.

When I arrived in Goroka in 1967 it was a bustling Australian enclave. In addition to serving as the headquarters for the Australian administration of the Eastern Highlands region, the township of Goroka was a thriving business center for a colonial plantation economy based on coffee. Australians and other expatriates owned the major plantations, coffee mills, and exporting firms, and controlled virtually all the retail and service establishments in the township. Even then, however, the Gorokan people were beginning to participate widely in the coffee industry and other sectors of the cash economy. Despite the fact that they had received only sporadic encouragement from the Australian administration and virtually nothing in the way of agricultural and business loans, the Gorokans were beginning to produce more coffee than was being grown on the expatriate plantations, and they were pooling their coffee proceeds and investing them in trade stores, trucking ventures, and other businesses (see Finney 1973b).

PIONEERING GOROKAN ENTREPRENEURS

Leading this Gorokan initiative were a number of indigenous business leaders known in New Guinea Pidgin as *bikpela man bilong bisnis*, or "big men of business." They were the first Gorokans to start growing coffee on a large scale, and were pioneering diversification into retail, trucking, and other enterprises.

These entrepreneurs were not, however, traditional leaders who themselves had made the transition to the cash economy. Traditional big men had been too involved with the old life and too inexperienced in the new ways to become successful entrepreneurs in the introduced economy. In contrast, all the main business leaders, even those who had been born well before 1930 when the first Europeans arrived, had either some formal schooling or extensive work experience in the cash economy, or both, before they started their own enterprises. Nonetheless, despite their exposure to modern life and their concentration on the market economy rather than the traditional one, these business leaders were actually following a career trajectory analogous to that followed by the traditional big men. Instead of working their way to the top through pig raising and wealth exchange, they were gaining status through growing coffee and other commercial activities. In the way they began with minimal resources, built up their holdings through hard work and skillful recruitment of support from their clansmen and others, and then converted their economic accomplishments into enhanced social status, these men were following the style, if not the substance, of the traditional Gorokan way of achieving status.

The case histories of Bimai Noimbano, Sinake Giregire, and Hari Gotoha, three of the most outstanding entrepreneurs in this first generation of business leaders, illustrate how these new big men built up their economic standing and repute as leaders.

Bimai Noimbano, who was born just before the first Europeans entered the region, was one of the first Gorokans to grow coffee on a large scale. He first became interested in cash crops in 1949, when he worked on Manus Island as a plantation laborer. From Manus he moved back to the Highlands to work as a trainee at an agricultural station. There he became so intrigued with the idea of growing coffee himself, that he left the station with a load of coffee seeds and seedlings and walked to his home village some 70 miles to the west. But he could not get the seedlings to grow. Bimai then sent some young boys back to the experiment station for more seedlings and seed, but these too failed to take hold. Although by this time Bimai had a thriving business selling chickens to expatriates, he was still interested in growing coffee and enthusiastically welcomed the technical advice offered by an Australian agricultural officer who happened by. Following the officer's instructions, Bimai set out a model nursery to grow seedlings, and then transplanted these to a carefully laid out plantation that started bearing after several years.

A key element in Bimai's success was his knack for gaining support and assistance from his clansmen and neighbors. As an adoptive member of his clan, Bimai had no secure land rights there. Nor did he have money to pay people to clear land and plant his coffee. Bimai overcame this lack of resources by successfully appealing to his clansmen for help. Although at the time he was a relatively unimportant man, the people were nonetheless willing to support him by giving him land, by contributing their labor, and even by making cash contributions for tools and supplies, because Bimai seemed to them to know something about the workings of the cash economy and promised to develop coffee-growing and other enterprises that would eventually benefit everyone.

By the early 1960s, Bimai was well established as a coffee grower, and, using trucks he had purchased from his coffee proceeds, was buying coffee from small producers and selling it to the processing factories. In addition, he ran a trade store and several other small enterprises. He was widely admired throughout Goroka as a successful "big man of business" who had mastered the art of making money in the new economy and was showing the way for other ambitious Gorokans.

Sinake Giregire was born in the mid-1930s, right after Europeans first came into the valley. After two years in the local Lutheran Mission school, he was sent to the Lutheran headquarters on the coast for further schooling. A near fatal attack of malaria forced him to return to Goroka, however, where, after recuperating for several years, he took a job as a mechanic's helper for a small air service operating from the Goroka airport. At age twenty, after working there for three years and then briefly holding a job at an agricultural experiment station, Sinake decided it was time he went into business for himself.

His goal was to start a coffee plantation, but, to do that, he needed capital as well as some credibility among his clansmen. Accordingly, Sinake turned to lumbering after observing the administration's need for building lumber. Sinake took his meager savings, purchased a hand-operated pit saw, and hired some local youths as laborers. Although Sinake made some money, he soon found that he could not compete with the sawmills then being introduced by Australians. So he abandoned lumbering to try his hand at panning gold to be found in small quantities in streambeds around the region. With a crew of a half dozen or so laborers, Sinake worked the streams for several years until 1958 when, with the equivalent (in Australian pounds, the currency of the day) of about $2,000[1] in his pocket, he returned to his home village.

Sinake's clansmen were impressed by the amount of money he had accumulated, and, overlooking his youth and lack of status in the traditional system, allocated a large tract of land to him for planting coffee. They even contributed some start-up money and offered their labor. Sinake then used his savings and their contributions to buy tools and supplies and to hire a crew of laborers from the adjacent district to help clear the land, set up a nursery, plant the seedlings, and then care for the maturing coffee trees. The resulting plantation soon became the largest owned by any Gorokan, and probably by any Papua New Guinean at the time.

Like other business leaders who were then getting their start in coffee, Sinake invested some of his profits in trade stores and trucking ventures. His ambition, however, was to own a coffee factory for processing his own crop of ripe coffee berries, and those of his neighbors, into green coffee which he could then sell directly to exporters, thus cutting out the expatriates who then controlled coffee processing and sales. In 1970, using his accumulated profits and one of the first major bank loans given to a Papua New Guinean, Sinake was able to erect his factory and start buying and processing coffee on a large scale.

"It all started with thirty cents of self-rising flour," was how another Gorokan entrepreneur, Hari Gotoha, began telling me the story of how he got into business. Unlike Sinake and most other major business leaders, Hari was not able to start his commercial career by planting a large tract of land in coffee because his clan was land-poor, having sold much of its territory to the administration as a site for Goroka township. Instead of following the coffee route to success, Hari was forced to build up his business holdings by catering to the nascent demand among Gorokans for goods and services in the new economy.

Continuing his story, Hari told me how one day while working as a domestic servant for an Australian, he used his store-bought flour and his employer's stove to bake some scones, which he readily sold to Gorokan customers at the local vegetable market. He then reinvested his profits into buying more flour, sold more scones, and so on until he had a flourishing business—so flourishing, in fact, that his employer suggested he leave her employ and devote himself full-time to his baking business.

This he did, earning some $700 in his first year, which he used to set up a small restaurant adjacent to the market. This venture proved even more popular, and he used his growing cash flow to build a small retail store on his property, the first such store in Goroka township to be owned by a Gorokan, and then to equip his restaurant with running water, electricity, a modern stove, and refrigerator-freezer.

By 1968, through reinvesting his profits and also the contributions of some of his clansmen, Hari had started a trucking business to haul freight between Goroka and the coastal port of Lae, and, using some $28,000 from his profits, he rebuilt and expanded his store to serve the hundreds of Gorokans who came each day to shop at the adjacent municipal market. Although he specialized in such urban businesses, Hari also tried his hand at more rurally oriented pursuits. After gaining rights from his clansmen to use some of their land, he started a small coffee plantation in partnership with another Gorokan and also experimented with raising cattle and pigs.

Both Sinake Giregire and Hari Gotoha were looked up to by their fellow Gorokans because of their success in the world of *bisnis*, the Pidgin English term Papua New Guineans use to refer to all commercial activities from cash cropping to ventures we would normally refer to as businesses. Although they were not considered to be traditional big men, the Gorokans did regard them as "big men of business," as they refer to those men who have shown great skill and leadership in the new economy. Their clansmen, in particular, were proud that one of their number had become a successful and famous business leader. These business leaders, in turn, took great pains to emphasize how much their clansmen had aided them in building up their enterprises. In addition, they also liberally donated money, pigs, and other traditional valuables to provide the bride price necessary for their young followers to marry, and contributed to the group in other ways, such as paying for children's school fees. In so doing, they of course further enhanced their reputation and cemented their ties with their clansmen.

It was clear that these business leaders were behaving within the context of the introduced cash economy much like the successful big men of previous, precontact generations. Coffee plantations, stores, trucking firms and other ventures were the new ways of gaining wealth and achieving status. Furthermore, in pioneering these activities, these business leaders acted as role models for other, less-daring Gorokans, and so were helping to promote the general level of economic participation while they themselves became comparatively wealthy.

GOROKA IN TRANSITION

Yet, however fascinating this entrepreneurial response and the degree of traditional support for it, looking ahead from the late 1960s, it was easy to foresee problems for the Gorokans on the horizon. While the Gorokan business leaders might have been able to walk the tightrope between utilizing clan support for their own and group goals and downright exploitation of their clansmen for personal gain, it seemed open to question whether or not their heirs might form an entrenched, exploitative economic elite. In addition, the very basis for Gorokan prosperity, coffee, was problematic, for as the people in one Third World country after another have learned, dependence on a single cash crop can be dangerous. Furthermore, no matter how much coffee the Gorokans produced, in the late 1960s the coffee industry itself was still firmly in the hands of Australians and other expatriates, and it seemed difficult to imagine how it could be peacefully and efficiently transferred into local hands as the decolonization of Papua New Guinea unfolded in the coming years.

During the 1970s and early 1980s, a number of disturbing reports concerning Gorokan economic efforts began to appear in the literature. For example, a geographer wrote about how a faltering coffee industry and local population growth was pinching off growth prospects for the Gorokans, and would eventually cause them to stagnate economically as an "infinite pause" in development settled over Goroka (Howlett 1973). A number of expatriate economists and political scientists were even more pessimistic about Gorokan prospects. They were particularly incensed by what they considered to be the rapacious behavior of the Gorokan entrepreneurs. They charged that these men were destroying the autonomy of the local village economy and pushing the Gorokan masses into a vulnerable dependency on the world economy with all its inequalities (Amarshi et al. 1979; Connell 1979; Fitzpatrick 1980; Gerritson 1979; Good and Donaldson, *in press*). To these neo-Marxist dependency theorists, the Gorokan business leaders were "rich peasants," "big peasants," or "kulaks" who were exploiting their fellow clansmen and turning them into a downtrodden, Third World peasantry.

Reading these analyses, as well as brief newspaper and magazine stories about falling coffee prices and how formerly expatriate coffee plantations were being grossly mismanaged by the Gorokans who took them over, gave this author cause to wonder if the promising entrepreneurial start of the late 1960s had indeed faltered. A chance to return to Goroka and restudy Gorokan business development came in 1986[2].

GOROKA IN THE LATE 1980s

The changes that greeted me when I returned to Goroka mirrored the contrast between the sleek Fokker jet of nationally owned Air New Guinea of the late 1980s, and the venerable DC-3 operated by an Australian airline that flew to Goroka almost two decades earlier. In those intervening years the Goroka township had expanded greatly, but what was most striking was that these facilities were now filled with seemingly affluent Gorokan customers, whereas before, virtually the only Papua New Guineans to be seen in the stores, banks, and other businesses were those sweeping the floor or engaged in other menial tasks. Even without current income figures, it was obvious that the Gorokans were far wealthier than they had been in the late 1960s, when their per capita income was less than $20. In 1986, they had the money to buy everything from groceries and whole sides of frozen New Zealand lamb and beef to the latest Japanese video tape recorders and pick-up trucks. Furthermore, although some of the old expatriate trading companies had survived into the modern era, it was apparent that virtually all of the new businesses in town were either owned outright by Gorokans, or were leasing space in Gorokan-owned buildings.

Even more impressive was the degree to which Gorokans had taken over the coffee industry. Virtually all the expatriate plantations had been taken over by Gorokans, and all the coffee buying and processing, formerly an expatriate monopoly, was now in the hands of Gorokan individuals and firms or nationally owned companies in which Gorokans had equity. Even in coffee exporting, the sector of the industry that requires the most capital and business experience, Gorokans had a stake in two of the largest firms serving the region and other coffee-growing areas of the Highlands.

A SECOND GENERATION OF GOROKAN ENTREPRENEURS

Upon investigating these economic developments, it became clear that the policies favoring indigenous enterprise put into effect with self-government in 1973 and the granting of full independence to Papua New Guinea in 1975 had greatly aided this Gorokan takeover. Nonetheless, it was equally clear that it was the Gorokan entrepreneurs who had actively seized the opportunities made possible by new legislation and government lending programs, and had made this economic transmutation really work. Only two or three of these entrepreneurs were the same ones who had been prominent in the late 1960s, for only a few, like Hari Gotoha, of the first generation of Gorokan entrepreneurs were still economic leaders. Some of the prominent entrepreneurs of the late 1960s, like Bimai Noimbano, had died, others had retired from business, while others, like Sinake Giregire, had suffered severe financial reverses and had declined in prominence. Most of the leading Gorokan businessmen of the 1980s were younger entrepreneurs, men in their mid-to-late-forties who had just been starting their commercial careers twenty years ago.

The enterprises that they, and the few first-generation businessmen still active, have developed can be roughly divided into two broad categories: individualistic and group-oriented. Most of the new entrepreneurs have followed the individualistic style of their predecessors in that they have built up businesses that they wholly or largely own and operate. Although they sometimes received financial help and donated labor to help them get started from their clansmen and other Gorokans, and although there may still be some degree of clan or tribal identification with their enterprises, there is no question who is the primary owner and boss. A case history of how Akapite Wamiri built up his business empire illustrates this individualistic style of entrepreneurship.

In the late 1960s, Akapite Wamiri was a schoolteacher in his late twenties. He had other ambitions, however, and was regularly putting aside money from his teacher's salary and from carpentry work he was doing on weekends and vacations toward the day when he could start his own business. In 1970, using $1,800 of his own savings and several hundred dollars from a clansman, he bought a used station wagon and started a local bus service. This was so profitable that he was soon able to purchase several buses and trucks to carry passengers and freight between Goroka and the coast. Then, in 1974, he sought to take advantage of the exodus of expatriate planters who were leaving the country just before independence by buying one of their plantations. With some $50,000 of his own savings, another $10,000 from some fifty of his clansmen, and a bank loan of $75,000, Akapite bought a plantation from a departing Australian.

Soon thereafter, coffee prices jumped following a frost that destroyed much of Brazil's crop, and Akapite was able to pay off the bank loan within the year and gain full title to the plantation. Akapite has not been content, however, with a single plantation. He has formed a holding company, the Anego Company, which now includes three more former expatriate coffee plantations, a cattle ranch, and a sugar plantation in the lowlands which were developed with partners from there. In addition, Akapite has invested in income property in coastal ports and in Australian cities, and in commercial property in Goroka on which he plans to build a shopping center. He now owns the newest commercial building in Goroka, the bottom floor of which he leases to the bank that gave him his initial loan. Although Akapite likes to stress that he owns only about 75 percent of the

Akapiti Wamiri, a leading Gorokan entrepreneur of the 1980s, in his office (photo by Ben Finney)

Anego Company and that it benefits a wide range of clansmen and other shareholders, at the same time he is not shy about stating that it was his vision and initiative that created this multi-million-dollar enterprise and that he alone runs it.

The great personal wealth of Akapite, and a number of other individualistic entrepreneurs who have been similarly successful in taking over plantations and other expatriate enterprises as well as in starting new ones, contrasts greatly with the economic status of the great majority of Gorokans. While the ordinary Gorokan is better fed and generally much more affluent than before, the economic gulf between these big businessmen and the average person is tremendous. According to Kenneth Read (1959), who extensively documented traditional Gorokan culture in the 1950s before major economic changes had occurred, individual and group interests should be balanced in Gorokan life: the success exhibited by a big man was supposed to be equalized by his generosity to his clansmen and others. The entrepreneurs of the 1960s recognized this obligation and sought to allay jealousy and retain their clansmen's support through contributing to bride price and other traditional payments and through such modern avenues as paying the school fees of their supporters' children.

Since many of the individualistic businessmen of today run plantations and other enterprises located outside their clan surroundings and operate through formal corporate structures, professional managers, certified public accountants, and the like, the translation of traditional leadership obligations into meaningful modern deeds is no longer easy. Some do not even try, and thereby earn the enmity of their clansmen and neighbors. Most, however, try, like Akapite, to keep clansmen and other supporters satisfied by traditional and quasi-traditional transactions, as well as with the direct distribution of dividends.

However, some prominent Gorokan business leaders explicitly reject this individualistic model of entrepreneurship on the basis that it is unhealthy for the society as a whole—and personally dangerous for the entrepreneur—to develop solely owned enterprises or enterprises largely owned and controlled by one man. Instead, they argue that group enterprises should be promoted so that everyone can participate in business, and they have implemented their philosophy by founding large businesses owned by thousands of persons from a number of clan and tribal groups. Among such companies, the biggest is the Gouna Development Corporation.

The largest structure in Goroka township is the Gouna Centre, a L-shaped, two-story structure located across the street from the provincial government headquarters. It houses two banks, a supermarket, and various others shops and offices, including that of the Gouna Development Corporation, which owns the building. Gouna also owns several large coffee plantations, a newly constructed coffee factory, a coffee-plantation management service, a petroleum products distributorship, an auto and truck agency, a print shop, and a number of other local businesses, and has a major share in a large coffee-exporting firm. While no figures were available as to the value of these holdings, they probably totaled well over $10 million in 1986.

Gouna is not only the largest Gorokan firm, but it is also the one with the widest ownership base. Thousands of Gorokan shareholders own Gouna. This firm did not arise, however, from purely group initiative or government fiat. It was created by Gorokan entrepreneurs who, wary of being too individualistic, went out of their way to create a large group enterprise for general benefit.

A prime mover behind the foundation of Gouna was Auwo Kitauwo, a Gorokan now in his late forties who started his business career much like Akapite Wamiri and other entrepreneurs of his generation. In 1966, after working first as a laborer in an expatriate-owned coffee factory, then in a store owned by a Chinese merchant, he built a small trade store in his village. Upon discovering that such ventures were not very profitable, he started raising and selling chickens, and founded a business selling traditional artifacts to the tourists who were then beginning to come to Goroka. But, Auwo was not satisfied with such small ventures, and, in the early 1970s, closed his artifact shop, sold his poultry farm, and began looking for something new.

He invested some of his savings in a new helicopter firm that had just been started to serve the mining companies and other organizations that needed to fly into remote areas. Although this proved to be a profitable investment (the firm has thrived with the minerals boom, and now has scores of helicopters serving all of Papua New Guinea and the neighboring Solomon Islands as well), Auwo was not content to be merely an investor. What really excited him was the prospect of starting a business organization in which the mass of Gorokans could become co-owners. Inspired by the speeches of the country's first prime minister, Michael Somare, about how the people of the country should buy out expatriate plantations, Auwo resolved to found a company with thousands of Gorokan shareholders for the purpose of buying and operating expatriate coffee plantations.

He began talking about this with his old friend, the well-established entrepreneur Hari Gotoha. In the late 1960s, Hari had already been concerned about promoting group-oriented businesses as opposed to the more individualistic ones that he and the other entrepreneurs of the day had already started, but had been unsure how this could be done. Now, however, as Papua New Guinea was moving toward independence, and the new national government was calling for nationals to buy out expatriate plantations and giving them legal structures and financial and technical aid to do so, Hari readily joined with Auwo and a third entrepreneur now deceased to develop an ambitious plan to start buying up expatriate plantations and other businesses.

They first collected over $100,000 from thousands of individual contributors. Then, with the aid of the newly independent government's Business Development service and a newly promulgated statute that allowed traditional social groups such as clans or subtribes to form simplified corporations called "business groups," they organized these contributors into business groups, which, in turn, became the owners of the newly founded Gouna Development Corporation. With the aid of bank loans made possible by their wide membership and capital subscription, Gouna began buying plantations and other businesses. Although Gouna has not been immune to business problems, the company has gone on to improve and expand most of the enterprises they purchased, and most recently has bought a major share of the largest coffee-exporting firm.

Auwo, Hari, and another Gorokan are the executive directors of the company; they and nine other Gorokans chosen to represent the interests of the contributing groups form the Board of Directors and set policy to be executed by a management team composed mainly of expatriates from Australia and Europe. However, although they may not directly participate in the day-to-day running of Gouna, Auwo and Hari are active directors and take particular pains to make sure that the Gorokan shareholders know what is happening in the company and gain a feeling of participation beyond the dividends they periodically receive.

Both Auwo and Hari like to stress that Gouna is being operated "to benefit all the people." Their choice of the name Gouna reflects this motivation: it is composed of letters from the three main tribal areas from which its members are drawn (Goroka, meaning the region around the township, Unggai, and Bena); and, in addition, the term means "united" in one of the local languages. Although Auwo and Hari may emphasize that they are only minority shareholders and that Gouna was founded to benefit all the people, at the same time they do not hesitate to say that Gouna was their idea and to brag how they worked long and hard to put the organization together and how they now spend their time looking after the welfare of Gouna and its thousands of shareholders. Such boasting is not out of place in Gorokan circles. Traditionally, big men were not shy about their accomplishments, either of an individual nature or for group benefit. In fact, these two are among the most popular of today's business leaders. Although they may not be as personally wealthy as Akapite Wamiri and some of the other more individualistic entrepreneurs who have recently become prominent, these founders of Gouna have earned great stature locally as men who have helped project the mass of Gorokans into the former expatriate preserve of big business. As one Gorokan put it to me, these men are "working for the interests of all the people," while the other more individualistic entrepreneurs are "too selfish."

A THIRD GENERATION OF GOROKAN ENTREPRENEURS

Although the entrepreneurs discussed so far had far more schooling than did most of their contemporaries, none had completed high school. Now, after the expansion of education throughout Papua New Guinea, high school graduation is becoming commonplace in such centers as Goroka, and a growing number of Gorokans are going on to the University of Papua New Guinea or other tertiary educational institutions. Although most of the graduates of these institutions take positions in government or in large national or multinational firms, a growing number are striking out for themselves in business.

An outstanding young Gorokan businessman is Benais Sapumei. Benais, who is now in his late thirties, was one of the first graduates of the University of Papua New Guinea. After graduation he joined Papua New Guinea's Department of Foreign Affairs. In 1978, however, after serving with Papua New Guinea's delegation to the United Nations, he resigned to return home to take a management position with Angco, a large, nationallyowned, agricultural exporting firm headquartered in Goroka.

Once back in Goroka, Benais became a leader in the Eastern Highlands Development Corporation, a group-oriented company founded, like Gouna, to buy out expatriate coffee plantations, and also went into business for himself, purchasing and operating a supermarket, a hotel, and a number of other enterprises. Although Benais finds it difficult to reconcile his cosmopolitan lifestyle with that of his fellow tribesmen, he still identifies himself closely with his native tribal area of Bena. In fact, when I last interviewed him he was totally preoccupied with defending the shareholding interest of the Eastern Highlands Development Corporation—which is essentially a Bena tribal corporation—within Angco when the latter was in danger of being taken over by investors headed by Papua New Guineans from another province.

Pepe Gotoha is a young, university-educated Gorokan entrepreneur who has specialized in small business. In the late 1960s, Pepe was a high school student and worked as a part-time clerk in the store owned by his older brother Hari Gotoha. After Pepe graduated from high school, Hari sent him to the government cooperative school so that he could come back to Goroka and help people start cooperatives. Pepe, however, was not satisfied with the level of training he received in the cooperative college, and transferred to the University of Papua New Guinea where he took a degree in accounting. Pepe then took a job in the central government's Commerce Department where he was assigned to a program designed to enable Papua New Guineans to purchase and operate retail stores formerly owned by expatriates.

After working in the program for a few years and seeing how some of his clients went on to earn much more from their stores than he could ever hope to as a civil servant, Pepe resigned and enrolled in the program himself. Upon completion of the course, he was assigned to a store in the coastal port of Lae that had been owned by a Chinese merchant who had gone to Australia. With the aid of a government loan and his own extensive training and experience, Pepe quickly turned the store into a profitable enterprise. Since then, he has gone on to buy several other stores, including one in Port Moresby, the capital of Papua New Guinea, where he now makes his home and serves on several government and community boards.

Pepe would like to return to Goroka, but claims that it is too hard to be a success there. All the good commercial sites in the town are already taken, he complains, adding that, besides, there is too much competition there from all the other "business-minded" Gorokans. So, for the time being at least, he is content to manage his stores in Lae and Port Moresby and to invest in a variety of other enterprises around the country where land is cheaper and the competition is less intense.

I also interviewed a number of other young Gorokan businessmen, some of whom, like Pepe Gotoha, were seeking their fortune elsewhere in Papua New Guinea, and some of whom, like Benais Sapumei, were trying to make a go of it in Goroka. In the years to come, it will be interesting to see how this third generation of entrepreneurs develops. Will, for example, intense local competition propel most ambitious Gorokans to go elsewhere in the country, or will continued local development provide still more opportunities for emerging businessmen, or will the outcome be some combination of the two?

DISCUSSION

The Gorokan case provides an example about how—contrary to many stereotypes about "tradition-bound" societies found in the literature on economic development—indigenous values and institutions that evolved in a nonmarket economy context can promote rather than hinder adaptation to the modern world economy. In their rapid transition from stone-age isolation to commodity production and consumerism, the Gorokans have, in a sense, applied traditional cultural resources to the task of adapting to the opportunities and demands of capitalism. In particular, it can be said that the traditional emphasis on wealth and status mobility and the way in which would-be big men were able to rise within the society through their own efforts and skill at recruiting followers preadapted the Gorokans to entrepreneurship in the cash economy. Yet, however smooth and felicitous the fit between traditional Gorokan values and institutions and the capitalist economy might seem, by so wholeheartedly plunging into the world of coffee production and commerce, the Gorokans are hastening the transformation of their own society.

To be sure, the activities of the first entrepreneurs were, despite their modern context, at least partially embedded in the traditional culture—as witness, for example, the way in which they solicited cash and labor from their clansmen to help start their enterprises and then later dispensed patronage to their clansmen and other followers, although mostly in cash rather than traditional items of wealth. Although some of the second-generation entrepreneurs have worked out ways to continue this pooling of resources to initiate enterprises and the judicious distribution of profits to contributors, even they admit that it is increasingly difficult to operate in a quasi-traditional manner. Most of their colleagues have disengaged themselves even further from the traditional context, and some of the young entrepreneurs now emerging have only minimal ties with their clans or other traditional groups. It may turn out that the lasting traditional contribution to Gorokan business success will not be particular cultural forms of economic behavior, but rather a basic psychological orientation to wealth and achievement which continues to make Gorokans "business-minded" (see McClelland 1961; LeVine 1966).

What about the charge that Gorokan entrepreneurs form a new elite class that is widening socioeconomic divisions within the society, transforming the mass of people into a downtrodden peasantry? While these class-formation implications of Gorokan entrepreneurs might seem self-evident, they should be looked at in the context of alternatives. For the Gorokans to have remained as isolated subsistence farmers and warriors was out of the question. Among other things, the Gorokans themselves were more than enthusiastic about joining the modern world in order to gain a share of its technology and other wonders. In an economic sense, the Gorokans entered the world system as poorly paid plantation laborers, but they hardly wanted to be proletarians in an expatriate-controlled plantation economy forever. While some theorists might imagine a scenario in which the government would have bought out all the expatriate plantations and other businesses and then have operated them as socialist enterprises, given the dismal record of socialist agriculture and business around the world, and, more importantly, Gorokan commercial ambitions, such a collective alternative was never even in the running. The Gorokans chose the route of cash cropping and business as the way they wanted to participate in the world economic system.

Of course, Gorokan's participation in capitalism has affected the structure of Gorokan society. Actually, the neo-Marxist critics of Gorokan entrepreneurs underestimated the Gorokan entrepreneurs when they called them rich peasants and kulaks. If anything, they should be called big businessmen who, through their enterprise in starting new ventures and taking over and expanding ones formerly owned by expatriates, are accelerating the transformation of Gorokan society.

One important change in Highlands' society has been increasing participation in business by women who are struggling to break through the male domination of both the traditional economy and the introduced one (see Chapter 8, by Lorraine Sexton, in this volume; Sexton 1986; Finney 1987:53–55). If women become outstandingly successful, their business prominence could greatly affect the nature of Gorokan society, particularly the structure of gender relations.

It is important to note that Gorokan society has not been transformed into a simple, two-class structure composed of a business elite and a peasantry. The coffee plantations and other local businesses need thousands of workers, particularly at harvest time. Although some Gorokans are full-time workers, wages, particularly on plantations, are too low to attract the coffee-rich Gorokans, and most laborers come from the poorer, more remote regions of the Highlands. In addition, a growing number of government employees, ranging from highly paid administrators to ordinary office workers, populates the urban center of Goroka. As a recent socioeconomic survey indicates, it is they, not the businessmen, who stand out from the majority of the Gorokans in terms of living standards and consumption patterns (Yupae 1986). A complex social system is therefore emerging in Goroka composed of plantation workers, government civil servants, and rural cash crop producers, as well as the dynamic business leaders whose careers and achievements have been discussed here.

NOTES

1. Three different units of currency—Australian pounds, then Australian dollars, and finally Papua New Guinea kina—were used during the course of this study. For simplicity's sake, amounts of money are quoted in U.S. dollars.

2. I returned to Goroka as a member of the project on Pacific business enterprise of the Pacific Islands Development Project of Hawaii's East-West Center.

8

Pigs, Pearlshells, and 'Women's Work':
Collective Response to Change in Highland Papua New Guinea[1]

Lorraine Dusak Sexton
The Vanderveer Group, Inc.

The entrance of Australian gold prospectors into the high central mountains of the Territory of New Guinea in 1930 was a turning point for the people of the region. In the intervening fifty years, the small-scale, isolated tribal societies of the Highlands have been drawn into the independent nation of Papua New Guinea, as well as into the international market economy. Highlanders continue to cultivate sweet potatoes, raise pigs, and engage in prestigious transfers of wealth, confirming social relationships between groups. But stone technology has been superseded by steel, warfare has been outlawed (although there have been serious eruptions in recent years), and Christianity has been adopted. Money earned from coffee cash cropping, wage labor, and commercial activities has become necessary for traditional exchanges and newly created needs and obligations.

In response to changes that adversely affected their economic rights, women in the Chuave District, Simbu Province, and the neighboring Goroka District, Eastern Highlands Province (Map 8–1), have, since about 1960, developed a savings and exchange system called *Wok Meri*, 'women's work' in the Neo-Melanesian lingua franca. Small groups of women collect and save their earnings from selling vegetables, small amounts of coffee, or their labor. Each group also enters into two kinds of exchange relations with similar Wok Meri groups. The first type of exchange mimics the payment of bride price and entails the re-enactment of birth and of marriage rituals. The second type of exchange is described by informants as a banking system in which Wok Meri women from a wide area make small loans to one another.

Female and male informants have a standard reply when queried about the reasons for Wok Meri's development and the goals of the movement. Wok Meri began because women disapprove of men's expenditure of money for playing cards and drinking beer.

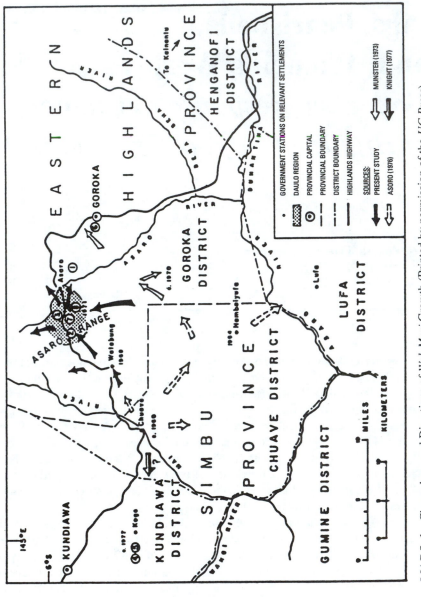

MAP 8–1   Chronology and Directions of *Wok Meri* Growth (Printed by permission of the *UC Press*).

118

In response to what they describe as men's negligence, women save a portion of their own money. By doing so they hope to safeguard their small incomes from importunate husbands, to demonstrate their competence as money managers, and to show how much money could be accumulated if men were more provident with the bulk of the household income that they control.

Beyond these modest aims, however, I perceive broader goals embedded in the financial and ritual activities of Wok Meri. Men's control of most money has enabled them to continue monopolizing prominent roles in ceremonial transactions and business enterprises, which are primarily financed by investment of income from coffee sales. In Wok Meri, women have developed their own exchange system in which they play all the roles, and they have established a modified Western-style banking system. The capital that Wok Meri women accumulate through savings, loans, and exchange payments (in effect, a customary type of loan) is usually invested in the same kinds of businesses that have attracted Highland male entrepreneurs since the early 1960s.

WOK MERI

Wok Meri is a network of autonomous groups ranging from two to thirty-five women. Members are recruited from the wives of lineage or sublineage mates who live in the same village.[2] Thus, the organizational unit of Wok Meri is based on a kinship unit already carrying out important social functions. The wives of older lineage or sublineage mates have worked together for many years to organize a variety of events, including exchange payments and rites to mark the members' passages through different stages of the life cycle. Thus, the women in a Wok Meri group are able to embark on their new social and exchange activities by building on the firm structural foundation of an existing kin group.

Each group engages in savings and exchange activities under the leadership of one or two *vena namba*, "big women," a new title for women used only in Wok Meri. The term and its duties are modeled on the traditional role of the *ve namba*, "big man," who attains his status through leadership in exchange, politics, and (previously) warfare. There may be more than one "big man" in a lineage, as there may be more than one "big woman" in a Wok Meri group. Both "big men" and "big women" achieve and maintain their positions through their ability to recruit supporters and to motivate their cooperation. Neither big men nor big women have the authority to coerce people to follow their dictates.

Successful male entrepreneurs have become known as *bikpela man bilong bisnis* "business leaders"; literally, "big businessmen" in Neo-Melanesian. These entrepreneurs have been able to adapt traditional skills to modern business conditions by enlisting their kin to invest labor and money in their business activities (see Chapter 7, by Ben Finney, in this volume). The Wok Meri movement is concerned with women's participation in both traditional exchange and modern business activities, and the role of the Wok Meri big women encompasses the task of the old- and new-style big men.

The big woman is the prime mover in organizing a new group. She establishes and maintains ties with big women from other groups, organizes meetings and ceremonies, and leads the rituals. Wok Meri big women encourage their group members to save money and to participate in exchanges with other groups by exhortation and by their own example. Big women compete with their opposite numbers in other groups to accumulate large sums of money. The reputation of a big woman, like that of a traditional big man, depends not only on her personal wealth but also on the group's successful completion of the cycle of exchanges and on the amount of money controlled by the group. The attainment of big woman status is not dependent on the position of a woman's husband; that is, big women are not generally the wives of big men.

Women most active in Wok Meri tend to be at least forty years old, while most big women are in their mid-fifties. The participation of younger women is sought when the group's activities become public and large numbers of workers are required to hold ceremonies. By the time a woman has reached middle age, she has established a solid relationship with her husband and has earned a place in the community, having proved her loyalty by bearing children, caring for gardens and pigs, and participating in kin-based activities. Without the demands of raising children, older wives also have greater autonomy and more time for market gardening. As a result, they appear to have more input into decisions about family income. In addition, older women command respect and share responsibility with male elders for the well-being of the community. In the past, a few outstanding elderly women were even inducted into the male cult, one of whose basic tenets was the exclusion of women.

Men play important supportive roles in Wok Meri as women do in traditional exchange. Each group has a male *kuskus* "bookkeeper" and a *siaman* "chairman" (both Neo-Melanesian terms) selected from the lineage or sublineage. Most women have had no formal education and find it difficult to count large sums of money. A young man in his late teens or early twenties with a primary school education is appointed bookkeeper and is responsible for keeping written records of money accumulated by members and money exchanged with other groups.

The chairman accompanies women on visits to other Wok Meri groups, acts as their spokesman at these meetings, and serves as a general adviser. The chairman, in his late thirties or early forties, is usually not the big woman's husband and is generally younger than the big woman. Younger men have a patina of sophistication acquired through first-hand experience with the world beyond the village. Most men under forty-five have spent several years as contract laborers on the Papua New Guinea coast or islands. They speak Neo-Melanesian fluently, are well-acquainted with money, and have had the opportunity to observe foreigners closely. The older woman's status as classificatory "mother" (*orabo*) to the younger chairman helps her to maintain her status as group leader. She can enjoy the chairman's assistance but can also ignore his advice if it suits her to do so.

A group meets sporadically in the big woman's house to collect money and bring members' accounts up to date. These meetings generally take place on Friday evening when a woman can deposit her earnings from the morning's village market before she spends it on tobacco or before her husband or children ask her for spending money. Each woman retains individual ownership of the money she saves. Her deposit of one or two *kina* (unit of Papua New Guinea currency; abbreviated as K) is added to her previously collected coins. Her money is tied up in a separate cloth bundle or mesh bag, placed in a common suitcase or box, and stored in a locked room built into the back of the big woman's house. As well as recording amounts in a ledger, the bookkeeper also writes each woman's contribution in her own small notebook with the word passbook inscribed on the cover. Villagers are familiar with "passbooks," as many have savings accounts at the savings and loan society or banks in the town of Goroka, the provincial capital.

Each new Wok Meri group is formed under the aegis of an existing group whose members teach neophytes the movement's ideology, rituals, and financial practices. Members of the more experienced group are known as "mothers" of participants in the new group, who are called their "daughters." The term *orabo* has the dual meaning of "mother" and "owner," and both denotations are drawn upon in Wok Meri. As a mother cares for her child, so, ideally does an owner look after her property; as a child grows, so, ideally, does property. Pigs grow and reproduce; coffee trees mature and bear fruit; money is invested to earn a profit. By the use of the term *orabo*, Wok Meri women not only base their relations with other groups on fictive maternal ties but also claim control of money by describing themselves as its owner.

The bond between Wok Meri mothers and daughters is described as similar to the relationship between real mothers and daughters. Wok Meri mothers loan their daughters small amounts of money to stimulate saving by the daughter group, to make the work of the daughter group grow. They teach daughters Wok Meri ideology and rituals and admonish them if they become lax in saving money. Eventually the daughters become knowledgeable enough to sponsor their own daughter group, described as "bearing a child" (*yahipa gendaiye*). Shallow genealogies of group relationships are kept, and members of related groups refer to each other using the appropriate kin terms such as "my grandparent," "my mother," "my daughter." Mothers urge their Wok Meri daughters to become mothers in their own right and chastise them if they are slow to find a daughter group for themselves. Mother-daughter ties are not developed at random; rather, they are based on agnatic or uterine kin links between women.

Birth and marriage are major themes of Wok Meri rituals. Fictive affinal as well as fictive consanguineal ties are established between mother and daughter groups, by the daughters/bride-receivers paying a cash bride price to the mothers/bride-givers for the knowledge of Wok Meri, metaphorically described as the *noiri* ("girl"). The girl is represented by a Western-style rubber doll and/or a mesh bag filled with coins given to the daughters/bride-receivers at a private meeting between the two groups. The doll and/or mesh bag is decorated like a bride, and after an all-night gathering patterned after the eve of a betrothal, the symbolic bride is given in marriage and the "mothers" ritually give birth to their daughters. The payment of bride price and marriage of the Wok Meri bride are later repeated at the "washing hands" ceremony (*anemo kuiyono*: "we wash hands"), the climax of the group's participation in Wok Meri.

Three major events take place during the "washing hands," a public ceremony jointly organized by two or more groups from the same clan or phratry after they have been saving money for five to nine years. First, the sponsors announce the amount of money each has accumulated, which thereby ends a prohibition on spending money totaling up to K2,500 per group. Second, bride price is paid again and the symbolic "girl" is married once more, a sign that the daughters/bride-receivers are empowered to hold their own washing hands ceremony in a year or two. The largest exchanges of cash in

Wok Meri are those between the mother/bride-givers and the daughters/bride-receivers, which approximate the cash component of a real bride price, about K200 to K250. Unlike a real marriage, however, in Wok Meri the bride price is a loan and must be repaid to the daughters/bride-receivers when they hold their own "washing hands." Third, women from Wok Meri groups throughout the region attend the "washing hands" to make small loans, from K2 to K20, to the ceremony's sponsors. At one "washing hands" in 1977, attended by over 2,000 people, 140 loans were made. Informants say that the sponsors are like banks, and loans made to them are like bank deposits. The debts are repaid when the creditor's group "washes hands."

Investment

The money saved by a group, added to the bride price and loans received at the "washing hands," totals a substantial amount of capital, ranging from K1,000 to about K4,500 for the seven groups whose records were made available to me. Most Wok Meri groups invest their capital in business enterprises similar to those men have chosen, not a surprising fact since women have access to the same information as men. Specifically, most groups invested in trucking, which along with storekeeping, have been the most popular businesses for Highlanders since the early 1960s. Trucks are the only form of transportation available in the Highlands for both people and freight. Undoubtedly, the women employed male operators (the oddity of women drivers would have been known far and wide), and it is likely that male bookkeepers kept the accounts. Some vehicles bought by women's groups in the Chuave District have been turned over to local businessmen for management, with the expectation that the women will share the profits (Anggo 1975:221).

Although trucks remained attractive in the late 1970s, women began to consider and adopt alternative investments in large-scale and potentially more lucrative enterprises, such as buying coffee for resale to processors, wholesale trade, plantation ownership, and truck leasing for fuel transport. In the 1970s, for example, successful Highlands entrepreneurs diversified businesses they had built on trucking and storekeeping; the most outstanding formed million-dollar holding companies. Wok Meri women have not escalated their investments to this level; women have, however, kept current with trends in rural businesses.

In the following section, I discuss the impact of socioeconomic change on women in the Daulo region in Goroka District (Map 8–1) and examine the economic and historical factors that contributed to the emergence of Wok Meri in neighboring Chuave District.

SOCIOECONOMIC CHANGE AND WOMEN'S ROLES

Gold prospectors and government patrol officers skirted the Daulo region in the early 1930s, but the presence of Australian administrators and Christian missionaries was soon felt in the area. The first European to settle nearby was Georg Hofmann, a German missionary who established the Asaroka Lutheran Mission east of the Daulo in 1935.

Because early contacts between foreigners and Highlanders were not always peaceful, the Australian administration restricted European movement in the Highlands and forced Hofmann to withdraw periodically from Asaroka. Members of one tribe, who blamed the missionaries for government intervention, attempted to burn the Asaroka station buildings in retaliation (Hofmann 1938). When relations between the Lutherans and their neighbors were less antagonistic, the missionaries bought food from local women and quickly became enmeshed in other kinds of transactions with the local people.

Both missionaries and government officials paid Highlanders for goods and services with trade items, including shells and steel axes. Before the advent of Europeans, shells and plumes (which, along with pigs, were the major valuables in ceremonial exchange) were acquired by participating in exchanges or by trading pigs to the Waitsan people across the Bismarck Range. Some shells were also acquired through trade with Simbu peoples to the west.

The influx of large numbers of shells and the introduction of steel axes had far-reaching effects on Highland economies. Salisbury (1956; 1962a; 1962b) has documented their impact on the Siane west of the Goroka Valley. These items made their way to Siane territory through traditional trading networks (see Hughes 1973), and, by 1936, steel axes, used as ceremonial valuables as well as tools, were no longer unusual among the Siane. The Siane big men who first received the axes lent them to other men for gardening. Gradually, as more men obtained them, they lost their cachet as valuables; by 1953, steel axes were no longer used in ceremonial transactions (Salisbury 1962a:118).

The substitution of steel axes for stone reduced the proportion of time men spent on subsistence production from 80 percent to 50 percent. The time men gained was spent on more frequent tribal fighting and on more and larger exchanges accompanied by increasingly elaborate ceremonials (Salisbury 1962a:118–119). Higher payments were made possible by the flow of shells from people closer to European settlement. By 1940, the value of bride-price payments had doubled (Salisbury 1962a:116).

The end of World War II, which had interrupted government, business, and mission activity, marked a turning point in the Daulo region and throughout the Highlands as European-instigated changes resumed at a faster tempo. Daulo people were soon in regular contact with missionaries and government officers and were introduced to a cash economy. By 1947, enrollment at the Asaroka mission school had increased to two hundred young men being trained to teach Christianity to their people (Goldhart 1947). The first baptisms were held in 1951 (Goldhart 1951). Acceptance for baptism required individual and group commitment to the new way of life, certified by relinquishing male cult rituals and other institutions contrary to Christian teaching, such as polygyny (Read 1952:234). In some villages, converts were required to display the sacred bird flutes (*nema*) to the women from whom they had been hidden. The revelation of such an important secret and sacred symbol created a great deal of unrest among adherents of the traditional religion (Goldhart 1951; 1952; 1953).

Secular as well as religious life was changing rapidly. The government appointed a leader and an assistant for him in each clan, called *luluai* and *tultul*, respectively. The *luluai*, was responsible for organizing participation in public works projects, such as road building and constructing rest houses for visiting patrol officers, negotiating conflicts or referring disputants to government headquarters, and administering government regulations, such as sanitation rules. Except for occasional outbursts, tribal warfare had ceased.

Transforming the entire economic system, money was introduced into the Goroka Valley in 1947. At the time, however, there were no stores in which to exchange it for goods. Jim Taylor, then district commissioner, recalls the unfavorable reaction when money was first substituted for trade goods in payment to laborers. Some of the men "burst into tears, threw the money on the ground and demanded shell instead" (quoted in Finney 1973:40). Daulo people were at first puzzled about the use of money. Some used bills to roll up their tobacco into cigarettes. But they learned quickly. After the first trade store opened next to the Goroka airstrip in 1947, Jim Taylor saw these men run into town en masse to make purchases. They carried their pound notes attached to long sticks which they waved in the air (Finney 1973:41). Money is still displayed this way at certain ceremonial exchanges.

In concert with the movement towards a cash economy, labor patterns began shifting as well. In 1950, young Highland men were first recruited to work on coastal plantations through the government-regulated Highlands Labour Scheme. Youths contracted for an eighteen-month period and were allowed to sign up again after spending six months back in the Highlands. Large numbers of young men from Daulo and throughout the Goroka Valley went to the coast on the Highlands Labour Scheme until local possibilities, such as tending their own coffee, became more attractive (Howlett 1962:261–263, 266). While on the coast they learned the Neo-Melanesian lingua franca, met people from other areas in Papua New Guinea, and gained a certain sophistication with European technology and customs (*pasin* in Neo-Melanesian). The first Siane laborers who returned in 1953 spent most of their wages on luxury items and shells for themselves and their kin and reserved the rest for future purchases, often of shells (Salisbury 1962a:127–130). Soon a pound note became accepted as a valuable, and money became an expected component of bride price and other payments (Downs 1953:20; Salisbury 1962a:126).

Economic changes increased dramatically as coffee production moved into the area. From the early 1950s, expatriate European planters were allowed to buy land in the Goroka Valley (Finney 1973:42–43), and their plantations set an example of how coffee trees should be grown and harvested. In 1954-1955, the Department of Agriculture, Stock, and Fisheries began to instruct villagers about raising arabica coffee on their own lands. Government officers visited villages to train people in coffee production, set up demonstration nurseries, and distributed seedlings (Howlett 1962:92–93). People quickly took to the new crop. During the 1960s and 1970s, villagers continued to grow coffee, although their enthusiasm waxed and waned as prices fluctuated on the world market. Today smallholders (that is, persons growing coffee on their individual plots) account for 70 percent of Papua New Guinea's coffee production (Beil 1977: see also Howlett 1973, Meggitt 1971).

A few farsighted men were quick to invest their coffee incomes in other ventures. Trucking and trade were the first businesses to attract Highlanders for two reasons. First, they were the most tangible enterprises at the time. Highlanders could see the utility of trucks and stores and understand their basic operating procedures. Second, trucking and storekeeping required relatively small amounts of capital which Highlanders could accumulate, in contrast to more capital-intensive businesses, like airlines. In 1963, there were five commercial vehicles owned by Highlanders in Goroka District; by mid-1967, there were sixty-eight. The number of licensed trade stores operated by Highlanders in Goroka District jumped from five in 1963 to 447 in mid-1967 (Finney 1973:72–73).

Like the traditional political leaders known as big men, the "business leaders" who seized the opportunity to become entrepreneurs recruited labor and money from their kin to begin their ventures. However, these business leaders tended to maintain individual control over the enterprises. They were attracted to business not only by the profit motive, but also by the desire to help their kin and to enhance their own and their kin's reputations; according to Finney (1973:80, 124) these traditional goals had "preadapted" Gorokans to commercial activities. The traditional emphasis on manipulation of wealth as a means of achieving status made entrepreneurship doubly attractive (see Chapter 7, by Ben Finney in this volume).

Most of the changes which had taken place since 1930 affected men more directly than women. These included the replacement of men's stone axes with steel and the recruitment of males for wage labor. But these and other changes have reverberated in the lives of women as well as men. When we examine events since 1930, we see that changes in the economy have had, on the whole, a detrimental effect on women's economic rights, while the relative weakening of male authority brought about by pacification and missionization has allowed women to take steps to respond to the deterioration of their economic rights.

Since the introduction of steel axes reduced the amount of men's time required for subsistence labor, it upset the previously balanced contributions to production made by both sexes. Comparison of data I collected in the Daulo region between 1976 and 1978, with those previously gathered by Salisbury (1962a:108) among the Siane, indicate that in precontact society, both men and women spent about 80 percent of daylight hours on gardening, pig husbandry, and household work. By 1978, men spent 18 percent and women 43.5 percent of their time on these subsistence tasks. When cash-generating activities were introduced, including coffee production, wage labor, and commercial activities, men spent 35.4 percent and women spent 53.1 percent of their time working.

Although women earn income in addition to their greater work load in subsistence production, they do not control the products of their labor. Property rights are the key to understanding the genesis of Wok Meri. Women's dissatisfaction with their restricted access to and control of money has been the major motivation for the movement.

PROPERTY RIGHTS

There is a history of intersex conflict over property rights in the Daulo region and areas bordering it—the Upper Asaro to the north, the Gahuku to the east, and the Siane to the west and southwest (Newman 1965:38; Read 1965:89–90; Salisbury 1962a:62). Moreover, this type of conflict is not limited to the vicinity of Daulo. Marie Reay (1980) notes that Minj women in the Wahgi Valley west of Simbu have engaged in similar struggles since before contact with Europeans.

Western notions of ownership are inadequate for discussing property rights in Highland Papua New Guinea. In Western culture, the term *ownership* implies individualized and absolute control over the acquisition and disposal of property. In the Daulo area, ownership is more complex. There are two types of ownership, also identified by Salisbury (1962a) among the Siane, with qualitatively different kinds of control over property:

> *Merafo* is the ordinary word for "father," and the *merafo* of property looks after it (*bentaiye*) just as a father looks after his son, acting in his best interests, and being responsible for his well-being to the community, to the ancestors, and to posterity. The property an individual *merafo* looks after is thus comparable with an entailed estate, while his position is that of a trustee. Estates usually consist of land, sacred flutes, and incorporeal property such as pigs' souls, *gerua* [decorated boards used in the pig feasts] designs, ritual knowledge, and rights to make speeches. (Salisbury 1962a:61)

The other type of owner is the *amfonka*, a term linguistically derived from the word "shadow." The *amfonka* is the owner of "personalty," a legal term Salisbury uses for personal property, including pigs, trees, crops, houses, ornaments, tools, and clothing. Only a Siane man can be a *merafo* ("father"/"trustee"), but men and women can be *amfonka*, "personal property owner," of certain items (Salisbury 1962a:62). The contrast is between trusteeship and ownership of personal property with rights of disposition.

These different kinds of ownership are also found among Daulo people, although the same linguistic distinctions do not prevail. Daulo men, with a few exceptions, are the *merafo* ("trustees") of land, the remaining type of estate property. Flutes and "incorporeal property" lost their value with the demise of traditional religious rituals. Both women and men can be "owners" (*orabo* for women and *merafo* for men) of specific kinds of personal property.

In the following discussion of ownership, the term *jural property rights* refers to formal, publicly recognized claims to property sanctioned in village courts and in traditional moots led by male elders. A major point to be made about ownership is that an individual's formal right to dispose of property is often restricted by the rights and desires of others. This holds true whether we consider trusteeship of land or disposition of minor personal property such as betel nut or cut tobacco, which people routinely demand from each other in bantering tones. An owner is hard pressed to maintain absolute control over personal property, and few would want to do so. In a society in which a person's long-term well-being depends on mutual assistance and exchange, it would be shortsighted to refuse the demands of kin consistently. This point should be kept in mind, particularly in reference to men's and women's property. For example, while men have jural rights to most coffee income, women often make informal claims to this money based on the labor they contribute to production.

The most valuable resources in the current mixed subsistence and cash-crop economy are land, coffee trees, pigs, and money. Consideration of each of these kinds of property shows that men's trusteeship of land placed them in a favorable position to claim ownership of introduced coffee trees and of the major share of their crop. Although men have begun to acknowledge women's claims to pigs within the last generation, on balance, women's economic rights remain inferior to men's.

Land and Coffee Trees

Individual men are trustees of land that is owned by the phratry as a corporate group. Each patrilineal clan has rights to separate land within the boundaries of the phratry territory. A man generally works the ground his father used, but there are informal land reallocations within the lineage or sublineage as older men die, as younger males set up households, or as people move to other villages. Each man has rights to arable land and to bush for planting and cutting timber and for cultivating nut pandanus trees. Members of clans constituting a phratry can exchange land among themselves, but they cannot alienate it outside the phratry without approval of leaders from all the clans. Alienation of land for coffee plantations sets the precedent for land sales, which are rare.

In this virilocal society, women usually give up their ownership rights to land at marriage, but they can maintain or renew them in certain circumstances. A few young married women who live near their natal villages garden on their fathers' land without claiming permanent title or inheritance rights for their children. A wife, however, generally activates her use rights only to her husband's land.

It is the relationship of coffee trees to the land on which they are planted that has facilitated men's possession of them. Ownership of coffee trees follows the same rules as those for nut, red pandanus, and timber trees valued in the subsistence economy. A son owns or inherits the trees he or his father planted. A married daughter or sister may be given pandanus nuts or fruits at her request or when she visits her family, but she cannot take them without asking. Young married couples sometimes pick coffee from trees that they or the wife's parents planted on her father's land. This practice usually tapers off when the couple establish their own coffee gardens on the husband's land. People may lay claim to coffee trees they planted and tended on someone else's land, but a claim based on work alone is tenuous and usually does not prevail over the landowner's title.

Labor contributions to coffee gardening give a wife restricted rights to the crop produced by her husband's trees, but not to the trees themselves. Informants unanimously state that these limited rights are canceled by divorce. A divorcee is expected to grow coffee, often called *wokim bisnis*, "make business" in Neo-Melanesian, with her new husband.

Pigs

Today spouses share ownership of their pig herd. Some earlier researchers claimed that men had sole rights to pigs, but there is evidence suggesting that the situation was more complex (Salisbury 1962a:61; Newman 1965:38; Howlett 1973:255; Read 1952: 21, 1965:89–90). Women's rights to pigs were in dispute up through the post–World War II period, as women individually and collectively demanded that men acknowledge their title to pigs. For example, Newman (1965:38) describes group protests in 1959–1960 by Upper Asaro women fed up with the men who had killed too many of their "children" (pigs they had tended) for use in exchange.

When asked about pig ownership, the majority of Daulo respondents said that pigs belonged jointly to them and to their spouses and that couples discuss the distribution of their pigs before a gift is pledged. Most of those who consult with spouses about gifts of pigs stated either that they never disagree about these contributions or that neither spouse dominates the decision when there is a disagreement. As one elderly woman said, she and her husband do not compete with each other; each spouse listens to the other's opinion. Of course, what people say and what they do are different matters. However, I was impressed by the dearth of marital quarrels about pigs. Women commonly complain about men's misuse of money, but no woman ever told me that she or other women were dissatisfied about the distribution of pigs.

Upon divorce the herd is split, each spouse claiming the pigs or the descendants of pigs she or he brought to the marriage. (Several mothers in long-standing marriages said that, should they divorce, they would leave their pigs behind for their children.) If the husband has initiated divorce after a lengthy marriage with children, the wife may also be awarded compensation for her labor in the form of cash and/or additional pigs.

The shift in women's rights to pigs over the last generation is important for several reasons. As a focal point for conflict between the sexes, disputed pig ownership provided the impetus for women's individual and collective action since before European contact until at least 1960. Women's recognized rights to pigs increased as the significance of the animals declined in relation to money.

Women's recent gains in pig ownership may be illusory. Data on nuptial transactions for ten of the eleven Yamiyufa men from Daulo who married during my 1976–1978 fieldwork suggest that pigs may be losing their cachet. In two of ten cases, the bride's family did not bring pork to the betrothal feast for the customary exchange of cooked pork with the groom's family. Even more striking is the absence of live pigs in four of the ten bride prices, while money was a component of all of them. At one of these four betrothal ceremonies, speeches were made supporting the elimination of live pigs from future bride-price payments. These four brides did not bring live pigs with them for their marital herds, an omission that traditionally enabled a husband to belittle his wife during arguments. If further investigation supports this trend, pigs are undergoing the same process of devaluation as shells and plumes did beginning in the 1950s, which would leave only money in the cycle of marriage exchanges and women with short-lived economic gains.

Money

The major sources of income in most households are coffee and vegetable marketing. A few entrepreneurs, almost all men, engage in commercial activities, including middleman coffee buying for resale to processing factories, truck operations, and storekeeping. Initial questions about control of money elicited the common response that women earn cash by selling produce and small amounts of freshly picked cherry coffee. Men's much larger income is derived from selling the bulk of the crop after it is processed into higher-priced parchment coffee. In fact, the relative sources, control, and use of money by women and men are more complex than these responses reveal.

Marketing

Women benefited economically from their early experiences with missionaries, explorers, and government officials. In 1930, Mick Leahy bought vegetables from women on the first exploratory trip by European prospectors through the Gahuku and

BenaBena areas of the Goroka Valley. Leahy remarked that "women appeared to be the gardeners and traders, and when we bought food, we traded with the women" (Leahy and Crain 1937:109). A few years later missionaries at Asaroka Lutheran Mission provided a steady market for women near the Daulo region (Hofmann 1937, 1938). By 1952, the government was regularly buying vegetables for its staff and hospital patients in Goroka.

In Daulo, spouses share ownership of garden crops and both spouses have the right to harvest food, although men usually do not because they consider it women's work. It is likely that there has been a shift toward joint ownership of produce (in addition to pigs) in the Daulo region as crops became commodities. It is relevant to note that, although vegetable marketing is women's work and demeaning for men, large-scale truck gardening is considered appropriate for men.

Today vegetable marketing is the source of small but steady earnings for women, providing a mean estimated annual income of K51 for fifteen women who participated in a budget survey. Although this income is said to be women's money, half the respondents who market said they regularly share their earnings with their husbands. Because this money is earned in small amounts, it is likely to be used for purchases of imported foods, kerosene, and soap for the household, and for personal pleasures such as tobacco and card playing. Since women are the food providers, they buy as well as sell at the market. However, women do manage to save some of their money in their Wok Meri accounts.

Coffee Production

A small portion of the coffee crop is sold as soon as the ripe cherries are picked, but most of the harvest is pulped, washed, and dried into the more profitable parchment coffee, which jurally belongs to men. Fifteen women surveyed earned a larger mean annual income from cherry coffee sales (K62) than from produce vending, but neither source of income nor their total compares favorably with men's parchment earnings. The majority of women queried about control of resources reported they do not share cherry coffee income with their husbands, although most noted that they use some of this money to buy food and sundries for household consumption. Women are less likely to share their cherry coffee income than their proceeds from vegetable vending, because their access to cherry coffee is considered remuneration for their labor in cash crop production. Wives are more willing to share their market earnings with spouses because husbands own the land and participate in establishing gardens.

Men obtain most of their income from sales of processed parchment coffee. For example, sixteen men earned a mean of K321 in 1977. A husband should ideally share a portion of this money with his wife, but she cannot legally claim it nor money he may earn from wage labor or entrepreneurial activities. Fellow villagers sympathize with a wife whose husband squanders money, but the elders and the Village Court magistrates have no authority to compel him to change his behavior. Should a couple with children divorce at the husband's initiative, a wife receives a standard compensation for her years of labor and child care that does not reflect the particular couple's current parchment coffee income or their savings.

Of course, few men spend most of their income on beer and cards. Informants agree that money should be used for certain purposes: to make exchange payments; to save for future ceremonial needs; to pay tuition fees; and to make investments, such as buying a coffee pulper or a truck. Women support their husbands' use of income for ceremonial payments and enthusiastically fulfill their limited roles in the organization of payments and in the rituals marking them. Women also approve of business investments. But wives do object to large sums being spent for personal pleasures, such as card playing, drinking beer, and buying truck fares for frequent trips to town.

An individual's right to dispose of property is constrained by other people's often conflicting rights and desires. This is especially true within marriage. Spouses informally negotiate the allocation of money and pigs. At times, however, negotiations fail and fights ensue. Money appears to have replaced pigs as the cause of many marital conflicts. As early as 1959–1960, for example, disputes over money arose as Gururumba women in the Upper Asaro were occasionally employed to pick coffee on an expatriate-owned plantation. Husbands tried to force their wives to quit work after the women refused to give them their earnings (Newman 1979).

The absence of women's jural rights to the main source of income is the motivation for the development of Wok Meri. Wok Meri women call themselves the *orabo* ("mothers"/"owners") of money. By using this term, women not only claim ownership but also emphasize their role in producing wealth.

ORIGINS OF WOK MERI

The economic foundations of women's discontent are clear. Two questions about Wok Meri's origins remain. How did such a women's movement, unparalleled in the ethnographic literature on Highland New Guinea, develop? Since a similar sequence of economic changes is taking place throughout the Highlands, why did a women's movement arise in a particular area?

A major underpinning for long-term group action by women in the eastern end of the Highlands where Wok Meri is found is the regular informal and structured cooperation of female coresidents married to patrilineally related males. Marilyn Strathern (1980) suggests that nucleated villages, in contrast to the dispersed settlement patterns in the western Highlands, allow daily interaction among women that supports a cooperative undertaking like Wok Meri. Women in Chuave and Goroka districts also have a tradition of working together to organize menarche rites and to play a limited part in the now-discontinued male initiation ceremonies.

Women customarily protested against their limited property rights. Upper Asaro women decried the slaughter of "their" pigs for ceremonial occasions in ritualized stick fights with men (Newman 1965:38). Women were also galvanized into action by noneconomic issues. Read (1965:136–137, 196–198) documents two occasions when Gahuku women's stylized protests against men's social arrangements erupted into brawls. In one case, women reacted against men's harsh treatment of young male initiates. In the other, women expressed anger at the marriage of a prepubescent girl.

Women's larger-scale collective activities were responses to colonial policy. H.F.W. Bergmann, a missionary in the Ega Lutheran Circuit in the Simbu region, notes the existence of a women's movement in his annual report for 1955.[3]

> In the beginning of this year there appeared a queer new movement. I called it the women's movement. It was going on already when we arrived here. First we noticed the women, not only the girls, dressed up, singing and dancing when we travelled from one place to another. Soon we heard that the men were bitterly complaining about the behavior of their womenfolk. They did not work in the garden, they did not prepare the meals properly, etc. The men kept quiet, but they said, We have still our axes... All that I could find out about how this movement started concerned a misunderstanding about the English Queen. As she is a woman, the women here thought to play a big role in the native life now too. They wanted to be appointed Luluais...etc., etc. When I heard about it, I suggested to the [Lutheran] teachers to quiet the men down and told them this movement would die out soon. And so it did. I have not heard anymore about it now for several months. (Bergmann 1955)

This tantalizingly incomplete description suggests that women were well organized and articulate in expressing their grievances. Bergmann says that women wanted to hold the office of "government-appointed leader"; unfortunately, he does not specify their other demands. The location of the movement in the Simbu region, along with similarities in self-decoration, singing, and dancing suggest this may have been a forerunner or an early stage in the development of Wok Meri.

Another example of collective response is a 1964 strike in the Minj area in the Wahgi Valley west of Simbu. Reay (1975) describes this incident as a successful group action resulting in changes in property ownership. After World War II, roadwork became corvée labor for Highlanders. Men's and women's participation in unpaid highway maintenance was required. The government did, however, remunerate groups for heavier tasks and road construction. This money was distributed among the men by local government councillors or committeemen, despite female participation in the work (Reay 1980). In an apparent bid to win women's votes in future elections, a newly elected House of Assembly member set aside women's obligation to take part in roadwork. Although all adults are eligible to vote in Papua New Guinea, Minj men perceived their wives' votes as extensions of their own. Thus the men interpreted the ban on women's forced labor as a political ploy to gain their votes:

> The Minj men were outraged by what they saw as a move to alienate the votes of their womenfolk...When the roadwork included tasks for which the men received payment, the women of several groups near Minj insisted that they should receive their share of the pay. The men tried to assert their authority and ignore the demand, but the women went on strike. They told the men that if they wanted to take all the pay for themselves they could also do all the work since they themselves were not legally obligated to help them. The successful strike of the Minj women marked the beginning of a new era.... From this time it was easier for women to keep for themselves at least some of the money they earned from marketing vegetables. (Reay 1975:6–7)

Minj women protested their exploitation by men, who profited by using female labor as a substitute for their own and by pocketing the money women earned themselves. After successfully acquiring their share of cash for roadwork, some women pointed out that they also took part in coffee production. Men perceived women's statements as an ultimatum before another strike, although it is not certain that women intended a similar action. As compensation for their wives' labor, some husbands began sharing coffee income with their spouses, and others gave their wives use rights to specified coffee trees (Reay 1980). Similarly, Wok Meri women protest against their lack of access to income they help to generate.

The immediate impetus for Wok Meri was the establishment of Lutheran women's fellowships in Simbu. In 1957, local male teachers were trained to conduct women's Bible study groups (Theile 1957) and were encouraged to establish them in their own villages (Habu 1981). Members usually made an offering at their weekly meetings to pay church expenses or the evangelist's support. In the early 1960s, women there tired of donating their earnings to the church and withdrew to form savings associations of their own (Anggo 1975:209).

It is clear that church-affiliated groups in Chuave District introduced women to a significant infrastructure. Through these associations, they learned important skills which they put to use in Wok Meri—skills such as how to sustain and work in all-female groups for nontraditional purposes. Members also gained experience in collecting and saving money. The impetus for the development of Wok Meri should also be understood in the context of the more stringent economic conditions characteristic of Chuave District (for example, poor soil and dense population), and thus to the possibly more intense intersex conflict over money.

CONCLUSION

I have described Wok Meri, a twenty-year-old exchange system and network of savings associations. Wok Meri is a collective response by women to the restructuring of their economic rights over the last fifty years, since Western contact. Both sexes claim that women developed Wok Meri to register their disapproval of men's expenditures on cards and beer. Women save their own small earnings in Wok Meri, demonstrate their capability, and set a good example of what can be accomplished if money is prudently saved. Women's actions belie their modest words. In Wok Meri women have established quasi-Western banks and a series of exchanges patterned after customary transactions initiated by marriage. By investing their capital in business ventures, women increase their participation in both the modern and traditional sectors of the economy.

The long-range implications for gender roles remain to be seen, but Wok Meri has the potential for bringing about radical change in relations between the sexes. As its "washing hands" ceremony approaches, members make larger deposits in their accounts to enhance their personal renown and their group reputation when their savings are announced publicly. At this point women draw on the parchment coffee income, which jurally belongs to their husbands, as well as on their own modest earnings from the sale of produce and cherry coffee. This indicates male support of Wok Meri activities, which reflect favorably on the lineage and clan; moreover, it also establishes women's claims to increased rights in parchment coffee income. It is easier to build on such precedents than it is to retreat from them, once established. If women collectively, or even individually, invoke these rights outside of Wok Meri, they could have a dramatic social impact.

Only if certain conditions are met will women's augmented rights to parchment coffee income transform property relations between the sexes. Individual males own coffee trees because they are planted on land controlled by men as members of corporate patrilineal descent groups. While women's access to land, the major means of production, depends on their relations to fathers, brothers, and husbands, men remain dominant economically.

However, an alternative route to achieving control of the means of production that bypasses land ownership could be created by Wok Meri investments in profitable businesses and capital accumulation. In this way, women could parlay rights to parchment coffee into their own means of production. In the late 1970s, Wok Meri groups began to expand investment choices beyond marginally profitable trucking and storekeeping. They became involved in potentially more lucrative, complex, and longer-term ventures such as coffee plantations and fuel-truck leasing. If their businesses are successful and expand, Wok Meri groups could conceivably control extensive capital investments.

Greater control of capital investments would allow groups of women to achieve increased economic autonomy. It seems unlikely, however, that women will opt for economic independence from men. Through Wok Meri, women strive to participate alongside males rather than to cut themselves off from men. Wok Meri is not a separatist movement; women express a desire for greater, not less, cooperation between the sexes. The collective nature of the movement and the organization of units based on established ties of kinship support the traditional value placed on cooperation. Wok Meri is significant because it institutionalizes collective female action and enables women to redefine property rights vis-à-vis men and, thus, to enhance their participation in the ceremonial and commercial sectors of the economy.

Acknowledgments: My research on Wok Meri from October 1976 through February 1978 was funded by a National Institute of Mental Health Predoctoral Research Fellowship no. 5F31 MH 05366. I also conducted research on Wok Meri from October 1980 through May 1981, with funding from the Institute for Applied Social and Economic Research and the Programme Division of UNICEF. I thank the Yamiyufa people with whom I lived in the Daulo region, and the neighboring Manto, Zoita, and Korepa peoples for their gracious assistance and patience. I gratefully acknowledge the assistance I received in my research on Wok Meri in conversations with David Anggo and his family; Judith Munster; James Knight, S.V.D.; Peter van Oostrum, S.V.D.; Dorothy James; and Denise Potts; and in correspondence with Robin and Carolyn Hide and Robert Smith. I would also like to thank Denise O'Brien, Cathy Small, Regina Oboler, Diane Freedman, Sharon W. Tiffany, Andrew Strathern, Terence Hays, and participants in the Women in Oceania Symposium for comments on previous drafts of material presented in this chapter. I am, of course, solely responsible for any errors of description or analysis.

NOTES

1. This chapter was first published in a lengthier version in *Rethinking Women's Roles: Perspectives from the Pacific*, Denise O'Brien and Sharon Tiffany (eds.) (Berkeley: University of California Press, 1984). The editors wish to thank the University of California Press for permission to reprint it in revised form in this volume.

2. Lineage members trace their descent patrilineally from a common male ancestor. Members of a lineage branch, which I call a sublineage, may act as a unit, but the sublineage is not a kinship group recognized in this society.

3. I am grateful to Robert Smith (personal communication, 1978) for sharing this information collected during his research on missionization in the Highlands.

9

The Cult of Custom Meets the Search for Money in Western Samoa

Tim O'Meara
University of North Carolina, Wilmington

"Tradition dies hard in Samoa. The many aspects of the Samoan way of life are vigorously and steadfastly protected. Nowhere else in the Pacific is innovation so resolutely resisted, and in few other territories is the cult of custom so deeply revered." (Farrell and Ward 1962:232–233)

In many ways, Western Samoa still fits the thatched-roof image of traditional Polynesia. Western Samoans are proud of their customs and of the enduring beauty of their volcanic islands. Two hundred years after European contact, traditional life remains more intact and more vibrant in Western Samoa than in any other major Polynesian society. Elected chiefs, or *matai*, still rule over their families, and a council of chiefs governs each of the more than three hundred rural villages. Village women still plait the intricate *'ie toga*, or fine mats, from pandanus leaves for presentation at traditional ceremonies. Young men still endure the pain of tattooing with implements cut from the tusk of a boar. Coastal villages still resound with the rhythmic clapping of hands that signal the beginning of chiefly kava ceremonies. And the smoke from traditional stone ovens still wafts out over the lagoon at the first light of dawn.

But Samoa has also changed considerably. Before Tongan Methodists arrived in 1828 to preach the gospel, Samoans prayed to a pantheon of Polynesian gods. Today Samoans pride themselves on being among the most devout Christians in the world. Before European traders established a commercial center at Apia harbor in the mid-1800s, every village and every extended family was nearly self-sufficient. Today even the most remote village relies on income and services from the outside world. Samoa was once a society of family chieftainships that often fought among themselves in shifting alliances.

Colonial intrigues soon fanned these traditional rivalries into a lengthy civil war. Warfare finally ended in 1899 when the United States annexed the eastern islands of Tutuila and the tiny Manu'a group (making them the Territory of American Samoa), and Imperial Germany annexed the larger, western islands of Upolu and Savaii. The German colony fell quietly to New Zealand forces only fifteen years later at the outset of World War I. During World War II, forty thousand U.S. Marines (more than the total Samoan population) occupied the colony, preparing for a Japanese invasion that fortunately never came. In 1962, the New Zealand territory became the Independent State of Western Samoa—the first Pacific territory to gain independence.

Samoans *were* culturally conservative during that century of colonial domination. It is clearer now in hindsight, however, that their conservatism during that era was largely a protective reaction against European incursions, rather than an expression of inherent conservatism among Samoan people or their culture. Samoan oral history recounts that in the centuries before European contact, Samoans freely adopted cultural items from Fiji, Tonga, and their other island neighbors. During the initial contact with Europeans, Samoans readily—even eagerly—adopted Christianity, literacy, commercial trading, European styles of education, singing, boat building, and many other Western practices.

Since colonial control ended in 1962, Western Samoa has once again changed swiftly and dramatically. Funded almost entirely by foreign aid, the country rapidly built new roads, schools, hospitals, a satellite telecommunications system, hydroelectric dams and power stations, an international airport, and then a larger international airport. Today the word on the lips of government officials, city merchants, and village farmers alike is *atiinaa'e*: "development."

Many Western Samoans now harbor dreams of material wealth, their aspirations buoyed by a flood of unearned income and video values from overseas. Yet very few Samoans can realize those dreams in their home islands. Though the material signs of modernization have increased rapidly in Western Samoa since independence, internally generated development has been illusive. The local economy stumbles along, selling cheap agricultural commodities abroad and importing expensive processed foods and manufactured goods. The value of imports is now six times that of exports. There is little industry to create new jobs, and local salaries are so low that the departure of well-trained Samoans overseas has increased from a modest "brain drain" at independence to a dangerous torrent today (see Chapter 10, "The Samoan Exodus," by Paul Shankman, in this volume). Western Samoans, for example, now hold half of the managerial jobs in the American Samoan government—drawn there by salaries that are five to ten times higher than those at home.

Back on the remote and sparsely populated island of Savaii, Samoan villagers still live in a world of thatched and corrugated-iron roofs, of machetes and firewood, pebble floors, muddy footpaths, and dugout canoes. It is a delightful world in many ways, but it is not Eden. Breadfruit and coconuts do literally drop from trees. But this is not a world of ease and leisure, except for those few who have attained old age and importance. Nor is it a world where people can afford many of the things they want—pick-up trucks, more substantial houses, books for the schools, better medical services, a better and more varied diet, electricity and the household fixtures that go with it, and clothes they do not have to stitch themselves or buy second-hand from Australia.

Savaii villagers often boast of the good life they enjoy as semisubsistence farmers and fishermen, secure in the knowledge that they can always *'ai fua*—"eat for free"— whether in their own homes or the home of a relative or neighbor. But these villagers increasingly measure their economic well-being by the new yardstick of urban and overseas incomes. By that yardstick, most villagers now consider themselves *mativa*, "poor." Some people chafe at the lack of economic opportunity or the slowness and conformity of village life, and they hope to leave soon for Apia, Pago Pago, Auckland, or Honolulu. Many other people enjoy village life, wishing only that they had more money. My friend, Nu'u Vili, expressed the common village sentiment: "Samoa is good. Food is easy to get. But Samoa is also bad. The search for money is very hard!" Today that search for money is profoundly changing Samoan culture, even in the more remote and traditional villages of Savaii.

THE TRADITIONAL *MATAI* SYSTEM AND THE CONTROL OF RESOURCES

The foundation of the *fa'a-Samoa*, or the Samoan way of life, is the *matai* system. In the traditional *matai* system, extended families reside together under the leadership of one of their members whom they elect by consensus to hold the family's chiefly *matai* title. Once elected to the family title, the new *matai* gains authority over the resident members of the extended family and their labor. By tradition, each extended family owns both a house site and agricultural lands. A newly elected *matai* also gains authority over these family lands and the produce derived from them. The chief's authority over his (over 99 percent of *matai* are males) extended family and its resources is limited only by his responsibility to care for the family, by its power to remove his title if he does not, and by the overriding authority of the entire village council of chiefs in all interfamily matters. The traditional *matai* system is thus a social, political, and economic system organized around extended families led by their elected chiefs.

In rural villages, land is the most important resource. Extended families traditionally acted (and sometimes still do act) as corporate groups, owning land in perpetuity. According to this traditional system, when members clear and plant new land, it belongs to their extended family as a whole. Individual members come and go, but ownership remains with the family, in the name of the family's *matai* title. An individual can gain control over this family land only indirectly by acquiring the specific *matai* title that holds authority over those plots. However, members of the extended family compete for election to that title, so in the traditional system control over family land is only as secure as control over family elections.

Any adult who can demonstrate descent from a previous holder of the title and who maintains active service in the affairs of that title-descent group is eligible to participate in family title elections. Samoans can trace their descent through either male or female links to many different titles, and they often maintain active membership in several of those groups. Thus, many more people belong to any particular title-descent group than actually reside on and cultivate that family's lands.

Different factions within this large title-descent group may support different candidates for election to the family *matai* title. The personal qualities of candidates are important, along with three other election criteria. First, and often most important, is the candidate's factional loyalty, which is almost always a matter of relatedness. Second is the service a candidate has rendered to the extended family and to previous title-holders. Third is the person's line of descent from previous title-holders. Individuals with direct male links to prominent earlier title-holders have the advantage. Occasionally a family will elect an adopted son or a son-in-law, but only if he has shown exceptional service and if there is no deserving heir.

In this traditional system, whoever is elected to hold the family title then moves onto the family house site (if he is not already living there) and immediately takes control of the family and its lands. One of the resident sons of the previous title-holder usually acquires the title, and there are additional safeguards to protect the use rights of those people who have been living on and working the land. A distinct possibility remains, however, that a nonresident or other rival will gain the title and wrest control from some or all of the current occupants.

CHANGING ECONOMIC CONDITIONS

Economic conditions have changed considerably over the last few generations. As a result, Samoans have changed the way they control their land, labor, and income. Rather than working together with other members of their extended family as they did in the past, people now usually work and earn money individually through cash cropping and wage labor. Because they can earn their own cash incomes, individuals are less willing to pool their labor, resources, and incomes with other members of their extended family under the control of their *matai*.

In order to safeguard these new, individually derived incomes, villagers have been shifting the ownership of productive resources and the control of incomes from extended families to nuclear-family households. During recent research in a village on the southeast coast of Savaii, I found that few of the thirty-two recognized extended families still pool their resources for either production or consumption. Instead, the extended families have fragmented into fifty-five nuclear-family households that now control their own economic affairs. A quarter of these economically independent households are not even headed by *matai*. Even adjacent households headed by siblings do not normally pool their resources, and they may not even be privy to information about each others' incomes.

THE CHANGING LAND TENURE SYSTEM

With the increase in cash cropping and the construction of expensive, European-style houses on family land during the last century, almost all Samoans have come to want exclusive control over their own lands and incomes. They no longer want to share rights with nonresident or even other coresident members of their extended families. And they no longer accept the risk—inherent in the traditional *matai* system—of losing control over their resources through family title elections. Villagers have changed their system of land control, or "land tenure," accordingly.

Over the last seventy-five years, villagers have developed and gradually adopted a new tenure system that has now almost replaced the traditional system. In Savaii, villagers first began claiming individual ownership and inheritance of cash-crop land shortly after World

War I. Since that time, villagers have increasingly accepted the new principles that a person who first clears and plants a plot of land may own it as an individual, and he may pass the ownership of that plot directly to his children, regardless of his or their *matai* titles.

Villagers now apply these new principles of ownership and inheritance to almost all newly cleared plots. They have also come to apply these new principles to most of the older agricultural lands that their parents and grandparents first cleared and held under the traditional tenure system. Many extended families have even divided their ancient village house sites among individual heirs. Villagers recognize that this new system of individual ownership and inheritance is not traditional (that is, it was not used during the time of their parents and grandparents), but has become established during their own lifetimes. Nevertheless, everyone accepts the validity of the new system and nearly everyone claims at least one plot of land under the new tenure system.

The change to individual tenure is currently without legal sanction, however. The nation's constitution charges the Land and Titles Court with adjudicating disputes over customary land and *matai* titles according to the "custom and usage" of the Samoan people. This charter causes much confusion today, as past custom increasingly conflicts with contemporary usage. The Court officially opposes modification of the traditional land tenure system, but in their legal decisions and in their own private affairs, the judges often support the new system (Land and Titles Court Records, Mulinuu and Tuasivi). Even without official legal support, the change in tenure has proceeded to the point where Samoan villagers now claim the majority of their lands as individuals, without regard to specific chiefly titles.

Traditionally, even though Samoans lived and worked in extended families, chiefs usually tried to favor their own children by passing their titles on to one of them. In order to assure that one of their children acquired the title and the authority over resources that went with it, chiefs would try to influence title elections, or even circumvent the traditional rules by force or guile. The important point about the modern system is that under current economic conditions, all villagers feel that it is essential for their children to inherit their cash-crop lands and house sites. Thus, what villagers once might have accomplished only indirectly or by subterfuge, they now accept as the social norm.

The new tenure system explicitly denies the traditional use rights of the extended family. It also denies the former claim of the extended family's *matai* to authority over land that has always been worked—and is now owned—by individuals living in separate households. Those "communal" rights to family land and labor were at the heart of the traditional *fa'a-Samoa*. Their denial is thus a significant development in the individual-ization of rights in the modern *fa'a-Samoa*. These changes have generally escaped notice because the villagers and the Land and Titles Court have both maintained a public ideology of traditionalism, and because they both legitimize the new, individualistic claims by citing four—slightly modified—traditional principles:

Principle 1.   Land belongs to those who clear and plant it. Traditionally this meant that land belonged to the entire extended family (under the authority of the particular matai title) to which the people who cleared the land belonged. In the new system, however, people advance the same principle to justify their claim that land belongs only to those specific individuals who physically clear and plant the land, not including even a person's siblings if they did not share in the work.

Principle 2. A planter may gain authority over land that he cleared previously, but only when he acquires a *matai* title. Until he acquires a title of his own, land that he clears remains under the formal authority of the *matai* he is currently serving. In the new system, however, control of the land passes to the person who cleared it as an individual by virtue of acquiring any *matai* title. Land is no longer vested in a particular title name.

Principle 3. It is not possible to take the land of another without cause. Extended families formerly invoked this rule to defend their land against competing claims by other extended families. Today, individuals invoke the rule to protect their cash-crop lands against claims by other members of their immediate families, including even siblings who share the same title name.

Principle 4. *E pule le matai,* "The chief has the authority." This means that *matai* have final authority over virtually all matters affecting their family and their family lands. An untitled person still cannot legitimately claim authority over land.

Villagers apply these traditional principles differently than before, however, and in different economic and political circumstances, with the result that their new claims directly contradict the old system. Individuals need only clear their own plots and gain their own *matai* titles for the system to be transformed from "communal" ownership by title groups to individual ownership.

The Land and Titles Court, in turn, adjudicates village disputes according to the villagers' accepted contemporary "usage," even though in doing so they contradict traditional "custom" (see O'Meara 1987:109–110). The Court cites the same four traditional principles as justification for their decisions, so that the appearance of traditionalism is maintained throughout.

The earliest explicit application of the new land tenure system in Savaii that I recorded was in the mid-1920s. At that time, a man who is now an elderly high chief cleared and planted his own plot, intending to use the cash crops to support his wife and children. His testimony is particularly relevant because he prides himself on his traditionalism and because he still claims authority over many other plots by his *suafa,* or *matai* "title," according to the traditional system. He says that when he dies, control of those family lands will go to whomever acquires his title. The old chief claims only the one plot as an individual—by his *tino,* or "body," as he says. When he dies, his children will inherit this individually owned plot regardless of whether they acquire his *matai t*itle.

Villagers are quite explicit about their reasons for changing to individual ownership of land. They say that the primary causes are their increased access to and desire for income from cash cropping. They earn this income individually, and they want to control it individually as well. Before the advent of cash cropping, there appeared to be little reason for conflict between a chief and his untitled men over the control of plots or over the disposition of crops. As long as they produced only food to feed their families and to support family social activities, there was probably little divergence between the interests of individual workers and their *matai*. Conflict has increased, however, with the growing importance of agriculture as a source of cash (or, in the case of subsistence production, as a way to avoid cash expense). High Chief Asiata Iakopo explained it this way:

> In the old days there was no copra, no cocoa, no taro sales. Everyone worked together to help each other, but it is different today. Now people want to get the fruits of their own sweat in order to raise their children.

Ironically, a secondary cause of the change in land tenure is that parents also want to retain the fruits of their children's sweat for their own support in old age. According to Samoan custom, parents support their children when the children are young, but when the children are grown, they support their parents. Almost all modern houses in rural villages are built with money sent by a couple's children who are living and working overseas. Villagers increase the security of these investments by claiming ownership of these house sites as individuals.

MONEY, POPULATION GROWTH, AND FAMILY ORGANIZATION

Villagers are increasingly free to claim individual ownership of resources because individually produced income from cash cropping, wage labor, and remittances is removing the main economic rationale for the extended family. For example, the construction and repair of traditional houses, large paddling and sailing canoes, fishing nets, and other items formerly required a pool of labor that was drawn largely from within the extended family and was organized by the extended family's *matai*. Today, modern purchased materials greatly reduce labor requirements while placing a premium on control over the sources of monetary income. At the same time, increased competition over those sources of income increases strife between extended-family members. As a result, the tradition of and the traditional need for cooperation within the extended family may no longer contain intrafamily rivalries. Villagers universally say, for example, that the immediate cause of their dividing up old family lands between individual heirs is their frequent disputes over jointly held house sites and cash-crop lands.

Individual incomes are still low, however, and often subject to high risk. Thus, most households still need to pool several incomes from different sources. This adds to the household's total income while reducing risk through diversification. Everyone wants to pool those diverse incomes, however, in such a way that they maintain tight control over them. Villagers have solved this problem in two ways: first, by claiming individual ownership and direct inheritance of resources within the nuclear family; and second, by increasing the size of the nuclear family. Recent population growth has thus facilitated the reorganization of village economics.

The shift from an extended-family to a nuclear-family-based village economy began around the 1920s when Western Samoa began recovering from the catastrophic depopulation of the preceding century. Family genealogies show that even a generation or two ago many people had no offspring, while other people had, at most, a few children who survived to adulthood. Many of the parents themselves did not live long. Under those demographic conditions, cooperation between nuclear families, or fragments of nuclear families, was necessary in order to pool a large enough labor force. Today it is common for couples to have six, eight, or even more children who reach adulthood. Once the oldest children reach productive age, the need for economic cooperation between nuclear families is thus greatly reduced.

POLITICAL OPPORTUNITIES AND THE CHANGING *MATAI* SYSTEM

While nuclear-family "individualism" has grown at the expense of extended-family "communalism," most Samoans still uphold the principle that only *matai* can hold authority over land. A major reason for this apparent conservatism is undoubtedly that national law does not allow otherwise. But real conflict over the issue is being defused because of another, very unconservative development—the wholesale granting of *matai* titles. The number of *matai* has been growing very rapidly since independence, so that now the great majority of Samoan men hold titles. In rural areas such as Savaii, more than three-quarters of all men twenty-one years old and older are *matai*. That is more than double the percentage of thirty years ago, and the percentage is increasing every year.

The main reason for the explosive proliferation of *matai* titles has undoubtedly been the law governing the election of district representatives to Parliament. Only *matai* may stand for election; and, more importantly, until 1991, only registered *matai* could vote in district elections. Members of the constitutional convention intended this law to forge an enduring compromise between traditional Samoan political organization and British-style parliamentary government. While the compromise has generally been successful so far, it has also produced an unintended and increasingly disturbing side-effect.

The assumption that Samoans held their traditional *matai* system sacred and therefore above electoral manipulation has proved to be unfounded. Many candidates immediately perceived the electoral advantage of bestowing as many new *matai* titles as possible on their loyal constituents. Politically united families (and even whole villages) have commonly bestowed dozens or even scores of new titles in preparation for an election. In some districts women, youths, and even children received titles, many without any or with only peremptory installation ceremonies.

Family members can elect people to their family titles at will. Thus, all that was required to "stack" an election was that no one in the family lodge a complaint with the Land and Titles Court or with electoral officials. Certain high titles also have the traditional power to create new titles and to bestow them freely. Many influential chiefs abused these traditional prerogatives for political gain, and some of the most honored and highest status *matai* led the way.

In order to satisfy electoral and court officials, and thus prevent a successful court challenge, the installation ceremonies for new *matai* should conform to traditional standards. According to these standards, all leading members of the title family should attend the ceremony to show their support. The other chiefs of the village should also attend, for this signifies their public acceptance of the new *matai* in village affairs. The host family should also distribute at least the equivalent of a small pig or a case of tinned fish and one or two fine mats to the guests for each new *matai* they install.

Once the individual has been installed, he (or, rarely, she) should also fulfill the public role of a *matai*. For example, new *matai* should attend council meetings and contribute to church and village affairs in the name of their new titles. These obligations can be very burdensome for a young man, especially since he often continues to serve the senior *matai* of his family as before. One twenty-three-year-old man ran away twice to avoid being installed as a "ballot *matai*" by his in-laws. He succumbed to the political will of his wife's family, with whom he was then living, only when his father-in-law directly ordered him to accept the title. His father-in-law mollified the young man by assuring him privately that he would not be responsible for his own contributions to village affairs. Instead, the father-in-law told the young man he could take the contributions for his new title from the general resources of the larger family.

In order to maintain the electoral status of new *matai*, the family and other members of the village should also treat new title recipients as legitimate chiefs—that is, calling them by their new title names instead of their given names, and treating them with the modest respect and deference due a minor chief (though in the most flagrant cases, even this pretense is not maintained). Thus, all of the rights, obligations, privileges, and honor of *matai* status have been dissolving rapidly into the wider population—ennobling younger and lesser people at the expense of the institution itself.

In short, Samoans reacted rapidly to the new election laws by subverting the *matai* system—their most fundamental and most revered social institution. This should be ample evidence that there is no "cult of custom" in Samoa today. Once again, Samoans have shown their ability and willingness to adapt their culture in order to take advantage of new opportunities. In the case of parliamentary elections, those opportunities were mainly political. In the case of land tenure and family organization, the opportunities are mainly economic.

Many Samoans objected to subverting the *matai* system for political purposes. They fear that the *matai* system is now in danger of collapse. Yet there is also widespread support for some of the consequences of the electoral maneuvering since it was paving the way for the individualization of contemporary Samoan society—enabling and speeding some of the social, economic, and political changes that many Samoans desire. Since only *matai* may own land, for example, the politically inspired spread of *matai* titles has facilitated the shift to individual land tenure. On the other hand, desire for *matai* status as a means of controlling land greatly reduced people's resistance to subverting the *matai* system for political purposes.

The politically motivated spread of *matai* titles rapidly enfranchised thousands of younger and often better-educated men who would otherwise have had little or no say in village and national politics, thus initially helping to defuse mounting pressure for universal suffrage. More recently, however, one of the strongest arguments *for* universal suffrage has become the fear that wholesale creation of ballot *matai*, if left unchecked, would utterly destroy the *matai* system—and perhaps the entire *fa'a-Samoa* with it. Since the vast majority of men have already gained the privileges and responsibilities of *matai* status, the significant question became whether or not the same liberalization would be extended to women. That question was answered in an historic plebiscite in late 1990, when Western Samoans voted to allow all citizens twenty-one years old or older to vote in parliamentary elections, with the first such elections held in early 1991. Whether this dramatic change to universal suffrage will halt erosion of the *matai* system, or only quicken its demise, remains to be seen.

ECONOMIC RESOURCES AND THE CHANGING *MATAI* SYSTEM

While electoral maneuvering recently fueled the increase in *matai* titles, economic forces have been changing both land tenure and the broader *matai* system since long before parliamentary elections began, and they will continue doing so now that election laws have changed. The first documented title splitting occurred on the island of Savaii in the 1920s, at the same time the change in land tenure began there. The population was then at its lowest ebb following the devastating flu epidemic of 1918, so population increase cannot account for the title splitting. By the time the wholesale bestowal of titles for election purposes began in the early 1960s, both the new tenure system and the sharing and splitting of titles were well established.

An important reason that individuals want *matai* titles is to legitimize their control over economic resources. The system also works the other way around. Having already gained personal control over economic resources, individuals can now support their own candidacy for a title even if no appreciable segment of the extended family is united behind them. Thus, title groups often split their titles among many contenders simply because each candidate has a relatively large and independent source of income from cash cropping, wages, or remittances that he can use to provide goods for distribution at his title bestowal ceremony.

Different factions within the title group no longer have much reason to work for unity in title elections. Each contender can hold out for victory, and the family eventually divides the title among several contenders. By sharing their titles among several candidates, extended families recognize (and sometimes increase) the already existing independence of their constituent households. Title sharing rarely (if ever) causes the breakup of an extended family that was formerly intact. Instead, the sharing of titles itself results from the earlier breakup of the extended family as a productive unit.

Even individual claims to village house plots, which are now common, are having a profound effect on the election of *matai*—as I learned at the formal gathering of an extended family as they met to elect their new *matai*. They chose their new *matai* primarily on the basis of who was occupying the traditional house site of that title. One of the two main contenders for the title had been born and raised on the site, and he had already built a European-style house there. The second main contender for the family title lived in another part of the village. Recall that a newly elected *matai* is supposed to take up residence at, and assume authority over, the traditional house site of his title. Since the assembled members of the extended family all accepted the new tenure system, however, they never entertained any thought of forcing the current occupant to give up his expensive house to the other candidate. Had they given the title to the nonresident candidate anyway, the current occupant of the site might have prevented the family from meeting there, and they all agreed that it would be most unsightly for the title family to meet elsewhere. The unavoidable result was that the man already occupying the traditional site received the title. The disgruntled loser then took the matter to court. The family eventually settled the dispute by bestowing the title on six contenders (one from each main faction of the title-descent group) at a single ceremony. Such joint-title bestowal ceremonies can be grand affairs, fueled by the donations of several new chiefs and their families.

One might easily wonder how an extended family could operate as a unit with several equal leaders, each jealously guarding his own rights, privileges, and authority. The answer is that it does not. None of the men acquires authority over any new land or laborers by virtue of his new title, and he gains little new authority over the members of even his own faction. Except in honorific matters pertaining directly to the title, little changes.

In the past, a *matai's* social and ceremonial prerogatives were symbols of the real authority he held over his extended family and its lands. An installation ceremony was the public investiture of that authority, and the ceremony itself was primarily the means to that end. Today, most of the title's authority is gone. Villagers continue to hold installation ceremonies, but they have become largely ends in themselves—grand but increasingly hollow ceremonies that proclaim rather than affirm the importance of men.

Although the honor and power of *matai* status are significantly diluted today, *matai* still bear their titles with dignity and pride. Low-ranking ballot *matai* often told me proudly of the great weight and profound dignity of their chiefly status, boasting that "In Samoan custom, power belongs to the chief." A *matai's* power is now usually restricted, however, to simple patriarchy over his own nuclear family, and the tokens of his prestige are usually limited to politeness of speech from fellow *matai* and modest deference from untitled people.

The prestige and power of *matai* status must remain relatively scarce if the status is to be worth achieving. By creating new titles wholesale, and by splitting and sharing old titles among many people, Samoans have approached a critical juncture in their cultural history. In broadening the base of the *matai* system, they may have adapted it to serve them into the twenty-first century, or they may have created a pointless and lifeless system in which by giving everyone something, no one gets anything.

The traditional power of *matai* is based on two complementary principles: *pule* and *tautua*. The first is the chief's *pule*, or authority, over the extended family's land, labor, and income. The second is the *tautua*, or service, of the extended family members to their chief. The system is organized largely on seniority: those who are older receive obedience and service from those who are younger. Ironically, this kind of system remains stable only as long as the participants believe it will continue. As long as the system is closed and the cycle secure, young people perceive their current service as a tolerable burden, knowing that one day they will, in their turn, likely command the respect and service of others.

But the cycle of *tautua* has been broken in the minds of many young people today. New technology, a market economy, and mass migration make individual production, profit, and accumulation of wealth possible. In these circumstances, village people no longer render their service gladly to another, for they see little benefit in such a system for themselves or their children. And as thousands of young men and women prepare to leave the village entirely, seeking their futures in Apia or overseas, they know that their own service will never be repaid by a younger generation.

Group installation for new Samoan *matai*.Thirteen men received newly created titles at this ceremony. They sit in the line at the right, garlanded with flowers. On the left sit the current *matai* of the village. At the far end stands the pastor delivering the blessing. The stick in the left foreground is the stem of a kava, the root of which will be used in making the ceremonial kava drink. (Photo by Tim O'Meara)

THE CHANGING CEREMONIAL SYSTEM

In spite of the dramatic changes in the *matai* and land tenure systems, in family organization, and in village economics, Samoans continue to participate enthusiastically in traditional social ceremonies, called *fa'alavelave*. In rural areas, the most frequent ceremonies are funerals, *matai* title installations, and kava ceremonies to greet *matai* who are visiting or returning from overseas. Since these ceremonies are founded on traditional social relationships between members of extended families and their *matai* titles, the continuing importance of the ceremonial system might appear to confirm the cultural conservatism of Samoans. But, like the rest of contemporary village life, the ceremonial system is far less traditional than it appears on the surface.

One of the central features of Samoan social ceremonies is the exchange of gifts between hosts and guests. Generally speaking, guests give fine mats, small amounts of money, and (on certain occasions) kava roots to their hosts. Guests may also present formal speeches, and they honor their hosts as well simply by attending the ceremony. In return for these material and nonmaterial gifts, host families give pigs, a few fine mats, money, and both local and purchased foods to their guests. The exact mix of gifts and counter-gifts depends on the type of ceremony and on the material circumstances of the parties.

An important reason the ceremonial system continues to flourish is that villagers want more opportunities to exchange the goods they produce themselves for cash and purchased goods. Many of the items they produce for exchange, such as the fine mats that women laboriously plait from pandanus leaves, have no other utility outside the ceremonial system.

Distribution of food to guests after a church dedication. After the dedication, host families reciprocate by giving their guests gifts of food. Each of the piles of food in the photo is intended for a particular group of guests. The cardboard boxes contain canned mackerel and the plastic buckets contain salt beef. Each pile is augmented with strips of pig blubber for use in cooking. In the background, untitled men butcher and distribute more pigs under the direction of the host family's talking chiefs. (Photo by Tim O'Meara)

My year-long survey of household economic activities in a Savaii village shows how important these ceremonial exchanges are as a source of cash and purchased goods, or "monetary income," for village households. This village has a reputation for being relatively traditional and strongly agricultural. During the survey year, fifty-three of the fifty-five village households obtained a significant portion of their income from agriculture. Total income for these fifty-three "farm households" averaged about WS $440 (U.S. $350) per capita and was evenly divided between monetary and subsistence income (see O'Meara 1990:184–190).

Even though the village has a reputation as an agricultural village—and in fact has no other visible means of support—the average farm household received only one-fifth of its monetary income from cash cropping. In comparison, fully one-sixth of the average farm household's monetary income came as gifts from other people living within Western

Samoa. Most of these gifts result from participating in *fa'alavelave* ceremonies. Villagers received another one-fourth of their monetary income as gifts from people living outside Western Samoa. While most of that money comes as private remittances from family members, a significant portion of that "overseas income" is distributed at local ceremonies—for example, at kava ceremonies where village chiefs honor traveling parties coming from overseas, or at funerals where much of the gift distributions are funded by relatives visiting from overseas.

Thus, in addition to their more traditional social reasons for participating in *fa'alavelave* ceremonies, villagers now often attend or contribute indirectly to ceremonies for the specific purpose of gaining monetary income. Guests at even modest ceremonies may receive WS $2 or WS $3 in cash or purchased goods, as well as food and perhaps a fine mat. When the alternative is slashing brush in the family coconut plantations for a return of WS $1 or WS $2 (O'Meara 1990:190–193), *fa'alavelave* ceremonies present stiff competition for villagers' attention.

Gift exchanges are socially and ideologically distinct from the market sales by which villagers also earn cash income, but they recognize that the material outcome is often much the same. For example, a couple may take two fine mats and WS $2 (U.S. $1.70) to a funeral. In return, they might receive one fine mat, five tins of fish, and WS $1 for "bus fare." There would be little or no material difference had they taken the one fine mat to the market, sold it, and then bought five tins of fish and paid the bus fare with the proceeds.

Samoans are quick to argue that gift exchanges are social exchanges, rather than economic transactions. On the other hand, they are very aware of and concerned with the economic results of their gift exchanges. The following conversation with Milo Faletoi, who is a chief in a neighboring village, gives an indication of villagers' material interests in these social formalities.

MILO: What did you all take?

TIMO: Seven small pigs, thiry-eight chickens, and baked taro.

MILO: Who went?

TIMO: All the talking chiefs of Vaosasa, plus Tafuli from Pitosili, and another chief I don't know.

MILO: Where was it held?

TIMO: At Toeaina Agalelei's house.

MILO: The one by the sports grounds?

TIMO: Yes, the big European-style house.

MILO: Who gave the speech for the family?

TIMO: Pe'ape'a.

MILO: What did they give you?

TIMO: Most of us got one fine mat and $5, but some of the men got $10 and Lauga So'o got $20 for his speech. Then we got $200 for the going-away present. [Milo paused for a moment to calculate and then, scowling with displeasure, announced his evaluation of the trip.]

MILO: Bad! You should have sent only four or five chiefs to represent you and left everyone else at home. That way you wouldn't have wasted all that money on travel expenses. Your trip would have been "square." As it is, when you came back you were "broke."

Another indication of villagers' material interests in *fa'alavelave* is that they commonly judge ceremonies according to how well they make out in the exchange. For example, I was lounging idly one afternoon with my friend and sometime assistant, Panoa, when my host, Nu'u Vili, returned home from a funeral.

"How was the funeral, eh Nu'u?" Panoa asked. Nu'u shook his head and smiled sheepishly. "*Gau*," he said. "Broke."

Nu'u had taken two fine mats that morning to a funeral held by the family of some relatives in a distant village. He returned with nothing but the curried gravy and breadfruit in his stomach, and three cans of mackerel rattling around in his briefcase.

"What about that, Nu'u?" I asked. "Is it bad to give things at a funeral and receive little in return?"

"*Tusā*," he replied. "All the same. Sometimes you get a lot, sometimes little, sometimes nothing. We don't give, just wanting something in return." Nevertheless, Nu'u was clearly dejected over the short-term imbalance in gifts.

He returned from another funeral two weeks later.

"How was the funeral?" His two young sons peeled back the layer of wilted banana leaves that covered the top of the large, coconut-leaf basket, revealing a shoulder of half-cooked pork, several thick strips of pig blubber, and half-dozen greasy cans of fish.

"Beautiful," Nu'u announced, smiling broadly. "Lots of food."

Nu'u and other Samoans express the traditional sentiment that their gifts are given freely at ceremonies, with no expectation of return or reward. When their hosts are planning their return gifts, however, they pay very careful attention to the number, size, and quality of the fine mats and the amount of money they have just received from each group of guests. For example, when Falanika was married in American Samoa, her family from Western Samoa gave the groom's family 300 fine mats. Leaders of the groom's extended family decided that $3,000 cash was an appropriate return gift. They explicitly chose that figure because $10 was then the market rate for fine mats in the city. The six branches of the groom's family each contributed $500 toward the total, and when they divided the fine mats among themselves, each branch received 50 fine mats—one for each ten dollars they had contributed.

Villagers pursue both their social goals and their economic goals through participation in the ceremonial system. By combining the two sets of goals in one system, people can shore up one with the other. For example, people can apply their social and political leverage to gain material support when they need it, or they can give away their material goods to gain needed social and political support. Thus, in any particular situation, an individual's own economic and social goals may conflict, just as their short-term goals may conflict with their long-term goals. In addition, different individuals and different families may come into conflict with each other as they pursue their respective—and often competing—goals. Such conflicts and competition add a good deal of emotional spice to the ceremonial system, which provides another strong incentive for participation. Host families try to give away more gifts than they receive from their guests (or at least they try to appear to give away more). But while hosts may give away many goods at these ceremonies, that does not mean that they covet material possessions less than other people do. They give gifts to demonstrate their material wealth and their generosity, both of which are in high esteem. No glory could be gained from gift giving if neither givers nor receivers really wanted the gifts.

Distribution of fine mats after the funeral of a high chief. The leading chiefs of the deceased's family sit outside his house while the highest-ranking orator stands with his speaking staff, announcing the gifts to the other chiefs who were guests at the funeral. They sit together on the grass outside the picture to the right. In the background the women of the family, wearing their black mourning clothes, crouch on the steps of the house with more fine mats that they will take from the house for distribution to the guests. (Photo by Tim O'Meara)

Nor do hosts necessarily incur significant loss through their generosity. Hosts at one ceremony become guests at many subsequent ceremonies hosted by other families. Acting as guests, they now hope to receive more than they give. Receiving large gifts demonstrates their high rank, since people give the greatest gifts to those of highest rank. When guests receive large gifts, it may also demonstrate their personal power, especially the powers of persuading and cajoling, in which chiefs try to excel. Of course, people also like to receive large gifts just because they desire the money and goods. Host families play on these material desires as a way of attracting guests to their ceremonies. Some guests would come anyway out of friendship or obligation, but the promise of generous gifts attracts a throng.

Hosts and guests exchange gifts at a ceremony, but that is just the public portion of the event. Before the ceremony, neighbors, relatives, and friends often contribute to the respective stockpiles of both the guests and the hosts. Sometimes both hosts and guests solicit such contributions. Other times people bring a fine mat or two of their own accord, saying that they have come to "help" the person with his or her *fa'alavelave*. When the public ceremony is over, both hosts and guests redistribute a share of their receipts privately to everyone who contributed to their stockpile earlier. Thus, some of the *fa'alavelave* exchanges occur privately, outside the arena of the main event. This creates the possibility of both hosts and guests manipulating their exchanges to portray a public image of generosity while actually achieving a net gain in resources.

Traditionally, adherence to two implicit principles ensured that gifts were reciprocal, so that in either the short or the long run families came out relatively even in the exchanges.

The first principle is that *high-ranking* people should both give and receive larger gifts than other people. Gifts between extended families always flow according to rank. Villagers give no consideration to the recipient's economic need. While the recipients may consume these gifts as part of their daily fare, the gifts are not intended to, and do not, level incomes between wealthy and poor families. If a particular household needs charitable assistance, they get it from other members of their extended family, not from the general public.

The second principle is that *wealthy* people should give larger gifts than other people. Ideally, rank and wealth go together. Traditionally, both depended largely on the number of supporters a person or family could muster, although today wealth is more often an individual or household matter. Today, as in more traditional times, families bestow their *matai* titles on an individual partly to recognize that individual's talents and accomplishments, including his economic accomplishments. More importantly for the family, however, they bestow the title on an individual in order to formally bind him in obligation to the family, thus securing his talents and resources for the benefit of the group.

Sometimes an individual's rank differs significantly from his wealth. In those cases, the size of the gifts he gives varies upward or downward with his resources, but still within the range appropriate for his rank. For example, a wealthy high chief might give a large pig and a poor high chief a medium-size pig, while a talking chief would contribute a chicken. The size of each gift depends on the donor's particular rank, current resources, his future aspirations, and perhaps his current pretenses. In addition, at family-centered ceremonies such as funerals, the size of each gift will depend on the closeness of the genealogical or title relationship between guest and host. Whatever the size of the initial gift, later in the ceremony the host family will give each donor group a return gift that is roughly proportional to the original gift. Of course, all of this still leaves considerable room for maneuvering and manipulation on both sides.

As villagers apply these traditional principles in current circumstances, they often intentionally upset the balance of reciprocity. If only village planters participated in the ceremonial system—as they once did—no one would gain much material advantage over the long term from the exchanges. But today, local (often part-European) business owners and both urban and overseas relatives also participate. They tend to give more cash and purchased goods than fine mats or other subsistence goods. Village planters, on the other hand, give more fine mats, pigs, and social honors (such as *matai* titles and honorific speeches) than money or purchased goods.

Some of the fine mats that village planters give were plaited by the women and older girls of their respective households. When people attend ceremonies, however, they may also take fine mats they have collected from previous ceremonies, and often a few other fine mats that friends or relatives have contributed for the occasion. Rather than being the direct-labor product of the household women, those additional fine mats are the indirect product of the entire household's agricultural, pig raising, and ceremonial activities. Thus, by participating in ceremonial gift exchanges, a household can convert some of the household women's surplus labor, some of the household's agricultural and pig-raising labor (most of which is done by adult men and by children), some of its social status, and some of its earlier ceremonial efforts into monetary income.

Villagers now also gain much of their income from a few members who live permanently in the city or overseas. Many of those migrants still want to help support their relatives back in the village, and they often want to achieve traditional status for themselves. Thus, when these migrants return to the village for *fa'alavelave*, they contribute generously. But since the migrants almost always lack high chiefly status or an immediate presence in local social and political affairs, their village relatives do not feel equally obliged to reciprocate the migrants' generosity. The result is that migrants visiting from Apia and from overseas usually give much and receive little at village ceremonies. Their losses make it possible for local host families to put on generous public displays at little or no cost to themselves. As in the following example in Savaii, some families now actually profit from hosting funerals and other ceremonies.

Faletele arrived from Apia in a hired pick-up truck to attend the funeral of his father, a high chief. It was the first time Faletele had returned to his natal village since he first left to attend school in Apia sixteen years ago. Over the years, he had risen to become a mid-level manager in a department store, and he earned a good salary by local standards. In the back of the pick-up truck were four cases of tinned fish and 100 loaves of bread (worth about WS $240, or U.S. $200) that Faletele brought as a contribution to the funeral, to which he added the roll of bills totaling WS $248 that he carried in his pocket.

Faletele's combined gift cancelled 43 percent of the local host family's monetary expenses and 28 percent of their combined monetary and subsistence-item expenses at the funeral (see Table 9–1). Faletele deposited the gift with his family and then, having fulfilled his obligation, departed without receiving any return gift. This case is somewhat extreme, but even by generous standards he would have received only a cooked pig and a few fine mats, together worth perhaps WS $100 to WS $150. Shortly after the funeral, the host family also received another large cash donation (of WS $275) from relatives in New Zealand. This donation, which was earmarked for construction of the concrete tomb, also went unreciprocated.

Table 9–1 shows that the local host family ended up with large net surpluses of fine mats, cash, and purchased goods. About half of that surplus they balanced by their own contribution of pigs at the funeral. Subtracting the approximate cash value of the pigs, the local family of the deceased earned a net profit of WS $1,024 from hosting his funeral, largely on the strength of the two unreciprocated gifts from two of the deceased's children—Faletele, who lives in Apia, and a daughter who lives overseas. When the funeral was over, the local members of the host family divided the surplus among themselves, with shares going to the three constituent households according to the number of fine mats and the number and size of the pigs each had contributed.

The extreme imbalance in the gift exchange noted above appears to be the rule, rather than the exception. While custom dictates that the generosity of the host family should leave it "broke" after a funeral, the host family made a net profit at two of the three funerals I recorded. The balance sheet at the third funeral was unclear due to charges of embezzlement made against the family member who had recorded the incoming and outgoing gifts for the family. After another funeral, a *matai* of the host family boasted to me that they had ended with a surplus of WS $300. Shortly after that funeral, the host family built a large addition onto their European-style house, a sure indication that they had not suffered materially in the funeral exchange. Moreover, the funds for the construction probably became available to them because of the funeral, which drew in relatives from overseas and gave them an opportunity to reaffirm their family ties by improving the family residence.

TABLE 9–1   Accounting of Host Family's Funeral Receipts and Expenses

VALUE OF RECEIPTS

Gifts retained from visitors:			
Fine mats (156 small, 4 large)	$1,356		
Cash	849		
Purchased goods (4 cases fish, 8 rayon cloths, 100 loaves bread)	280		
Subtotal		$2,485	
Cash received from overseas		275	
Total Receipts			$2,760

VALUE OF EXPENSES

Gifts given after burial:			
Pig (1 large)	$100		
Cash	191		
Purchased goods	58		
Subtotal		$349	
Lagi and tomb construction:			
Pig (1 large)	$100		
Fine mats (33 small)	264		
Cash	40		
Purchased goods (cement, etc.)	275		
Subtotal		$679	
Burial materials (casket, etc.)		258	
Pigs provided at funeral (4 large, 2 medium)		450	
Total Expenses			$1,736
Net Income			$1,024

Accounting of the local host family's receipts and expenses at the funeral of a high chief. The accounting shows that the family received a net income of WS $1,024—which they divided among their three constituent households according to the number and size of pigs and fine mats each had contributed earlier.

My consultations with other people confirmed that it is now common, although still shameful, for families to profit from hosting funerals or other ceremonies. Such profit is possible largely because the hosts reciprocate gifts from their urban and overseas relatives very lightly, if at all. Sometimes the local family just reciprocates by giving the urban or overseas relative a *matai* title, for which honor he (or, rarely, she) must then provide even more money and goods. By attending these ceremonies and participating in the gift exchanges, other cash-hungry villagers gain a share of the monetary income that the host family attracts from its urban and overseas relatives. Thus, it is now possible for all of the local villagers—hosts and guests alike—to come out ahead in their *fa'alavelave* exchanges.

Fa'alavelave ceremonies are important not only as foci for giving and receiving goods, of course. Villagers also attend these ceremonies for socializing and for diversion. *Fa'alavelave* ceremonies have an air of importance, tension, and excitement that interrupts the usually pleasant but often dull routine of daily life. In order to create that excitement, villagers combine in their ceremonies many of the things that matter most to them: family, food, money, competition for status in a public forum, a chance for men to display their knowledge and their skill at oration, a chance to command and to impress, a chance for women to take center stage for a moment as they display their fine mats, a chance for young men and women from different villages to meet and talk amid the turmoil of their constant labor.

These social and political affairs are the prime arena of chiefs. If there is a temporary lull in these activities, energetic chiefs begin searching more and more widely for affairs to engage them. I recall going to the house of an elderly chief named Umusa one day and finding him sitting alone, drumming his fingers on the pandanus-leaf mat. Too old to work the plantations with dignity, he sat and stared out across the empty village green. Umusa directed our conversation to the many chiefly affairs that currently occupied him. During pauses he plucked frayed leaf strands from the plaited floor mats around him. As he fiddled, he seemed to search the future for new engagements, for when he spoke again it was of a distant ceremony that he must attend, or an obscure court case that he must press. All the while he complained of the great burden of responsibility that men of his rank must bear.

Most *fa'alavelave* ceremonies are still the public affairs of large extended families, and few Samoans are yet so wealthy that they can afford to withdraw from the mutual support and security system that is the ultimate foundation of the extended family. Nor is there any significant national insurance or social security system to take over that function of the extended family. Independent incomes and larger nuclear families have largely eliminated the need for extended families to produce together. But because of the small size and insecurity of those incomes, most Samoans must still rely on their extended families for security. I suspect that the ceremonial system endures partly in response to this reduction in economic cooperation within extended families. Since related households no longer cooperate in their everyday economic affairs, people may participate in *fa'alavelave* in order to maintain their positions in strong extended families, which are still important to them for security. Ceremonial exchanges provide frequent opportunities for people to demonstrate their own (and check other people's) ability and willingness to come to the support of their kin. As Nu'u once told me, "If we give generously now, when we have a *fa'alavelave* of our own, the house will be full."

Like the land tenure system and the *matai* system of which it is a part, the ceremonial system endures today not because Samoans are caught in a "cult of custom," but because Samoans have adapted their customs to serve their present needs. The newest and most powerful force supporting and modifying Samoan custom today is the search for money. Men increasingly head nuclear-family households that own their own resources and control their own incomes. They, and a few women, have been able to legitimize that individual control by gaining their own *matai* titles. Yet they continue to maintain the wider social affairs of their extended families as important sources of pleasure, power, and prestige, and as a major source of both immediate monetary income and of long-term economic security. Villagers have very little power or influence over urban residents in most other matters. Villagers still control custom, however, and they know how to manipulate it to their advantage.

Acknowledgments: I wish to extend my sincere thanks to the government and people of Western Samoa, and especially to the Chiefs and Orators of Satupaitea District for their support and friendship. The research presented here was supported by grants from the National Science Foundation, The University of California at Santa Barbara, Sigma Xi Scientific Research Society, and by a research contract with the Food and Agriculture Organization of the United Nations and the University of the South Pacific. Parts of this chapter appeared in print earlier. I thank the University of the South Pacific and Holt, Rinehart & Winston for permission to reprint that material here.

10

The Samoan Exodus

Paul Shankman
University of Colorado, Boulder

In the spring of 1989, Vice President Dan Quayle traveled to the Far East on a major foreign policy tour. In transit, Quayle stopped briefly in American Samoa, a small American territory about twenty-five hundred miles southwest of Hawaii. There the Vice President addressed an offical delegation of Samoans, declaring:

> You all look like happy campers to me. Happy campers you are. Happy campers you have been, and as far as I am concerned, happy campers you will always be. (*Newsweek* 1989: 13)

Quayle then boarded his plane and departed for the bulk of his tour.

To most outside observers, including the Vice President, Samoa is a place where people should be happy. The sheer physical beauty of the archipelago evokes the mystique of a tropical paradise. Swaying palms, blue lagoons, and soft breezes are some of the ingredients of the romantic imagery so vividly conveyed in the writings of Margaret Mead, Somerset Maugham, and Robert Louis Stevenson. There is the temptation to think of Samoa as a Polynesian idyll bound by the rhythms of indigenous life, a place to get away from it all. Yet if this idyll ever existed, it has long since vanished. As Tim O'Meara demonstrates in Chapter 9, Samoa today is part of the modern world. And Samoans are leaving paradise in large numbers. While tourists seek refuge from the fast lane in the islands, Samoans are migrating overseas in an exodus of significant proportions.

Who are these Samoans leaving the islands and why are they doing so? Where do they go and how do they fare at their destinations abroad? What kinds of ties do they have with the relatives they leave behind? Will the migrants remain permanently abroad or will they return to the islands? These are some of the questions to be addressed in examining the contours of the Samoan exodus.

This chapter focuses on Western Samoa, the largest independent country in the South Pacific to be significantly affected by migration.[1] Nearby American Samoa is an important destination of this migration and has experienced a major exodus of its own. Few Americans are aware that there are two Samoas, perhaps because they are culturally identical and only 70 miles apart. Yet they are politically and economically quite different, and the recent migrations from both island groups reflect these differences.

Western Samoa has a population of one hundred sixty thousand people. When it became the first independent country in the South Pacific in 1962 after over four decades of New Zealand colonial rule, Western Samoa was politically advanced, but it had a fragile economy based on export agriculture. In fact, economic stagnation has been a major reason for Western Samoan migration to areas with greater opportunity such as New Zealand, American Samoa, and the United States. By the mid-1980s, one-third of Western Samoa's population was overseas.

In contrast, American Samoa (population thirty-two thousand) is relatively affluent. It has been an American possession since the turn of the century, and, since 1960, the United States has poured in large amounts of money through federal programs. The average cash income in American Samoa is many times that of neighboring Western Samoa. But this relative prosperity has not satisfied the aspirations of American Samoans who see better opportunities in the United States. Over 60 percent of American Samoans have now left the islands for Hawaii and the mainland.

Western Samoans have not merely watched as their American Samoan relatives have prospered and migrated; they have followed them. Western Samoans are now the majority of the population in American Samoa. When Vice President Quayle visited Pago Pago in American Samoa (pronouncing it "Pogo Pogo"), he probably did not realize that many of the "happy campers" he addressed were of Western Samoan rather than American Samoan origin. Many other Western Samoans in American Samoa are only temporary sojourners waiting for the necessary immigration papers that will allow them to join their American Samoan kin in the United States.

THE BACKGROUND OF WESTERN SAMOAN MIGRATION

The destinations of Western Samoan migrants have shifted with changing migration opportunities. In the 1960s and early 1970s, Western Samoans migrated primarily to New Zealand and American Samoa. Since then, they have increasingly sought entry into the United States itself. In 1981, there were an estimated 68,700 Western Samoans overseas, including 42,000 in New Zealand, 13,000 in American Samoa, 13,238 in Hawaii and the continental United States, and 500 in Australia. Today these figures would be much higher.

Western Samoan migrants are concentrated in major cities such as Auckland and Wellington in New Zealand, Honolulu, the San Francisco Bay area, and the Los Angeles and San Diego metropolitan areas on the West Coast. They also live in smaller cities and towns such as Oxnard, California. They reside as far east as New York City and Chapel Hill, North Carolina, and in such unlikely places as Denver, a mile high in the Rocky

Mountains. Western Samoans can be found in many parts of the world, including over thirty different nations (Sutter 1989). In this far-flung exodus, Western Samoans maintain networks that keep them in touch with relatives abroad and back home. In the larger urban areas, they have formed overseas emigrant communities that act as powerful magnets for future migration. But the story behind these numbers and overseas destinations begins in the islands themselves.

Western Samoa has a reputation for being one of the most traditional and conservative cultures in Polynesia. Although the port town of Apia is the focus of much economic and government activity, Western Samoa is still a country of rural villages and subsistence agriculture. These villages, ranging in population from a few hundred to several hundred people and larger, dot the picturesque coastlines of the large islands of Upolu and Savaii. Each village is composed of large extended kin groups, known as *aiga*, each of which has one or more titleholders, known as chiefs or *matai*. These titleholders govern the village through a village council. Also playing an important organizational role in the village are the wives of titleholders. Village pastors and storeowners occupy vital niches in the village as well.

The daily round of subsistence activities includes cultivating taro, bananas, breadfruit, and coconut palms; coconuts, cacao, taro, and bananas are also grown as cash crops. The day and week are punctuated by religious observances, since most Samoans are devout Christians of various denominations, and by political meetings of various village organizations. These and the other activities that comprise village life have been described in detail in the novels and short stories of Samoan author Albert Wendt (1974a, 1974b, 1977), in the anthropological works of Bradd Shore (1982) and Tim O'Meara (1990 and Chapter 9 in this volume); and in the popular, humorous works of Fay Calkins (1962) and John O'Grady (1961).

If the initial impression of village life is that it is simple, static, and unchanging, these authors remind us that villages are not self-contained or isolated. They are linked to the wider world by education, by media, by travel to the port town of Apia and overseas, and by their relatives and peers who share these links. They are also linked by their participation in a cash economy. Samoans need money to participate in this wider world—money for education, church participation, imported foods that are now part of their diet, and for clothes; for radios, TVs and videos, and travel; for tin roofs and more modern housing. They need higher incomes for maintaining social status and for improving their individual and collective lives. In selecting traditional titleholders, cash increasingly influences votes. And in village agriculture, cash can buy chainsaws, pesticides, fertilizer, and other kinds of modern technology to improve production. Western Samoan villages, tranquil and traditional as they seem, are dynamic and changing, especially in the economic arena. It is the villages that are currently producing the bulk of Western Samoa's migrants.

During the 1960s and early 1970s, migrants from Western Samoa were more likely to come from the Apia urban area and were more affluent and better educated than today's migrants. Migration from villages is a recent trend that reflects the increasing incorporation of rural areas into the national and international economy. Apart from increasing monetization and urbanization, there have been four convergent trends over the last several decades that have encouraged migration by Western Samoans, both urban and rural, including: (1) population growth, (2) education, (3) the stagnation of the islands' economy, and (4) the lack of opportunities for young people in villages. Let us review each briefly.

Since the turn of the twentieth century, the population of Western Samoa has more than quadrupled. Indeed, if the migrant population is included, the population would have grown by a factor of almost six. The country's population is not only increasing, it is a young population that will live longer due to better health care; average life expectancy is now sixty-five years. Young people between fifteen and twenty-nine comprise the bulk of the migrants, with men and women almost equally balanced among the migrants. As more of these young Samoans leave the islands, those remaining behind must work harder to support the proportionally larger number of old and very young. Working for their families can be a major burden for the young who, as a result of their education and rising expectations, envision a more promising future.

The Samoan educational system, like most in the Third World, is Western-based. The curriculum implicitly teaches students to aspire to wage-labor jobs in urban areas, and many students go to school in Apia. Young graduates are eager for higher-paying wage-labor employment in town or overseas; they have been educated to expect it. When asked what they want to become, high school students overwhelmingly desire "white collar" employment (Fairbairn-Dunlop 1984). They do not want to return to village agriculture where, by comparison, the work is hard, dirty, and not financially rewarding. Yet many young people will have to remain in or return to their villages. The educational system in Western Samoa helps create a set of expectations that the islands' economy cannot meet.

Of course, if village agriculture were more remunerative, the situation might be different. But Western Samoa's agricultural exports, especially copra and cocoa, are subject to wide fluctuations in price and demand. Western Samoa is only one producer among many, and it is a small, marginal country that is not a major player on world markets. Furthermore, even when prices are good, the income potential of village agriculture is limited, in part by the percentage taken by government and commercial traders in the export process. An internal market for village agriculture products has developed in the port town of Apia, but it, too, is limited. Thus, while agriculture provides adequate subsistence for villagers as well as some cash, it does not provide the income levels that Samoans want and need as consumers in an increasingly cash-based economy.

For young Samoans, all of these trends are compounded by the limited opportunity structure of village life itself. In the village, authority is based on a gerontocracy of titleholders and pastors. Young people are expected to work for their family, for their chief, for their church, and for their village. They are expected to be obedient and dutiful, and to wait until they become old enough to become part of the gerontocracy. Individuality is not encouraged, and sanctions, including physical punishment, can be harsh. To become an influential titleholder is now an expensive proposition; becoming a pastor or entrepreneur is a limited option for most young people.

Limited opportunities are reflected in low cash incomes. In 1988, the yearly cash income of the average Western Samoan was $166, according to the World Bank. Although such figures can be misleading, there is no doubt that young Samoans can make many times this amount overseas. And these young people have often been abroad and have relatives overseas. They are aware of the money they can make there and know of opportunities that are not part of Western Samoan life. They realize that they can help their families by migrating and remitting, and their families have carefully weighed the benefits and costs of migration too. During recent decades, the lack of opportunity at home in comparison with opportunities overseas has led to an increasing desire by young Samoans to migrate abroad.

THE MIGRATION PROCESS

As opportunities opened up overseas, Western Samoans left in increasing numbers. By 1966, roughly 8 percent of the population was abroad; by the mid-1970s, this percentage doubled, and doubled again by the mid-1980s. By then, one-third of the islanders were living abroad, with many more traveling overseas on a temporary basis.

In the 1960s and 1970s, when many Western Samoans were taking their first trips to New Zealand, travel itself could be a traumatic experience, especially the first plane ride. But relatives helped, assisting with jobs, housing, and social support that made the migration process much easier. Families and individuals migrate under the auspices of relatives already abroad who provide sponsorship, temporary housing, food, social support, and even employment. After the new migrants become established, they in turn facilitate the migration of other relatives back in the islands. It is an almost classic case of chain migration, the same process that brought many European migrants to America.

The most common migrants are young men and women, frequently single, who are employable and begin remitting money back to relatives in the islands almost as soon as they find work. In New Zealand, relatives already there will help migrants obtain work permits and jobs even before they arrive. Yet while families can provide many forms of assistance to new arrivals, permanent migration to New Zealand or the United States also involves adapting to a new social environment in which Western Samoans are a relatively poor, negatively stereotyped minority group. The overseas environment is almost entirely urban and industrial, in contrast to the Western Samoa which is mostly rural and agricultural. Typically, the new arrivals live in large cities like Auckland, Wellington, Honolulu, Oakland, and Los Angeles where simply finding one's way around can be difficult. Furthermore, although well-educated by Third World standards, young Samoans are not always well-educated by the standards of the countries to which they migrate, and many do not speak English fluently. The kind of employment opportunities they have abroad are limited. Most Western Samoans enter the urban work force in low-paying, blue collar jobs at the bottom of the occupational hierarchy. Of course, among the migrants there are upwardly mobile Samoans, often well-educated overseas. Since they provide a voice and role models for other Samoans, they are an asset to the overseas community. At the same time, though, their education and skills could be valuable back in Western Samoa; they are thus part of a "brain drain" in which better prospects draw upwardly mobile and talented Samoans abroad.

The overseas social environment also includes the sometimes difficult problem of being a minority group. In Western Samoa, Samoans are the vast majority of the population and have a strong, resilient cultural identity. They are proud of being Samoan. But overseas they are an ethnic minority, a new minority, and one among several minorities who are in the process of establishing an expatriate identity for themselves and for the majority population as well. Western Samoans are a small minority not well understood by the majority. As a result, negative stereotypes of Samoans are common among the majority. In New Zealand, where since the mid-1970s the government has cracked down on illegal migrants or "overstayers," the majority sometimes think of Samoans as part of a Polynesian "brown peril" that they fear will overrun their country. Tabloids in New Zealand portray Samoans as dangerous, as rapists, as drunks, and as noisy and violent, even though many in the majority have Samoan neighbors who are every bit as quiet and law-abiding as they are.

In the United States, very few Americans know of or understand the important differences between Western Samoans and American Samoans; for most, they are all simply Samoans. In Honolulu, Samoans are popularly associated with crime, including organized crime, or they are stereotyped as wrestlers, Polynesian dancers, or football players. In fact, Samoans growing up in Hawaii, American Samoa, and California are heavily recruited by college football programs and the National Football League, where they have enjoyed a remarkable record of success, as *Sports Illustrated* noted in a story entitled "Shake 'Em Out of the Coconut Trees." Even better known is Olympic diving gold-medalist Greg Louganis, a part-Samoan. Overall, however, Samoans overseas are not regarded as a model minority. Their hard work and the millions of dollars they send back to their families in the islands are overlooked, and negative images abound in the media. It is almost as if Samoans, regarded as "noble savages" or "happy campers" in the islands, become dangerous and threatening when they migrate.

For Western Samoans themselves, even the limited opportunities they have overseas appear bright in comparison with their opportunities back in the islands, and almost all migrants agree that migration has been a good choice. Yet as an ethnic minority at the bottom of the social hierarchy, Samoans are having trouble abroad. In Hawaii and the continental United States, Western Samoans often live in government or substandard housing in crowded living conditions; they are poor, unemployment is high, and they live in or near crime-ridden areas. They suffer from stress, high rates of obesity, and high rates of hypertension (Janes 1990). Since some Western Samoans are illegal aliens, they are apprehensive about their status. While there is some evidence of upward mobility across generations, there is concern that these migrants will become a permanent part of the underclass.

Samoans themselves are acutely aware of these problems and their effect on young Samoans. In Seattle, where there are six thousand American and Western Samoans, Samoan activist Betty Patu described the situation candidly:

> So many of our children have gone by the wayside here.... Our kids are in and out of jails, they have the highest dropout rate in the Seattle public schools, they're joining gangs, they're using drugs. What is it? What is going on? Unless we train our kids right, our community is going to die. (Redmond 1989:1)

Patu had just won an award for her work with Samoan teens in local high schools.

Despite the hardships they face, Samoans persevere. Because Samoan migrants tend to live near each other, this concentration in communities allows Samoan churches of various denominations to flourish. Other organizations, including work groups, musical groups, sports groups, and political organizations, also thrive. As they adapt, Samoans have developed a distinctive overseas Samoan lifestyle. Yet there has been difficulty establishing organizations that speak for all Samoans; indeed, there has been competition and factionalism. And Samoans intermarry with other groups at surprisingly high rates. In New Zealand, one study in the 1970s indicated a rate of intermarriage of about one-third among young migrants, while in Hawaii a more recent study suggested a rate of intermarriage of over 40 percent. Samoan communities overseas, then, are both coalescing and changing in the migration process.

THE EFFECTS OF MIGRATION AND REMITTANCE ON WESTERN SAMOA

As more Western Samoans have left the islands for new lives abroad, migration has changed life in the islands. A complex of demographic and economic changes has occurred related to the exodus that, in turn, has encouraged even more migration. One of the most obvious of these changes has been in the rate of population growth for the islands. Migration has dramatically reduced growth and altered the distribution of population within Western Samoa.

For the past three decades, the islands have experienced increasing urbanization as well as external migration, both of which are closely related to the availability of wage-labor opportunities. By 1976, the Apia town area proper contained just under one-quarter of Western Samoa's economically active population over the age of fifteen and provided just under one-half of the country's wage-labor opportunities (Walsh 1982:95). When taken in conjunction with the urbanizing Northwest Upolu area, much of the country's population and wage-labor opportunities were in this single region; the population of this area grew more rapidly than other areas of Western Samoa.

The entire country grew at a rate of increase before migration of just under 3 percent a year. After migration, however, between 1971 and 1976, the overall population growth rate was 0.8 percent per year while the Apia area grew at 1.2 percent per year. Migration thus limited the growth of both urban and rural sectors. In 1974 and 1975, migration to New Zealand alone was so pronounced that the net population growth rate for the islands fell to 0.2 percent, alleviating the pressure put on the job market by high school graduates and providing millions of dollars in remittances.

Wage labor, whether in the port town or overseas, accelerated dependence on cash and more closely linked the people of Western Samoa with the outside world. The income benefits to Samoans were sizable as cash income and remittances supplemented other sources of money such as cash cropping. In fact, remittances increased at ten times the rate of agricultural revenues in the late 1960s and early 1970s. By the mid-1970s, remittances had become the most important source of cash income for most Samoans and a major component of the national income, exceeding agricultural exports. Yet in underdeveloped areas, wage labor and remittances, while benefiting individuals and families, can accentuate the economic vulnerability of the country as a whole. And this is what happened in Western Samoa.

In the 1960s, as incomes from cash cropping fell, cash income from wage labor in town and remittances from abroad allowed many families to preserve and/or increase their standard of living. But the benefits accruing to families back in the islands were offset by four economic trends, including: (1) a distortion of Western Samoa's balance of trade, (2) inflationary pressures fueling further dependence on wage labor and remittances, (3) corresponding changes in cash cropping, and (4) greater vulnerability to shifts in international economic trends. These trends are worth exploring in more detail.

For a family in the islands receiving $500 per year from a migrant son or daughter abroad, migration and remittances are obviously beneficial. For a family of eight, $500 might comprise one-third of its annual income. But what happens when millions of dollars in remittances flow into an underdeveloped nation? At the national economic level, remittances helped to alter the balance of trade in Western Samoa. Prior to the 1950s, when there was little capital investment, little foreign aid, and less wage labor in the government and private sectors, the cash economy was regulated almost entirely by production of agricultural exports for the world market. People could only purchase imported goods with money earned either directly or indirectly from agriculture, and any decline in agricultural earnings almost automatically resulted in a decline in import demand. By the late 1950s and 1960s, however, declines in agricultural income occurred without a subsequent fall in import demand. Indeed, demand increased, leading to ever-larger balance-of-trade deficits. Between 1969 and 1981, the value of imports increased by a factor of nine while the value of exports remained almost stationary. Much of this import demand was due to increased wage-labor employment in Western Samoa and to remittances from abroad.

The sums remitted were usually not large enough for investment in large-scale development or capital equipment, nor was there much incentive to invest. Remittances were also not large enough or regular enough to do much more than supplement other forms of cash income. Partly as a result of this and partly as a result of the institutions through which money and goods flow in Western Samoa, the bulk of remittances was spent on the kinds of things that money had been spent on in the past—consumption items, religious contributions, ceremonials, family events, education, and further migration. These expenditures led to an increase in economic activity and increased import demand, but did not improve the overall performance of the economy. In 1981, the cost of food imports alone exceeded the value of all exports. The islands were consuming more than they were producing.

The increasing reliance on imports fueled inflation. The cost of imported goods continued to increase much more rapidly than local income, whether generated in agriculture or wage labor. Between 1972 and 1981, the consumer price index for food quadrupled as inflation in Western Samoa rose more rapidly than in any other part of the South Pacific. Air fares increased and so did the cost of education and church contributions. Maintaining or improving a given standard of living therefore required having more wage earners either in town or overseas or both. Many households in Western Samoa opted for a strategy of multiple income streams—some subsistence and cash income from village agriculture, some cash income from relatives working in town, and some income from other relatives abroad. Since it was less difficult and more remunerative to obtain wage labor overseas in the early 1970s, more families sent sons and daughters away, especially to New Zealand; families themselves went as units, but in smaller numbers than single immigrants. Work parties, visiting groups, and other Samoan organizations also circulated through New Zealand, soliciting and bringing back remittances.

As a result of increasing incomes from remittances and wage labor in town, monetization of the rural sector increased in pace and the cost of participation in village activities also began to rise. This was due not only to inflationary increases in items purchased for ceremonials and church openings, but also because some of the traditional items formerly exchanged could now either be replaced or supplemented with cash and manufactured goods or with traditional items purchased with cash. Families with larger incomes could enter into such exchanges at a level impractical under the former lower-income, largely agricultural regime. Moreover, as cash led to the greater independence of the household economic unit within the extended kin group (a point discussed in detail in Chapter 9), inequalities within and between kin groups became more apparent. Local inequality encouraged migration and so, to obtain more money, Western Samoans sought more visas in the early 1970s. In some households, so many young people left that neither cash cropping nor subsistence activities could be sustained at previous levels.

As village agriculturalists became more reliant on other sources of cash income, the status of village agriculture itself diminished. The contrast between village agriculture and wage labor was not lost on those who had experienced both. As noted earlier, invidious comparisons favored wage labor, with its higher income paid at regular intervals and its more prestigious occupations. People who had grown up in Apia or who had worked or been educated there often found it difficult to return to the village; they viewed it as a step down. Migrants who had been abroad for several years, if they planned to return permanently, also found it difficult to return to village agriculture. Most often, returnees hoped to set up some kind of small business or to be retained in government service, the private sector, or the churches. Some saw the potential for making money in commercial agricultural ventures, but not in village agriculture. Many bought land near Apia, far from their home villages.

All of these trends—dependence on wage labor, balance of trade deficits, inflation, and the decline of village agriculture in areas most dependent on cash—were related. Individual households, pursuing multiple income strategies to respond to these trends, continued to be vulnerable to shifts in an economic environment that they could not predict. In responding to these changes, general economic trends were often aggravated rather than relieved. As Graham Harrison noted:

> A situation which had been changing over the past decade was triggered off by a period of low rainfall in 1972 causing a shortfall in the taro production, which in turn led to extra consumption of bananas and coconuts and the importation of staple foods such as rice, forcing more pressure on the import of protein foodstuffs, due to both inflation and fixed import allocations.... This lack of goods, and especially foodstuffs, required by large numbers of people now dependent upon the wage labour force, forced prices to rise dramatically, and people were only able to meet costs by getting large sums of money from New Zealand. (Harrison 1974:2)

Harrison was writing about the early 1970s when pressures for increased wage-labor opportunities were rising. When New Zealand increased its migrant quota, thousands more young Samoans left. Then, at the end of 1975, New Zealand began to sharply curtail migration from Western Samoa and a new set of problems arose.

RESTRICTIONS ON MIGRATION FROM WESTERN SAMOA

The restrictions on migration by the New Zealand government underscored the economic and political vulnerability of Western Samoa. As the world economy went into recession in the mid-1970s, overseas labor markets that employed Western Samoans shrank; Samoans were no longer needed or even necessarily welcome. In 1976, the new restrictions caused conflict between the governments of Western Samoa and New Zealand. The New Zealand government issued two categories of visas: temporary visas for short-term visits and permanent visas that allowed Samoans permanent residence in New Zealand. The new restrictions limited both, but there was particular friction concerning the Western Samoans who had overstayed their temporary visas and were to be shipped back to Western Samoa. Bitter words were exchanged over the issue, but, more importantly, between 1975 and 1976, the number of Western Samoan migrants to New Zealand was dramatically reduced; there was a drop of almost two-thirds in the permanent visa category alone. Waiting times for visas, already ranging from four months to two years, remained lengthy despite the cutback in overall volume.

This slowing of migration in the mid-1970s led to a temporary but steep drop in remittances. Without increases in other sources of cash income, the decline in remittances led to hardship for relatives back in the islands. Moreover, Samoan migrants in New Zealand, coping with recession and inflation in that country, found it difficult to send enough money home to offset the decline caused by changing New Zealand immigration policy and the increasing cost of living in Western Samoa.

The reduction of wage-labor opportunities in New Zealand in the mid-1970s brought another problem to the surface. For a number of years, the government of Western Samoa had explicitly viewed migration to New Zealand as a "population safety valve." As mentioned earlier, in 1974 and 1975, the growth rate after migration approached zero. Following the reduction in New Zealand migration, the specter of rapid population growth once again raised its head. The group most affected by the reduction in migration opportunities was the fifteen- to twenty-nine-year-old age bracket. Now these young people faced unemployment and underemployment. The problem was so serious that it was the central topic of the address by the Head of State at the opening of the Western Samoan Parliament in 1977.

One solution that the government of Western Samoa pursued was an ambitious multi-million-dollar rural development program aimed at moving the islands toward greater self-reliance and revitalizing rural agriculture. Beginning in 1977, the program attempted to reduce the past effects of migration by strengthening the rural sector. The rationale, in part, was that the multiple income strategy of most Samoan households could be modified with changing economic conditions; households had been flexible and could readjust to a more agricultural way of life.

The government's rural development plan, however, did not provide major incentives and rewards that would lead to a more long-term commitment to village agriculture by potential wage laborers and migrants. By the mid-1980s, this program had largely failed. By then, the economic situation in Western Samoa had deteriorated as balance-of-trade problems, stagnating agriculture, runaway inflation, a paralyzing strike, failed development plans, and limited migration opportunities crippled the nation. Foreign loans borrowed to pay for development plans could not be serviced, and, in 1982, the local Monetary Board intervened to devalue Western Samoan currency and limit imports. With austerity measures in force, this was an especially difficult period for young Samoans. From the mid-1970s through the early 1980s, youth suicide increased dramatically to among the highest rates in the world (Macpherson and Macpherson 1987).

While the availability of opportunities for migration to New Zealand and wage labor within the islands diminished after the mid-1970s, opportunities were still there and no less desirable. In the late 1970s, as New Zealand became more difficult to enter, Western Samoans emigrated by the thousands to American Samoa, the United States, and, to a lesser extent, Australia. At that time, American Samoa had extended an "open door" to temporary migrants from Western Samoa who were visiting their relatives. From there, Western Samoans found it relatively easy to enter Hawaii and the continental United States. However, by the mid-1980s, American Samoa became concerned that literally thousands of Western Samoans were staying for long periods of time, many without employment. And the U.S. Immigration Service in Hawaii began to tighten its screening of Western Samoan migrants after expressing concern over large numbers of illegal aliens. Australia also curtailed Western Samoan migration.

The most dramatic incident involving Western Samoan migration occurred in New Zealand in 1982. A Western Samoan facing deportation for overstaying a temporary visa filed a lawsuit, arguing that people born in Western Samoa before the end of New Zealand colonial rule in 1962 were really New Zealand citizens and were therefore entitled to live in New Zealand as New Zealanders. In a legal ruling that sent shock waves through the New Zealand government and the majority population, the Privy Council in England upheld this argument, which would have recognized New Zealand citizenship for roughly one hundred thousand Western Samoans, or about two-thirds of Western Samoa's population.

But New Zealanders feared a massive influx of Western Samoans as a result of this ruling. The New Zealand government sidestepped the Privy Council's ruling by granting New Zealand citizenship to all Western Samoans then in New Zealand rather than all Western Samoans eligible according to the ruling. At the same time, the New Zealand government negotiated an accord with the government of Western Samoa to prevent any substantial increase in migration from Western Samoa. Western Samoans, who favored open migration and New Zealand citizenship, protested and accused the New Zealand government of racism. But the restrictions remained in place (Macdonald 1986).

For Western Samoans, there was an historic irony in this incident. The islanders had worked for two generations to become independent from New Zealand and had succeeded in becoming the first independent country in the South Pacific twenty years before this case came to court. Yet, the situation in the islands had become so difficult that Western Samoans were now suing to become New Zealand citizens. The final outcome left little doubt as to just how far Western Samoans were willing to go to increase their economic opportunities. It also left little doubt about how far other countries were willing to go to restrict Western Samoan migration.

PROSPECTS FOR RETURN

Given the antagonism and hostility that they have faced overseas, Western Samoans might be expected to return to the islands. For older migrants, return is possible. Many older Samoans overseas talk about the better quality of life in Western Samoa, and there is a public ideology of return. Although New Zealand and the United States have considerable appeal for younger islanders, for older migrants, Western Samoa promises a satisfying way of life, security, and companionship. Furthermore, older Samoans are sometimes disenchanted with their lives abroad, having watched the acculturation process transform their sons and daughters. Many potential returnees contrast their lives in New Zealand with a more abundant and less-demanding way of life back in the islands.

However, despite rapt idealizations of their island homeland, few Western Samoans on permanent visas abroad permanently return to Western Samoa. Privately, they acknowledge a variety of influences keeping them overseas, including the number and kinds of kin in the area, jobs, income level, education, financial commitments, and the development of an alternative Samoan lifestyle abroad (Macpherson 1985). They may wish to stay with their children who have grown up overseas and prefer to stay there. Since there is a relatively high rate of intermarriage between Samoans and non-Samoans, this too may hinder permanent return. The fact that travel to Western Samoa for brief vacations is possible lessens the necessity for making a choice between one place or the other. Western Samoan citizenship can still be maintained for those permanently in New Zealand.

The factors that lead people to remain overseas are compounded by factors in Western Samoa that lessen chances for permanent return. Although people in Western Samoa can proudly point to families who have made a successful return, particularly those who have been able to set up a business or joined the civil service, these same people do not believe that most migrants will return to the islands permanently. Western Samoans note that many younger migrants left the islands precisely because they could not obtain wage-labor employment in Apia or because they lacked the education necessary for better employment. Without more education or unless they have been able to save while overseas, they are not likely to be in a competitive position upon return. Younger migrants are also reluctant to return permanently because they anticipate their reincorporation into the extended kin groups which they sought to escape.

There is also resentment toward those who have left the islands. Samoans who have remained behind sometimes feel that migrants left in order to avoid the family obligations that are ever-present in the islands. As one titleholder commented, reflecting on his responsibilities: "It takes real guts to live in Samoa and to have to reach down into your pockets when there is no money there. The people that went to New Zealand could not do this and that is why they left the islands." Resentment also arises because some of those who return tend to think they are "better" for having lived in New Zealand. Their relatives at home believe that they made the migrants' sojourns possible by their sacrifices; hence, in expecting money on the migrants' return, they are receiving only what is rightfully theirs. Returnees quickly learn that they are judged by what they can provide when they come back as well as by what they have accomplished abroad.

On their shorter visits to Western Samoa, permanent migrants visit their families, distribute what money and goods they have, and return overseas. Since the pressures to redistribute and to appear wealthy and successful can be intense, visitors attempt to calculate rather carefully how long appearances can be maintained and plan their visits accordingly. One returnee, in a rare discussion of impression management (*Samoa Times* 1977), explained that, while migrants desire to help their families and migrate partially for this reason, those who are left behind have only a limited understanding of life abroad, and the migrants themselves do not always want to convey what has actually happened to them since it may reflect poorly on their family's expectations of them. And so, unwilling to admit that money is scarce, migrants are pressured into giving at higher levels than they are able to afford. As this returnee confessed, "our families don't realize that money doesn't grow on trees [but] the fault lies with us because we do not tell them the whole truth which is why these illusions persist!"

Redistributive pressures on returnees are sometimes joked about; at other times, there is open apprehension about obligations to their relatives. In some cases, this concern may be so severe that individuals refuse to return to the village at all. One woman in her mid-forties visited from New Zealand on a number of occasions and, in 1977, was in Apia for two months in order to settle a land case. Although she would at times describe the village in glowing terms, at other times she was quite harsh, and she adamantly refused to go to the village due to the anticipated demands of distant relatives. Since the village was less than an hour by car from Apia, a visit would have been easy. This woman and her husband had been very generous to her mother and other close kin in the village, and she and her husband had given up a great deal to put their own six children through schools in New Zealand. What she objected to in the village was the pressure from more distant members of her extended kin group who also had claims on family resources. Her brother, a titleholder in the village, lived in town and went to the village only rarely for the same reasons. This woman was carefully planning her family's eventual return to the islands on a permanent basis, but the anticipated return would be to Apia rather than the village, partly in the hope of avoiding obligations to more distant kin. As she said, "We like Samoa, but not fa'a-Samoa ('the Samoan way')."

Other Samoans contemplating return cite different reasons for not doing so. One Samoan professional in New Zealand had purchased a piece of land near Apia for his family's return. However, subsequent visits convinced him that he could not afford to return. His salary in Western Samoa would be too low for him to build a proper house, and he felt he would not be able to afford education abroad for his children. He also believed that crime made Apia more dangerous to live in than Auckland.

Still another potential returnee found his visits to the island very stressful. He was a candidate for a high chiefly title that had been contested by various segments of his extended kin group for years. Each time he returned, competition for the title produced more anxiety and bitterness. He would ultimately remain in New Zealand.

Even under the best of circumstances, return is not easy. A firm commitment to village life and the sharing it entails do not ensure a positive outcome. In the village described in my earlier work (Shankman 1976), there was only one attempted return between 1966 and 1976 from among the dozens of permanent migrants to New Zealand. This young man, in his thirties, was particularly gifted and well-educated; he had planned his return carefully over a period of several years with brief visits to the village that were characterized by generosity. Having saved a substantial amount of money, he returned with his wife, purchased a car and piece of land in town, and set up a store in the village. He then gave the car to his wife's family and purchased a second car. Unfortunately, the store could not compete with the other stores already present in this village of about three hundred and fifty people, despite the heavy remittance-dependence of the villagers. He was forced to sell his land in town to compensate for the store's losses and to pay off the two cars. The second car, however, was repossessed and, rather than face the prospect of having to take up village agriculture, he and his wife took what money was left and purchased tickets for a flight back to New Zealand.

In the very process of returning home, then, visiting migrants are often confronted in a personal manner with the abstract trends that influence behavior and attitudes. As Pitt and Macpherson remark:

> ...the migrant himself has changed while he has been abroad whether he realizes it or not. He has built up new attitudes, new networks of commitments, constraints, and comforts which are hard to break. He may think he wants to go back to Samoa but if he does go—on holiday, for example—he is often glad to return to New Zealand. It seems that the closer the contact with the reality of home, the stronger is the migrant's resolve to consolidate his new life in New Zealand. Thus if the dream remains it seems likely that it is nostalgia for the past rather than a plan for the future. (Pitt and MacPherson 1974:15–16)

Samoans weigh, at different stages of their lives, the relative satisfactions and dissatisfactions of life overseas with life in the islands, including their limited mobility and the discrimination against them (Macpherson 1976, 1985). Interestingly, the wave of negative feelings toward Samoans during the New Zealand "overstayer" crisis of 1982 and the citizenship turmoil that followed did not produce a major return to the islands. Rather, it led to renewed efforts by Western Samoans to gain more security abroad.

The overwhelming direction of migration continues to be overseas. Return migration, in comparison, has been insignificant. Indeed, the return of more than some of the over sixty-eight thousand Western Samoans abroad in 1981 would be almost impossible for Western Samoa to accommodate. The task of increasing wage employment by even a thousand jobs is a staggering one for the financially weak Western Samoan government. Economic circumstances in Western Samoa and the opportunities abroad continue to make the pressure for migration as great as it has ever been.

CONCLUSION

The Samoan exodus has been a mixed blessing for Western Samoa and Western Samoans. For a tiny independent country, migration has meant lower population growth rates and increased national income from remittances; but there have been costs, too, mostly unanticipated, including national economic problems and inflation. Most of all, once the migration process has reached a certain momentum, it requires more migration to keep remittances flowing, to dampen population growth, and to provide employment that the islands cannot provide. As a result, Western Samoa has become more dependent on the wider world for migration opportunities. A recession overseas or restricted migration worsens the situation in the islands. In search of ways to reduce vulnerability, Western Samoa has received millions of dollars in foreign aid in recent years, but the projects thus funded have difficulty succeeding as long as migration is an alternative to local economic development.

For Western Samoans, national problems exacerbated by migration are of less concern than their families' futures. If migration increases economic dependency and vulnerability for the country, it is nevertheless advantageous for families to have sons and daughters abroad. Without them, their standard of living in the islands would certainly fall. Western Samoans want much of what we have; the question is how to get it in a country that cannot provide what its people want. Migration has become, over the past three decades, the major means by which families have improved their lives. People have become Western Samoa's most valuable export.

The future of Western Samoa is analogous to the experience of a character in a short story by Samoan author Albert Wendt (1974). In the story, a young man from a poor urban neighborhood in Apia migrates to New Zealand on a temporary basis. When he returns, he brings with him a suitcase full of European clothes and other goods. Everyday he reaches into the almost magical suitcase to impress his relatives and friends. Then, one day the suitcase vanishes. The young man has nothing, no clothes, no goods, no ability to impress. He is a Samoan again, just a poor Samoan.

Like the young man in the story, many Western Samoans have left their island homes to remit, to adapt, and to cope. Those fortunate enough to have permanent visas will not return except to visit; to do otherwise would be to risk the fate of the Samoan with the magical suitcase. Their lives abroad may be difficult, but their situation back in Western Samoa would be even more problematic. If Samoans ever were "happy campers," their lives today are more complex as the Samoan exodus from the islands continues.

NOTES

1. This paper builds on my earlier work in 1969–1970 and 1973 on Western Samoan migration sponsored by the National Science Foundation. The University of Colorado Council on Research and Creative Work provided funds for field work in Western Samoa in the summer of 1977. Additional short visits to Western Samoa were made in 1984 and 1986. A number of individuals have been very helpful in encouraging my research and thinking about the issues involved, including: Cluny Macpherson, Loia Fiaui, Robert Franco, Martin Orans, Karla Rolff, Craig Janes, Michael Bellam, John Connell, Bradd Shore, and Murray Chapman. Although my work has benefited from their research, they are not responsible for the ideas expressed herein. I am also grateful to Tim O'Meara for his detailed comments on an earlier draft of this paper.

   For reviews of the migration process and its wider context, a partial bibliography would include: Bedford and Lloyd (1982), Bellam (1982), Connell (1981, 1983, 1990), Douglas (1977, 1986), Fairbairn (1985), Franco (1987), Gibson (1983), Government of Western Samoa (1976), Janes (1990), Lewthwaite et al. (1973), Macpherson (1976, 1981, 1985), Pitt and Macpherson (1974), Shankman (1976), and Sutter (1989). I have drawn on these sources for this chapter.

11

Keeping Options Open:
Copra and Fish
in Rural Vanuatu

Margaret Critchlow Rodman
York University

Coconuts are so much a part of South Pacific life that palms and islands just seem to go together. Throughout the Pacific, island after island offers swaying palms and sandy beaches, scenes that are remarkably uniform from place to place and that have changed little over the past fifty years. Across the Pacific, the ways in which islanders have responded to a cash economy are also similar. Yet the introduction of cash-earning activities followed historical courses that were different in each region, each colony, and even each island.

   This chapter examines, first, what happened with the introduction of dried coconut (copra) as the major cash crop in Vanuatu (the former New Hebrides). Why did islanders (ni-Vanuatu) transform subsistence gardens into small plantations? How did they keep open their options for earning cash from other sources, and for social security through traditional activities? I then move stepwise from the hamlet to the global level. I discuss the implications of rural islanders' copra production for the monocrop export economy that emerged in Vanuatu and describe the vulnerability of that economy to world market forces. Islanders' responses to a copra crisis in the early 1980s illustrate both their flexibility and their reluctance to become too dependent on a single cash crop in times of uncertainty. Finally, the chapter evaluates a recent attempt to diversify the economy through the development of village fisheries in terms of the following question: Could fishing today have an impact on the rural islander's mode of production comparable to that of copra half a century ago? The development program's impact on women is of particular interest.

RURAL ISLANDERS AND COPRA PRODUCTION

Through the sandalwood trade in the first half of the ninteenth century and the labor trade in the second half, the people of Vanuatu became familiar with a wide range of new goods and practices. Commercial quantities of sandalwood were found between 1825 and the 1840s in the southern part of the archipelago, attracting traders who were soon followed by missionaries (Brookes 1969). Despite the traders' reputed ruthlessness, the islanders were not easily intimidated. They were very selective about what they would accept in trade (Shineberg 1967). Nor did they take kindly to the first missionaries. The London Missionary Society representative John Williams, his assistant, and three Samoan teachers were martyred as soon as they landed on Erromanga in 1839. Nevertheless, increased missionary activity on the part of Anglicans, Presbyterians, and Roman Catholics brought Christianity to most of the islands by the end of the nineteenth century.

Along with the missionaries and traders came new goods. Islanders at first sought such items as fishhooks and calico; later they also wanted tobacco, knives, other metal tools, muskets, and ammunition. New tools and such items as cooking pots and cloth changed the way of life in the islands, reducing the amount of time spent on daily tasks and increasing mortality in armed conflict. Islanders continued to cultivate swidden gardens and, by and large, to provide for their own subsistence; but they began to sell their labor as well as their resources, such as sandalwood, specifically to obtain these new goods.

Those with access to the white men's goods had a new source of power. Part of that power consisted of increased knowledge of the world beyond the village. Anglican missionaries brought young men from Vanuatu to New Zealand, and later to Norfolk Island, to attend college. In 1847, sixty-five Vanuatu men were recruited to work in Australia, the first of thousands to participate in what became known as the Labor Trade. Most went to Queensland, where the sugar industry needed a steady supply of cheap, docile labor. The abuses of recruiting ships, also known as "blackbirders," are well known and the inadequacy of attempts to regulate the trade helped to end recruiting by the turn of the century.[1] In some instances, islanders were kidnapped and abused, but other men—and in smaller numbers women—signed on willingly.

The reasons for going to Queensland often had to do with a desire for adventure and for the goods that were offered in payment for one's labor. As in the days of the sandalwood trade, islanders' participation in the labor trade (at least insofar as that participation was voluntary) was linked to consumption goals. Laborers wanted the trunk filled with cloth and, at times during the trade, a musket that was their due at the end of a contract. Leaders extracted goods from the less powerful, returned laborers, and again as with sandalwood, islanders quickly established the best terms of trade that they could. There were clear preferences concerning destinations as well as trade goods.

Plantations within Vanuatu, compared to those in Australia or even Fiji, were never popular destinations with islanders. Until the 1880s, foreigners cultivated relatively little land in the archipelago. During the American Civil War, planters grew cotton for British markets. After 1880, coconuts became the main crop, supplemented by cocoa and coffee in some areas. During this period, French interests acquired large landholdings in the islands. Conflict between the British and French led to the establishment of the Condominium of the New Hebrides, formalized by the Protocol of 1914. This was an unusual and inefficient form of colonialism whereby France and Britain jointly administered the islands. Paired institutions proliferated under the Condominium, including two currencies, two health care systems, and two police forces.

The requirement that both resident commissioners had to agree on everything that was done ensured that very little was accomplished and that everything took a great deal of time. The missions had limited funds and manpower to provide social services, but, until the 1950s, they ran the only systems of health care and education in the islands. Thus, it was in everyone's interest that the islanders continue to provide for their own social security, even if they were urged to abandon those aspects of customary behavior deemed to be at odds with their new Christian lives. In many places, the islanders kept alive their customary systems of land tenure, reciprocity, ceremonial exchange, kinship and traditional medicine, and so could attend to their own well-being. This they did, even developing their own legal systems in some islands (see Chapter 4, "The Law of the State and the State of the Law in Vanuatu," by William Rodman, in this volume), and maintaining a deep-rooted sense of their fundamental autonomy that shrugged off the rivalries of the British and French, or *tufala gavman*, as a white men's problem.

During the first half of the twentieth century, ni-Vanuatu became more deeply involved in the market economy. They began to produce their own copra and form small trading companies. Experience gained working on white men's plantations, along with encouragement from missionaries and traders, led ni-Vanuatu to start their own small coconut plantations on customary landholdings in the outer islands where large plantations had not been established. Missionaries encouraged coconut production as part of their efforts to introduce a work ethic and to provide islanders with a source of cash with which to purchase cloth and other Western goods. Traders encouraged rural coconut production to transform islanders into both suppliers of copra and consumers of trade store goods. They also provided the market linkages essential to local copra production.

People planted coconuts in lowland gardens, so that once the food crop had been harvested, the palms could continue to grow in the abandoned garden. As more people followed this practice, moving from garden to garden year by year and sometimes clearing larger tracts of land expressly for plantations, some areas of Vanuatu were given over entirely to coconuts. A canopy of coconut palms rising from hundreds of smallholder plots came to cover entire coastal plains.

Islanders sold their coconut meat to traders who lived locally or who dealt from ships. At first, raw coconut meat was sold, but ni-Vanuatu soon learned to dry the coconut flesh, turning it into copra and earning a higher price for their product. The technology was simple. Minimum requirements were an ax to split the coconuts and a curved metal blade to scoop out the meat. The coconut could then be dried in the sun or smoke-dried on a "bed" made of local timber and a wire-mesh screen. Copra production fit easily into the rhythm of rural life as a part-time activity to pursue when one wanted cash.

By 1930, rural smallholders produced about one-sixth of all copra exported from the country (in 1982, they produced three-quarters of all copra exports). As their own plantations grew and islanders were able to gain the Western goods they wanted through labor on their own plantations, they were less and less willing to work on white men's plantations, except when the copra price was low; but, of course, when the copra price was low, white planters were reluctant to hire more labor. In times of prosperity, ni-Vanuatu began to employ other islanders as plantation labor.[2] Some started their own trading enterprises with copra profits and did well because they could live more cheaply than white traders and could therefore undercut their prices

Chiefs often took the lead in adopting cash cropping in Vanuatu, as elsewhere in Melanesia (Finney 1973). In Longana (E. Ambae), the part of Vanuatu with which I am most familiar, chiefs were feared and respected as warriors and probable sorcerers before pacification in the 1930s (M. Rodman 1983).[3] The aura of this power over life and death seems to have remained throughout their lifetimes, despite the end of warfare. They used the communal labor of their many wives and the followers who had lived under their protection to clear large tracts of bush for coconut plantations. Much of this land was brought into coconut production on the basis of what other Longanans recognized, even in the 1940s, to be flimsy land claims, but few were willing to protest their leaders' actions. In this way, a handful of men came to control far more plantation land than others. These were the men described as "masters of tradition" (Rodman 1987b). They were able to use their mastery of the graded society (based on pig exchanges) and their traditional knowledge of kinship, land tenure, and other customary domains to dominate the new sphere of cash-cropping coconuts. Often, their heirs have been able to keep these large holdings intact. In 1979, 5 percent of the landholders controlled 31 percent of the land planted in coconuts. Their annual incomes from copra averaged $9,500 (Australian), while overall the average copra income per landholder was only A$2,300.

Income differences are one sign of increasing social differentiation in Longana. Wealthier landholders employ fellow islanders as wage laborers. But differentiation has not proceeded very far for several reasons. First, tradition has masked new forms of inequality, making wealthy landholders appear to be nothing more than exemplars of a customary model of success. Second, redistribution of wealth in the form of pigs and mats exchanged ceremonially, and both money and business opportunities provided for kinsmen, have helped to level income inequalities. Third, there have been few ways for the rich to get richer in Longana. Development projects and investment opportunities were rare before independence and are only beginning now to reach the rural areas (M. Rodman 1987b).

The Domestic Mode of Production

Today, a domestic form of production rather than a communal or village mode predominates in much of Vanuatu. In Longana, the household is the basic unit of both copra and subsistence production. Now that plural marriage is no longer practiced, a husband and wife are the nucleus of the household, with dependent children and/or parents included for some periods of the domestic cycle. A healthy adult male could produce a metric ton of copra (1,000 kilograms) in about nine days. A husband and wife working together with some help from children or older people could expect to make a ton of copra in three or four days.

While the labor time involved in producing a ton of copra is predictable, the price is not, even with the price stabilization provided in recent years by the Vanuatu Commodities Marketing Board. For example, in July 1987, a ton of copra sold for A$320. One year earlier, it was worth half that amount. Consequently, rural islanders work to achieve particular targets or goals. Instead of making copra to make money, small producers make copra to buy things. Notably, the producers in my sample (sixty-eight people) remembered how much they had produced in terms of the specific reason they had made the copra, such as to buy a sewing machine, pay school fees, or finance a wedding.

Most islanders remain intermittent copra producers, following a well-documented "targeting pattern" of making copra to achieve specific consumption goals (Brookfield with Hart 1971:262; Bollard 1978:326; M. Rodman 1987b). The only Longanans who make copra regularly are a few entrepreneurs who have inherited larger plantations (often established by chiefs in the 1930s and 1940s). Most people cut copra when they need money, and otherwise tend their pigs, their gardens, and their family obligations. When they make copra, they make enough to achieve a particular consumption goal.

In summary, by the 1930s, islanders had learned to produce their own copra and to trade in the Western economy to which they had been introduced first by sandalwood traders, then missionaries, planters, labor recruiters, and finally by the colonial Condominium. The people of Vanuatu took active roles as participants in these new marketplaces. They insisted on particular goods, particular destinations as laborers, and other terms of trade. The most powerful took particular advantage of the goods, and especially the guns, that Westerners brought. These men also took advantage of local traditions to bring large areas of land under coconut production, land to which other less-powerful people also had claims that they feared to press. Except for those among the heirs of these large landholders who have become entrepreneurs and regularly harvest their coconuts, most islanders are intermittent copra producers. Coconuts have become an important part of the domestic economy, alternating with, but not replacing, subsistence gardening and pig husbandry. Coconuts provide a ready source of cash that supplements the social security islanders obtain through customary exchanges and kinship networks. Coconuts, then, offer one option among other more traditional ones for islanders to ensure their self-reliance.

VANUATU COPRA IN THE GLOBAL ECONOMY

Vanuatu's domestic export earnings from copra have ranged from 46 percent of total exports for the decade 1967–1977 to 76 percent in 1981. Clearly, copra exports dominate the country's economy, a dependence that has made the government vulnerable in bargaining with copra buyers overseas. Revenue earned from copra fluctuates due to climatic conditions, such as cyclones and drought, but erratic movements in the world price of copra account for most of the variation in domestic export income. Vanuatu's other major exports include cocoa and coffee, commodities whose price variations often coincide with those of copra. Moreover, the quantity of copra exported by the country is insignificant on the world market. In contrast to Vanuatu's 1981 copra exports of about forty thousand tons, the Philippines produces over two million tons of copra annually, or 85 percent of the world's coconut product exports. The economy of Vanuatu is at the mercy of a market it can scarcely influence, much less control.

The average rural Vanuatu family has 3 hectares under coconuts with annual yields of only 600 to 700 kilograms of copra per hectare.[4] Until the introduction of a marketing board in 1982, there was no government control over production and little regulation of trading. What has been described elsewhere as the "chain of copra" (see M. Rodman

1987b) passed most of the marketing costs back to the rural producer. The "beach price" he or she received for a bag of copra was relatively unresponsive to international price increases and more responsive to a falling market. Islanders responded to instability by withdrawing from copra production when the prices were very low. They could do this because coconut palms are hardy and require minimal attention (Brookfield 1971:148). Small producers also tended to work toward cash targets, so that they might actually sell less copra at higher prices.

Historically, France purchased as much as 90 percent of Vanuatu's copra exports because copra from the ex-colony enjoyed duty-free entry. But France and northern European copra buyers discounted the price paid for Vanuatu copra because of the poor quality of the product. The economist J.S.G. Wilson recognized the precariousness of the archipelago's copra market position in his 1966 survey:

> If there were no import duty and New Hebrides copra was offered at the same price as foreign copra, the importers in Marseilles would tend to prefer foreign copra, because on the whole it is of rather better quality. It has only been because of its relative price advantage that New Hebrides copra has been able to hold its own for so long....(Wilson 1966:101)

In the late 1970s, demand for copra began to decline markedly. A general destabilization of the soft edible-oils market followed the commodities boom of 1972-1974 (FAO 1982:12). The subsequent fluctuation in world prices for soybeans, which dominate the edible-oils market, together with a slowdown in the growth rate of demand for tropical oils, limited the marketability of low-quality coconut oils. Then, in 1980, vegetable-oil prices plummeted due to higher output, the world recession, and the U.S. embargo on food sales to the Soviet Union associated with the war in Afghanistan. The Soviet grain embargo glutted the soybean market and affected coconut oil prices for the entire year (Sacerdoti 1982:45).

Given Vanuatu's traditional dependence on copra sales to France, the closing of a single, antiquated, and unprofitable copra crushing mill in Marseilles was enough to precipitate a national crisis in the islands. In February 1981, the mill that purchased most of Vanuatu's copra exports ceased operations. The bulk of Vanuatu's copra then was sent to Unilever mills in Germany that previously had processed only about 3 percent of the country's copra. But Unilever pronounced the copra quality unacceptable; the June shipment, for example, contained "pieces of plastic, timber, and string as well as burnt and wet copra" (*TamTam* 1981:1). Vanuatu was given six months to improve the quality of its copra or lose its one remaining market for the export commodity on which the country's economy depended. As Prime Minister Lini put it, "If copra producers do not succeed in improving the quality of their copra by then, Vanuatu's prospects of future copra exports are almost nil" (*TamTam* 1982:1).

Initially, the Prime Minister's exhortations had little effect. Producers in the islands were fearful that they could not make acceptable copra, so rather than wasting their efforts producing an unsalable product people simply stopped making copra. This response was identical to rural smallholders' responses to very low prices in the past when an inadequate return on the investment of labor led to a cessation of cash crop production in favor of subsistence production, despite an almost total absence of alternative sources of cash.

The copra quality crisis of 1981-1982 took Vanuatu by surprise. Planners knew that world demand for copra had declined by about 10 percent annually for the preceding decade (FAO 1983:165), but postindependence attempts to diversify the export economy had only begun, and structures for improving both the quality of copra and the vertical integration of the copra market were only in the planning stages in 1981. Reduced to dealing with a solitary and skeptical buyer, Vanuatu had no choice but to show a determination to improve the quality of its product. This meant finding a way to motivate rural producers both to resume making copra and to make it better.

A media campaign with a great deal of radio time was the core of the government's plan. The work of agricultural staff supplemented the media campaign in areas producing the worst copra. The goal was to achieve an immediate improvement in copra quality simply by eliminating practices that produce an unacceptable product (such as too hot a fire or too short a drying period). "Kopra Man" t-shirts and comic books helped to convince smallholders that they could produce good-quality copra without making major changes in the production process.

The process of educating rural copra growers was tricky. They often responded to uncertainty by withdrawing from the market, and the uncertainty during this crisis was great. Patient, repetitive explanation in a context of respect for rural people was important. The Kopra Man comic book encapsulated a Vanuatu style of knowledge transmission in an effective literary form. Kopra Man's appearance was youthful, but his moustache suggested a stylish maturity. His facial expression was nonthreatening, his eyes and mouth had a friendly expression, and the set of his brows was neutral. Kopra Man was willing to answer the comic-book farmers' questions. He did not deliver an unsolicited lecture on agricultural techniques. The problem of copra quality, as presented in the comic, lay not with the producer but with the use of confusing technical terms concerning copra quality. The assumption was that once the terms were clearly understood, the islanders would be able to recognize—and therefore control—the quality of the product.

The information phase of the copra-improvement scheme was successful in raising the standard of Vanuatu smoke-dried copra and in overcoming the initial withdrawal of small-holders from copra production. By April 1982, agricultural officers noted an improvement in copra quality due simply to slower and more complete drying over smaller fires, better storage, rejection of sprouted coconuts, an improvement in general cleanliness, and cessation of the practice of ramming sacks of dried copra to increase the bag-weight.

Although rural farmers were willing and able to improve production techniques in a crisis situation, price incentive would be crucial to the long-term improvement of copra quality. A problem facing planners in Vanuatu is that the country must export a higher-quality product just to maintain its market. The few transnational corporations who buy copra, such as Unilever, can afford to be increasingly selective as the demand for coconut oil drops steadily relative to other edible oils, and supplies remain fairly constant.

As essential as the production of good copra is to the Vanuatu economy, the difference between world prices for high- and low-grade copra is too small to make conversion to hot-air drying economical for Vanuatu producers. Deep subsidies would be necessary to raise the standard of production. Even then, there is no guarantee of a secure position vis-à-vis the transnationals. In sum, the copra crisis of 1981–1982 is simply a dramatic illustration of a chronic condition, highlighting the economic vulnerability that

dependence on copra as a predominant export has produced. The crisis contributed to the
national government's determination to diversify the economy. Deep-water, artisanal fishing
is one such attempt at diversification that began at the time of the copra quality crisis.

DIVERSIFYING THE COPRA ECONOMY: VILLAGE FISHERIES DEVELOPMENT

The ocean is an obvious resource for Vanuatu to develop in efforts to diversify the
monocrop coconut economy. The land area of the archipelago is small (less than 14,000
square kilometers) compared to territorial waters that span 680,000 square kilometers of
sea (Ridings 1983). In 1976, offshore resources began to assume new importance when
the South Pacific forum introduced 200-mile nautical zones.[5] The United Nations sanctioned 200-mile Exclusive Economic Zones in 1982 (Bergin 1983:20–21; *Asia Yearbook*
1984:112). Vanuatu Islanders are not known for their maritime orientation, perhaps
because many lived in the interiors of the larger islands prior to pacification. Nevertheless,
a recent survey found that ni-Vanuatu depend considerably on the sea for food. About half
of the rural households in Vanuatu regularly take some of their food from the sea. The
total annual catch of finfish and shellfish was estimated to be 2,403 tons in 1985 (David
1985:6). More than three-quarters of this total was for subsistence. Two-thirds of these
fish and shellfish were found within the reef, where a large variety of seafood is relatively
easy to catch. Outside the reef the variety of fish is much less and there are few shellfish.[6]

My research in Port Olry (Santo Island) indicated that households eat fresh fish at about
three evening meals a week. Ample supplies of fish were part of the diet, and this had been
the case long before the introduction of fisheries development schemes. On the Longana
(Ambae) coast, the consumption of fresh fish from within the reef is low by comparison with
Port Olry. Sea crabs or reef fish are sometimes featured at a feast, and a few households eat
fresh fish often, but in contrast to Port Olry, fresh fish is not common in the Longana diet.

In 1982, Port Olry became host to one of the first projects in the Village Fisheries
Development Program (VFDP). I conducted an evaluation of this project in 1985 for the
Canadian volunteer organization CUSO,[7] and later wrote a book about this project and
others in the group (M. Rodman 1986, 1989). The expressed intent of the VFDP as a whole
was (1) to meet demands for fish in both urban and rural areas and to substitute
progressively for imported tinned fish; (2) to generate employment and income in the
rural areas; and (3) to provide an important source of protein (Vanuatu 1984:117). The
Port Olry project grew into one of the program's largest. By 1985, it consisted of fifteen
privately owned fishing boats and a fish-buying association with a cold room. A much
smaller VFDP project began in 1983 in Longana. It involved a single, 8-meter, catamaran
fishing boat. Both projects had the assistance of volunteers from CUSO, a Canadian
nongovernment organization, for the first two years. By 1985, nearly one hundred VFDP
projects were scattered throughout Vanuatu. Most were similar to the Longana project in
that they were very small. And most involved only men.

Women's options regarding fisheries development are limited, in any case, by the
rarity with which women traditionally fish from canoes in many parts of Vanuatu. Most
often, women fish and glean within the reefs, and fishing from boats in deep water is
men's work, where it is done at all. But, as elsewhere, Vanuatu women are involved in fish

marketing. In this area they, like the men, seek to keep their options open and pursue strategies of self-reliance through diversification of productive activities. And, of course, they have been affected as consumers of fish.

In fact, a woman was the prime mover behind the establishment of a fishing association in Port Olry. Women were both the biggest beneficiaries and the biggest losers in this fishing project, as this story of the strong woman behind the fishing association reveals. In 1985, Celia Sarsom was forty-four years old, and she was probably the most influential person in the village, although she held no office. Celia's style was to be tough, direct, and outspoken. But in public, she conformed to local expectations of feminine behavior. She dressed like the other women in bright-colored Mother Hubbard dresses. She sat with the other women on the fringes of social gatherings.

Celia's father had been the village chief when she first considered the idea of starting a new fishing association. It seemed a risky undertaking, partly because her father's reputation had foundered on an earlier community venture. Subsequently, the leader of a rival faction in the village had attempted to establish a fishing association, but participants felt that the organizer was absconding with their money and the enterprise failed. Still, the possibility of building up a viable fishing business intrigued Celia.

In 1980, she and her husband began buying fish to sell at the town market. Soon there were times when she had more fish than she could chill. The fish-marketing business was bigger than she had expected.

In February 1982, Celia was approached at the market by a white man, a Canadian CUSO volunteer whose job was to organize village fisheries development in the north of Vanuatu. Gradually, the Canadian and Celia began to make plans to start a fish-marketing association in the village. The Canadian was careful to be sure that Celia felt the local people really wanted such an association. And he was careful to point out what the association might cost her personally. He told Celia that a new fishing association would drive her out of business. She would no longer be able to sell fresh or frozen fish at the market because, first, the association would handle all the fish from the village and, second, a fish market with proper cold storage in town would mean that for health reasons, market women would no longer be allowed to sell fresh fish.

He remembers Celia's response well because it surprised him. "That's great!" she said, "I don't need that work. I have more fish than I can handle, and I have more than enough other business." She seemed quite happy to put herself out of a job, but in a way she was only putting the other women who sold fish at the market out of work, for she immediately invested her own money and time in organizing the fishing association.

Just as the Canadian volunteer saw potential in village fishermen, Celia quickly recognized the potential benefit to her family in organizing the fishing association as a village fisheries development project. First, she knew she would have the government and the expertise of Canadian fishermen on her side. Second, as a woman, she could deal more directly with a white Canadian male than with Melanesian men in her village. Third, she could put the Canadian and the Vanuatu fisheries department between herself and the rival faction in the village, and hopefully avoid drawing a connection in local peoples' minds between this venture and the previous fishing association fiascos. Fourth, she was able to mediate the local impact of both CUSO and the Fisheries Department and serve as the mouthpiece for local opinion on which the outsiders depended. Finally, she encouraged the career of a close male relative who became manager of the association when the CUSO volunteer returned to Canada at the end of his contract.

Clearly, one woman benefited greatly from the fishing project—Celia. Just as clearly, the other market women suffered. But, less obviously, another category of women who had the least to begin with has quietly benefited. These are the 14 percent of the households in the village (population six hundred) headed by single women. Unless there is a boy in the household big enough to catch fish for the family, these women could only depend on the generosity of others who might share their catch of deep water fish. Single women who are household heads have little money, and they recognize that fresh fish offers good food value for a reasonable price (about A$1 per kilogram). So the fishing association became a convenient, regular source of fresh fish that especially helped these women. Although the market women who could no longer sell fresh fish suffered in the short run from the project, their options were not ultimately curtailed. They simply began to prepare cooked fish which they could still sell legally at the market.

The expectation behind this small-scale fisheries development program was that participants would at least go fishing regularly, if not full-time, and that they would sell their catch either locally, as in the Longana case, or to two urban fish markets, as in the case of the Port Olry fishing association. The program sought at least to extend the depth and breadth of islanders' participation in the cash economy. It sought to develop domestic markets for fish, with the possibility of building an export market, as part of a long-range plan to achieve national self-reliance.

The Fisheries Department of the Vanuatu government intended for the VFDP to prepare the way for a second generation of commercial fishermen. These islanders would fish full-time in 10-meter, diesel-powered boats, for which larger loans obviously would be necessary. Greater indebtedness would require the captain to fish regularly and productively. Such fishermen would have little time for gardening or making copra. Instead, they would become participants in a capitalist mode of production.

For many reasons, this has yet to happen. So long as islanders retain relatively easy access to gardens and coconuts, they are not compelled to sell their labor on a full-time basis, as either crew members or captains. The Vanuatu state so far has made little effort to impose constraints that would force people to enter a capitalist mode. It is clear that the state lacks the resources to provide the social services that would be necessary if capitalism supplanted the domestic mode of production, and social reproduction in rural areas. The collection of a head tax has a long history of rural opposition, as have attempts to alienate or even register titles to land. Customary land tenure is enshrined in the constitution, and the idea of someone having no access to land remains anathema. For all of these reasons, the government has not used, nor could it use, a big stick to transform the mode of production in Vanuatu.

In addition, there are particular reasons why fishing has had little impact in this regard. Fisheries development so far has failed to achieve a transformation of the mode of production in Vanuatu partly because of problems with the program. First, the prototype of the larger fishing boats sank during maiden trials in 1985. Second, the extent of the resource remains uncertain, and ongoing research indicates that 100 small projects may be the maximum that can be sustained, partly because of the slow maturation rate of deep-water species. Third, problems associated with intermittent production, widely scattered projects, the expense of reliance on air freight, and the perishability of the product continue to inhibit the development of a marketing infrastructure. But, more fundamentally, the VFDP projects have yet to become viable businesses that can stand on their own without subsidies of various kinds. They remain imitations of real businesses, and they would not be financially viable even on paper were it not for government grants and loans, subsidized fuel, and "cargo"—that is, capital goods such as motors, freezers, and cold rooms provided as foreign aid to Vanuatu, especially by Japan. "Cargo" is often more available than staff and therefore becomes the "solution" to problems. A new motor may be easier to obtain than a mechanic, for example.

THE IMPACT OF COPRA AND COMMERCIAL FISHING COMPARED

Even without basic changes to the mode of production, might the VFDP at least have had an impact equivalent to that of the introduction of copra? Theoretically, the program's objectives could be met simply by extending participation in capitalist markets without other changes in the traditional economy. This was the way in which copra had earlier been incorporated. That is, if islanders could be motivated to fish on a frequent and regular basis, the program's goals could be met without fundamental changes to the domestic mode of production in the islands. People would still tend their gardens, raise their pigs, look after ceremonial and other social obligations, and make copra. They would simply add fishing to these options as they added copra a half-century or more in the past. But this would help to diversify the country's economy only if people who fished generated at least as much cash as their forgone copra incomes had generated, or if they took up fishing as a net addition to commercial activity, perhaps filling some of what had been "leisure time" in this way.

Commercial fishing has indeed been incorporated into the local economy, following the pattern established with cash-cropping coconuts—that is, a pattern of intermittent, targeted production for the market without participating in a capitalist mode of production. Like copra production, commercial fishing is intermittent, not only because there are alternate ways to earn money, but also because it competes with noncommercial demands on peoples' time. Villagers reserve time for subsistence gardening, leisure, social obligations, and recreation. The 1984 agricultural census found that Santo men spend 16 percent of their working time in their gardens and 31 percent in leisure activities. In fact, diversity seems to be valued for its own sake. In research I conducted on work, ni-Vanuatu ranked desk jobs among the most difficult because these jobs were seen to be the most monotonous. But diversity also is important to rural people because the state provides no pension, unemployment insurance, or the like for its citizens. Social security remains a matter of custom, informally looked after in the villages. Only by maintaining access to their means of production and reproduction—in other words, by maintaining a variety of potential sources of income, food, and social support—can rural islanders ensure continued self-reliance. Ironically, this strategy of individual self-reliance inhibits the achievement of national self-reliance and constrains capitalist development (M. Rodman 1987a).

Another similarity between fishing and copra—and another reason for intermittent participation in both activities—is the possibility of opting out. Islanders withdraw from fishing for the market in response to social and economic conditions in much the same way as they cease copra production when a low price or poor terms of trade reduce producer motivation. Elsewhere I have described some of the ways in which islanders, who have no control over the prices they receive for their copra, nevertheless control other terms of trade (Rodman 1987b). For example, on one occasion when Longana was completely out of gasoline, islanders refused to sell their copra until a ship brought them fuel in exchange. Most producers maintain an "exit option" (Hyden 1980), so that they can withdraw from one kind of commercial activity into another, or into gardening, when social or economic conditions make production for the market unattractive.

Islanders can use this exit option to gain bargaining power in commercial fishing in much the same way as they do in the context of copra production. For example, the fifteen fishing boats of Port Olry village have a reputation for "going on strike." If they are unhappy with the manager, as was all too often the case in this project, which was beset with local political problems, or if the return to labor seems inadequate, Port Olry fishermen don't stop fishing for food, but they do stop fishing for money. There, fishing boats have supplemented but not replaced outrigger canoes, of which twenty-nine were in use in October 1985. Most subsistence fishing continues to be done from canoes on a daily basis because these vessels are convenient and cost virtually nothing to operate. The availability of both fishing boats and canoes have provided village fishermen with new options to fish commercially or to feed the family. It is, however, a relatively minor option.

Despite similarities in the ways islanders have made commercial fishing part of their way of life, it remains an insignificant source of cash compared to copra. A range of activities compete with fishing for the time a producer devotes to earning an income. In Port Olry, alternate activities include copra and cocoa production, ten stores, sixteen truck-taxi businesses, market gardening, collecting and selling lobsters and coconut crabs, sales of pigs, and sales of cattle to the Luganville abattoir. The people of Port Olry (population approximately six hundred) earned an estimate total income of more than A$500,000 in 1985, of which fish sales constituted about A$18,000, a distant third as a source of income after copra (A$331,000) and cattle (A$34,500). All but three Port Olry fishermen earned more money from copra than they did from fish in 1985. At that time, one could earn A$150 per week from copra. In comparison, those who sold fish averaged a mere $5.68 per working week from these sales. Of the 79 men who sold fish to the association in my sample of 1,044 cases, only four earned incomes of more than A$1000 per year from fish.

Why has the impact of fisheries development not been as great as that of copra a half-century earlier? The answers to this question also suggest what it would take for real diversification of the copra economy to occur, even without basic changes to the mode of production. One reason for the minimal impact of fisheries development is simple. Intermittent copra production has become so deeply a part of life in the islands that, so long as there is a market, no other commodity is likely to displace it as the main source of cash in rural areas. Islanders learned how to make copra on expatriate plantations before they planted their own commercial stands. There have been no such learning opportunities with deep-water handlining, except for the projects assisted by expatriate volunteers.

Moreover, the pattern of intermittent production characteristic of the island economy works better with coconuts. So does the pattern of allowing kin and affines access to plantation land that a chief controls. A neglected palm tree will survive longer than a neglected fishing boat or outboard motor. Lending a boat holds much greater risks to the owner than lending access to a plantation. Copra itself is less perishable than fish. Finally, it has usually been easy for islanders to find a buyer for their copra, although the price they receive may be very low, but markets for fish are less fully developed. Fishermen unable to sell all or part of their catch may be discouraged from continuing. This in turn means an unreliable supply for those attempting to develop fish markets. To a much greater extent, the copra market preceded smallholder production.

CONCLUSION

Since the introduction of copra production, rural islanders have had one foot somewhat tentatively in the capitalist marketplace and the other squarely in a lifestyle based on values and relationships that are very different from those underlying a capitalist way of life. They have participated in the cash economy mainly through small-scale copra production, although a variety of other activities offer alternative ways to earn money, and islanders have done so instrumentally, to reach limited target incomes oriented to specific consumption goals. Copra production historically was incorporated into the islanders' way of life on their own terms, as well as the terms dictated by the international and domestic market. Copra has remained an adjunct to an economy based on subsistence gardening and elaborate exchanges of mats and pigs. It has deepened islanders' ties to the cash economy, but it has not made the major changes in the domestic mode of production that would signal a transition to capitalism. By and large, people retain access to plantations and the land they need for gardening, even where the accretion of smallholdings into large plantations has been a legacy of warrior leaders. They have been able to do so partly because of the selectiveness for which islanders became known in the days of the sandalwood and labor trades. By opting out of copra production or by withholding copra from the market, islanders can affect terms of trade that are otherwise beyond their control.

However effective islanders' attempts are to manipulate terms of trade in copra locally, the country as a whole has virtually no influence on the international copra market. The copra-quality crisis of 1982 dramatically illustrated this dependence, and encouraged national efforts to diversify the monocrop economy. The Village Fisheries Development Program was one such strategy for diversification.

The results of the VFDP have been disappointing at the national level, in that it appears not to have increased the overall productive activity of the islanders. Commercial fishing has been incorporated as an intermittent activity, but not as a net increase to the cash economy. Working to earn money is still tied to specific consumption goals. Islanders use fish, as they have used copra, as a way to reach particular consumption targets. Thus, fishing projects have diversified the economy only minimally. So far, they have simply strengthened the subsistence sector and extended the options facing islanders who want some access to cash.

Acknowledgments: I am grateful to The Social Sciences and Humanities Research Council of Canada for supporting my research in 1978–1979 as doctoral student, in 1982 as a postdoctoral fellow, and in 1985–1986 as an independent scholar. McMaster University and the University of Waterloo also provided funding for portions of this research, which I acknowledge with appreciation. As always, I am grateful to the people of Vanuatu for sharing their way of life with myself and my family.

NOTES

1. See, for example, Corris (1970) and Scarr (1967).

2. MacClancy (1981:88). See also W. Rodman (Chapter 4) for a description of current practices of employing local labor among Ambae smallholder plantation owners and analysis of the implications of this practice for social differentiation.

3. See W. Rodman (Chapter 4) for a discussion of our reasons for using the term *chief* rather than *bigman* to refer to men of wealth, rank, and influence.

4. Republic of Vanuatu, *First National Development Plan, 1982–1986*. Port Vila: National Planning Office, p. 128.

5. The Law of the Sea Convention held in April 1982 by the 3rd United Nations Conference on the Law of the Sea further sanctioned 200-nautical-mile Exclusive Economic Zones for the South Pacific States, although the U.S. refused to sign this treaty (Bergin 1983:20–21; *Asia Yearbook* 1984:112). The data on Vanuatu's sea area come from Penelope Ridings (1983).

6. Etelidae are the most common species caught on the deep reef slopes of the tropical Pacific, comprising 62 percent of the fish caught in a study conducted in Vanuatu by ORSTOM. These are the snappers and *poulet fish*, of which Etelis carbunculus, Etelis coruscans, Pristipomoides multidens, and Pristipomoides flavipinnis are the major species. The ORSTOM study estimated that the mean sustainable yield for fish at depths of 100–400 meters in Vanuatu is about 1 kilogram per hectare per year. Consequently, the mean sustainable yield for Vanuatu as a whole is less than 750 tons annually (Brouard and Grandperrin 1985). Thus one of the most fundamental constraints on capitalist development in this fishery is biological.

7. Until 1980, CUSO was an acronym for Canadian University Services Overseas. Since then, the organization, which serves as the primary placement agency for Canadian volunteers working in overseas development, has been known simply as CUSO. It has moved away from its association with universities and emphasized recruitment of more mature volunteers with considerable practical experience.

12

Some Pohnpei Strategies for Economic Survival

Glenn Petersen

Baruch College
and
The Graduate Center of the City University of New York

Despite variations in the social and cultural lives of the Pacific Islands peoples, a common element runs through many of their respective political economies: social status and economic redistribution are closely linked. In general, leaders are seen as providers. In most cases, they truly are; in others, their productive efforts may be more or less restricted to the ideological realm (that is, they are a lot less productive than they claim to be).

During the colonial and postcolonial eras, the introduction of mass-produced, imported goods has consistently had an impact on this intertwining of politics and economy. The character of this impact has, however, varied according to circumstance. Leaders have sometimes sought to enhance their own status by establishing monopolies over access to imported goods; the flow of goods has at other times contributed to the disruption or disintegration of existing political relations; and in yet other cases, successful efforts have been made to preserve the status quo in the face of these new conditions.

Until quite recently, anthropologists and others have tended to focus largely on changes wrought by the imposition or growth of new economic relations. Relatively little attention has been paid to deliberate attempts at turning these forces aside or rendering them ineffective. Indeed, some would argue that in cases where change has been less dramatic, it has been a result of chance rather than intent.

In this essay, I consider a case in which an island people has not merely accepted certain opportunities for social change, but has identified other trends as undesirable and taken deliberate steps to halt them. These people are not simply affected by changes. They work deliberately to exercise a degree of control over their lives, and they have been remarkably successful.

The people of Pohnpei (Ponape), in Micronesia's Eastern Caroline Islands, rely on aspects of their "traditional" political economy to provide a secure platform from which they can deal with the political and economic pressures placed upon them. Asserting the primacy of their own economic categories, they now have access to a flow of imported goods—without having the presence of those goods substantially transform social relations among them.

Some have argued that the mere presence of imported goods—that is, "affluence"—is enough to transform cultures (Salisbury and Tooker 1985). Events on Pohnpei are significant because they remind us that the imported goods themselves do not cause changes in people's lives. Rather, these changes are products of new developments in interpersonal relations, which are, in turn, marked by the distribution of goods. When a people is able to control the movement of goods and continue to distribute them in a socially acceptable manner, then the goods have a very different impact on the lives of its members.

I intend: (1) to show how the close interdependence between Pohnpei cultural categories and the realities of political and economic life are mutually enhancing; (2) to describe the deliberate bankruptcy of the small retail trade stores that channel goods into Pohnpei communities; and (3) to demonstrate that these efforts are the result of deliberately pursued strategies and not merely the chance products of something known as "preadaptation."

MODERN MICRONESIAN HISTORY

If we look at the history of modern Micronesia, or at least of the islands which are now emerging out from under American trusteeship, we find a startling array of responses to the availability of an extraordinary amount of money and all the imported goods it can buy. Chapter 5, "New Political Statuses in American Micronesia, " by Robert Kiste, details this history; I want only to summarize some of the more salient points.

The people of the Northern Marianas Islands seek to ensure the flow of cash by becoming an American commonwealth with a status much like that of Puerto Rico. In the Marshall Islands, nominally a republic, the government has traded American control over the vast missile range at Kwajalein for large sums of American money.

In Belau (Palau), the situation is a bit more complex. Guarantees of American funding are contingent upon an agreement that will permit the U.S. to store nuclear weapons in the islands. The people continue to vote in an absurd series of plebiscites forced upon them by the U.S. government.

In the eastern and central Caroline Islands, which constitute the Federated States of Micronesia (FSM), the situation is markedly more complex. The FSM, like the Marshalls and Belau (if it ever resolves the weapons issues), has agreed to a relationship with the U.S. known as free association. But the aspirations of the various island peoples within the FSM are not at all in harmony with each other. While the people of Truk, for example, seem to be pursuing a course of increasing dependency, the people of Pohnpei continue to seek genuine independence from the U.S., with the expectation that this will bring an end to, or at least markedly curtail, American funding. The source of this divergence in political attitudes is not immediately apparent.

The larger FSM islands have undergone essentially common colonial histories and are comparable in many other ways as well. There are differences in population sizes, rainfall, soil quality, the frequency of typhoons, and so on, but these are hardly great enough to explain the considerable variation in attitudes toward American dollars. All experienced a mid-nineteenth-century era when whalers, traders, and missionaries were the primary source of commerce. Then followed a rapid succession of four different colonial administrations: Spain, Germany, Japan, and the U.S.

This sequence of regimes resulted in a rather peculiar colonial history. No blueprint for transformation was in place long enough to have much effect. The policies of each new administration contradicted and cancelled out those of its predecessors to such a degree that it is difficult to speak about any clear consequences of most of this colonial history (Petersen 1990b).

American rule has now been in place considerably longer than the earlier regimes, although it has passed through several stages which have themselves been quite contradictory. Following World War II, when the U.S. first occupied the islands, there were two decades of neglect (1944-1963). Then came two decades of intense change (1963-1983) as the U.S. spent large sums in hopes of convincing the Micronesians to join in a permanent alliance. Since the mid-1980s, the islands have been nominally self-governing under their various pacts of free association with the U.S., and the United Nations finally terminated American trusteeship in 1990.

THE INTEGRATION OF POLITICAL ECONOMY AND CULTURE

According to Pohnpei mythology, political life on the island has always been in flux. When the Europeans first arrived (circa 1830), Pohnpei had five generally recognized paramount chiefdoms (*wehi*), though there were areas within these that exercised considerable autonomy. Local communities formed local chiefdoms (*kousapw*) within the larger chiefdoms. Both the larger and the smaller polities had two lines of ranked titles surmounted respectively by sacred and secular (or "talking") chiefs.

Men achieved chieftainship through a complex, perpetually shifting mix of matrilineal descent, competitive feasting, prowess in battle, and political acumen. Women shared their husbands' titles, organizational responsibilities, and status. For all but a few of the highest titled people, the affairs of local chiefdoms played a much greater part in daily life than those of the paramount chiefdoms. Most decision making seems to have been done in public councils that were convened during the course of the frequent public feasts. Political life was something for all to participate in, and was tied integrally to the feasting economy.

In the course of the half-century between the Europeans' first appearance on the island's shores and their imposition of colonial authority (1886), the Pohnpei managed to incorporate commercial activities and a growing dependence on steel tools, factory-made cloth, and firearms into their thriving subsistence economy. Indeed, the introduction of pigs and new yam varieties helped spark an agricultural boom that replaced warfare as the primary focus of individual and community competition (Petersen 1982).

There is, perhaps, a degree of historical irony in this. Their desire for tools, cloth, and firearms spurred a people who already held productivity in high regard into increased production, providing fresh foods for whalers and traders. New livestock species and crop types helped them pursue and achieve these higher goals. The new weaponry made fighting entirely too dangerous a pastime for recreation's sake, while simultaneously enabling the Pohnpei to maintain their control of the island. They gradually stopped battling each other, and instead fought the interlopers—until the combined impact of hired Melanesian troops and modern gunboats gave the Germans the upper hand in 1910.

What had been an active complex of first-fruits rituals and sociable feasts centered on kava-drinking, dancing, and talk then grew into a potlatch system rivaling those of the Northwest Coast and Melanesia. Saul Riesenberg, who has described the feast-types in great detail, suggests that at first glance "the multiplicity of feasts…and the development of the feasting complex seem almost hypertrophied," but goes on to demonstrate their importance to the political economy (1968:83; see also Bascom 1948). Traditional competitiveness expanded in two directions.

On the one hand, pursuit of prestige lies in the number of different crops and cultivars (including items with medicinal or utilitarian functions) a family or individual can produce in response to a challenge. These feasts (known generally as *kourepwerepw*) are sometimes undertaken in friendly spirit, sometimes in response to insult.

While they do not often take place, the possibility of being challenged to such a competition is certainly on people's minds. I once observed the gauntlet thrown down in response to a political disagreement. A man well into his seventies said to a man twenty years his junior, "All right, you go to your land and take one of everything. I'll go to my land and get one of everything. Then we'll see who knows what they're talking about."

The second sort of competition is more common, appearing in its most developed form during the annual "honor feasts." These were introduced by the Germans in an attempt to replace first-fruits and other feasts for the chiefs, in hopes of converting the Pohnpei into a peasantry. Competition at these is focused purely on size. Although the term "honor" (*wahu*) supposedly refers to the process of honoring the chief, in reality most of the honor is reaped by those who contribute the largest pigs, yams, and kava plants. These, however, are not necessarily (nor even often) exclusive categories of people.

As a result of the complex, cross-cutting levels, grades, and lines of chieftainship in the Pohnpei political world, only a tiny handful of individuals are ever secure in their rank (Petersen 1990a). It is not unusual to find that the highest-ranking participants in a feast are vying to make the biggest and best contributions.

This integration of political status and distributive activities is hardly peculiar to Pohnpei. But on Pohnpei it continues to grow, it is ceaseless, and it remains central to political success.

For historical reasons detailed elsewhere (Petersen 1990b), a sequence of attempts to establish indirect colonial rule, alternating with periods of utter disregard, has left the traditional chiefs in place and with most of their status intact (see also Fischer 1974). Leaders in the new electoral and bureaucratic systems draw heavily upon their participation in the older political economy for the status they need to gain and hold positions in these systems. Put concisely, unless Pohnpei men and women participate successfully in the traditional political economy, they cannot in any meaningful way manifest *mana*

(Pohnpei *manaman*). They cannot, therefore, accrue any "honor," and they are entirely without political standing. By the same token, Pohnpei who aspire to success in the traditional system often seek to advance in the electoral and bureaucratic systems. These provide yet other avenues along which to pursue prestige and demonstrate the political skills that simultaneously grow from and manifest the quality of one's *mana*.

This means, without exaggeration, that Pohnpei's leaders—whether they are chiefs or legislators, deacons or judges, curers or administrators—all raise pigs, yams, and kava. I have spent time feeding the pigs of governors and college presidents, bearing the yams of magistrates and merchants, and pounding the kava of teachers and land commissioners.

In the end, one is reduced to making the simple statement that all this agricultural productivity confers meaning on Pohnpei lives. It is fundamental to the essence of Pohnpei culture. To be a successful farmer is simultaneously to be able to take care (*kopwel*) of oneself—thereby asserting and establishing one's personal autonomy—and to be a real member of the community (*uhdahn ohl en Pohnpei*), two of the highest values in Pohnpei culture (Petersen 1985).

All these ideas and cultural behaviors provide the material underpinnings of Pohnpei's success. In a 1975 referendum and a 1983 plebisicite, the people of Pohnpei called for independence from the U.S., even though they believed that this would cut off American funding and leave them effectively broke. (Because theirs was a minority vote within the FSM, it had no immediate impact on their political status.) This is in contrast to most other Micronesians, who argue that American dollars—and thus continued American rule—are essential to their survival. The Pohnpei's willingness to "go for broke," as it were, is grounded in a recognition that their thriving domestic economy can provide enough food to carry them through until they develop commercial resources.

They are neither comfortable nor arrogant about this. They believe they will suffer if and when it comes to pass. And they are hardly unanimous in expressing these sentiments: about one out of three Pohnpei voted for the free association agreement that now provides cash in return for American dominance in island affairs. Nor are they the sole arbiters of their homeland's opinions: large numbers of immigrants from coral atolls and other Micronesian islands now reside and vote on Pohnpei. These people, without the Pohnpei commitment to farming and lacking some of the Pohnpei access to land, see their future more closely tied to the U.S.

CONTROLLING COMMERCE

While a substantial majority of Pohnpei are *willing* to see the cash flow end, few are *eager* to bring it to a halt. Most people on Pohnpei enjoy the good life that American dollars bring. However, the Pohnpei's long-standing familiarity with commerce and with colonial boom and bust cycles has taught them how to defuse the time bomb that others hear ticking away.

Pohnpei and other Micronesians have been dependent on copra sales and imports for generations and were well-integrated into an educational and wage-labor complex during the Japanese era, but they had never experienced anything on the scale of

American spending in the last quarter-century. Vast amounts of money have coursed through the island's commercial economy since the mid-1960s, when American policies toward the islands shifted radically.

In the first fifteen years of the new policy, before the U.S. had agreed to the terms of Micronesian self-government, American expenditures on Micronesian wages alone rose from $2.69 million to $42.15 million, a fifteen-fold increase. Government employment in the islands went from 2,200 to nearly 11,000. Most of these employees work at providing services to the other islanders in education, health, public works, and administration.

The government employees spend their salaries on imported goods. Imports climbed from $5 million to $40 million during this period, and the import-export ratio went from about two to one to seven to one (Peoples 1985:10, 20–23). Total U.S. expenditures in Micronesia have exceeded $100 million per year for the past decade 1981–1991. For the fiscal year 1985, U.S. funding in the Federated States of Micronesia amounted to more than $128 million (U.S. State Department 1985:51). In Pohnpei alone, the 1983 balance of trade figures (the most recent available) are $13,356,303 in imports, $446,737 in exports: a ratio of nearly thirty to one (Division of Economic Planning 1986:15).

In addition to the large sums earmarked for salaries and thus channeled directly into consumer goods, a recent FSM official audit of capital spending found that a great deal of this funding—intended to provide an infrastructure for economic development—was spent on private vehicles, outboard motors, air conditioners, and, on Pohnpei, on yams, pigs, and kava. The report concluded that after more than $15 million in appropriations between 1980 and 1987, the FSM "does not have anything concrete to show for this huge commitment of public funds" (JK Report 1989:1–3).

I have observed the flow of this money through a host of small stores over the course of nearly two decades. Each Pohnpei community has one or two, occasionally more. These sell most of the imports.[1] We might guess that storekeepers accumulate a great deal of the cash that is force-fed into the Pohnpei economy, and, over the long haul, establish themselves as a local economic elite. We would be wrong; their stores are unsuccessful and ephemeral.

In eastern Awak, where the population has grown from approximately two hundred and fifty to five hundred during this period, eight stores have opened since the late 1960s. Six are no longer in business, one is doing little business, and the one that in 1990 was still doing significant business had opened in 1981. Stores in this community operate for an average of four to five years; in time, their business tapers off and they close. Their absolute number grows along with the population and the amount of cash in circulation.

These small stores do most of their business on a credit, not cash-and-carry, basis. The proprietors readily admit that their main problems are credit-related, and the few expatriates who work in island businesses report that overextensions of credit and the accumulation of unpaid debts bankrupt almost all small stores in the course of a few years of operation. A brief sketch of a typical small store's life history will show how this pattern unfolds.

An individual or family builds or remodels a structure that serves as both home and store, and stocks it using funds that may be drawn from savings (for example, from the salary of a man who has returned from a period of service as a merchant seaman), proceeds from a land sale, or a loan secured by wages from a government job. Accounts with one or more of the island's wholesalers are established. Credit is extended to a few families, while others are expected to pay cash. In time, the number of families allowed to buy on credit grows, as does the size of the debts of some of the families. While families do make payments against their debts, the payments tend to lag well behind growth of these debts.

Gradually, the store's cash flow contracts as its own debts to wholesalers mount. Wholesalers sometimes cut off the store's credit and it finds itself unable to keep the shelves stocked. In the former case, with a growing debt of its own, the store keeps extending credit in hopes of doing enough business to maintain its own credit standing. In the latter case, with credit from wholesalers cut off, and with little stock, business drifts away and outstanding debts are left unpaid. In either case—the difference between the two is essentially a matter of the length of the period over which the process is extended—the store eventually finds itself bankrupt. The owner takes a financial loss and the store is closed.

In a common variation on this, a new store opens nearby and the older business finds itself in a dilemma. Some of its customers establish new lines of credit with the interloper. The proprietor of the older store must decide whether to terminate entirely the credit of those who shop at the new store and thus cut off any chance of having them pay off their debts, or continue to extend them credit while knowing that they are simultaneously incurring debts at the other store and thus making it even more unlikely that they will ever be able to pay off their debts.

In sum, we see that a store that did not offer credit would do little or no business, while those that do offer credit eventually go broke. An unending series of small stores open, despite the obvious fact that small stores do not turn a profit. A degree of historical perspective makes it clear that on Pohnpei the point of pursuing a business career is not profit making; these stores are not ends in themselves. Rather, storekeeping is one of the many prestige-enhancing strategies the Pohnpei employ as they strive to advance their political status and rank.

Pohnpei feasts are by no means the only arena for redistributive activities. In the same way that an ambitious person is expected to participate in a range of social activities, distribution is expected in a variety of fashions. Ownership of a store is but a new way of engaging in distribution.

Pohnpei notions of distributive activities call for both productive abilities and humility. Grand gestures are admired, but must not be clangorous; one should not call too much attention to an act of generosity (*sapan*), a virtue everyone is expected to exercise. To be simultaneously great and modest is the Pohnpei ideal. The trick, then, is to embed these activities in an expanse of time; to have them unfold in an ongoing process that can be maintained at a discreet level throughout the course of an ambitious life.

Individuals seek ways of demonstrating prowess and generosity over a long period of time, and it turns out that a store is an excellent means of doing so. It allows one to lose—while the community benefits—slowly and publicly. It converts an accumulation of cash into stock and a business that is visible for years. The loss itself, then, is the investment; it is converted into a social gain.

With a few exceptions, these storekeepers are ambitious, active people who play leading parts in some or all the basic Pohnpei community activities, or are young men bent on entering into them. They are usually in their thirties and forties, although older men and women and younger men sometimes open stores. One interesting exception to this pattern was the late Sisanando Seneris (who is quoted below). Sis, a dynamic participant in Pohnpei sociopolitical life, was paraplegic and used his store for political theater in the way that other men perform at feasts. Intent on remaining in business, he would not forgo what was owed him. Every few years he had to move to a new community, as he antagonized those whose debts he refused to cancel.

Today, as in the past, Pohnpei in quest of prestige, whether it lies in the traditional chiefly hierarchy or the realm of elective politics, must both possess and distribute pigs, kava, and yams. These acts manifest one's *soar*, one's quality or substance as a human. "*Ih soaren ohl*," someone once said: to give things away, "That is the substance of a man." One's personal *mana* likewise manifests itself throughout the entire nexus of activity entailed in production, accumulation, and distribution. Opening a store, extending credit, going broke, and then moving on to other activities: these now provide one more course of action for a Pohnpei leader to pursue.

The people of Pohnpei disarm the monetary time bomb that threatens them by directing dollars and goods through the channels of their own political economy. This means that in the Pohnpei economy, production, possession, and distribution—which capitalism defines as three distinct phases that can be uncoupled from each other in the course of daily life—cannot be carved into separate spheres. Putting it bluntly, to possess is to distribute. Money and goods move through the system at such a high rate of speed that there is little chance for accumulation.

Doing so, however, is not necessarily easy. Not everyone participates fully in traditional prestige competition and not everyone applies its principles to the commercial economy. But the majority of Pohnpei do. Moreover—and this is the main point of this essay—they understand precisely what they are up to. They see how participation in agricultural competition shores up their ability to assert autonomy, and how such cultural values as autonomy promote agricultural activity. And, they see that by forcing money into traditional economic channels they limit its power to weaken the autonomy they prize.

INTENTIONAL STRATEGIES

It is surprisingly difficult to convince people that the Pohnpei, in pursuing this course, know what they are doing—that they act deliberately, consciously, purposefully. I once presented a portion of this material at a conference on the impact of multinational business culture. The discussant (an economist) rose and, displaying his erudition, pointed out that the Pohnpei political economy rather resembled that of the Kwakiutl potlatch described by Ruth Benedict. It was an interesting cultural artifact, he said, and it was interesting that the Pohnpei had integrated storekeeping into their traditional ways, but it was hardly a conscious economic strategy. It was, he explained, merely a chance—and temporary— result of the intersection of business and feasting; it would in time, as the Pohnpei learned better, be replaced by more appropriate economic behavior.

His argument is one of a set of disparate, but nonetheless related, positions taken by a number of anthropologists who have written about small-scale business activities in the Pacific. These viewpoints share a common assumption that the island entrepreneurs do not see that traditional patterns help them to shape the development of new economic forms.

Ben Finney, for example, suggests in Chapter 7 that prestige competition in the New Guinea Highlands serves as a "preadaptation" for capitalism—that is, it provides pre-existing means for the mobilization of labor and capital and promotes rapid economic development. A.P. Vayda, on the other hand, has pointed to the misguided efforts of several Cook Islands storekeepers, who put kin obligations ahead of profit-and-loss statements (1959). Romola McSwain described Karkar storekeepers as "bewildered" by their failures (1977:116).

Different peoples, dealing with differing historical circumstances, have made a variety of responses to commercial opportunities. Many on Pohnpei are as committed to prestige competition as any Highlander, but they work to preserve an economy that could well be called socialist. It is not necessary, and may in fact be dead wrong, to assume that these economic activities are done randomly or in ignorance—that is, that they are not strategies.

Nor should we think that this interest in commerce is a new phenomenon. In the mid-nineteenth century, local Pohnpei communities "adopted" European beachcombers to act as go-betweens with whalers and traders. In the late 1800s and early years of this century, a number of missionary-educated Pohnpei opened stores, including Soumadau, leader of Sokehs chiefdom's ill-starred 1910 rebellion against the Germans. People on Pohnpei have long been interested in obtaining foreign goods—they are determined, however, to retain control over the impact these goods have on their lives.

Thoughtful Pohnpei are quite conscious of the security their political economy provides them, and they deliberately apply its principles to their participation in the commercial realm—a realm of activity in which they have been participating for nearly a century and a half. The degree of consciousness, of course, varies with individual acumen and relative maturity. Younger people with ambitious plans understand that stores now serve as elements in the redistributive culture; older people tend to have a fuller and more appreciative view of the role these stores play in their people's struggle to preserve that culture and work actively to preserve the overall pattern.

In some cases, cash probably *is* invested with a relatively conscious goal of monetary profit. Business activities tend, however, to evolve into investments in the community in much the way that feasts do. Individual ambition is harnessed by the same values that transform men and women who pursue prestige into extraordinarily generous members of the community.

Since prestige is so much a part of Pohnpei social life, ambitious men and women are always seeking out avenues for advancement (Pohnpei speak of traveling the "*al*"— "road"—of advancement in the traditional title system). Many will work to rise in local church hierarchies, in civic affairs positions, or in government jobs. Running a store provides one more venue. For a short time, a storekeeper occupies a highly visible position. Some assume, however briefly, that they will be able to both succeed socially and turn a profit, though few have ever managed to do so.

Several well-respected men, individuals who have been eminently successful in every possible sphere of Pohnpei life, argue that those who go into retail business know what lies in store for them. The basic problem that accompanies proprietorship—debt—is so well understood, they say, that anyone going into business has some underlying awareness that his or her store will go bankrupt. One described the basic pattern of individual business activity on Pohnpei by tracing an arc through the air: "Businesses go up, and then go down." After a business fails, he said, you wait a while, then begin a new project.

Failure in this context, men have told me, is success. They emphasize the Pohnpei code of *luhs laud*—losing in a grand fashion. It is well worth bankruptcy to gain in status.

Underlying these Pohnpei observations about their own lives is an enormously sophisticated appreciation of the singular context in which the pattern unfolds. These men speak with frankness about the wealth of contemporary Pohnpei. There is so much food available in Pohnpei's gardens, so much money flowing through its peculiar economy, they say, that people can live easily, with little exertion or stress. As a consequence, Pohnpei have no fear of failure, nothing to lose, no need to worry about going broke in any commercial venture. They can always fall back on the land and their relatives' money. "The Pohnpei haven't yet encountered hard times," they tell me. "When we do," said one, "things will change."

These men, like most adult Pohnpei, are fully aware of the island's high rate of population growth and the impending shortage of land. And like most Pohnpei, they have long assumed that in the unlikely eventuality that the Pohnpei achieve their goal of independence from the U.S., funding will be cut drastically, if not completely. After the 1975 Referendum on Future Political Status, when the Pohnpei first called for Micronesian independence, two little girls asked if it was true that they would have to begin making their clothes from bark cloth; their mothers told them this would be a consequence of independence (Petersen 1979). And in 1970, older women asked Martha Ward to help them relearn soap-making techniques for the same reasons (Ward 1989:97). When the Pohnpei vote for independence, as they continue to do, they understand the possible consequences and are willing to take their chances.

In 1990, while the Federated States of Micronesia Constitutional Convention was underway at the national capital on Pohnpei, a number of Pohnpei cited an old epigram, *Sohte me kin kapara inen Katau.* Loosely translated, this means, "Don't get involved with that which breeds foreignness." Its roots can be traced back in the mythology that chronicles Pohnpei's earliest days. In 1990, however, it was meant to call attention to the dangers of becoming too dependent on foreign goods and procedures, since this dependence has a way of transforming people's lives without their being aware of it. It is better, therefore, to hold these things at a safe distance.

In this context, the reference was specifically to the form of government fostered during the U.S. administration of the islands and embodied in the new Micronesian federal system. There is on Pohnpei nearly universal agreement that the FSM's strong national government has to be stripped of most of its power. But the expression was also used to communicate a more general sense, shared by many on the island, that the best hope for the future lies in constant skepticism about the direction of history, and the possibilities of shaping it.

Few scholars would think twice when encountering a phrase such as "a far larger part of the French story, *the long contest between* centralized, regularized and somewhat bureaucratic monarchical power and *the proud vitality* of an aristocracy *resisting the direction* in which monarchial order was moving" (Bernstein 1990, emphasis added). Americans are continually harangued by claims and counterclaims concerning the "original intent" of the men who drafted the U.S. Constitution. Why then should it come as a surprise to learn that the people of Pohnpei are actively and consciously engaged in the shaping of their history?

At evening kava sessions, small groups sometimes discuss the capacity of Pohnpei's farms to feed the island's people if all imports were cut off. There would be hardships at first, it is concluded, but in time there would be plenty. The people of Pohnpei recognize the possibility of a radical change and understand the hardships it would bring, likening them to the privations they suffered during World War II.

Indeed, one of the few older Pohnpei who spoke in favor of the free association relationship with the U.S. referred explicitly to the wartime era, arguing that buying kerosene for hurricane lanterns is decidedly preferable to boiling down coconut oil for wick lamps. But his opinion does not reflect the majority of the Pohnpei people, whose sentiments are much more accurately captured in the words of the late Sisanando Seneris, an unusually outspoken man. On the day of the 1983 free association plebiscite, he said, echoing the timeless phrase *Carpe diem*—"Seize the day":

> If we Pohnpei want independence we must vote for it now. If we wait till the 15 years of Free Association are finished, all the tough people—people like myself—will be dead. The only ones left will be those who who've grown so accustomed to life under the terms of the Compact that they'll be afraid to strike out on their own. They'll never be able to call for independence.

Carefully weighing the alternatives, the Pohnpei pursue a deliberate course. Their extraordinary emphasis on competitive feasting serves much more than cultural needs. Redistribution requires production: Pohnpei's extraordinary agricultural productivity is not an accident of history. The Pohnpei know they can live this way because of their island's fertility, *and* that this fertility is a direct result of the labor they expend in the pursuit of culturally defined prestige. They see the circle.

CONCLUSION

One unfortunate aspect of an overly functionalist social science (and functional analysis is not without an important place in science) is its tendency to view the development—or evolution—of social institutions as purely a result of impersonal social forces. It is easy to fall into the habit of supposing that people do not reflect on the kind of social relations they wish to enjoy, nor actively work to achieve them. Theories thus stress the inevitability of certain kinds of changes, ignoring the possibility that in some times and some places peoples might well analyze and reject them.

A viable alternative to this way of framing history can be found in Pierre Clastres's *Society Against the State* (1977). In his iconoclastic study of lowland South American Indians, he maintains that these societies are strangers to what we call political power. "The chief is there to serve the society; it is society as such—the real locus of power—that expresses its authority over the chief," and any chief who tried to reverse this relationship by asserting power would be abandoned as a threat to the group (Clastres 1977:175, 131, 35).

Clastres portrays people who are able to imagine things being different, who judge the possibilities, and who opt for preserving what they have. In South America, colonialism, capitalism, and industrialism—among other things—have subsequently been making such resistance moot. But Clastres's point is that people do not act blindly, borne in ignorance before the winds of change.

The Pohnpei, too, understand what they have. They see what they might have in its stead, judge it inferior, and work as active preservationists. They have enjoyed more fortunate historical circumstances than most native Americans, having managed to retain their land. It is easy to imagine that the weight of American dollars and the blandishments of consumer goods will now accomplish what coarser forms of colonialism could not. But the people of Pohnpei think otherwise.

Acknowledgments: This chapter draws on research conducted on Pohnpei in 1974-75, 1979, 1981, 1983, 1985, 1987, and 1990. I thank the National Institute of Mental Health, the National Endowment for the Humanities, the National Science Foundation, the Wenner-Gren Foundation, and the Faculty Research Award Program (PSC-CUNY) of the City University of New York for the funding that has made this work possible.

NOTES

1. I am limiting my analysis here to the operations of the small local stores. There are a few large wholesalers in Kolonia, Pohnpei's only town. An explanation of their operations, as well as more detailed data on the smaller stores, can be found in Petersen 1987.

13

Education Is Development on a Ten-Acre Island

Alice Pomponio
St. Lawrence University

Many rural parents in the Pacific Islands view their children's school education as a "development project." The following pages document the rise and fall of interest and participation in formal schooling on Mandok Island, in the Siassi Islands of Morobe Province, Papua New Guinea (PNG). The Mandok case illustrates two perennial problems in education faced by all developing nations, both in the Pacific Islands and elsewhere. The first is how to balance the public aims of a national education system with the private goals of parents who send their children to school. The second is how to reconcile different and sometimes conflicting definitions of development held by the people involved— government administrators, educators, missionaries, and rural villagers.

This chapter has three parts. The first gives a brief sketch of national development and education history in PNG since European contact. Against this general background, the second part focuses specifically on the Mandok case and how this community experienced the development process. Education was just one of many possible "development projects" offered to the Mandok within a specific time period. This particular project involved a minimal initial investment and reaped substantial financial returns. Through the years, however, the Mandok developed the notion that education had become a "losing investment." The third part considers the lessons that might be learned from this case.

EDUCATION AND DEVELOPMENT IN PAPUA NEW GUINEA

Education and development in PNG have long been recognized as inextricably linked. "Education," as used here, means formal schooling. "Development" has meant several things to different governments over the years since first European contact, but each new definition reflects a Western preoccupation with progress. Early colonial administrators defined development in terms of the pacification of "natives" in order to provide a labor force for the colonial plantation economy. Later administrations defined development in terms of economic and technological change aimed to create a self-suffcient, independent nation. Together, education and development imply deliberate movement away from a "traditional" society toward a "modern" one. School curricula in PNG reflected these goals and were organized over the years to foster social change. Several authors have documented the evolution of PNG's education system through several stages (reviewed in Pomponio and Lancy 1986; see also Weeks and Guthrie 1984). These stages reflect changing national administrative priorities regarding development during the colonial era and after independence. What follows is a brief overview of these stages, with specific reference to the Mandok case.

In the prewar Mandated Territory of New Guinea, the government took little interest in education as a policy rule. In this "mission phase" (Pomponio and Lancy 1986:41), missions established and managed education without government interference. Their aim was to teach rudimentary literacy, numeracy, and religious instruction in order to convert the indigenous population to Christianity. The precise timing of this phase varied across the country according to the pattern of European contact and establishment of colonial rule.

The post–World War II Australian administration unified the Territories of Papua and New Guinea and launched a concerted effort to unite the various mission and administration schools in both regions into one unified system. The educational policies of this administration embodied a "rural bias" and stressed a "blending" of the country's numerous Melanesian cultures in the schools.

By 1955, a movement had begun to achieve universal literacy in English through Universal Primary Education (UPE) in the Territory. UPE became the official guiding motto of the education system of the 1950s and early 1960s. Fearing the rise of an indigenous and potentially exploitative elite, this administration allowed little provision for education beyond the primary level. Its successors criticized the policy as paternalistic and insufficient to prepare the country for sovereignty and independence.

Education in the 1960s was characterized by expansion. A 1962 United Nations report on schooling in the territory had called for the development of indigenous secondary and tertiary education and an increase in the number of personnel who could replace expatriates as civil servants and elected political leaders. The motto of the Education Department became "Education for Development." In this context, "development in education" came to mean national development. Although it lasted less than ten years, the changes implemented during this phase had a tremendous impact nationwide.

All levels of the education system benefited from the expansionist policy. Rural areas not previously served by primary schools now received them. Secondary education was expanded, and PNG's university system was created. Various other vocational, technical, teachers' training, and subprofessional training institutions also were established at this time. Education policy had shifted from a gradual, rural-bias approach to one that emphasized the rapid production of a technically skilled (mostly urban) labor force. Foreign teachers, mainly Australians, were recruited to carry out the new mandates.

In 1968, an Advisory Committee on Education was formed as part of a Five-Year Plan to create a national education system within existing financial constraints. The resulting Education Ordinance of 1970 brought the mission schools (except for the Seventh-Day Adventist schools) into one unified system under the auspices of the national government. For the first time, major control of the school system was held by the government; missions maintained only an advisory capacity. English became the official language of instruction for the whole country.

The ensuing phase, beginning in 1970, involved a retrenchment from the expansionism of the 1960s. It began with two major policy shifts, one inside and one outside the country. From outside, Australia's newly elected Labor government sped up the process of PNG independence. Inside the country, administrators recognized the rise of cultural conflicts and the rapidly closing job market. In response, the goal of the Education Department shifted to "Education for Community Development," and the notion of the "community school" was introduced in 1969. Elementary schools were renamed and reorganized. Students were now educated not to leave their villages to find employment in the already overcrowded towns, but rather to gain practical skills useful for rural life. At this time, nonformal education (including vocational and technical training) was given a new legitimacy.

Papua New Guinea achieved self-government in 1973, and associated with it was a new era of "nationalism" in education. For the first time, Papua New Guineans themselves were designing the education program for the country. The new government shifted to a policy emphasis on community development.

As might be expected, national independence in 1975 brought with it still more policy changes in education. Partially in response to the copper-rich North Solomon Islands' threat to secede (Weeks and Guthrie 1984:39), the power to formulate government policy was decentralized. Newly established provincial governments now shared responsibility for education with the national government. Today the national government controls larger issues, such as teacher conditions, the curriculum, languages, and standards of instruction. Provincial governments oversee primary education and retain administrative control over provincial high schools, nonformal education (including vocational centers), as well as "aspects of curricula, and associated provincial educational planning" (1984:40).

Weeks and Guthrie (1984:42) observe that "one of the major effects of the school system is to create failure." During the late 1970s and early 1980s, achievement scores of community school children did show a decline, and the number of "school leavers" increased. The focus of educational policy became educational "standards." Weeks and Guthrie describe an overriding "pragmatism" motivating the new focus (1984:40–41).

In 1986, a Ministerial committee reviewed the nation's education system and concluded that although PNG had had some fourteen education ministers since independence, it did not have any guiding philosophy of education. This review produced one based on "Integral Human Development" (IHD) (Matane 1986). This approach, in line with constitutional priorities, stresses the following: (1) a recognition that spiritual and social needs are basic human needs, equally important as physical and economic needs; (2) greater cooperation between all agents involved in children's education (parents, teachers, churches, media, leaders); and (3) better integration between the content of schooling and community needs (Matane 1986:6). The review also formulated a set of aims and goals for formal schooling consistent with this philosophy. These goals reflect the lessons learned from the disillusionment and artificially produced "failures" of the 1970s. They encourage a more holistic, pragmatic approach to the education of a "whole person" who is more likely to live in a rural than an urban area.

But "pragmatism" here is the pragmatism of government administrators educated in European educational philosophy. What happened in rural areas? In the next section, the case study of Mandok school children illustrates some of the problems that ensued from the continual changes in administrative priorities for education.

EDUCATION ON MANDOK ISLAND

Mandok is a ten-acre, raised coral islet that lies just south of the high volcanic island of Umboi (Map 13–1). Historically, the Mandok were middleman traders in the Vitiaz Strait trading network. This system extended from Madang to West New Britain and along the Rai Coast of New Guinea as far as the Finschhafen area of the Huon Peninsula, up to and including Tami Island and Malasiga on the coast (Harding 1967). The Mandok garden a plot of about 300 acres in the Muru River area of Umboi Island. Gardening is supplementary; the Mandok generally trade their fish and shellfish for vegetable foods with Umboi Island horticulturalists. The resident population in 1987 was 537. Over 75 percent of this population was under the age of 30.

Students marching in front of Por-Mandok Community School. (Photo by A. Pomponio)

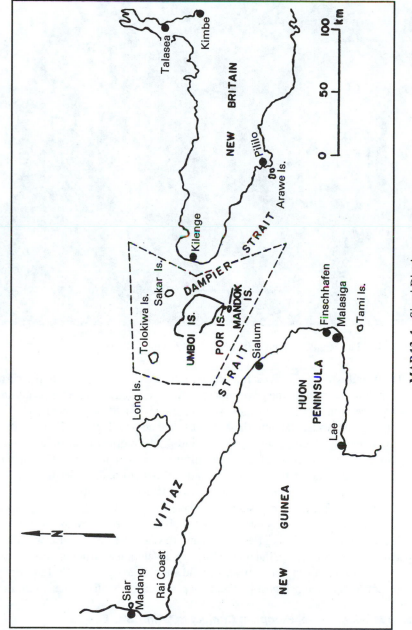

MAP 13-1 Siassi District

Classroom life, Por-Mandok Community School. (Photo by A. Pomponio)

The Mandok people view schooling as a development project. On the surface, this view seems consonant with the government's. A closer look, however, reveals an entirely different conception. Whereas the government associated "development" with economic and technological modernization, the Mandok defined development in terms of personal access to cash and valued goods. For the Mandok, development became a metaphor for a more complex process of adopting a new cultural system that included European Roman Catholic spirituality and Christian values but did not supplant older beliefs. The stated purpose of education was to send children to school to get jobs, earn money, and send money and material goods back to parents and other relatives on Mandok. Those goods and cash were recycled into the local feasting and status mobility systems (Pomponio 1992).

The government's views of education and development changed from education for national development to education for community development. But the Mandok's views on the value of education did not change, nor did they alter significantly their definition of development. What changed most for them over the years were the routes to earning cash.

Phase I: Mission Phase, European Contact to World War II

The first documented European contact in the Siassi region involved traders and explorers. The Englishman Dampier explored the northern route around Umboi Island in

1700, but did not sail around Umboi's southern point, so he never visited the small islands (see Ball 1982). German traders came in the late 1880s to collect pearlshell, tortoise shell, and sea cucumber. Traders and explorers did not, as a rule, interact much with "natives" except to exchange trade goods. Extended personal contact with Europeans began with the arrival of missionaries.

Mission history in Siassi shows an interesting pattern on both sides of the pulpit. French Marist priests settled on north Umboi Island for a brief time in 1847. Concerted missionary activity was minimal until after 1884, however, when the Germans took control of northeastern New Guinea. In 1886, German Lutherans settled at Finschhafen and controlled mission activities in what is now Morobe Province, including Siassi. They established the first Lutheran school at Finschhafen in 1890. The Lutherans contacted the Mandok early on in their evangelizing enterprise, and they educated four Mandok girls at the Awelkon mission school (west Umboi Island) in the early 1930s. (Although the education of girls remains a struggle across PNG, the Mandok are proud of the fact that from the beginning, they sent both girls and boys to school as opportunities arose.) There were some conflicts with the Lutherans, however (see Mulderink 1980 and Pomponio 1992), so the Mandok chose to become Roman Catholics in 1937.

In 1938, the Mandok sent four young men to the Catholic mission's catechist school at Taliligap, east New Britain, where they received basic literacy and catechistic training for three years. Schooling was suspended during World War II and resumed around 1948, again with the purpose of teaching basic literacy, numeracy, and religious instruction. Those who had gone to school before the war became catechists. They traveled around the Siassi area, teaching and proselytizing.

After the war, the Catholic mission resumed its activities, teaching the "three Rs" to Mandok children and young adults. Although the government had effected two policy changes by 1955, the Catholic mission retained exclusive control over education on Mandok until the 1970 Education Ordinance was implemented. There was thus some consistency in the educational system presented to Mandok villagers.

From the beginning, contact with Europeans had a material aspect to it, exposing the Mandok to heretofore unimagined forms and quantities of material goods. These possessions were subsumed under the more general Tok Pisin term *kago* ("cargo"). Mandok people, like other New Guineans, wanted access to this "cargo." Recruitment for plantation labor began during the German colonial era in the late 1880s. Plantation owners seeking labor, traders looking for shells or trepang, armies seeking soldiers, and missionaries seeking converts and plantation workers, all paid for labor and local goods with various kinds of European goods: steel axes and knives, cloth, glass beads, tobacco, cash, and so on. Mandok middlemen, traders with a keen eye for investment, wanted access to European goods and cash. With European contact came missionization. In particular, the Catholic mission introduced a new philosophical and value system that went along with formal schooling, labor migration, and cash.

Improved commercial shipping after World War II brought an influx of more desirable European goods, coupled with easier access to distant places for all. This meant that other Papua New Guineans who previously depended on Mandok and other Siassi traders for valued goods could now get them for themselves. The overseas trade system was starting to disintegrate. The introduction of cash into what previously had been a barter system, as well as government-imposed "head taxes," meant that along with the rest of the country, the Mandok needed and sought employment from Europeans. This employment took several forms over the years.

World War II: Labor Migration and First-Hand Experience

World War II brought with it a series of unique educational experiences and occupational opportunities. These are not always recorded in the literature for this period, however, and consequently an important aspect of the wartime experience goes underreported. This is the experiential, first-hand, individual, and very personal expo- sure to European ways of doing things, as well as to European mentality. Mandok war veterans experienced a unique apprenticeship with the American and Australian soldiers with whom they served.

Before World War II, Mandok migrants were few. No more than a handful of men took jobs as ship's crew, cooks, or servants for short periods of a few months or less. The war marks the first big wave of labor migration.[1] Twenty-three men went off to be soldiers, cooks, and scouts for the Allied forces in World War II. All returned safely with many entertaining stories about European cargo and generosity.

Post-World War II: Reconstruction and Development

After World War II, administrators focused their energies on rebuilding the country and initiating economic and technological development. Government patrol officers in Siassi, alarmed at the drop in small-island populations (largely the result of adult male absenteeism during the war years), closed the area to plantation labor recruitment and encouraged local people to "repopulate," improve their subsistence gardens, and cultivate cash crops (*Patrol Report Finschafen 1*, 1952:4).

From an administrative standpoint, "development" in Siassi has always focused on cash cropping. This has been true even though the small islands lack land; and some, including Mandok, lack a fresh-water source. For the Mandok, intensive cash cropping requires that they relocate from their tiny overcrowded island to their Umboi Island garden land. Although the Mandok and other small islanders engaged in limited copra production over the years, patrol officers were never impressed with their output. Moreover, each new patrol officer had a different idea about which new cash crop should be planted. Rice, coffee, and even corn were all tried at one time or another and all failed. Although this failure can be attributed to climate in part, patrol officers were never convinced that the Mandok tried in earnest to produce cash crops.

Islanders explained to administration officers that they were fishermen and not gardeners. The Mandok perceive themselves as a maritime people oriented towards mobility and middleman trade, not sedentary horticulture (Pomponio 1992). They also claimed that the distance between the small islands and the garden areas was a deterrent. The canoe journey from Mandok to Muru takes about two-and-one-half hours in calm seas. Garden plots are at various walking distances inland. The Mandok consid- ered this journey, as well as gardening, to be "hard work." They would much rather go fishing and trade surplus fish for vegetables with their Umboi horticulturalist neighbors.

In spite of these obstacles, administrators believed that if the Mandok (and other small islanders) would only move to Umboi, their cash cropping ventures would succeed. Consequently, there were several government, school, and mission attempts to move the Mandok community to Muru. Time and again, they refused to move (Pomponio 1990a and 1992).

Some Mandok earned money in the postwar years by collecting and selling trochus and green snail shells. This was a lucrative, if undependable, source of money. There was a temporary slump in the trochus market in 1952, but business picked up within a few years. By 1955, the shells being collected were so small that patrol officers tried to close the area to collection and allow the species to replenish (*Patrol Report Finschafen 3*, 1955–1956:2). Private traders ignored the ban, however, for fear of losing the market altogether (*Patrol Report Finschafen 6*, 1957–1958:3). From the islanders' perspective, shell collecting, although traditionally categorized as "women's work," became viewed as "easy money." Married men with children could stay home with their families. They could "repopulate" for the government and still earn cash for themselves. Plantation labor increasingly became an adventure for single men looking for excitement before they settled down.

Siassi was reopened to labor recruitment by 1954. The number of Mandok men who migrated for labor had always been low compared with that of other Siassi islanders (Harding 1967:205). But although the numbers might be low, the percentage of male absenteeism for the population as a whole was high. The twenty-three men who went to war in the 1940s, for example, constituted 50 percent of the adult male population. Their absence reshuffled an entire set of marriage alliances and caused other disruptions in the village. Their families might have been hesitant to repeat this process quickly (see Harding 1967:205).

The Expansionist Bonanza: 1960–1969

The expansionist climate of the 1960s brought an educational and economic bonanza for the Mandok. In 1960, a permanent mission house and a "Primary T" School[2] (grades K through three) were constructed on Por Island, adjacent to Mandok. Students who graduated from this school then went to mission schools at Vunapope for grades four through six, and then to high school or technical school in Rabaul.

Parents felt some misgivings about sending their children off to distant shores to attend high school, but their monetary investment was negligible. Moreover, the children were in town centers and thus within reach of either family trade relations or kinsmen who worked at the mission-owned plantations. In fact, the first students to go to school were accompanied by an older man who was their father or uncle and who "took care of them" while they were away from home. These children experienced the modernization taking place in town centers and became absorbed in the movement toward national independence. During this phase of "Education for National Development," students attended high school in a political and emotional climate of hope and promise. Most of the community school teachers were expatriate lay missionaries dedicated to helping the Mandok "develop" in a Western sense of the term. They were idealists whose image of development included Christian mores, European notions of ideal family life, and a quest for high personal achievement.

Traditional Mandok ideas about valued knowledge are typically "Melanesian" in their emphasis on personal experience and extended apprenticeship with an expert. Although on Mandok these experts are usually relatives, there was a consistency between Mandok traditions of learning and achievement and those presented by European formal schooling. By attending school at mission and town centers they were ensconced at the source of the knowledge they sought. From 1964 to 1969, an increasing number of boys *and* girls went off-island for secondary education (including technical and vocational schooling). As young adults they secured jobs in towns, some of which were located along traditional trade routes, and they enjoyed rapid upward mobility during the expansionist era of administration policy.

These events created a situation in which Mandok traders were able to increase their trade networks in two ways. First, in visiting children at schools, they also visited towns and established new connections. Second, the employed children themselves became "new trade partners" by recycling new wealth back into the traditional system of formal distributions and status mobility. By sending cash and goods back to the village, they subsidized the declining trade system and staved off its demise. They also evaded what they felt were intrusive government attempts to relocate the village to Umboi Island and turn the people into sedentary horticulturalists. Education gave the Mandok more than literate children. The rewards earned through wage employment sustained the declining trade system and subsidized the local feasting and ritual prestige systems, making it possible for the Mandok to stay on their island.

Nationalism and Retrenchment: 1970–1975

The government's reduction of educational resources during the "retrenchment" phase preceding independence (beginning with the Education Ordinance of 1970) hit the Mandok hard for several reasons. First, education that had been free or required only token payments for school fees now cost a great deal, with charges for tuition, clothing, and transportation. Second, the school nationalization program pushed Papua New Guineans out of school and into teaching service with six to ten years less education than the expatriates they replaced. Teachers who came to Mandok possessed less education and less first-hand knowledge of "European things." Teachers no longer were symbols of achievement in the European domain, and the presence of strangers in the village caused many unanticipated problems (Pomponio 1985).

The school localization program, initiated originally to encourage children to stay in school, had the opposite effect on the Mandok. Instead of going to high school in town centers, Mandok students now attended high school on Umboi Island. The students no longer were surrounded by kinsmen, no longer lived in urban centers, and no longer were supported by the Catholic mission. Worse still, from the students' point of view, they now were required to work in the school gardens. To children raised in a maritime environment, gardening was unpleasant, demeaning work. The "first-generation" Mandok students who went to Vunapope during the mid-1960s were seventeen to nineteen years old at the time they entered Form I (grade seven). According to Mandok concepts of physical and moral development, they were on the verge of adulthood. In contrast, students attending high schools on Umboi Island from

1970 onward were only twelve to fourteen—too young by Mandok standards to be expected to do hard garden work. The students complained that they were being over-worked and underfed in their bush high schools. Their parents, already wary of this new policy, felt sorry for them and angry at the school teachers for what they felt to be unreasonable and cruel exploitation of "mere children." They went home.

Added to these problems were other changes associated with the "retrench-ment" phase; in particular, a quota system for high school entrance begun in 1971. No longer could any student who had adequate grades be admitted as before when the Catholic Mission controlled education. Now each district of each province had a quota system by which students competed for limited high school places. The quota intro-duced a new concept of "failure" on Mandok. Parents were angry at what they judged to be an arbitrary and unfair barrier along their children's path to high school and town careers.

From the Mandok parents' perspective, the closer the country came to indepen-dence, the more they lost by participating in "development." By 1971, fewer Mandok students were allowed to go to what the Mandok felt to be an inferior location for

String band competition on Por Island (1979). (Photo by A. Pomponio)

substandard "European education." Early Mandok graduates noted that the standards of excellence even at the elementary level had declined drastically. As one early graduate of the school system remarked in 1979:

> When I was in school [early to mid-1960s], the teachers were much stricter—we were not allowed to speak Pidgin [Tok Pisin] or our language; we always had to speak English only. Now, the teachers are not strict about this, and the kids can't speak English. I saw the sixth grade exam that they just took, and it's a disgrace—they can't do in sixth grade what we had to do in the fourth grade.

Parents recounted bitterly the meteoric rise in school fees: no school fees in 1964; K40 annually per child in 1970; K150 in 1981; and by 1989, the fee at Lablab High School (Umboi Island) had risen to K241 (approximately U.S. $265). While school fees were rising, the access that the average Mandok family had to money had either remained constant (for those selling carvings or crafts) or had declined (for men migrating for temporary employment). Although by 1986, the Mandok had almost doubled the prices of local crafts, their earnings could not come close to keeping up with the phenomenal increase in school fees. This prompted one father of school children to comment, in 1981:

> If one hand holds a pen, then the other must hold a bushknife. We need to read and write and do numbers, yes. But first, we need to eat.

A Losing Investment

In most Melanesian societies, the spiritual realm and the material realm are interwoven. Veneration of ancestral spirits involves the acquisition, accumulation and exchange of material wealth with contemporaries. Europeans had power, money, important forms of knowledge (including sacred and religious knowledge), and many material "things." Papua New Guineans wanted access to European "cargo." Specifically, they wanted their children to learn "Europeans' knowledge" so they could earn money and send much valued "European things" back home. The promises of education soon caught on, and villagers in rural areas, eager to gain the wealth that education brought, sent their children to school in increasing numbers.

Parents also believed that through formal schooling, their children would become "like Europeans." Melanesian cultures typically stress learning by example, through an extended apprenticeship with an expert. Sending children off to school to learn from Europeans was analogous to their own system of apprenticeship. Through the European spirituality introduced by missionaries, people thought they would also gain access to European gods and their spiritual and cosmic power (see especially Lawrence 1964; and Swatridge 1985). Thus, the material and spiritual union central to Melanesian cosmology found reinforcement in missionaries' approach to education. An essentially "religious" element was inherent in these experiences all along.

If parents' and students' expectations were "materialistic," the government did nothing to dispel them. Administrative predictions estimated growth in the demand for skilled labor to equal twenty- to thirty-five thousand new positions between 1968 and 1973

Students entertain villagers with a skit at the end of the year school concert (1979). (Photo by A. Pomponio)

(McKinnon 1968:102). For a time, villagers' materialistic expectations could be met through these new employment opportunities. Students were pushed through the education system in anticipation of independence and were able to gain well-paying jobs in towns immediately after secondary, tertiary, or vocational training. For highly skilled and ambitious graduates, there was ample opportunity for rapid upward mobility to still higher-paying positions.

As independence approached, however, the job market flooded. Employment opportunities declined, and placement requirements escalated as more people competed for fewer jobs. By the end of the 1960s, three major problems had become apparent to the national government. The first was that the education system in its present form was too dependent on foreign (especially Australian) aid. The second was that jobs no longer awaited educated and skilled graduates of the school system. As a result, many students who were still in school, along with those who had just completed their studies, started returning home to their rural villages.

The third problem was a product of the first two: what to do with these unemployed "school leavers." A widening gap had grown between "traditional" expectations of village society and "modern" values of the urban educated. There was evidence of a burgeoning educated elite who were experiencing problems of personal identity and "cultural fit" in their villages. School leavers, disappointed by their apparent personal failures, were often involved in conflicts at home. Their parents, equally frustrated, labelled them *bikhets* (Tok Pisin for "stubborn," "recalcitrant," "contrary"). These problems of values, change, and continuity are not dissimilar to those faced by other developing countries.

Teenage girls play basketball on Por Island. (Photo by A. Pomponio)

The Mandok had come to count on the remittances received from their educated and employed children in towns to supplement village earnings from local activities and financial expenditures on Western items. This additional income, however, proved to offer only a temporary reprieve for the villagers. Whereas, until the late 1960s, anyone who was literate and numerate could expect to find a well-paying job, by 1970, a tertiary degree or diploma was necessary for all but the most menial jobs. And even finding a menial job was difficult. From the villagers' perspective, they were paying much more for their children's schooling and getting less in return. Their children were having trouble finding jobs and the parents were receiving much less in the form of remittances. As one educated town worker explained in 1979:

> Today, many parents have already seen their older children go to school and not get into high school and come back to the village, or go to high school and then quit and come home. Either way, the children are back in the village, living as their parents are living. Money is so hard to get, the parents figure, "Why should I spend my money and send them to high school at all if the kids come home and live the same way I do anyway, in the end?" The smart kids are pushed, so they are more motivated. The not-so-smart ones are left alone because the parents know they'll wind up back in the village anyway.

Moreover, those early graduates of the system who did succeed in finding urban careers had delayed marriage during their school years. These people were now adults with their own families and their own increasing living expenses.

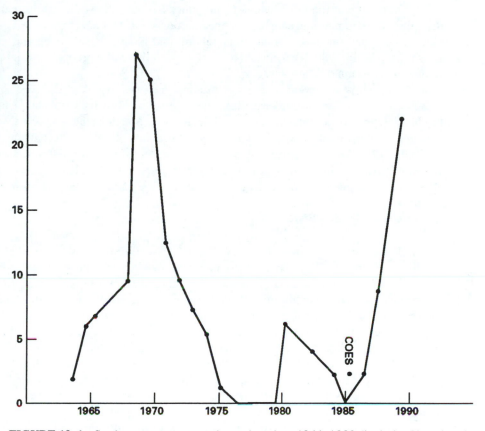

FIGURE 13–1 Students sent to secondary education, 1964–1989 (includes Vocational and Technical Schools)

These disincentives accumulated to a breaking point in the mid-1970s. Parents came to view schooling as a "losing investment." With decentralization of the government, the mission's role in education suddenly had become unclear. The expansionist era of educational and employment opportunities had created a "brain drain" of the village's brightest youths. There was no strong leadership anywhere. This was clearly a period of transition, but to what? No one seemed to know. Interest in school at all levels plummeted.

The number of Mandok children sent off the island for secondary schooling since 1964 reflects these changing attitudes (refer to Figure 13–1). This number rose consistently to a peak in 1969. The 1971 class was the first class to attend Gelem High School (Umboi Island), and after that the numbers dropped suddenly to zero between 1976 and 1980.[3] From 1980 to 1987, a dozen or so started, but fewer than a handful graduated. With a missionary priest's guidance, some school leavers pursued correspondence courses through the College of Extension Services (COES) in 1985. A few stayed with the project, but only one finished and took the final examination. Lack of materials, electric light for night work, and a place to study in the village posed constant obstacles even for the extraordinarily motivated.

Attendance at the Por-Mandok Community School[4] showed a similar pattern of dropping out, and parental support has been inconsistent. In 1979, for example, twenty children dropped out of the community school, and none was sent back and made to finish the year. In 1980, teachers had to work especially hard to get recalcitrant parents to pay the K3 annual school fees.

Comparative achievement levels of past and present Mandok graduates also reflect changing attitudes. The early graduates in the work force quickly earned a reputation for being bright, highly motivated, and upwardly mobile. In 1978, Mandok children scored well on a battery of cognitive tests, indicating a high level of cognitive development (see Lancy 1978, 1983). By 1979, Mandok students' reputation had changed. High school teachers expected them to drop out within the first year of high school, especially at Lablab. In that year they also achieved an all-time low score of 42.22 percent in the national grade-six exam.

Pragmatism, Mandok Style

Mandok parents adjusted their participation in schooling to reflect the likely return on their investment. They also expressed their dissatisfaction with shifting educational policies. From a ten-acre island in the middle of the sea, they were powerless to change government policies and educational rules, so they controlled the only thing they had: their children. They voted against administrative and educational policies, in a sense, with their children's feet. It seems that these attitudes were transmitted to the children, who moderated their classroom performance in a similar fashion (demonstrated by the low achievement scores of 1979). By 1986, attendance at the community school had improved. But this renewed commitment to their children's schooling had not carried over to improve teachers' status in the village since 1980: the three new teachers expressed the same complaints I had recorded seven years earlier (Pomponio 1985).

In the meantime, the island's population had continued to increase, as did the prices of trade store items. There were new movements afoot, this time from within, to move the community to Muru. On February 9, 1987, an earthquake measuring 7.4 on the Richter scale terrified the entire community (see Pomponio 1990b). Fearing a tidal wave, more Mandok took more seriously the proposal to move. The village remained underinhabited for several months afterward. Toward the end of 1987, a much-loved missionary priest returned after an eight-year absence, and by Christmas of that year most of the Muru settlers had moved back to Mandok (Mulderink 1988). As of March 1989, twelve students were enrolled in Lablab High School, and nine boys were at St. Joseph's Technical School in Lae (Mulderink 1989). Only time will tell if this cohort marks the beginning of a "new optimism" on Mandok.

DISCUSSION

I am not the first to observe that from the beginning, parents' interest in schooling in Melanesian communities and elsewhere was motivated by pecuniary concerns (see, for example, Conroy 1970). Nor am I the first to state that the entire notion of education was oversold to Papua New Guineans as a panacea for local and national problems (see Swatridge

1985). Such issues, however, usually pale in relation to national-level budgetary, curricular, and administrative concerns. The Mandok are not an isolated instance or an exceptional case. They are not alone in their frustrated efforts at "development" or in their pecuniary motives for "education." They may represent more of the norm than government officials of many developing (and some developed) countries would like to admit.

If anything, the short duration of each stage of Papua New Guinea's education policy displays an extraordinarily self-conscious attempt to produce and maintain an efficient school system. The concern for higher standards in the early 1980s was followed by a complete overhaul of the curriculum. Teacher training is beginning to acknowledge the importance of "community relations" in defining teachers' jobs. The IHD philosophy seems to provide a synthesis of the best of previous educational policies. It stresses early vernacular education aimed at quicker achievement of UPE, local resource development, and a more integrated approach to "local culture," "modernization," and the individual. IHD thus institutionalizes a characteristically Melanesian blend of the spiritual with the material.

The task is not easy. At the same time, the impediments to education—particularly in rural areas—are many. Since 1973, there have been several concerted attempts to give rural students equal access to a system that has favored students from more urban, cosmopolitan areas. Continual increases in school fees for secondary schools remain a barrier for rural school children whose parents have little income and virtually no disposable cash. Nationwide, fear of illegitimate pregnancy and other cultural constraints keep the provision of equal opportunities for girls and women problematic. Increases in urban violence and horror stories told by older siblings living in towns are retold in the villages during school holidays. These add more fear in the minds of parents who may already consider schooling to be a high-risk investment. Many parents are also disappointed with the actual remittances they receive. They do not understand that housing, electricity, transportation, and water, for example, siphon off earned wages. Town workers simply do not have the disposable cash their village relatives think they have.

While comparing education histories in three different PNG societies to 1980, David Lancy and I discovered that communities go through stages of "attitude development" that parallel those described above for the educational system (Pomponio and Lancy 1986). In the initial "supportive" stage, the newness of the school and the promises of Western education foster excitement and hope (Pomponio and Lancy 1986:44–46). Rather than becoming independent and participating in "development," this is often followed by a stage in which villagers become "dependent" on their educated and employed offspring (Pomponio and Lancy 1986:50–51).

An example of this phenomenon has been described for Ponam Island, Manus Province (Carrier 1981; Pomponio and Lancy 1986:50–51; see also Carrier and Carrier 1989, and Chapter 10, "The Samoan Exodus," by Paul Shankman, in this volume). Convinced from the outset that they could not "develop" their tiny sand quay, Ponam Islanders turned instead to education. They gained cash from remittances sent home to village parents from the formally educated, employed Ponams working in towns. Carrier asserts that on Ponam, "the strong elements of consciousness, rationality, calculation and intention which surround education and remittance" on Ponam justify calling education an "export labour business" (Carrier 1981:239).

There are many contrasts between Ponam and Mandok (Pomponio and Lancy 1986:50–53). First, Ponam students always went to the same high school at Lorengau, while Mandok students attended several different high schools in completely different locations over the years. They were unable, therefore, to build up a substantial support group once they were moved away from town and mission centers. Second, Ponam Islanders viewed themselves as "poor fishermen" who traded fish for vegetables on the Manus mainland. The U.S. government had built an airstrip on Ponam during World War II, which ruined Ponam for cash cropping. Ponam Islanders believed that the only way to obtain cash was from their children's remittances. For the Mandok, education was only one of several kinds of "development projects" they had tried since World War II (Pomponio 1992). In the precontact era Mandok formed part of the central hub of the entire Vitiaz Strait trade system, controlling access to valued goods within this system (Harding 1967). Rather than "poor fishermen," they liked to see themselves as "kings of the sea."

Whereas Ponam represents an educational "success" story, the Mandok case illustrates "failure." But whose failure was it? Mandok is an example of a third stage of attitude development: "disillusionment." For the Mandok, education was clearly a new type of investment. This investment involved more than financial gain. The entire package involved a moral commitment to a new value system that included Roman Catholicism, schooling, different perceptions of family life, social relations, and so on. The twisting and turning of government policies in education turned a "good investment" into a frustrating series of disappointments (Pomponio and Lancy 1986:46–50). When education stopped reaping adequate returns, the Mandok stopped investing (that is, they stopped sending their children to secondary schooling). The government did little to mitigate the results of this judgment. The school localization program and the quota system of the 1970s added insult to injury. Is it any wonder the Mandok were skeptical?

Change in external (that is, administrative) priorities does not necessarily produce changes in the expectations and goals of those who are most directly affected—parents and students. These problems were widespread throughout PNG and recognized at the government planning level even in the 1970s (Lancy 1979a, 1979b).

In the meantime, there seems to be a revival of interest in schooling on Mandok. Some graduates of the school system who have succeeded in their own lives are also old enough to convince village parents to send their children to school and to encourage and support them to pursue education beyond primary level. Younger parents who were themselves denied secondary schooling are working hard to procure it for their children. New kinds of technology have encouraged a new appreciation for schooling, and exposure to English-language movies and videos have heightened people's sensibilities regarding the desirability of learning English. Mandok's secondary education figures for 1988 and 1989 are encouraging, especially considering the long stretch of time since any substantial cohort was sent. They may mark a turning point in Mandok attitude development. In ten years, I would like to be able to describe the current era as a new stage of cautious optimism and recovery, born of a more realistic notion of the possible benefits of schooling.

Acknowledgments: This article is based on over twenty-four months research in PNG, conducted in two field trips. Research during the period 1979 to 1981 was funded by the PNG Ministry of Education, Research Branch and the Frederica deLaguna Fund for Predoctoral Research, Bryn Mawr College. A return trip to PNG for eight months (six in Siassi) in 1986–1987 was funded by the Wenner-Gren Foundation for Anthropological Research and a St. Lawrence University Faculty Research Grant. The write-up was conducted as part of an Andrew Mellon Postdoctoral Fellowship at the University of Pittsburgh. My thanks to all of these institutions for their support. Special thanks are also due to David Lancy, previously Research Officer for the PNG Department of Education for his continued encouragement, and to Lewis Kusso-Alless, Fr. Anton Mulderink, Richard Perry, Richard Scaglion, and Sara Sturdevant, for their critical reading of earlier drafts. Responsibility for interpreting their comments is, of course, mine.

NOTES

1. Although Mandok men did fight in World War II, they never considered it "their fight." It was something that "belonged to the Europeans." At the time, they were paid with trade goods. Much later (beginning in 1985) veterans received K1,000 for their services. Most Mandok men bought outboard motors with their money. For these reasons I categorize wartime participation with "work" and "labor migration."

2. The "T" stands for "Territory." The colonial administration maintained for many years a dual education system that recognized the profound background differences of native and expatriate children. Primary "T" schools served native Papua New Guinean children. Primary "A" schools catered to (primarily) Australian children, maintaining Australian standards of excellence for the children's eventual return to Australian or other Western school systems. Though this particular system no longer exists in government schools, a tripartite system still exists in the country. "Community schools" are the contemporary equivalent to "Primary T" schools. Mission schools are subsumed under the category of community school, but include religious instruction in their curricula. They are also likely to receive church subsidies. Although they require a fee, it is minimal for both at the elementary level. Both these schools follow a PNG-based curriculum. International schools, on the other hand, are private, and much more expensive. They follow a New South Wales, Australia, curriculum, and cater to expatriate and elite Papua New Guinean children.

3. During this period, the villagers experienced a devastating economic failure when they tried to purchase a boat and start a transport business. The entire process became a fault line for a political split in the village. This schism also contributed to the decline in secondary school students.

4. Mandok's community school is located on Por Island, about one-half mile across a channel from Mandok— hence, the name.

Identity, Community, and Social Relations

INTRODUCTION

The chapters in this section of the volume consider a number of themes in the social transformation brought on by intensified Western acculturation, rural to urban migration, and modernization in Pacific Islands societies. These themes include (1) the changing construction of social and personal "identities," (2) new patterns of community organization and social interaction, including gender relations; and (3) an increasing prevalence of Western-style social problems.

Dawn Ryan (Chapter 14) looks at the changing nature of village-town interactions and the new patterns of community organization that have resulted from rural to urban migration in Papua New Guinea. Since the end of World War II, rural Toaripi from the village of Uritai have migrated to Port Moresby in search of jobs. The first migrants established urban squatter settlements and maintained strong links to their home villages. Over time, however, these links have weakened and many Toaripi have become permanent "towns-folk." Nevertheless, Ryan notes that village affiliation continues to be an important component of urban Uritai social identity, as well as a determining factor in urban social interactions.

Frederick Errington and Deborah Gewertz (Chapter 15) consider changing gender relations among the Chambri of Papua New Guinea. They specifically focus on how notions of what constitutes male domination of females has changed over time. Errington and Gewertz compare the lives of two Chambri women (Sepik Province), one belonging to the era of the 1930s and the other a "modern" young woman of the 1980s and recent migrant to the town of Wewak. In the 1930s, Chambri women defined themselves as "persons" in terms of their embeddedness in kin networks. A woman's marriage partner was chosen by the senior males of her clan, yet Errington and Gewertz argue that this did not constitute male domination by Chambri women's own assessment. By the 1980s, however, Chambri youth living in Wewak town believed that rights to individual choice were central to "modern personhood." The "modern" young woman of the 1980s expected to choose her own partner; not to do so would have constituted her domination by males.

Dorothy Counts (Chapter 16) describes the culturally accepted pattern of wife beating and subsequent female suicide among the Lusi-Kaliai of West New Britain (Papua New Guinea). Although a part of traditional family relations, Counts argues that this pattern has been exacerbated by the rapid social and economic changes that have taken place in the island nation. In particular, national economic crises and a fluctuating standard of living (linked to rapid development), challenges to male authority posed by new educational and economic opportunities for women, and increasing abuse of alcohol and drugs have led to a higher frequency of wife abuse by husbands.

Mac Marshall (Chapter 17) analyzes a growing social problem in Pacific Islands societies related to Western acculturation: an increasing prevalence of drug and alcohol abuse. He notes that certain drugs (kava and betel) had been used socially in precontact times, but goes on to add that not only was their use culturally controlled and routine, but their effects were neither physiologically nor mentally damaging. Beginning with the first Western contact, alcohol, tobacco, marijuana, and other drugs were introduced and at least partially incorporated into island society. However, there are few existing cultural controls that can curtail their abuse. Marshall proposes that the aggressive media campaigns organized by the multinational corporations that sell cigarettes and liquor in the region contribute to this pattern of abuse.

14

Migration, Urbanization, and Rural-Urban Links:
Toaripi in Port Moresby

Dawn Ryan
Monash University

The homeland of the Toaripi-speaking people is in Malalaua District of the Gulf Province of Papua New Guinea, where they live in villages located on, and around, the mouths of the Tauri and Lakekamu rivers. The language group is divided into three socially distinct categories: Moveave, Toaripi, and Moripi, the respective descendants of people who lived in three large, autonomous villages until late last century. This chapter is concerned with the Toaripi; specifically, with those who come from, or who are identified with, the large village of Uritai.

Uritai is situated on a small island at the mouth of the Lakekamu river, on the site of the original Toaripi settlement, most of whose population dispersed to other locations following a large washaway in the estuary in 1928 (Ryan 1985:256).

Traditionally, the staple foods were sago, fish, and coconuts, and these are still important, although people also eat a great deal of store-bought foodstuffs. The terrain is low-lying and swampy, unsuitable for commercial exploitation, and the only local source of cash is copra. There has been no European settlement in the area apart from government officials and missionaries, but the impact of Western institutions has been profound, the church, in particular, having become an integral part of village life.

This chapter is concerned with the process and effects of migration over a period of approximately forty years since World War II, and discusses changes in the lives of both villagers and town dwellers in that time. First, there is a brief outline of contact history until World War II; then, the beginning of family migration and the founding of urban settlements are described. The rest of the chapter relates to migration and its consequences for the village over a period of more than twenty years, from 1960 to 1984.

TOARIPI: EARLY CONTACT HISTORY

First contact with the West occurred in 1879, when James Chalmers of the London Missionary Society (now part of the United Church) landed at the Toaripi village, Mirihea-Uritai (Langmore 1974:56). The church was the earliest and most persistent influence, the first missionary settling in Mirihea-Uritai in 1884 (Langmore 1974:62). When Australia assumed control of Papua in 1906, officials conducted annual patrols through the area, but no local government post was set up until 1946.

In 1910, there was a small gold rush to the head of the Lakekamu river, but the Toaripi apparently played little part as laborers. Indeed, they showed little or no inclination to sign on for any kind of work at this time (Ryan 1985:256). However, in 1920, a head tax was imposed on all able-bodied Papuan males over the apparent age of fifteen years, unless they had more than five children. For the first time, Toaripi men needed cash on a regular basis and began to sign labor contracts. The preference was that groups of young, unmarried men who in the recent past would have undergone seclusion in the men's house together would sign up to go work on the same plantation. Within a few years, many employers had formed a very unfavorable impression of workers from this area and refused to take them on, so they had to take work wherever they could get it (Ryan 1985:257). Nevertheless, a pattern was established whereby young men went away to work, usually for no more than one contract period, then returned to the village to marry and settle down. As far as can be ascertained, their absence caused minimal disruption to village life, as men of this age played little part in productive activities, their earlier role having been primarily that of warriors. On the other hand, the returning laborers had undergone experiences outside the ken of the village and brought back stories of this wider world. When, in 1928, it became possible to engage in wage labor without signing a contract, some Toaripi men took advantage of this, generally going to spend some time in Port Moresby. The overall number who did so, however, seems to have been small.

World War II was a period of great disruption for Toaripi. A village near Uritai was evacuated to make way for an Australian army camp, and most of the men were recruited as carriers. Many worked locally, as provisions and ammunition were transported up the Lakekamu river; others were dispersed throughout Papua and New Guinea in accordance with the perceived needs of the Allied forces. In either case, they were separated from their homes for some years, and the women had to do as best they could to support their families.

POSTWAR MIGRATION

Port Moresby had been severely damaged by bombing, and at the end of the war there was a big push to rebuild it as the Australians began to return. Workers with building skills were in great demand, and this provided an opportunity for a number of Toaripi men.

In the 1930s, the London Missionary Society had provided basic trade training for youths in its Moru District, which included the Toaripi area, so that, in 1945, several men possessed greatly valued skills in carpentry, painting, and plumbing. Wartime experiences, however harrowing at the time, had widened horizons, and there had also been a change in tastes and expectations so that there was among Toaripi an increased reliance on cash for items that were coming to be seen as necessities rather than luxuries. The upshot was that a number of these skilled men went to Port Moresby to participate in the building boom.

Much of the reconstruction work was organized through contracts. The Works Department would offer a job, from digging a ditch to building a house, at a fixed price, to be completed within a stipulated time. If a contractor thought that he could meet the conditions, he bid for the job. It was the contractor's responsibility to organize, pay, and house his work force. This kind of employment suited the Toaripi, who did not always take kindly to being mere workers, as it gave them the chance to work with whomsoever they wished. The contractors chose their workers from among kin, affines, and age mates, almost invariably from the same village. Accommodation was usually arranged by activating ties with the indigenous Motu people of the Port Moresby area.

There were very long-standing trade-cum-exchange links between the Motu and the Toaripi and Moripi, which meant that there were recognized partnerships and even a few affinal ties resulting from occasional marriages. In addition, many Motu and Toaripi had shared war experiences which were the bases of bonds of friendship and obligation. The Toaripi contractors seeking to provide housing for their workers invoked these ties with the Motu landowners in order to obtain permission to build one or two houses, and soon small clusters of these dwellings sprang up all over town.

Such freedom was in marked contrast to the situation that had obtained before the war, when there were legal restrictions on movement out of the home area. Papuans and New Guineans in towns had to live in designated areas or in quarters close to their employer's place; and those without employment, or deemed likely to cause a nuisance, could be removed from town (Fitzpatrick and Blaxter 1976). The laws were still on the books, but were not enforced, as they would have made the task of reconstruction much more difficult because they would have restricted the growth of the desperately needed work force.

Toaripi, then, had several advantages in the competition for building contracts: they had the skills, they could arrange to house their workers, and it was easy to travel by coastal boat from the village to Port Moresby. They soon made up a significant proportion of the work force in the building industry.

So far, those who had come to Port Moresby were following the established pattern of migration: that of unmarried or unaccompanied men leaving home to obtain wage employment and presumably planning to return when the job ended or they had reached whatever goals they had. This pattern, however, now underwent a significant change. Married men began to arrange for their families to join them in town, and sought permission from the Motu landowners to build more houses. Thereafter, the number of Toaripi migrants continued to increase as more families moved to Port Moresby and other men came to join the work force. The size of the settlements increased accordingly.

At first, permission was still sought from the landowners before additional houses were built; but, after a time, they were bypassed and only the original settler was consulted. Understandably, relations between landowners and settlers deteriorated. Motu, however, were reluctant to complain to the authorities, as this would have violated norms and expectations regarding the provision of hospitality. When they confronted the Toaripi directly, asking them to leave, to curtail the growth of the settlements, or at least to pay some kind of rent, the latter generally refused and on occasion threatened either physical violence or sorcery.

By the mid-1950s, the "Kerema" settlements, as they were known, were viewed with alarm by the authorities as well as the landowners. Nothing, however, was done to remedy the situation. Although the settlements were seen as constituting a social problem, they served a very useful purpose: they accommodated not only the contractors and their workers but also other Toaripi employed by the Australian administration and by private firms, thus helping to relieve the desperate housing shortage. In 1954, housing for better-paid Administration servants began to be provided (Oram 1970:53), and some Toaripi families left the settlements. Their places were quickly taken by new arrivals from the villages, and those who had moved continued to make the settlements the foci of their leisure-time activities.

Late in the 1950s, the Port Moresby reconstruction boom ended, and so did the period of prosperity for contractors. The Toaripi, however, did not go back to their villages in large numbers. Generally, those men with some skills either moved on to other towns where reconstruction or new construction continued to provide ample opportunities for work, or they joined the Administration as tradesmen. Those who were unskilled had to compete for jobs with men from other parts of Papua and New Guinea who had also been attracted to Port Moresby.

The persistence of the "Kerema" settlements was disconcerting to the Australians, who saw the Toaripi as temporary migrants whose real homes were in the villages. It was decided to make the settlements unattractive, in the hope that it would induce the inhabitants to leave and deter further migration. To this end, settlements were denied water supplies and garbage and sanitary services, but these measures failed to have the desired result.

What had been overlooked was that the settlements were in many ways "urban villages" whose inhabitants were linked by preexisting socially significant ties and who were able to maintain frequent contact with those still in the villages so that there was no feeling of being cut off from home. These people had become used to living in and depending upon a cash economy and there was no way in which they could maintain that way of life in the rural area. Finally, the migrant population was large enough to make it likely that an individual would be cushioned against the worst effects of disasters such as loss of employment or housing. Against all these factors, lack of convenient water supplies and sanitary services was a small discomfort.

URITAI VILLAGE AND OUTMIGRATION

In the period 1960–1962, approximately 40 percent of those designated "Uritai villagers" in census records were in fact absent. Most of those were in Port Moresby, although some were located in other urban centers. There was a great deal of visiting between Uritai and Port Moresby, as villagers went up to town on one of the coastal vessels that called every few weeks to pick up copra and unload goods for the cooperative and trade stores in the local villages. Many returned after a few weeks spent with kin, but some men stayed on to look for work, and some women took their children and joined husbands who had settled in the town.

Marriage Payment, Uritai Village, 1984. (Photo by D. Ryan)

Return visits by town dwellers were less common, usually occurring at Christmas, when some of the people in Port Moresby would charter a boat and come to Uritai for a few days. They would bring with them large amounts of goods such as rice, flour, and canned meat and fish, most of which would be distributed at marriage payments, mortuary feasts, or some occasion associated with the church. These visits were also times when marriages were arranged and elopements took place, although the new wives were unlikely to go to Port Moresby until at least some part of the marriage payment had been made and accommodation arranged.

A striking feature of the absentee population was the large proportion that had been continuously absent for many years and the number that had returned only once or twice for brief visits. Oddly enough, however, they were not lost to the village: their where-abouts in the town were known; they provided hospitality to visitors, even those who took months to find work; and they were consulted before decisions were made over land use, allocation of house sites, and the timing of ceremonial occasions.

Toaripi society is one in which genealogical links are transformed into socially recognized kin ties through the constant exchange of goods and services. Only thus are claims to land going to be validated. The kinship structure is cognatic, and there are no landholding groups. Instead, every person inherits from both parents the right to use land in a large number of widely scattered, named plots. An individual does not necessarily activate all the rights inherited, but the children will have difficulty in obtaining permission from the current users of the neglected blocks to join them. Each named block has a very large number of potential users: all the known descendants of the

Preparing for a feast, Uritai Village, 1984. (Photo by D. Ryan)

original users, who may have lived six or seven generations ago. At any one time, however, only a small proportion of them are actually working on it. The genealogical claims of others may be acknowledged, but that does not guarantee permission to use the land if it is decided that the claimants have not behaved like kin by looking after the land through usage and by participating in constant exchanges.

Thus, an absentee needs to maintain links with those members of his or her personal kindred who have remained in the village in order to have a chance of activating land rights in the event of a return. During the period 1962–1964, three families who had been away for many years returned to Uritai, but, of these, only one was able to stay on. The two who had to leave had very few close kin in the village and were effectively denied permission to build a house. On the other hand, the husband in the third family had numerous kin and both his parents were in vigorous middle age, and the wife's father was also in good health and participating in village life. It seems that a family wishing to return has a much better chance of doing so successfully if one of the spouses has a surviving parent in good health who can act as a sponsor.

Most absentees maintained their place among their kin, at least to some degree, by providing both long- and short-term hospitality to visitors from Uritai and by fulfilling obligations on ceremonial occasions with contributions of large quantities of store-bought foodstuffs. Although they had not put their position to the ultimate test of attempting to assert land claims, they were generally spoken of by their close kin as constituting an integral part of Uritai social life.

The town population was indeed very important. Its members provided money, introduced foodstuffs without which ceremonies were no longer considered complete, and provided accommodation for visitors and those seeking work. Since cash was now an essential part of village life and copra and wage labor constituted the only means of obtaining it, the migrants from Uritai enabled villagers to live and work in Port Moresby for a short time if necessary, and their contributions to ceremonial outlays were a valuable supplement to the money and goods that could be obtained with income from copra alone.

URITAI VILLAGERS IN PORT MORESBY

In 1963–1964, there were approximately three hundred Uritai people in Port Moresby, one hundred and eighty of them living in two settlements adjacent to the large Motu village of Vabukori. The larger of the two settlements had begun prior to World War II, when an Uritai man had obtained permission to build a house on the site. Later, the settlements had grown in the way described earlier. By this time, relations between the Motu villagers and the settlers were poor, marked by disputes over the settlers' use of the village water taps and other signs of ill feeling.

The settlers frequently expressed a sense of insecurity, fearing that the landowners would have them removed, as they were well aware of the authorities' hostility to the existence of localities such as theirs. In fact, the Vabukori villagers did go to court and attempt to have the settlers moved, but because they could not legally demonstrate their title, in the Western sense, to the land, their action was unsuccessful.

The larger settlement was divided into three sections, only one of which contained people from Uritai; the smaller one consisted entirely of Uritai people. Social interaction was overwhelmingly with people from the same village: it was here, after all, that those most closely bound together were to be found. Not only those who had grown up together and whose current place of residence had been largely determined by village-based ties, but also recent arrivals who had come to stay with kin, whether visiting or seeking work, all formed a community whose social characteristics were very similar to those of Uritai itself. There was, of course, contact with other Toaripi, especially if they lived nearby, but it was not of the same order of intensity unless there were affinal ties resulting from intervillage marriage.

This recreation of the village in town meant that the same obligations and expectations applied: social relationships had to be maintained by the constant exchange of goods and services. Not only did this constitute the very core of the way in which social life was understood and enacted, it was also a vital part of a strategy for survival in town.

For the overwhelming majority of Papuans and New Guineans, there was at this time no job security whatsoever and anyone could become unemployed at any time. In many cases, loss of a job meant loss of housing, as accommodation was tied to employment. Whether or not this was the case, a man who lost his job could wait for a long time before he found another and, in the absence of any social security system, had to rely on relatives for survival until he found another position or tried to go back and settle in the village. The Uritai population in Port Moresby was large enough to ensure that most people had close kin who could provide such support. This meant, however, that those who were employed needed to look after the others as an insurance against possible future disaster, or as a return for such help in the past. Since many were employed in unskilled or semiskilled jobs, and usually had their own families to support, these obligations placed considerable strain on resources.

Maintenance of social ties with others in town, however, constituted only part of the obligations. It was also necessary to maintain links with village kin. At this time it was very rare to hear an Uritai adult declare that he or she was permanently in town; rather, the notion of village as truly "home" was widely held, and there was usually a vaguely expressed intention of returning sometime in the indefinite future. If this option was to remain open then in some way obligations to village kin had to be fulfilled, and most town dwellers did this in the ways described above.

Overall, then, at this time Uritai could be seen as a bilocal social system in which the rural and urban centers were interrelated in such a way that each was indispensable for the functioning of the other.

PORT MORESBY: HOUSING AND EMPLOYMENT

Following reconstruction after World War II, Port Moresby grew in size and complexity as it developed into the governmental, commercial, and educational center of Papua and New Guinea. People from many parts of the country were attracted to it, and, by 1966, migrants accounted for approximately 80 percent of the indigenous population (Oram 1976:97). Many of these were uneducated and unskilled, especially those from the inland areas, and, overall, there was high unemployment. With the passage of time, the concentration of Toaripi in the building industry had declined as men took whatever work they could find in an environment where jobs were not easily obtained. They were increasingly in competition with men from other groups who had similar educational opportunities, so that the Toaripi's earlier advantages were lost.

From 1966, the Australian administration began acquiring land on which the various settlements were located, and, by 1970, it owned more than 90 percent of the land inside the town boundary (Oram 1970:48). The number of settlements themselves had grown from eighteen in 1964 to forty in 1970 (Oram 1974:173), and the Toaripi were no longer such a visible component of the migrant population.

In the late 1960s, the Port Moresby City Council began to provide services such as water supplies to the settlements, and, in the period 1973–1975, the Housing Commission oversaw the upgrading of settlements and the initiation of self-help housing schemes (Flack 1979:72–75). This meant that settlers had the opportunity to improve or build houses on land for which they paid a nominal rent in return for security of tenure, and some Uritai people left the settlements at Vabukori. Housing that only the comparatively well-paid could afford was also being built, and new suburbs sprang up around the town, and older subdivisions were extended. Again, some Uritai people moved to these areas from the settlements, while others with high

Gordons, a suburb of Port Moresby, 1984. (Photo by D. Ryan)

educational qualifications and good jobs went there immediately on coming to town. Those who remained in the two settlements at Vabukori were not able to improve their housing, as they were located on land that the Australian administration had not been able to acquire.

Uritai people scattered throughout the town continued to keep in touch with each other, but the settlements were no longer of such central importance. Settlement population continued to grow, however, as people kept coming from the village and as the younger generation of settlers married and began raising their own families.

Coastal shipping had all but disappeared by the mid-1970s and communication between the village and Port Moresby was considerably more difficult than it had been during the 1960s, but movement between the two areas continued.

Until late 1974, Port Moresby offered expanding employment opportunities, although not for those with little or no formal education (Curtain 1980:53). Thereafter, fewer jobs were available and higher educational qualifications were demanded (Garnaut et al. 1977:187–188). Those coming from Uritai were less likely to find work, or at least would have to wait longer before doing so (Morauta and Ryan 1982:46), and those who had not at least completed primary school had virtually no hope at all. At the same time, the urban households were also feeling the effects of the recession, so that the provision of hospitality was even more of a burden, and, possibly, the rationale for it was no longer so strong as it had been in the past.

Boroko shopping area, Port Moresby, 1984. (Photo by D. Ryan)

RURAL-URBAN INTERACTION

By 1983–1984, the Port Moresby population of those labeled "Uritai" contained a significant proportion of adults who had either been absent from the village for periods up to forty years or who had been born and had spent their whole lives in town. For the latter, in particular, talk of Uritai as "home" was a symbolic statement, and many of those who had actually grown up in the village had by now been away so long that it would be difficult to say what the significance of Uritai as "home" could be.

Some town dwellers no longer had any close kin in the village because they had all died or had also come to town. These people no longer had a place in Uritai (Morauta and Ryan 1982). Even people who did have kin in the village would find difficulty in returning. Those who remained and cared for land and trees on behalf of their siblings had increasingly come to assume superior rights over the joint inheritance and would not necessarily care to share it. The case has not really been tested, since, by 1983, only one family that was in Port Moresby in 1963–1964 had returned and settled in Uritai. Others who had grown old had stayed on in town, being supported by their children just as they would have been had they been in the village.

The settlements in 1983–1984 were remarkably similar to what they had been twenty years earlier. More than one-third of the households were still there, usually living in the same building. Most of their children, many now married and with families of their own, were living with or beside their parents. Although there was considerable stability in population, there had been some notable changes in its socioeconomic character. Whereas, in 1963–1964, many Uritai people lived in the settlements because they could not afford other housing (Ryan 1977:149), now there were people who could well have gone into expensive accommodation who stayed on because this was their home.

Despite the fact that the village seemed to be becoming less relevant to a growing proportion of the town dwellers, there was a constant stream of visitors from Uritai. In 1979, it became possible to travel by road from Port Moresby to a canoe mooring place on the border of Moripi territory, where canoes from villages throughout the Toaripi language area met people and conveyed them to their various destinations. By 1983, this had become a twice-weekly service that was well patronized. Overwhelmingly, the traffic was of village people going to, and returning from, town.

Approximately three-quarters of the households in Uritai had a child or sibling living in Port Moresby in 1983. Some of these absentees had been away a long time; others were young people with secondary or postsecondary education who had left more recently. In either case, villagers were going to visit people with whom they had very close kin ties. Some had mats or sago to sell, but most were going "to eat rice" and obtain money.

As Morauta has pointed out in discussing another Toaripi village (1985:239), a consequence of out-migration and frequent contact between village and town is that tastes and expectations in the rural area become progressively assimilated to those of the urban area. Thus, over the years, Uritai villagers' need for cash had grown and many of them were wholly dependent on remittances from kin in Port Moresby to meet it. Whereas, in the 1960s, Uritai people in town were expected to provide money and goods mainly on ceremonial occasions, in the 1980s they were also expected to make frequent contributions to help meet their village relatives' everyday requirements. In part, this was a reflection of the fact that copra production had virtually ceased because of low prices and the near impossibility of getting it shipped out, so that there was no longer a local source of cash, nor was it any longer possible for those with little or no education to go away and work for a while. It was also partly an expression of parents' expectation that their adult children should support them, whether they were in the village or the town.

Many of the town dwellers were torn between the need to provide for their own children and the strong obligation to look after parents and help siblings. In households in which only the husband had a job, and these were the great majority, the wife was in a particularly difficult situation if she wished to send remittances to her parents or have them come and visit. To complicate matters, many villagers had exaggeratedly inflated ideas about the amount of money and goods their urban kin could provide.

When town dwellers visited the village they were expected to make a substantial contribution to the household in which they stayed, either bringing foodstuffs with them or buying from the local trade stores. In addition, they often brought household goods, petrol for outboard motors, and the like. In return, of course, they enjoyed the opportunity to eat sago, fish, and vegetables, which were too expensive in Port Moresby to be more than an occasional luxury for many people. Nevertheless, a village holiday was an expensive one.

Koki's Market, Port Moresby, 1984. (Photo by D. Ryan)

Overall, rural-urban interaction was frequently marked by tension and mutual misunderstanding, although on the surface amicable relations might be maintained as people attempted to conform to the norms of proper behavior.

URITAI TOWNSFOLK

In 1983–1984, approximately three-quarters of those who identified themselves as "Uritai" in Port Moresby had either been born and brought up in the town or had been absent from the village for more than ten years. Of those who had arrived more recently, a considerable number were under thirty-five and had at least some secondary schooling, so that either they were employed or had good prospects of getting a job. There were also some women who had come to join husbands, but very few individuals who were long-term unemployed dependents.

As discussed earlier, the kinship organization and land tenure system are such that a large, and increasing, proportion of this population in reality no longer has a village "home," although few would be prepared to accept that fact if it were put to them. It is not likely that the matter will be tested very frequently, as Uritai becomes less attractive as a place in which to live. There are virtually no opportunities to obtain cash, and a subsistence-based existence is not likely to be congenial to those who have become used to urban life or have known no other. Despite all this, however, the

'Uritai' identity was maintained and there was a high degree of interaction, although it was less intense than had been the case in the 1960s.

Young townsmen were now less likely to marry village girls, simply because they seldom met them. There was, however, still a strong tendency to marry Toaripi girls, even if they were not "Uritai." Children of these marriages were identified as "Uritai," so that the group continued to acquire new members, even if they had never been to the village.

Port Moresby was by now a city of more than one hundred twenty-three thousand who had come from all parts of the country, and, in the face of this threatening heterogeneity, association with familiar and trusted people was a powerful source of a sense of security. This applied throughout the city population, of course, but what made the "Uritai" unusual was the fact that so many of them had had little or no experience of the place of reference. The significant factor would seem to be the social interaction itself; shared activities reinforced the sense of common identity, and this, in turn, generated further interaction. The constant visiting from the village, for all the problems that it often engendered, also provided many reminders of Uritai as a common point of origin.

The most important factor in the maintenance of "Uritai" identity, however, was the United Church which, like its precursor, the London Missionary Society, has always been organized in such a way as to give individual village congregations a considerable degree of autonomy. In Uritai, and other Toaripi villages, many activities were organized around and through the church, and those who were prominent in its affairs tended to be influential more generally in village life. Throughout the 1960s, Uritai villagers were raising funds to build a large church of permanent materials, and absentees were active participants in this project. In 1983–1984, money was being collected with a view to building a house of permanent materials for the village pastor; but, in this case, most of the cash was being provided by the town dwellers. Indeed, given the heavy reliance on remittances, much of the cash raised in the village in fact came from Port Moresby. This activity provided a focus for Uritai identity and a framework for interaction between village and town as well as within the town. It will continue to do so for some years, as the money was being accumulated only slowly.

There had also grown up in the settlements the practice of having regular monthly church services for "Uritai" people only. Each month the service was held at a different house, led by an Uritai man who was a deacon in the formal Vabukori congregation, and followed by a meal provided by the hosts. These services were a focus of specific "Uritai" identity within the more general Toaripi category.

CONCLUSION

The twenty-four-year period covered by the study has seen some interesting continuities as well as changes in patterns of migration and rural-urban interaction. It has overwhelmingly been the case that those who leave the village do so permanently and live in town with their families. With the passage of time, an increasing proportion of the urban population no longer has close kin in the village and thus, as discussed above, have now in all probability lost access to land.

The case, however, is not a straightforward one of proletarianization as the land continues to be held in customary tenure, and the rules and norms can be varied to meet different contingencies. The situation remains obscure because the very low rate of return migration means that claims have seldom been made. Save in the unlikely event of there being discovered means of making Uritai land commercially productive, this state of affairs will probably persist. Meanwhile, "Uritai" identity within the Toaripi category has continued to be an important means of promoting interaction and organizing activities, although the substance of the concept has changed in significant ways for many of the town dwellers.

Despite the fact that the migrant population of the 1960s has increasingly become a truly urban one (Morauta and Ryan 1982), there are still enough town dwellers with primary kin links in the village for rural-urban interaction to occur on a large scale. And, migration is still taking place, although the migrants are now almost exclusively young men and women with enough education to make it likely that they will get jobs. There has not been a progressive withering away of primary links between the village and town.

In fact, rural-urban links continue to be important, although the form they take and the significance they have are different from what they were in the 1960s. It is no longer possible to see Uritai as a bilocal social system. The village needs the town for its continued existence, but the town no longer needs the village, even though this is not generally recognized by the people themselves.

Acknowledgments: The field work on which this chapter is based was carried out in 1960–1962, 1963–1964, 1972, and 1983–1984 and was funded variously by the University of Sydney, the Australian National University, Macquarie University, Monash University, and the Australian Research Grants Scheme.

15

The Historical Course of True Love in the Sepik

Frederick Errington
Mount Holyoke College
Deborah Gewertz
Amherst College

In 1987, while living among Chambri migrants settled on the outskirts of Wewak, the capital of East Sepik Province of Papua New Guinea, we were shown a letter Emma Kambu had written and was about to send to her Chambri boyfriend. Emma was a fourteen-year-old Chambri girl; in her words, one who "loved to wear smart clothes and go around the town," as did many other girls of her generation. She admitted to us with some giggling that she wanted to marry the young man to whom she had addressed the letter. The letter had been written with care, in English, on a piece of notebook paper. To it was glued a picture cut from a Japanese calendar purchased by Emma for just this purpose at Wewak's Christian book shop. The picture was of a crane standing on one leg under a tree. Below the picture was the caption, "Follow the way of love," attributed to First Corinthians, verse 14. Emma's letter continued with this theme of love:

```
Dearest bro,

    Hey, we are in trabel now. Please I want to see you at Kreer
market at 12 noon. Just today. Bro don't refuse my note. Please
come and I will tell you what they were talking about us.

    Please my one you must come and face me.

                        Thanks.

                        Love,

                        Emma Kambu
```

In 1933, while Margaret Mead was living in one of the three Chambri villages on Chambri Island, in the Chambri Lake region of the Sepik, she saw Yebiwali, a young widow, make an overture to the young man she wished to marry. Specifically, Yebiwali sent Tchuikumban the head of a fish. This action, like that of Emma, also precipitated some "trabel," which Mead describes at length.

As we shall see, the difference between calendar illustrations and fish heads indicates more than just an adjustment in the conventions of courtship during the fifty years that separates these events. The concern of this chapter is to determine the changes—as well as the continuities—in the lives of Chambri women from the time of Yebiwali's overture, shortly after "first contact," to that of Emma's, in the present. The lives of these two young women, viewed in their respective settings, can provide both illustration and evidence of the course of gender relations during a most important period of Chambri history. In our effort to compare the lives of these women and to understand the character of the gender relationships each participated in, special attention is given to the issue of domination. Although a concern with domination would be appropriate in almost any representation of gender relations, it is virtually essential in discussing gender relations among the Chambri. The Chambri, after all, were described by Mead as a society in which *women dominated over men.*

In order to examine Chambri gender relationships over time, one needs to recognize that domination must be understood with respect to specific—and changing—cultural circumstances. An essential component of domination is that persons actually *experience* control by others that they regard as unwarranted. To understand what might be experienced as unwarranted control, one must take into account the objectives and interests of actors in particular cultural instances. One must consider what men and women might actually seek to be doing, benefit from doing and, correspondingly, perhaps prevent others from doing. One also needs to consider cultural definitions (which may themselves be subjects of contention) of what is unwarranted—as opposed to appropriate or reasonable—control.[1] Given these concerns, the following is proposed as our working definition of domination for the Chambri: that which *they would regard as unjustifiable deprivation of the capacity to make reasonable decisions.*

In order to understand Chambri gender relations, we will explore in some detail the (culturally defined) objectives and interests of both men and women as well as the extent to which they are, respectively, able to pursue these without significant interference. In this latter regard, a focus on Chambri marriage arrangements, a major area in which the objectives and interests of men and women are distinct yet intersect and the context in which we meet Emma and Yebiwali, is especially appropriate for consideration of the possibilities of gender domination.

In the discussion of Yebiwali's case we examine not simply what Mead reported as happening, but the perspective Mead brought to her description of the events. Although partially correct about the character of Chambri gender relations—Chambri women did evidently have substantial control over their lives—Mead's account of Yebiwali's situation reflects an instructively significant misreading of the objectives Yebiwali was, as a Chambri woman, likely to have had. Thus, Mead's perspective is discussed with some care for two reasons: to show the necessity of understanding gender relations—including those of domination—in terms that do correspond to culturally defined and experienced objectives of men and women, and to construct a more accurate rendering of those events.

Finally and most generally, we argue that calendar pictures replacing fish heads signaled an important transformation in socioeconomic circumstances which, in turn, modified the objectives of, and relationships between, Chambri men and women. Specifically, *domination* (as defined in this chapter) has come to have a new meaning: over the years there has been a shift for Chambri with respect to their cultural standards concerning what would be an unjustifiable deprivation of the capacity to make reasonable decisions. That Yebiwali was not (as it turned out) able to fulfill her desire to marry Tchuikumban had, we think, a different import to her than would be the case for Emma if she were unable to marry the man of her choice. Simply put, Yebiwali was a different sort of Chambri than was Emma; that comprising domination for her would not be the same as for Emma.

YEBIWALI: HER LIFE AND TIMES

Yebiwali's case had interested Mead primarily because it seemed anomalous. Mead contended that Chambri women dominated Chambri men because individual Chambri women had economic autonomy: they were in charge of the underlying economics of life. They controlled subsistence fishing and, of even more significance, they wove the mosquito bags that were an important item of trade throughout the Sepik region of lowland swamps. In addition, Mead claimed, women controlled the shell valuables derived from the sale of these mosquito bags (Mead 1935:254).

Mead's interpretation of Chambri gender relationships, and thus of Yebiwali's circumstances, rested on certain Western—rather than Chambri—ideas of the importance of economic autonomy. She argued that because Chambri women controlled major economic resources, Chambri men lacked the economic individualism that would enable them to be themselves. Instead, they were forced to act against their own inclinations which, in turn, produced a crisis in their subjective experience of themselves—a psychosexual conflict which, in some cases, became a neurosis. Mead wrote:

> Here is a conflict at the very root of [a Chambri male's] psycho-sexual adjustment; his society tells him that he rules women, his experience shows him at every turn that women expect to rule him.... But the actual dominance of women is far more real than the structural position of the men, and the majority of Tchambuli [Chambri] young men adjust themselves to it, become accustomed to wait upon the words and desires of women. (1935:271)

However, Yebiwali, in Mead's view, lacked the basis of autonomy because she had never acquired the skill of weaving mosquito bags. Consequently, *unlike other Chambri women*, Yebiwali could not marry the man of her choice, Tchuikumban, to whom she had given the head of a fish. Thus, as part of her argument that it was their economic autonomy that enabled Chambri women in general to dominate over Chambri men, Mead claimed that, in this particular case, Yebiwali was dominated because she lacked vital economic skills (Mead 1935:261–262).

Although there appears to be no evidence to support Mead's claim that Chambri women dominated over Chambri men, our data do suggest that Chambri women were not dominated by Chambri men. They suggest as well that Mead was quite correct in linking

Chambri gender relations to their socioeconomic circumstances. Yet the position we take on the implications of those circumstances differs from hers in major respects. To begin with, we attribute far more importance than did she to the influence of regional and systemic factors on gender relationships.

The Chambri were known throughout the area as producers and purveyors of essential commodities. Not only did Chambri women weave mosquito bags, but men fashioned stone tools from quarries on Chambri Island. These they traded to their Sepik neighbors, especially to the Iatmul for the shell valuables central to their ceremonial exchanges. Because their trade items were so important, the Chambri were relatively protected from attack by their powerful Iatmul neighbors and, therefore, never developed a male-oriented military organization comparable to that of the Iatmul. Relations between Chambri men and women were, for this reason alone, much more egalitarian than between Iatmul men and women (see Bateson 1958; Hauser-Schaublin 1977). Moreover, Chambri relations of trade mitigated against the development of male dominance in yet another way. Specifically, because the access of Chambri men to shell valuables was substantially dependent on the availability of these to their trading partners among the Iatmul, Chambri men could not appreciably increase the flow of shells to themselves by increasing their production of trade items. Thus, the control of women and their products—mosquito bags in particular—was irrelevant to either the military or political viability of Chambri men (see Feil 1984; Josephides 1985; Lederman 1986).

Not only is there more significance in such regional and systemic factors in determining gender relationships than Mead allowed, there is another aspect of her analysis that we believe to be erroneous; she interpreted economic relationships as they affected relationships of dominance according to cultural assumptions that make much better sense to us than to the Chambri. As one can see in her discussion of male psychosexual neuroses, she viewed dominance as the extent to which Chambri were unable to act as subjective individuals—that is, were unable to achieve self-expression because they lacked an economically derived individualism (see Gewertz 1984; Errington and Gewertz 1987a). But Chambri women and men sought neither such a Western form of self-expression nor such a Western form of relationship. Mead, thus, was imposing on the Chambri—and, in this case, on Yebiwali in particular—her own cultural understanding of persons and objectives and, based on this understanding, her own cultural interpretation of what constituted dominance in gender relationships (see also Strathern 1988).

Let us, then, briefly reconsider the case of the remarriage of Yebiwali to see whether *in terms of Chambri assumptions* about the nature of persons and their objectives she was dominated. Was she, indeed, unjustifiably deprived by Chambri men of the capacity to make and enact what by Chambri standards were reasonable decisions? Was she, in other words, deprived of the capacity to pursue those strategies that were in fact important to her: those strategies that would enable her to become, what could be termed, a Chambri woman of worth?

During a debate in the men's house, Chambri men argued at length about whom Yebiwali should marry (Errington and Gewertz 1987b). According to our own Western cultural expectations about what constitutes dominance in gender relationships, certain data concerning this debate might indeed suggest that she was dominated by these men. After all: (1) Yebiwali was not allowed to be present—much less express her preferences—during the discussion. (2) Nor did these male debaters even address the possibility that she be allowed to marry Tchuikumban, the man to whom she had shown interest. (3) Instead, the discussion focused on the claims of two political factions, each asserting control of superior cosmological power. (4) Eventually, the wishes of her former father-in-law prevailed that she should marry his preference, a political ally named Akerman. Thus, Mead concluded that Yebiwali, lacking the economic power based on proceeds of mosquito bag sales, was dominated because she was forced, through the activities of these Chambri men, to marry a man not of her own choosing.

But what, from the point of view of *Chambri men and women*, would actually have been of concern in this case? Were they, as Mead suggests, concerned with subjective self-expression that could only come from an individualistic economic autonomy? In contrast to what one would expect from Mead's interpretation, those Chambri men and women we knew not only defined themselves by, but were thoroughly enmeshed in, social and economic networks. Indeed, for a Chambri, the importance of immersion in such networks virtually went without saying.

That they were the very stuff of life would have been apparent to any Chambri in a thoroughly redundant way from earliest experience. For example, the houses into which children were born were themselves embodiments and illustrations of patrilineal connection, solidarity, and affinal interdependence. Each house not only carried the name of the apical ancestor of the house-owning patriclan, but had its central post carved with clan emblems and draped with clan ceremonial gear. On either side of this central post, and supporting the thatched roof, were some five or six additional carved posts, each called by an ancestral name of the agnate whose domestic area surrounded the post. Each of a man's wives, in turn, placed her cooking hearth in his area of the house and fastened there the ancestral hook she was given by her own agnates on which to hang the basket containing her patrimony of shell valuables. Such a house, the very physical context of much of daily life, was hence a reiteration of the social relationships of the clan.

Moreover, in significant measure, Chambri were the incarnation of their patrilineal and matrilateral relationships. Chambri were given names by their patrilineal and matrilateral relatives that both reflected and affected their fundamental social relationships and identity. These names, which were public knowledge and used as terms of address, served in much the same way as did the clan house itself to define Chambri through reference to their social networks. In addition to these publicly known names, there were secret names used to evoke powerful ancestors and other totemic spirits. The most efficacious of these secret names were the carefully guarded possessions of particular men. They provided the basis of what might be regarded as a man's spiritual reputation—his reputation for having cosmological and other power. The specific names a man knew, when used correctly, enabled him to become his ancestors and thus to incorporate their efficacy.

Thus, rather than regarding themselves as unique subjectivities—as unique clusters of dispositions, capacities, and perspectives—Chambri considered themselves to be essentially the embodiment of their social networks, the embodiment of their relationships with both living and dead. These relationships were the basis not only of identity, but of long-term obligation. Both men and women were unequal to those who had provided them with their lives—their mothers and those, the wife-givers, who had provided their mothers—because they owed them a profound debt for life itself. However, women were able to pursue a much different strategy than men for achieving the relative equality and thus the relative worth which came through redemption from this ontological debt.

Women were able eventually to achieve equality with their mothers and those wife-givers who provided them by reproducing social persons. In this highly endogamous society (with over 30 percent of marriages with a matrilateral cross-cousin) after several generations, a woman's descendants became members of the same patriclan as those who had given her life. Moreover, given the Chambri assumption that identity was largely constituted by social position, these descendants were, in a fundamental way, those ascendants whose positions they had come to hold. Hence, a woman, because she could produce life, was able to pay her ontological debt and achieve equality through a kind of reproductive closure: through replacing—reproducing—those who gave her life, she would have caused her own existence (see Weiner 1976, for somewhat comparable circumstances).

Like other Chambri women, Yebiwali in all likelihood sought to achieve worth primarily through reproductive closure. Although, as other Chambri women, Yebiwali might prefer to marry in such a way that her daughter's daughter would eventually assume the social position of her mother, any children she might bear, *regardless of how she was married*, would be viewed as adequate self-reproduction.

In contrast to women, who could with time pay their ontological debts in full, Chambri men could never completely compensate their wife-givers for having provided the women who had given them life. That men could never entirely free themselves of ontological debt generated a complex politics in which they pursued strategies for dealing with unfulfilled (and unfulfillable) affinal obligations. Senior men, primarily, were engaged in continuing struggles to achieve relative worth by showing that they were at least equal, if not superior, to all other men in their capacity to deal with their debts by compensating wife-givers. The outcome of these struggles, as with the outcome of events most generally, was seen as determined by the relative power men held through their knowledge of secret and efficacious names. Because men were, in fundamental respects, their capacity to incarnate ancestral power, the course politics took provided an essential measure of worth and being.

Marriage decisions were thus political moves that required careful calculation by clansmen, especially clan leaders, of existing clan resources and obligations. Periodically, as with the case of Yebiwali, a decision might have to be made about the future marriage of a young widow. Those of her dead husband's clan could choose to perpetuate an existing affinal obligation by marrying her to one of her dead husband's agnates. Or, if overwhelmed by their current obligations, rather than face the humiliation of possible default or meager payment, they might decide to sacrifice a measure of prestige by letting the relationship lapse. Yet, even under these latter circumstances, they would still seek to play a political role. Because they had paid at least some bride price for her, they would attempt to influence her remarriage so as to derive some strategic benefit.

And so it went in this ceaseless competition between men to show themselves as persons of power and worth. In this Chambri context, the choices men made of marriage partners were not expressions of personal—subjective—attraction. Marriage choices were the playing out of their political strategies in a context of perpetual indebtedness.

Thus, in Chambri society, the objectives, strategies, and spheres of activity of men and women were essentially distinct and ordinarily did not conflict. Nor, it should be noted, were Chambri women considered of less cultural value than were Chambri men. Therefore, the fact that only men spoke in the debate concerning Yebiwali's remarriage and that the only concerns voiced were male political concerns did not engage or much affect Yebiwali, nor mark her as inferior. Because Yebiwali found the decision of the men acceptable—although for reasons other than theirs—she did not have to be coerced to marry her father-in-law's preference, Akerman, rather than Tchuikumban. Moreover, it must be stressed that *even a powerful man would not wish to marry a woman against her will* for she might disclose to his enemies names and other ritual secrets he had inadvertently revealed, perhaps while sleeping, and so entirely undermine his future efficacy and worth.

Hence, even in this singular case—the only one Mead encountered of a woman who appeared to be under male domination—Yebiwali was not dominated since marriage either to Tchuikumban or to Akerman would have satisfied her interests as a Chambri woman. Regardless of whom she married, she knew that her marriage was appropriately a matter for consideration by her agnates, affines, and others composing her social network and self. It would be they, after all, who would transact in the shell valuables, the symbolic wombs, that would convey her from one extended household to another. (Indeed, her present of the head of a fish to Tchuikumban anticipated her role as fish-provider in such a domestic context.)

Significantly, in 1984, when we met Yebiwali as a very old lady, some fifty years after Mead had first described her case, she insisted that she be addressed as "wife of Akerman" and, in addition, emphasized in several different ways her success in having reproductively replicated herself.

TRANSFORMATIONS

By the time that Papua New Guinea had achieved independence in 1975, most Chambri children were attending grades one through six in the local Catholic school. Money had completely replaced shell valuables in affinal exchanges, and a clan's viability in cere-monial matters had become less dependent upon the number and solidarity of its members than on the remittances of its wage-earners. Yet these remittances were used in affinal exchanges, as shell valuables had been, to construct the effigies that were symbolic women. These effigies were presented by wife-takers to wife-givers, as one presentation in a lifelong series, in return for the actual women received.

When women had been given as wives in exchange for shell valuables, they had not been regarded as purchased objects worth a certain number of shells, but rather as embodiments of affinal relationships of enduring inequality. The same had remained true when presentations were made in money. In the context of affinal exchange, money was used largely as the functional equivalent of symbolic wombs—it was part of a gift economy; however, in the context of most other transactions—as, for instance, at a trade store—it was a generalized medium of exchange—it was part of a commodity economy. It could be used to buy almost anything—radios, tape recorders, outboard motors—and did not necessarily generate further relationships.

The Chambri, then, had come to operate within both a gift and commodity economy (Gregory 1982). It was, however, unclear, at least in the Chambri instance, whether this separation of context and meaning would persist. Certainly there were some indications that the meaning money had in the commodity economy might displace the meaning it had in the gift economy so that, for example, the presentation of bride price might come to be regarded as the purchase of a woman rather than as a part of an affinal exchange. Now that the women were acquired with the same medium of exchange as were a vast array of commodities which could be owned and controlled outright, two related possibilities were likely to arise: one, affinal relations might become largely commercial; and two, gender relations might shift—women might acquire some of the attributes of commodities.

Indeed, during field work in 1983 we encountered several instances in which wife-takers speculated as to whether exceptionally high bride prices might be sufficient to retire the affinal debt. To the extent that social relations became substantially monetized in these ways, the concept and experience of ontological debt and, consequently, the way in which personal worth was defined and established, appeared likely to undergo substantial change. Wife-takers' contribution of money could be regarded as any commercial transaction might be regarded, subject to the same appraisals. Moreover, if affinal exchanges became comparable to other commercial transactions, there would be the possibility that payment of cash might confer disposal rights. Thus, if the acquisition of a bride came to be generally viewed primarily as a monetary transaction, not only might affinal relationships be terminated on the conclusion of the business deal, with no social relationship necessarily established between wife-givers and wife-takers, but also women might be dominated while pursuing their own interests.

Upon return to the Chambri some four years later, we expected to find that social relationships would have become increasingly monetized in just these ways, and that monetization had progressed furthest in the towns, where Chambri found themselves dependent on cash for even their subsistence. It was in one such town—Wewak—that Emma Kambu and the boyfriend to whom she planned to send her love letter lived.

EMMA: HER LIFE AND TIMES

By the early 1970s, Chambri came to Wewak in ever-increasing numbers, staying with those kin or co-villagers already living in the area known as Chambri Camp. They came primarily to earn money to take or send home. But they also came to see what town life was like. Women who came to sell fish might stay several months before returning to Chambri; the men who accompanied them or those who came alone might look for jobs and stay longer. They built houses or additions to existing structures for themselves from whatever was available—bush materials, scavenged pieces of sheet metal, and even cardboard—and squeezed these in as they could. The 117 adults living in the Camp came to describe it as the fourth Chambri village. Indeed, as many lived there as in any one of the three home villages.[2] And furthermore, many of those living in the Camp eventually considered it their home and did not plan to return to Chambri at all, except perhaps for brief visits. Virtually all, however, still considered themselves to be thoroughly Chambri, bound to other Chambri for their very identity as persons by ties of relationship and by complex and continuing histories of interaction.

(Dawn Ryan, in Chapter 14 of this volume, reports similarly that Uritai living in town rarely visit their village but still regard themselves as Uritai.)

For young people, in particular, life in town was preferable to that at Chambri because it provided them with experiences and opportunities that simply did not exist at Chambri. Moreover, it provided them with relative freedom from traditional forms of authority.

Young Chambri men and women found wandering around Wewak with their Chambri friends exciting, especially when they could present themselves in stylish clothes. They would spend hours in the trade stores looking at portable radio–tape recorders and at clothing, and at other products that would further embellish their appearances. And, as they circulated in little groups looking at the sights of Wewak, Chambri youth were also looking at other Papua New Guineans—a few from the Highlands or perhaps from Rabaul, but most from the various villages of the Sepik. Although there was ordinarily only minimal interaction between these Papua New Guineans, such as an occasional greeting in Pidgin English, most knew each other, often by name, and certainly by village or region of origin and by area of residence in one of the twenty-nine equivalents to Chambri Camp scattered throughout Wewak.

Encounters among these youths who were socially peripheral but not socially irrelevant to each other were charged with excitement stemming from a sense of freedom, potentiality, and danger. Such a sense was most palpable at night, when young men, and increasingly young women, wearing their most sophisticated outfits, congregated to drink and dance at the Sepik Club or another bar, or at some temporary dance ground. Although liaisons occasionally occurred, more typically the efforts by a young man to impress a young woman from another group provoked a fight between the young men of both groups. (In an instance that most Chambri found amusing, a young Chambri man asked a woman from another village to dance, and when she refused, he kicked her in the rear. His performance as seducer and fighter was regarded by even his friends as seriously flawed.)

Although everyday life in town was often exciting, it was also frequently hard, as well as dangerous. Only 17 percent of those adults living in the Chambri Camp had regular salaries. Most of the other men and women in the Camp were artisans—carvers or basket weavers— and relied for their survival on income earned from intermittant sales. The average yearly income of these artisans, we estimate, was only (U.S.) $230. They eked out a living somehow, depending for food at least partly on smoked fish occasionally sent from Chambri, green mangoes gathered from trees belonging to others, and small marsupials killed in the bush. Moreover, many had to rely on remittances from kin farther afield in Papua New Guinea.

There was also a widespread perception that crime, particularly in the towns, was rampant (see Morauta 1986; O'Collins 1986). During our research in 1987, three Chambri (in Wewak alone) were arrested for two separate thefts—robbery at knife point and burglary—and three Chambri suffered attack—one rape, one stabbing, and one death as a result of beating.

When those Chambri no longer new to the town and its excitements reflected on why they remained in Wewak, they recognized that if they were to return to Chambri Island they would have plenty to eat. Indeed, they talked nostalgically of low-water time when the lake literally overflowed with fish. They also recognized that one would be safer from criminal attack in the home villages than in Wewak.

Many migrants were nevertheless committed to town life because it enabled them to escape the constraints of the village. Young people, especially, sought the freedom from what they had, as moderns, come to regard as the coercion characteristic of traditional Chambri life. Rex Kamilus, a Chambri migrant, expressed these feelings, saying that in town, "you are free to walk about; you are the master of yourself." In contrast, he said that people at home practiced the "ancestral custom of killing people by poisoning [ensorcelling] them." When asked to elaborate, he said that if, for example, he tried to seduce a young woman at Chambri and her father found out about it, he would either ensorcell him or hire someone else to do so.

He continued by telling us that the "big men" at Chambri consistently prevented the younger men and women from holding all-night dance parties to modern music because they thought that such occasions encouraged young people to choose their own sexual and marriage partners. He stressed that big men liked to arrange marriages for everyone. (Indeed, as we have seen, the arrangement of affinal alliances was central to Chambri politics.) He described a recent debate that took place at Chambri concerning these parties. All of the older men sat on one side of the men's house, opposing the dances as new and pernicious, while all of the younger men sat on the other side, supporting them as new and desirable. The young men lost and the dances were discontinued.

A similar view, although reflecting a woman's perspective, was presented by Gabriella Apak, a woman of twenty-nine with two illegitimate children. She had been living in Wewak for seven years, supported largely by remittances from a brother working in the Bougainville copper mine. When we asked her why she did not return to Chambri, she at first said she was foolish for not doing so. Then, lowering her voice, she revealed that she and many other young women did not go home because they would be expected to marry old men whom they did not like and would be ensorcelled if they refused. If big men at Chambri were rejected, they would hire someone to place a bespelled object on a path frequented by the woman who had thwarted them. When she stepped over it, its magic power entered her body and she became sick and died.

Gabriella then told us of a recent dream that had warned her of this danger. She dreamt that a man she could not immediately identify had come to the house of one of her female friends at Chambri and said, "Here is some betel pepper for Gabriella. When Gabriella wants to chew betel nut, give her a little of this." She also described the man in her dream as holding the pepper, which was huge, at the level of his crotch. Gabriella knew that this had been a "real" dream—one which predicted forthcoming events—so she went to two other Chambri women living in the Camp to discuss it. They told her that she should avoid taking betel pepper from anyone. They also suggested the identity of the man wishing to ensorcell her. He had already poisoned another woman who had refused to marry him by providing her with poisoned betel pepper. As his intended victim bit into it, a bespelled leaf had emerged. Fortunately, she had the support of her father and brothers who had not wanted her to marry the sorcerer. They helped her to counteract the magic by gathering the youngest coconuts from the tallest trees, boiling the nuts and then washing her with the resulting liquid. This enabled her to be cleansed of the poison she had consumed, but it had been a narrow escape. Profiting from her dream and from the example of this young woman,

Gabriella did not intend to return to Chambri as long as this man desired her, lest she be doomed either to become his wife or to die.

It should be noted, however, that it was still the case that even a powerful man was not likely to wish to marry a woman against her will. Women back at Chambri said that the real reason Gabriella and other young women remained in Wewak was because they were too lazy to fish and gather firewood. One said resentfully: "They say we smell of fish; they like to walk around town smelling of perfume; they prefer to be supported by others rather than working hard themselves." Yet, regardless of whether Gabriella actually thought her only alternative to marriage was death if she returned to Chambri, she clearly did not want to be put under any pressure to marry someone not of her choice.

NICK AMBRI: THE LIFE AND DEATH OF A CHAMBRI ROCK-AND-ROLL STAR

Rex, telling us earlier of the repressive actions of Chambri big men, had mentioned Nick. It was over performances of Nick's Yerameri Drifters Band that the big men had instituted a ban on all-night dances. Nick's songs blended traditional and modern elements: the lyrics consisted of a brief Chambri phrase repeated over and over, yet were concerned with themes of love and rebellion and were set to string-band music. The following eight songs (in translation) were the entire corpus of Nick's music:

1. Come here. (This was addressed to his girl friend.)
2. Father, mother, I don't belong here.
3. Mama said slow down. (But he did not listen.)
4. Mama said so. (But he did not listen.)
5. She follows me when I walk about. (This referred to the devotion of his girl friend.)
6. You're too loud. (This was what the big men said about his music.)
7. You don't want to wait for your boy friend. (He was trying to convince a woman to reject the man arranged for her as husband and to accept him.)
8. Bernadette. (This was the name of his girlfriend, later his wife.)

It was clear to us that the power for Chambri youth of these songs of love and rebellion came in significant part from the circumstances of Nick's own life. Whereas young men and women—like Gabriella and Rex—had fled Chambri rather than be subject to arranged marriages or other forms of coercion, Nick had, after attending vocational school in Madang for a year, chosen to remain at Chambri and challenge his elders. He had, we discovered, defied his father by marrying Bernadette, the woman of his own choice. His subsequent and lamentable—although, in the view of young Chambri men and women, entirely predictable—death epitomized for these youth the problems they faced living at home. At his funeral, a young band member eulogized him as "a man who fought for the rights of all young men and women."

A most vivid account of Nick and his circumstances, substantially abbreviated below, was provided at Chambri some six months after his death by Theo Pekur, a young man who described himself as Nick's best friend. In answer to the question: "What kind of man was Nick Ambri?" he had said:

Nick was a good man…. He was not afraid to defy the big men when they told him whom he could or could not marry. He told the big men that we should be allowed to marry whom we choose because *we are young lives* [emphasis added]. His father was responsible for his death. His father didn't want him to marry Bernadette. One night when Nick's father and others were drinking, Nick's father promised that Nick would never marry Pombank's daughter [Bernadette]. But Nick insisted that he marry her because he already had made her pregnant. [Pombank, a church leader and catechist, insisted that the marriage take place.] Nick's father won't remain alive long now. Nick will fight back from the grave.

As has been stated, a senior man with any political aspirations would seek to gain renown for himself and the clan he led by displaying and augmenting his power through skillful manipulation of affinal relationships. To do this, he must ensure that his children—both sons and daughters—made strategic marriages. In his insistence that he determine who Nick married, Nick's father was, thus, acting as might any traditional senior Chambri male. (It must be added that, however reasonable his desire to designate Nick's wife might appear to other senior Chambri, no one would think that he should kill his own son over this or any other disagreement.)

Regardless of whether Nick thought his intransigence might end in his death, the extent of his opposition to his father was both impressive and instructive. It testified that representations of modern personhood were indeed attractive and persuasive to Chambri youth. These representations appeared in Western concepts of freedom of choice, in Catholic Church teachings about the freely entered "Christian marriage" and in popular literature, music, and advertising that extolled stylishness and the importance of fulfilling personal attraction, desire, and romance.

Indeed, many young Chambri men pinned sexy photographs—frequently bathing-suit advertisements—to the walls in their houses. Sometimes they added a text to these pictures, also clipped from magazines. For example, in one display of fifty or more photographs, a picture of several young Asian women in bikinis had affixed to it, by way of caption, a clipping with the words, "At what age did you first have sexual intercourse?" Another, of a woman sitting astraddle a man's lap, had scrawled on it, in Pidgin English: "Look at the two of them!"

Young women also clipped pictures from magazines, although they did not post them. One revealed an extensive collection, kept in an old school notebook. Her pictures were of white women, posed in romantic settings such as rose gardens, wearing formal, frilly dresses—frequently bridal gowns. She had underlined several of the captions, including: "With the rustle of silk and the hint of tulle, you will be the envy of all single girls. Make sure you choose the dress of your dreams on your wedding day."

THE COMMODITIZATION OF PERSONS

As mentioned, it seemed likely that Chambri social relationships would become increasingly commoditized as money continued to be used in ceremonial contexts. In other words, one might anticipate that the meaning of money in a gift economy would be displaced by its meaning in a commodity economy. In particular, one would expect that Chambri seniors might attempt to use money to break off certain of their entailments by retiring affinal debts and thus terminating affinal obligations. Significantly, such an objective (if any, in fact, wished to pursue it) was in certain regards becoming less rather than more feasible.

This was so because, regardless of whether affinal politics would continue to be based on enduring obligations or on the termination of these obligations, it remained clearly essential to senior men that they still control the marriages of young men and women. Whatever Nick's father's ultimate strategy, he could implement it only in response to the entailments that defined his political position. And, the only way to respond effectively to those entailments—whether to perpetuate or terminate them or to inaugurate new ones—would be to ensure, as had senior Chambri before him, that his son married appropriately. However, the representations of modern personhood—those focusing on choice—that now prompted Chambri youth to defy their seniors were also a product of the intrusion of the commodity economy. Since money, after all, could be used to acquire all manner of things, "strictly commercial" transactions left the future open by precluding or terminating obligations. Thus, money had become the embodiment of choice. While money gave senior Chambri men the possibility—largely still unrealized—of transcending at least some of their affinal obligations, it was, at the same time, affecting young Chambri men and women in such a way as to make it increasingly difficult for senior men to pursue any of their traditional strategies, much less ones that called for the termination of affinal obligations.

Moreover, the possibility that the young women acquired through affinal transactions might come themselves to be regarded increasingly as commodities, subject to the control of others regardless of their own objectives, did not seem to have materialized. Given the increasing importance to Chambri youth of exercising choice, certainly young women were unlikely to accept any redefinition of marriage that would give more control to men than previously.

Nonetheless, it must also be stressed that *no* Chambri—even the most rebellious youth—wished to be adrift without ties to other Chambri. Rather, the question central to the dealings of senior men with junior men and women had become who would initiate and shape the ties that bound, who would make the choices that defined the pattern of obligation. Indeed, so important had choice become for Chambri youth that Nick's decision to risk alienation from his father by marrying the girl to whom he had himself been drawn, had become quite reasonable.

ON FISH HEADS AND LOVE LETTERS: THE MODERNIZATION OF PERSONS

Yebiwali, like other women in the 1930s, defined herself as a person in terms of her embeddedness within kin networks, and as a person of worth in terms of her capacity to repay her ontological debts, which meant bearing children. Undoubtedly attracted to Tchuikumban (enough so to send him the head of a fish), she might have been happier, in some sense, with Tchuikumban than she was, at first, with Akerman. Yet, she was not prevented from pursuing her strategy for becoming a person of worth when the men arranged her marriage with Akerman. She was, therefore, not dominated by the men. She was, in other words, neither in her own view nor in that of other Chambri (women and men), unjustifiably deprived of the capacity to make what were regarded as reasonable choices in pursuit of her own interests.

Like Yebiwali, Emma, a young woman of the 1980s, also defined herself in terms of kin networks. She was the repository of both patrilineal and matrilateral names and powers, she lived in a Chambri community, and she interacted almost exclusively with other Chambri. And, it may be recalled that the boyfriend to whom she intended to send (and eventually did send) the love letter was a Chambri. Indeed, Emma expected to remain embedded in a kin network, to have her kin receive at least some bride price for her, to have children, and to have her agnates and affines engage in affinal exchanges focusing on her and her children.

However, rather than have the selection of her husband follow from, and be determined by, the politics of senior men, she expected that those politics follow from *her choice* of husband. In contrast to the criteria of strategic choice they would follow, she would choose to marry someone who was sophisticated and could provide her with the clothes, perfume, earrings, and so on, through which she defined herself as stylish. Yet, if she were able to marry a man with sufficient earning capacity to satisfy her, her agnates were likely to be well satisfied too. After all, such a man could, as his initial affinal presentation, provide a very generous bride price. Thus, in Emma, we do not see the development of a new sort of person as much as the modernization of one. She had herself become the embodiment of what Gregory (1982) describes as the mixed gift-and-commodity economy of contemporary Papua New Guinea. Whereas Yebiwali sent Tchuikumban the head of a fish, Emma chose to spend perhaps $3.50 for her love token.

To judge by the examples of Rex, Gabriella, and Nick, the trouble Emma—and the other "young lives"—feared was a collision of generational differences. Who in particular they married meant something more to these young Chambri than it had meant to Yebiwali and to the young men and women of her generation. It meant that to marry someone not of their own choosing would be a serious diminution of self. There had, thus, been a partial shift in the definition of *person* and, hence, in what constituted dominance. There had, in other words, been a shift in the definition of objectives and, thus, in what would be considered a matter of reasonable choice.

Mead was wrong when she argued that Yebiwali was dominated because she was precluded from choosing her husband. Yet, Emma would be dominated if she were not allowed to choose hers. Although neither Yebiwali nor Emma sought self-expression through an economically derived individualism—immersion in social networks was essential for both—the Western representations that defined personhood in terms of the capacity to choose have become of central importance to—indeed, definitional of—young lives. Domination for Emma—as for Rex, Gabriella, and Nick—would be, at least partly, through the curtailment of choice. (It is not yet clear whether these young men would, in their turn, ever try to control the marriages of their juniors.)

CONCLUSION

Despite the shift in what would cause domination, there had not, in fact, been a significant change in gender relationships. It was unlikely that Emma would be forced into a marriage she did not want. In fact, few Chambri women either of Yebiwali's generation or of Emma's were dominated. This was so in part because, as mentioned, then as now, women could cause too much trouble to their husbands by revealing, and thus undermining, the basis of their power. And it was also so in part because neither then, nor now, was it in male interests to control female production.

In this latter regard, the incorporation of their regional system into a world system had not had the same effect on gender relations for the Chambri as it often had elsewhere in Papua New Guinea and throughout the Third World. The economic factors affecting the lives of contemporary Chambri men and women, whether living at Wewak or at home, differed from those frequently reported where

> Western capitalistic systems…[impose] features such as the structure for general male dominance over females, based materially on preferential male access to strategic resources; private ownership of land and a money economy; overall inequality in the form of differential access to privileges and resources…; and an emphasis on the nuclear family, supported by a wage-earning male, as the ideal domestic unit. [Buenaventura-Posso and Brown 1980:124][3]

Just as the Chambri's protected position in their regional system as purveyors of specialized commodities had meant that the control of women and their products was irrelevant to either the military or political viability of Chambri men, so too was their position "out of the mainstream of [economic] development" (Philpott 1972:37), giving them a certain protection in the world system.

And, although Emma and other Chambri in Wewak existed on the edge of poverty (it was in fact unlikely that women like Emma would be married in dresses of "silk with a hint of tulle" to husbands with well-paying jobs), they could always return home. As long as Chambri Lake overflowed with fish, those in Wewak were not inevitably at the mercy of a cash economy in a Third World country. Emma, who pressed a "remembrance note" into our hands requesting that she be remembered with gifts of perfume and make-up from the United States, probably would not recognize how relatively lucky she was. After all, if calendar love notes and wedding dresses were to prove beyond her means and those of other Chambri, choice and consequent worth might still be expressed in other ways. Perhaps the head of a fish might again suffice.

Acknowledgments: We are grateful to the granting agencies and institutions that supported our field trips to the Chambri over the years: the National Endowment for the Humanities, the American Council of Learned Societies, Amherst College, the Research School of Pacific Studies at the Australian National University, the Population Institute of the East-West Center, the National Geographic Society, the Graduate School of the City University of New York, and the Wenner-Gren Foundation for Anthropological Research.

NOTES

1. We recognize that under some circumstances persons may not know what their (best) interests are—that is, what they should "reasonably" be allowed to do—and are, in consequence, "dominated" without their realization. In Errington and Gewertz 1987a and 1987b, we argue in detail that such a false consciousness is not characteristic of Chambri women.

2. In 1987, 43 percent of the adult Chambri population over the age of seventeen lived away from their island; 15 percent of those away lived in Chambri camp.

3. A handbook written by Papua New Guinean women suggests much the same thing:

> Modernization and the cash economy often make matters worse regarding the way we think about the work of men and women. The introduction of cash crops is usually called "development," yet it leads to lots of divisions in work which make men and women think differently about the usefulness of the different work they do (Mathie and Cox 1987:40).

16

The Fist, the Stick, and the Bottle of Bleach: Wife Bashing and Female Suicide in a Papua New Guinea Society

Dorothy Ayers Counts
University of Waterloo

Akono was a busy and important man with business in the provincial capital that kept him away from his village home for weeks at a time. Although his wife, Galiki, was known by her neighbors to be a woman of irreproachable character, Akono often accused her of having an affair during his long absences and, because he suspected she was unfaithful, he frequently beat her. Galiki was from a distant village and had no relatives living nearby to come to her aid, so when the beatings continued over an entire weekend other villagers became concerned for Galiki's well-being. Some of their neighbors attempted unsuccessfully to persuade Akono to stop the violence, and finally his own mother and brothers urged restraint. The outside interference enraged Akono and the beatings continued. On Monday, Galiki had been in her cook house preparing her children's meal when she stumbled into the compound yard crying, "Come help me! I'm dying," and fell unconscious. Some people said they heard her say she had swallowed poison; others heard nothing other than her plea for help. Some of her neighbors attempted to force her to vomit the poison they believed she had drunk, but she was soon dead.

Two months later I arrived in Papua New Guinea (PNG) to begin the 1985 research season. Before reaching Galiki's village, friends in Kimbe, the capital of West New Britain province, passed on the news that Galiki had killed herself and that Akono was in mourning. Later, another friend whispered that although the nurse from the nearby Kaliai Health Center had listed her death as suicide, Galiki did not commit suicide at all. He believed that she was, in fact, beaten to death by her husband.

While staying in the village, I had many conversations with female friends about Galiki's death, sometimes seeking their view of this "suicide" that might not be suicide. Sometimes women brought it up because they—especially the young women—were angered by the violence they had witnessed and frightened that no one had been able to stop it. Most people not directly related to Akono argued that Galiki had followed none of the procedures that usually precede suicide, and her death bore none of the usual characteristics of suicide by poison. They insisted that she had died of injuries sustained during the beatings she received that last weekend. They were angered by Akono's behavior—he wept loudly, dressed in filthy rags, refused to leave his compound or to drink anything but water and gave away the entire inventory of his trade store. One friend commented to me that she and other women had gone to mourn Galiki only briefly because they were offended by Akono's display of grief. She said, "We thought, 'Why are you crying? You killed her.'"

Although Galiki's abuse and death were upsetting for many villagers, they were not isolated events. During my four-month stay in the village, information surfaced about a number of wife beatings, some among my close friends, and two were witnessed at close quarters. And, during that time four women from the Kaliai region killed themselves, three of them following beatings by their husbands. These tragedies focused the attention of both villagers and anthropologist on a pattern of beatings followed by suicide that people feared might become epidemic. The relatives of young women who were beaten by their husbands watched them carefully, fearing that a weeping woman who left the village alone might intend to drink poison or hang herself.

DOMESTIC VIOLENCE AND SUICIDE IN KALIAI

The Lusi-speaking people of the Kaliai district of West New Britain province live in villages and hamlets along the northwest coast of the island of New Britain. Most of my research has been centered in Kandoka, the largest of the Kaliai communities with a population of between two hundred and fifty and three hundred. The people are slash-and-burn horticulturalists whose systems of descent and residence are normatively patrilineal and patrivirilocal. There is no ranked hierarchy and no formally inherited office among the Lusi-Kaliai, but people are not equal. Power differences exist on the basis of age, sex, and birth order. A first-born male has an advantage over women and younger men, and a man ordinarily has authority over his wife, daughters, and other female relatives—especially younger ones. Although he has this advantage, his ability to use it is restricted by a number of conditions including idiosyncratic differences in personality and character which, combined with birth order and relative age, may permit a strong-willed woman to dominate her younger male relatives.

Women in Lusi-Kaliai society do not share power equally with men, but they do have control over the economic resources they produce and, increasingly, they have a say in marriage arrangements made on their behalf. Bride wealth is given at marriage, and ideally marriages are arranged by parents. Village women have always attempted to influence marriage arrangements, but modern young Kaliai women—like the Chambri women Fred Errington and Deborah Gewertz discuss in Chapter 15 in this volume, who have been exposed to Western notions of courtship and romantic love—insist on participating in the choice of their mates. Today, attempts by parents to arrange marriages are successful only if the young couple approve of the match, and many marriages are arranged by parents after the couple is living together and the woman is pregnant. After marriage a woman remains a member of her own kin-group with all the duties and obligations of kin-group membership, if she resides nearby. However, postmarital residence is ideally virilocal and a woman may find herself many hours'—or even days'—journey from her relatives.

Divorce by mutual consent is easy in a customary marriage. The couple stop living together and the woman returns to her natal home, but their children remain with their father after they are weaned. Neither custom nor provincial law enables a divorced woman to claim custody of her children. If, for instance, a married man takes a lover or brings home a second wife, his actions do not give his first wife grounds to divorce him and retain custody of their children. If, however, she has an affair or leaves her husband because he has taken a second wife, he has the right both to divorce her and to keep their children. The probability that she will lose her children makes it difficult for a mother to end a violent marriage, especially if her natal home is far from her husband's residence.

Domestic violence is not an everyday event for most Lusi-Kaliai families, nor is village life a battleground. Laughter and good will are much more common than are anger and strife, and a village is a pleasant place to live. Nevertheless, domestic violence is not rare. Parents strike children, co-wives quarrel and fight, and married people hit one another. Episodes are usually brief and inflict neither injury nor bloodshed.

Although in most marital fights the husband hits his wife, who does not return his blows, occasionally a woman initiates the conflict. A woman is justified in doing this if her husband has an adulterous affair or brings home another wife. In this situation women usually use weapons—axes, bush knives, or boards. An angry wife brandishing a weapon may knock her husband unconscious or cause him to flee the village in fear for his life. When this happens, the expressed sympathy of both men and women is with the wife, while the husband is ridiculed and said to deserve the treatment he receives. The only suicide attempt by a man for which I have any record followed such an incident. He announced his intention to marry a woman who was pregnant with his child, and his wife chased him out of the village with an axe. Friends found him tearfully preparing poison and escorted him back to the village. He did not marry the second woman.

It is unusual for a woman to strike her husband, but it is common for men to hit their wives. One informant estimates that in a community of some fifty married men, there are six who often beat their wives severely and about the same number who never strike them at all. Others maintain that almost all men hit their wives occasionally. Both women and men say that a husband has the right—even the duty—to beat his wife if she gives him cause: if she flirts with other men or commits adultery; if she fails to meet her domestic obligations; if she draws blood in punishing his children; if she shames or insults her husband or his kin; if she fails to assist her husband in meeting his ceremonial obligations; if she fights with her co-wives. Women say that a man whose wife is careless about her domestic chores is responsible for the disheveled state of their household because he does not punish her for neglecting her duties.

Although both women and men accept wife beating in principle and are reluctant to interfere when it happens, there is a point when violence becomes unacceptable. There is no "rule of thumb" to signal when this point is reached, for people evaluate each situation on its own merits. A woman's kin will usually interfere if her husband shames her by pulling off her pubic covering, publicly exposing her genitals, or if he kicks her "as though she were a dog," draws blood, strikes her with a weapon other than a small stick, or prolongs the beating over several days. Others—even the husband's kin—may try to stop the beating if they think it may maim or kill the woman. It is in the villagers' interest to end the violence because the woman's kin may hold the entire community responsible for her bad treatment, shame them, and demand that the group pay compensation for injuries she suffers.

Regardless of the level of violence, a woman's relatives are unlikely to intervene if they think she is guilty of the offense for which she is beaten. For instance, the relatives of one woman whose husband attempted to kill her with an axe for suspected adultery agreed with his assessment of her behavior. Consequently, they not only failed to interfere, but when she begged them to take her with them out of Kaliai, refused to help her flee the area.

There are a number of options available to a Lusi-Kaliai woman who considers herself to have been unjustly beaten. Many require the support of her family and all have serious shortcomings. First, she may passively accept the punishment, hoping that, if she submits meekly, her kin may feel pity for her and attack her husband, shame him, or demand that he pay compensation to them.

Second, she may actively fight back. Women rarely take this option because in addition to the risk of being even more severely beaten or publicly shamed in return, they also chance losing the support of their own relatives. As a case in point, one woman whose husband beat her for fighting with her co-wife struck him back. He knocked her unconscious, and then, with the tacit agreement of her kinsmen, he called for masked spirit figures to shame her publicly and to forbid her to hit back in the future. The next time he beat her, she attempted suicide. As a result of her suicide attempt, her husband did not again publicly shame her, and he did not beat her again for over a year.

Third, a beaten woman may return to her own kin if they are willing to accept her and if she is willing to lose her children, a cost that most women are unwilling to bear. Fourth, she may charge her husband before court officials. While a few women successfully choose this option, it is an alternative that Lusi-Kaliai women have infrequently used. The difficulties they meet are similar to those facing other PNG women who appeal to the legal system for protection from domestic violence. This problem is discussed below.

Fifth, an abused woman may expose her husband to menstrual blood contamination in order to cause him to sicken or die. Or, she may collect his hair clippings, cigarette butts, or other effluvia for use in sorcery. These are considered by Kaliai to be effective strategies. Like many Papua New Guineans, Kaliai attribute almost all illness and death to either menstrual contamination or the use of malevolent magic. Although female friends insisted that these are effective ways for a woman to revenge brutal treatment, no one admitted to using either alternative herself. Sixth, she may commit suicide. Suicides in Kaliai are almost always committed by women and often (five cases out of twelve) follow an episode in which the woman was beaten by her husband (see Counts 1987).

Suicide often seems to Westerners to be the least effective of the responses that a beaten wife might choose. Why, then, do some Lusi-Kaliai women respond to abuse by turning fatal violence on themselves? To answer this question we must realize that Lusi-Kaliai women are not unique. Wives in North America also often respond to the despair, anger, and shame associated with abuse by killing themselves (Jacobson and Portuges 1978:223; Back et al. 1982; Pagelow 1984:318; Stephens 1985). The authors of a working paper on spouse abuse in the United States report that between 35 and 40 percent of battered women attempt suicide and conclude that "abuse may be the single most important precipitant for female suicide attempts yet identified" (Stark and Flitcraft 1985:22).

In PNG, suicide is a frequent response to interpersonal problems or to shame. Reported suicide rates in the country vary markedly from one society to the other, and the data may often be unreliable (Pataki-Schweizer 1985:140). For example, data for Port Moresby, the national capital, and its immediate area vary from 10.7 (per 100,000) in 1982 (Murphy 1983) to 5.5 in 1985; while in 1982, there was a suicide rate of 2.4 for the entire country (Pataki-Schweizer 1985:141). In contrast, reported rates in rural areas are much higher. In one Highland group, the suicide rate for people aged fifteen to forty-five is 34 per 100,000, with the rate for females in that age cohort being 61, in contrast to 7 for males (Pataki-Schweizer 1985:140). Other researchers report suicide rates of 23 for the Kandrian area of West New Britain (Hoskin et al. 1969:204); of 300 for the Gainj of the Central Highlands (1,200 for Gainj women aged twenty to forty-nine) (Johnson 1981:326). Compare these rates with figures from the West—6.8 in the Netherlands, 9.8 for England and Wales in the late 1960s (Tousignant and Mishara 1981:7), and 11.1 for Australia in the 1970s (Pataki-Schweizer 1985:140). Even though there is a wide variation in suicide rates, it is clear that in some PNG societies suicide is common—particularly among women. Its frequency also suggests that it is, under certain circumstances, expected behavior.

To return to the question of why beaten women kill themselves, part of the answer is that suicide is not an ineffective act. In many parts of PNG, suicide is a culturally recognized, appropriate, expected act that permits politically powerless, abused, and shamed persons to take revenge on those who have made their lives intolerable (see Counts 1980; 1984; 1987; 1988; 1990a). It may even be the only way a battered wife can take revenge on her brutal husband.

Brief examples from two Papua New Guinea societies illustrate how this works. Among the Gainj (who have an incredible female suicide rate of 1,200 per 100,000), only married women kill themselves. Gainj men dominate their wives, demand obedience from them, and sometimes publicly shame them by siding with other women with whom they are involved in a dispute (Johnson 1981). Any show of conciliation to his wife calls a husband's manhood into question. According to Johnson, although a woman's suicide threats may cause her husband to make concessions to her privately, he cannot publicly yield to her without acknowledging her power over him, a situation that a Gainj man would find intolerable. "Indeed," says Johnson, "the standard public response of men to a woman's threat of suicide is, 'there's a rope nearby'" (1981:333). When Gainj women kill themselves, the suicide almost always occurs after a husband has supported another woman in a dispute against his wife or after he has physically punished her in public (Johnson 1981:326). Her death is an eloquent statement of her anger and shame, it requires her husband to pay a large compensation to her relatives in order to avoid physical retaliation, and it humiliates him. She has bested him and has demonstrated to everyone that, in the final analysis, it was she and not her husband who was in control.

Maring women also kill themselves after severe, physically violent domestic arguments and frequently kill their young daughters as well. Healey (1979:96), who has worked with the Maring, says:

> Destruction of a child in suicide is particularly vengeful, for not only is the husband deprived of a wife, but also of children who can care for him in his old age, and who will forge new affinal alliances for him. Further, he must provide the customary death-payments for both wife and child to the woman's agnates, and face the anger and possible vengeance of his affines by physical attack of witchcraft.

In Kaliai, knowledge about the reasons why others have committed suicide, the results of a suicide death, and the ways in which it should be done is part of the culture. Suicide is, for example, a common theme in mythology where powerless people who are shamed or mistreated kill themselves, and stories about others who have committed suicide are frequently told around the evening fires. Most importantly, Kaliai who commit suicide are considered to be victims of homicide: someone else is culpable for their deaths. They are thought to be victims, either of a type of sorcery that causes suicidal depression, or of slander. Suicide victims are often said to have been "killed with talk," and those who slandered or shamed them must pay compensation or face retaliation from the suicide's grieving kin, just as if they had killed the victim with a weapon.

A beaten wife's decision to kill herself is a complex one in which the beating is only one component. In some cases, the way in which a woman is beaten may lead her to commit suicide. Women particularly resent beatings that they consider to be unjustified, and they expect that after a few blows, a reasonable husband will listen to their explanations. An unjustly beaten woman who is struck repeatedly when she attempts to speak is said to have *ailolo sasi*, "bad stomach," a combination of anger, shame, self-pity, and despair. If her relatives refuse to come to her aid and she feels powerless to change her situation, this powerful emotion may cause her to kill herself. Another factor is the interpretation that a woman places on the beatings. According to Chowning, a Kove woman—the Kove are the Kaliai's neighbors and frequent marriage partners—will kill herself if she believes that an "excessive" beating indicates her husband's preference for another woman (Chowning 1985:82).

In order for a woman who has chosen to commit suicide to be certain that her kin and neighbors know why she killed herself and whom she holds responsible for her death, she should follow certain procedures. First, she should warn others that she intends to kill herself. She may do this by asking detailed questions about others who have killed themselves, by talking about her own death, or by leaving messages that she intends to commit suicide. One sixteen-year-old girl scratched goodbye notes on the skins of green coconuts for several days before her death, but people failed to take her warnings seriously (see Counts 1980).

Next, she should prepare for death by dressing in her best clothing and wearing her finest ornaments, and by destroying her personal possessions. She should then kill herself in the presence of others or where they will be certain to find her body. Lusi-Kaliai commit suicide by hanging themselves, by jumping from the tops of tall trees, or by taking poison—rotenone fish poison, household bleach, or an overdose of the malaria medicine, chloroquine phosphate. Sometimes they combine two or more methods, so that a person may climb to the top of a tree, drink poison, announce to the audience why she is killing herself, and then jump to her death.

Finally, she should identify the individual(s) responsible for her death. She may do this by sending a letter to the guilty person telling him of her death, or she may call his name as she dies. The identification of the culpable party is so important for a meaningful suicide that villagers may report that they have seen the suicide's ghost wandering in the bush or along the beach and calling the guilty person's name.

If a suicide fails to follow the culturally expected procedures for killing herself, her death is ambiguous and the result is confusion. People may question whether the death was in fact a suicide, and they may disagree about the meaning of the death and fail to resolve the problems that the suicide wished to call attention to. At least two Lusi-Kaliai deaths—presumably suicides—of beaten wives are problematic for this reason. One is the death of Sharon and the other is the death of Galiki, whose story was told at the beginning of this chapter.

In 1979 Sharon, the pregnant mother of eight children, died after a violent quarrel with Paul, her husband. She was heard crying that she was dying, by a fellow villager who found her lying near a spring where women often went to wash. The villager smelled household bleach on Sharon's breath and found an empty bleach bottle nearby, but Sharon lost consciousness and died without explaining her actions or calling the name of the person who had caused her suicide. Sharon's death did not follow the rules. She gave no warning of her intention to kill herself, she made no preparations for her death, and she accused no one of culpability as she died. As a result, her death was the subject of controversy. Most villagers concluded that she killed herself because she was shamed by her pregnancy, alleged to have resulted from an affair with her husband's classificatory brother; in Kaliai, this is analogous to incest. They thought Paul was justified in beating Sharon and did not hold him responsible for her death. Others, however, thought he was culpable and a few even suspected that he killed her by forcing her to drink the bleach. Although Paul paid compensation to Sharon's parents for her suicide, her grieving father was not satisfied and engaged a sorcerer to kill Paul. After Paul's death in 1984, his relatives convened a public meeting where the sorcerer admitted that he had been employed by Sharon's father and that he was responsible for the death.

Galiki's death was also ambiguous and villagers could not agree how to interpret it. People not closely related to Akono pointed to the irregularity of the death as evidence that she died of injuries received during her beatings rather than by suicide, and argued that if her relatives had lived nearby, Akono would not have gotten off lightly. In contrast, Akono's closest kin considered Galiki's death to be suicide, but argued that both wife and husband were at fault in their quarrels and that her death illustrated the innate instability and unpredictability of women.

Akono accepted culpability for Galiki's suicide and paid compensation to her relatives. It should be pointed out that although traditional Kaliai norms do not distinguish between homicide and culpable suicide, the PNG legal code does. Culpability for suicide is not recognized as a criminal offense by the law; homicide is. Akono accepted responsibility for his wife's suicide, but he did not face the penalty of imprisonment for homicide.

DISCUSSION

The events described for Kaliai, the pattern of wife bashing and female suicide, are characteristic of a complex of problems that plague contemporary PNG. As we have already noted, suicide rates are high in some PNG societies, and suicide may offer otherwise powerless women a way to strike back at abusive, brutal husbands. Unfortunately, domestic violence, especially wife beating, is a pervasive problem in many Pacific Islands societies. Anthropologists and other social scientists are just beginning to research the subject and, as a result, there is little information yet available (an important exception is Counts 1990a). In the early 1980s, the Law Reform Commission of PNG began a series of studies on the problem of domestic violence with special focus on wife beating, and has published a set of excellent reports (see Toft 1985 and Law Reform Commission of PNG 1986 for examples).

Although there is still a great deal of research to be done, we may draw at least two tentative conclusions from the data in the available literature. First, wife beating is not just a contemporary problem but has a long history in the Pacific Islands and is considered by many to be a part of traditional family life. Second, the political, social, and economic changes that have taken place in the Pacific Islands since World War II are just beginning to make a difference in the lives of women in the region. Contact with the West and modernization have brought increased access to Western goods, technology, education, and medical care but, ironically, these advantages may lead to an increase in wife beating rather than to an improvement in women's lives. There are a number of reasons for this.

Although modernization may bring new wealth, labor-saving technology, and an improved standard of living into an area, women often do not share in the wealth, or other benefits, and have little opportunity to achieve positions of community leadership in these male-dominated societies (these points are elaborated upon by Sexton in Chapter 8 in this volume). And, when economic crisis strikes the modernizing economy—such as the one presently faced by PNG due to the closure of the Bougainville copper mine and the drop in the prices of copra and coffee—jobs are lost, the standard of living declines, and women and children suffer disproportionately. As Justice Brian Brunto, the resident judge for Eastern Highlands and Chimbu Provinces, observed, men may vent their feelings of anger and frustration on their families. He also warns that the present economic depression in the Highlands will force some families into poverty, causing an increase in wife beating and child abuse (Bromby 1990:25).

Even in those cases where women enjoy the benefits of education and the opportunity for paid employment, the consequence may be an increase in violence toward them. The findings of other researchers (see Toft 1985 and Scaglion 1990 for PNG; and Lateef 1990 for Fiji Indians) echo the sentiments expressed by a Kaliai friend, a well-educated professional woman: she noted that women whose educations and salaries equal that of their husbands expect to be consulted about family decisions and insist on sharing control of family resources. Their husbands resent their independence and assertiveness and beat them in an effort to assert their dominance and regain control. The result is an increase in domestic violence, especially when the couple live in an urban area far from the restraining influence of the wife's kinsmen.

Finally, modernization is accompanied by increasing use of alcohol and drugs (see Chapter 17, "A Pacific Haze: Alcohol and Drugs in Oceania," by Mac Marshall, in this volume). According to several Kaliai consultants, in PNG as a whole (see Law Reform Commission of PNG 1986), as elsewhere in the Pacific (see, for example, Nero 1990 for a discussion of alcohol use and domestic violence on Palau—now Belau—in Micronesia), alcohol is a major factor contributing to wife beating. The problem is multifaceted. Men use family resources, often demanding money earned by their wives, to purchase alcohol for themselves and their friends. If the wife protests or refuses to give her husband money, he will beat her. When the husband returns home drunk he is likely to be violently aggressive and beat his wife, especially if she expresses displeasure at his condition or if she does not prepare food on demand for him and his friends. Finally, if he is hung-over after a drinking bout, he may be irritable and beat her with little provocation.

Although modernization has its downside for Pacific Islands women, contemporary institutions may provide some relief for beaten wives. The courts will be particularly important sources of help for women in the future, and in some cases they already protect abused wives. For instance, in the Agarabi area of the Eastern Highlands, magistrates are severe with male defendants in cases of marital violence and do not tolerate men physically abusing their wives (Westermark 1985:114). Most of the recommendations of the Law Reform Commission of PNG focus on legal changes intended to extend the protection of the law to women (Toft 1985).

These changes are needed, for the courts have become available to women only recently, and in many cases they have had little influence on entrenched patterns of wife abuse. In some Papua New Guinea societies, a beaten woman who charges her husband in court has little chance of success. As one researcher observed: "Local government councillors and other village officials almost all strike their own wives and so are reluctant to prosecute other men except when exceptional brutality is involved" (Chowning 1985:88). Another researcher (Reay 1987) argues that the court system is of limited usefulness to women because local magistrates often do not recognize the pathological nature of chronic brutality. When an abused wife comes to them for protection, they recommend that she seek compensation from officials in her husband's village. "This is," says Reay (1987:77), "cold comfort for a woman whose husband beats her up every time he comes home drunk and sometimes holds a gun to her head or a bushknife to her throat."

The acuity of the criticisms leveled by Chowning and Reay is underlined by the response of the PNG parliament in 1987 when the Law Reform Commission recommended that wife beating be made illegal. Although some members warmly supported the Commission's proposals, most ministers opposed them because they represented an interference in "traditional family life." William Wi of North Waghi argued that wife beating "is an accepted custom and we are wasting our time debating the issue" (Heise 1989).

In spite of the shortcomings of the courts and the disappointing response of the PNG parliament to the Law Reform Commission's proposals, there are reasons to be optimistic. Educated women are increasingly becoming involved in public activities, are holding important and well-paying jobs in the government and civil service, and are insisting that society recognize their contributions to their nation's culture and economy. There is evidence that there is a change of attitude, at least among educated and urbanized Papua

New Guineans (Bradley, in press). For example, in 1989 both the Prime Minister and the Governor General of PNG publicly spoke in support of the efforts of the Law Reform Commission to reduce domestic violence. In 1989 and 1990, with the support of the Canadian High Commission and CUSO (the Canadian equivalent of the U. S. Peace Corps), the Law Reform Commission and the Women and Law Committee began a campaign to educate women about their legal rights and to inform local magistrates about national law making assault—including the assault of women by their husbands—an indictable offense. They have distributed throughout the country educational pamphlets in English, Motu, and Tok Pisin, the three national languages, and have produced a video film, *Stap Isi* ("Take it Easy"), explaining that wife beating is a crime, suggesting that aggressive violence is not necessary for a "real man," and proposing alternative ways in which men can express anger and frustration.

It is not certain that these efforts will result in a decrease in domestic violence. However, the efforts to educate both women and court officials about women's rights and about the procedures that should be followed when a woman brings a complaint of abuse before the courts have had promising results. More women are taking their cases to court, and village magistrates are moving away from customary practice—which worked to the disadvantage of women—and are giving judgments that are more consistent with national law (Bradley 1989).

CONCLUSIONS

This chapter began with the case of a personal tragedy, a woman who died because of her husband's physical violence. The circumstances that led to Galiki's death are not rare; wife beating is common in PNG, and one way in which women (in North America as well as in PNG) respond to "bashings" (as beatings are called in PNG) is to commit suicide. Women do this because suicide enables them to take revenge against brutal, abusive husbands. The friends and kin of a woman who kills herself will likely consider her to have been a homicide victim and, even if they were indifferent to her suffering before her death, they quickly coalesce into a grieving group anxious to see justice done. Following a suicide, the person who is held responsible for the death is in danger, for the suicide's kin may physically attack him or kill him by magical means. At the very least, he must expect to pay a large compensation to the suicide's survivors, and even then he lives in fear that the angry relatives may contract for his death by sorcery or witchcraft. This fear is not an unreasonable one.

Wife beating, and a suicidal response, are traditional patterns of interaction in PNG. These patterns are apparently being exacerbated, not modified, by the rapid social and economic changes taking place in the country. Women may not reap the benefits of economic modernization, but may suffer when economic crisis results in unemployment and a rapid decrease in the family's standard of living. Educated, employed women challenge traditional patterns of male domination and are beaten by their husbands who use violence to maintain control over their families. Increasing levels of alcohol abuse by men results in more wife bashing. Furthermore, the courts have frequently been unresponsive to the needs of battered wives.

Although the situation is a grim one, educated and sophisticated PNG women and men are working to change cultural attitudes toward violence against women and to make the courts more responsive to the needs of battered wives. These women and men, with the assistance of enlightened national government officials, are determined to create a society in which women's contributions are recognized and in which they and their daughters can live in safety and dignity.

Acknowledgments: The research on which this chapter is based was supported in 1966–1967 by the U.S. National Science Foundation and Southern Illinois University, in 1971 by the University of Waterloo and the Wenner-Gren Foundation, in 1975–1976 by the Canada Council and by the University of Waterloo, and in 1981 and 1985 by the University of Waterloo and by research grants from the Social Sciences and Humanities Research Council of Canada. I wish to thank Drs. Judith Brown, Ann Chowning, Victoria Lockwood, and David Counts for critical comments on earlier drafts of this chapter and Christine Bradley for unpublished material and for her astute comments on the problem of wife abuse in PNG. Earlier versions of the chapter were delivered as papers to the American Association of Suicidology in Atlanta, Georgia in April 1986 and in a symposium on domestic violence in the Pacific at the Association for Social Anthropology in Oceania (ASAO) meetings in San Antonio, Texas in February 1989.

17

A Pacific Haze:
Alcohol and Drugs
in Oceania

Mac Marshall
University of Iowa

All over the world people eat, drink, smoke, or blow substances up their noses in the perennial quest to alter and expand human consciousness. Most of these substances come from psychoactive plants native to different regions—coca, tobacco, and peyote, in the New World; khat, coffee, and marijuana in North Africa and the Middle East; betel and opium in Asia. Some people use hallucinogens from mushrooms or tree bark; others consume more exotic drugs. Produced by fermentation, brewing, or distillation of a remarkable variety of raw materials—ranging from fruits and grains to milk and honey—traditional alcoholic beverages were found almost everywhere before the Age of Exploration.

As European explorers trekked and sailed about the globe between 1500 and 1900, they carried many of these traditional drugs back to their homelands. Different exotic drugs became popular at different times in Europe as the explorers shared their experiences. In this manner, tea, tobacco, coffee, marijuana, and opium gained avid followers in European countries. Today, this worldwide process of drug diffusion continues at a rapid pace, with changes in attitudes toward different drugs and the introduction of new laws governing their use varying accordingly.

Oceanic peoples were no exception to the widespread quest to expand the human mind. From ancient times they used drugs to defuse tense interpersonal or intergroup relations, relax socially, and commune with the spirit world. Betel and kava were far and away the most common traditional drugs used in the Pacific Islands. The geographical distribution of these two drugs was uneven across the islands, and, in a few places (for example, Chuuk [Truk]), no drugs were used at all before the arrival of foreigners. Kava and betel were not only differentially distributed geographically, but they were also differently distributed socially. Every society had rules governing who might take them (and under what circumstances) that limited their consumption, often only to adult men.

In the four-and-a-half centuries since foreign exploration of the Pacific world began, the islanders have been introduced to several new drugs, most notably alcoholic beverages, tobacco, and marijuana. This chapter discusses substance use in the contemporary Pacific Islands by examining the history and patterns of use of the five major drugs found in the islands today: alcohol, betel, kava, marijuana, and tobacco. To the extent that reliable information exists, such recently introduced drugs as cocaine and heroin are also discussed. The primary concern of the chapter is with the negative social, economic, and health consequences that result from consumption of alcohol, tobacco, and marijuana in the contemporary Pacific Islands.

BETEL AND KAVA

"Betel" is a convenient linguistic gloss for a preparation consisting of at least three distinct substances, two of which are pharmacologically active: the nut of the *Areca catechu* palm, the leaves, stems, or catkins of the *Piper betle* vine, and slaked lime from ground seashells or coral. These substances usually are combined into a quid and chewed. In some societies, people swallow the resultant profuse saliva, while in others they spit out the blood red juice. Kava is drunk as a water-based infusion made from the pounded, grated, or chewed root of a shrub, *Piper methysticum*. Whereas betel ingredients can easily be carried on the person and quickly prepared, kava makings are not as portable, and its preparation calls for a more involved procedure. Betel is often chewed individually with little or no ceremony; kava is usually drunk communally, and frequently accompanied by elaborate ceremonial procedures.

Betel chewing appears to have originated long ago in Island Southeast Asia and to have spread into the islands of the Western Pacific from there. While betel use is widespread in Melanesia (including the New Guinea Highlands where it has recently been introduced), it is absent from the Polynesian Triangle, and it is found only on the westernmost Micronesian islands of Palau, Yap, and the Marianas (Marshall 1987a).

In most parts of the Pacific Islands where betel is chewed, its use occupies a social position akin to coffee or tea drinking in Western societies. For example, Iamo (1987) writes that betel is chewed to stimulate social activity, suppress boredom, enhance work, and increase personal enjoyment among the Keakalo people of the south coast of Papua New Guinea. Similarly, Lepowsky (1982) comments that for the people of Vanatinai Island in Papua New Guinea, shared betel symbolizes friendly and peaceful social relations. Iamo notes that betel consumption "is rampant among children, young people, and adults" in Keakalo; that is, it has few social constraints on its use, except in times of scarcity (1987:146). Similarly, "Vanatinai people chew betel many times a day," and they also begin chewing betel early in childhood: "By the age of eight to ten, boys and girls chew whenever they can find the ingredients" (Lepowsky 1982:335).

In those parts of Papua New Guinea where the betel ingredients can be produced in abundance, such as Keakalo and Vanatinai, they figure importantly as items of exchange or for sale as "exports" to surrounding peoples. The enterprising Biwat of East Sepik Province are remarkable in this regard. They trade *Areca* nut, *Piper betle*, and locally grown tobacco with other peoples in the vicinity, carry these products by canoe to the regional market town of Angoram (98 miles away), and occasionally even charter a small airplane to sell as far away as Mount Hagen in the Western Highlands Province (Watson 1987).

Traditionally, kava was drunk only in Oceania, the world region to which the plant appears native. Kava drinking occurred throughout the high islands of Polynesia (except Easter Island, New Zealand, and Rapa), on the two easternmost high islands of Micronesia (Pohnpei and Kosrae), and in various parts of Melanesia, particularly Fiji, Vanuatu, and New Guinea proper. Kava and betel were often in complementary distribution, although there were some societies where both were routinely consumed.

Whereas betel is chewed by males and females, old and young, kava is different. In most Pacific Islands societies, at least traditionally, kava drinking was restricted to men, and often to "fully adult" or high-status men. Although its consumption was thus restricted, young, uninitiated or untitled men, or young women, usually prepared it. These distinctions were notably marked in the elaborate kava ceremonies of Fiji, Tonga, and Samoa. Wherever it was used, however, kava played important parts in pre-Christian religion, political deliberations, ethnomedical systems, and general quiet social interaction among a community's adult men.

On the island of Tanna, Vanuatu, for example, Lindstrom (1987) argues that getting drunk on and exchanging kava links man to man, separates man from woman, establishes a contextual interpersonal equality among men, and determines and maintains relations of inequality between men and women. Kava is drunk every evening on Tanna at a special kava-drinking ground, separated from the village, and from which women and girls are excluded. Lindstrom argues that kava (which is grown by women) is both itself an important exchange item and symbolically represents male appropriation and control over women and their productive and reproductive capacities. Tannese men fear that women intoxicated on kava would become "crazed" and usurp men's control over them, become sexually wanton, and cease to cook. Lindstrom concludes, "Gender asymmetry in Tannese drunken practice maintains and reproduces social relations of production and exchange" (1987:116).

Among the Gebusi of Papua New Guinea's Western Province, the men of a longhouse community force their male visitors to drink several bowls of kava in rapid succession, usually to the point of nausea. This is done to prevent the chief antagonists at ritual fights or funeral feasts "from disputing or taking retaliatory action against their hosts during a particularly tense moment in the proceedings" (Knauft 1987:85). Forced smoking of home-grown tobacco is used in an analogous manner "to forestall escalation of hostilities" among a people for whom homicide tied to sorcery accusations is a leading cause of male mortality. As on Tanna, Gebusi women never drink kava. Both peoples link kava to sexuality: Lindstrom (1987:112–113) describes a Tannese-origin myth of kava that he calls "kava as dildo;" Knauft (1987:85–88) notes that kava often serves as a metaphor for semen in jokes about heterosexual relations or the ritual homosexuality practiced by the Gebusi.

As is typically the case in human affairs, these long-known and highly valued drug substances were deeply rooted in cultural traditions and patterns of social interaction. Pacific Islands peoples had developed culturally controlled ways of using betel and kava that usually precluded abuse.[1] Users also were unlikely to develop problems because of the relatively benign physiological effects of these two substances and because neither drug by itself seems to produce serious harmful disease states when consumed in a traditional manner.

Kava drinking leads to a variety of physical effects, perhaps the most pronounced of which are analgesia, muscle relaxation, and a sense of quiet well-being. In addition to its ceremonial and recreational uses, kava is a common drug in Oceanic ethnomedicine, and kava extracts also are employed in Western biomedicine. Of the various drugs discovered by human beings around the world, kava seems to be one of the least problematic. Its physiological effects induce a state of peaceful contemplation and euphoria, with the mental faculties left clear, and it produces no serious pathology unless taken (as by some Australian Aborigines since 1980) at doses far in excess of those consumed by Pacific Islanders. The most prominent effects of prolonged heavy kava consumption among Oceanic peoples are a dry scaly skin, bloodshot eyes, possible constipation and intestinal obstruction, and occasional weight loss (Lemert 1967). Even excessive kava use does not produce withdrawal symptoms, and all of the above conditions are reversible if drinking is discontinued.

The situation with betel is somewhat more complex. The main physical effect obtained by betel chewers is central nervous system stimulation and arousal producing a sense of general well-being (Burton-Bradley 1980). Arecoline, the primary active ingredient in betel, also stimulates various glands, leading to profuse sweating and salivation, among other things. Beginners typically experience such unpleasant symptoms as nausea, diarrhea, and dizziness, and prolonged use leads to physiological addiction. There is some preliminary experimental evidence that arecoline enhances memory and learning, and it is being explored as a possible medicine for patients suffering from Alzheimer's disease (Gilbert 1986).

Considerable controversy surrounds the health risks of betel chewing, particularly as regards its possible role in the development of oral cancer (MacLennan et al. 1985). This debate has been confounded by the fact that many betel chewers in Southeast and South Asia (where most of the clinical data have been collected) add other ingredients to the betel chew, most commonly, and notably, tobacco. A summary of the epidemiological evidence available to date leads to the conclusion that chewing betel using traditional ingredients without the addition of tobacco probably does not carry any significant risk for oral cancer (Gupta et al. 1982).[2] Occasionally, a betel chewer develops what Burton-Bradley (1966) calls "betel nut psychosis," following a period of abstinence and in response to a heavy dose of the drug. This acute reversible toxic psychosis is characterized by delusions and hallucinations in predisposed individuals, but it must be emphasized that its occurrence is rare. There is thus no conclusive evidence that regular betel chewing without the addition of tobacco results in physical or mental health problems for most people. Like kava, betel appears to produce a relatively harmless "high."

As usually taken in Oceania, not only do kava and betel consumption pose few—if any—health risks, but neither drug leads to intoxicated behavior that is socially disruptive (indeed, quite the contrary). The plants from which these substances are derived are locally grown and quite readily available, and the processes for making and taking these two traditional drugs do not require commercial manufacture. In the past twenty years, some cash marketing of both drugs has developed, but this is primarily by smallholders or local concerns, and neither substance is handled by multinational corporations. Thus, kava and betel do not have negative social and economic consequences for the Pacific Islands societies where they are used.

ALCOHOLIC BEVERAGES

Pacific Islanders, like most North American Indians, had no alcoholic beverages until Europeans brought them early in the contact period. Initially, most islanders found alcohol distasteful and spat it out, but eventually they acquired a fondness for what sometimes was called "white man's kava." During the late eighteenth and first half of the nineteenth century, whalers, beachcombers, missionaries, and traders arrived in the islands in growing numbers. Many of them were drinkers and provided models of drunken behavior for the islanders to copy. Some of them established saloons in the port towns, and alcohol was widely used as an item of trade with the islanders. By at least the 1840s, missionaries to the islands, reflecting temperance politics in the United States and Great Britain, began to speak out forcefully against "the evils of drink" (Marshall and Marshall 1976).

As the European and American powers of the day consolidated colonial control over Oceania in the nineteenth century, they passed laws prohibiting islanders from consuming beverage alcohol. While such laws usually had strong missionary backing, they were also intended to maintain order, protect colonists from the possible "drunken depredations of savages," and serve what were deemed to be the islanders' own best interests. Despite prohibition, production of home brews continued in some areas, theft provided an occasional source of liquor, and the drinking of methylated spirits offered a potentially deadly alcohol alternative in some parts of the Pacific (Marshall 1988:579–582).

Colonially imposed prohibition laws remained in place until the 1950s and 1960s, when they were set aside one after another in the era of decolonization. Since then, the establishment of new Pacific nations has fostered a maze of legal regulations surrounding alcohol use, and it has also led to the encouragement of alcohol production and marketing. In many different parts of the Pacific Islands, problems have accompanied the relaxation of controls and the expansion of availability.

It is generally true around the world that more men drink alcoholic beverages than women, and that men drink greater quantities than women, but these gender differences are particularly pronounced in most of Oceania. In many of the islands, there are strong social pressures against women drinking, reinforced by church teachings, that effectively keep most women from even tasting alcoholic beverages. With a few exceptions, it is usually only Westernized women in the towns who drink on any sort of a regular basis. Boys below age fourteen or fifteen seldom, if ever, drink, but by the time they are in their late teens or early twenties, nearly all of them partake of alcohol. So much is this the case that in Chuuk (Truk) drinking and drunkenness is called "young men's work" (Marshall 1987b).

These gender differences have resulted in profoundly different attitudes toward alcohol by men and women that sometimes have resulted in outspoken social opposition by women to men's drinking and its attendant social problems (see Marshall and Marshall 1990). Weekend binge drinking by groups of young men—especially in towns—frequently leads to social disruption and confrontations that have been labeled "weekend warfare" in one Micronesian society (Marshall 1979).

For many Pacific Islanders, alcoholic beverages have come to symbolize "the good life" and active participation in a modern, sophisticated lifestyle. Beer is usually the beverage of choice in Oceania, and, in some places, it has been incorporated into ceremonial exchanges surrounding such events as bride price payments, weddings, and

"Driving Under the Influence" Accident, Weno Island, Chuuk, Federated States of Micronesia (1985). (Photo by M. Marshall)

funerals. In the Papua New Guinea Highlands' Chuave area, beer is treated as an item of wealth and "has assumed a central role in inter- and intraclan prestations" (Warry 1982:84). Cartons of beer have been endowed with a number of social and symbolic qualities in common with pork, the most highly esteemed traditional valuable. For example, the success of a ceremony is judged, increasingly, by the amount of beer, as well as pork, available for display and distribution; beer in cartons has a known value and the twenty-four bottles are easily divisible; like pigs, the stacked cartons of beer (sometimes as many as 240!) are appropriate items for display; alcohol is a social facilitator in these sometimes tense feast situations; beer—like pork and other food-stuffs—is consumable; and, like pork, beer is used at feasts both as a tool to create relationships and as a weapon to slight rivals (Warry 1982).

The chief problems associated with alcohol use in Oceania are social ones, although it is difficult to divorce these from the interrelated public health and economic costs. Among the more prominent and widespread social problems are domestic strife, particularly wife beating; community fighting and disruption, often with attendant trauma and occasional fatalities; crime, and drunk-driving accidents.

In the post–World War II era, these alcohol-related problems have been a continuing concern of community-based and government agencies in Pacific Islands countries. For example, a seminar was held in 1977 on "Alcohol Problems with the Young People of Fiji" (Fiji National Youth Council 1977), and, in 1986, Catholic youth in the Highlands of Papua New Guinea rallied to oppose alcohol abuse (*The Times of Papua New Guinea 1986a*). Other examples of community-based concerns are church women's groups who

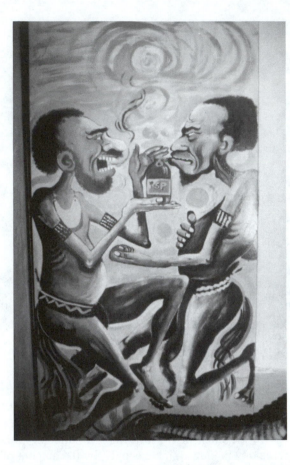

Wall Painting (by Robert Siune), Kuglame Taverne, Simbu Province, Papua New Guinea (1980). (Photo by M. Marshall)

championed a legal prohibition against alcohol on Weno, Chuuk (Moen Island, Truk) (Marshall and Marshall 1990), and an ecumenical Christian training center in Papua New Guinea (the Melanesian Institute) that has given voice to village peoples' concerns over abuse of alcohol for many years. Within a decade after it became legal for Papua New Guineans to drink, the government felt it necessary to sponsor an official Commission of Inquiry in 1971 to assess the widely perceived problems that had ensued. Less than ten years later, another investigation of alcohol use and abuse under national government auspices was launched in Papua New Guinea through its Institute for Applied Social and Economic Research (IASER). Such government commissions and groups of concerned citizens usually produce recommendations for action; however, serious and effective alcohol control policies are rarely forthcoming.

Although they have received less attention in the literature, primarily because of the absence of adequate hospital records and autopsy reports for Pacific Islands countries, the physical and mental illnesses linked to either prolonged heavy ethanol intake or binge drinking appear to be considerable. Among these are alcoholic cirrhosis, cancers of the upper respiratory and upper digestive tracts, death from ethanol overdose, alcoholic psychoses, and suicide while under the influence of alcohol.

In recent years, researchers have focused on non-insulin-dependent diabetes mellitus (NIDDM), which has increased in urbanized and migrant Pacific Islands populations (for example, Baker et al. 1986; King et al. 1984). With changes from traditional diets to "modern" diets of refined foods and higher intakes of fats, sugar, sodium, and alcoholic beverages, some Micronesian and Polynesian populations have shown what is thought to be a hereditary susceptibility to NIDDM, which apparently is only expressed with a change from the traditional rural lifestyle. Urban and migrant islanders typically engage in less physical activity and have higher levels of obesity than their rural nonmigrant counterparts. Given that individuals with diabetes are more vulnerable to the hypoglycemic effects of alcohol because alcohol interferes with hepatic gluconeogenesis (Franz 1983:149; see also Madsen 1974:52-53), heavy drinking that may produce complications for diabetics poses an added health risk.

TOBACCO

Although the Spanish and Portuguese introduced tobacco into the East Indies from the New World in the late sixteenth and early seventeenth centuries, and although this new drug spread rather quickly to the island of New Guinea via traditional trade routes, *Nicotiana tabacum* did not reach most Pacific Islands until the nineteenth century. It became a basic item of trade and even served as a kind of currency during the heyday of European exploration and colonization of Oceania. The first German plantations on the north coast of New Guinea near Madang were tobacco plantations, and the crop continues to be grown commercially in Fiji and Papua New Guinea. In the 1800s, pipe and homemade cigar smoking were quite popular; today manufactured cigarettes dominate the market in most parts of the Pacific Islands. The prevalence of tobacco smoking by both men and women in Pacific Islands populations is much higher than in the developed countries of Australia, New Zealand, and the United States, and higher than in most developing nations elsewhere in the world (Marshall 1991). In some isolated rural parts of Oceania, nearly everyone in a community smokes—including children as young as eight or ten years of age.

With the decline in tobacco use in the developed nations of the West, the multinational corporations that control global production and marketing of this drug have shifted their emphasis to the huge and rapidly growing market in the Third World. Developing countries offer few restrictions to tobacco companies: most such countries have no maximum tar and nicotine levels, no laws restricting sales to minors, no advertising limits, no required health warnings, and no general public awareness of the serious health risks associated with smoking (Stebbins 1990). As a result, tobacco consumption has grown steadily in Third World countries, leading public health experts to predict and document the beginning of a major epidemic of diseases known to be linked to chronic tobacco use. During the 1980s, numerous studies have been published by health care professionals and other concerned individuals noting these alarming trends and calling for action. Studies documenting these problems exist for Africa, Latin America, and Asia, and researchers have begun to chronicle the same sad story for Oceania (Marshall 1991).

Cigarette advertisements on the outside of a store, Goroka, Eastern Highlands Province, Papua New Guinea (1980). (Photo by M. Marshall)

As with the upsurge in alcohol use and its aggressive marketing by multinational corporations in Pacific Islands countries, so it is, too, with the production and sale of commercial tobacco products, particularly cigarettes. Almost any store one enters in Oceania today displays tobacco advertisements prominently inside and out, and has numerous tobacco products readily available for sale. Among the many ploys used to push their brands, the tobacco companies sponsor sweepstakes contests with large cash prizes which can be entered by writing one's name and address on an empty cigarette pack and dropping it into a special box for a drawing. Tobacco firms also routinely sponsor sporting events, with trophies and prizes in cash and in kind. In other promotions, those who present fifteen empty packs of the pertinent brands are given "free" T-shirts emblazoned with the cigarette brand name.

The association of tobacco smoking with serious cardiovascular and respiratory diseases—lung cancer, chronic bronchitis, and emphysema—is by now well known. These diseases are particularly linked to the smoking of flue-cured commercial cigarettes, which now have been readily available in Oceania for about thirty years. As the Pacific Islanders who have smoked such cigarettes for many years develop health problems, more suffer from these smoking-related illnesses (Marshall 1991). One New Zealand study shows that those Maori women who smoke heavily during pregnancy produce infants of a lower average birth weight than those of Europeans or other Pacific Islanders in New Zealand (Hay and Foster 1981). Another study shows Maori women to have a lung cancer rate that is among the world's highest (Stanhope and Prior 1982).

As yet, there have been few efforts to gain control over the smoking epidemic in Pacific Islands countries. In one, the Fiji Medical Association announced a campaign to ban cigarette advertising following a directive from the Fiji Ministry of Health to stop smoking in all patient areas in government hospitals (*Pacific Islands Monthly* 1986). But the most encouraging program has been mounted in Papua New Guinea. In the early 1980s, an antismoking council was established there by members of the medical profession (Smith 1983), and, following several years of public debate, Parliament passed the Tobacco Products (Health Control) Act in November 1987. This law mandates various controls on tobacco advertising, requires health warning labels on cigarette packs and cigarette advertisements, and provides the authority to declare various public places as nonsmoking areas. As of March 1990, these included all national and provincial government offices, the offices and buildings of all educational institutions (other than staff quarters), all hospitals, health centers, clinics and aid posts, cinemas and theatres, public motor vehicles (PMVs), and all domestic flights on scheduled airlines. While there are some enforcement problems, the Department of Health has mounted an aggressive antismoking campaign (tied to the anti-betel-chewing campaign), and this is likely to have a positive impact over the next few years.

Despite the encouraging signs in Papua New Guinea, public-health-oriented antismoking campaigns have met with relatively small success to date in the face of the large sums of money devoted to advertising by the tobacco multinationals. Much more effort is needed in community and public health education if this preventable epidemic is to be brought under control in Oceania.

MARIJUANA

Unlike the use of alcohol, betel, kava, and tobacco, marijuana smoking is uniformly illegal in Oceania. Nonetheless, the plant is now grown quite widely in the islands and has a substantial number of devotees. In part because its cultivation and use is against the law, fewer data are available on marijuana smoking than on the other four common Pacific drugs.

Native to central Asia, marijuana diffused to Oceania much more recently than alcohol or tobacco. While it doubtless was present in such places as Hawaii and New Zealand well before World War II, in other island areas like Micronesia or the New Guinea highlands, it appears to have been introduced only during the 1960s and 1970s.

While considerable controversy surrounds the long-term health effects of marijuana smoking, certain things are by now well known and give cause for concern. Marijuana induces an increased cardiovascular work load, thus posing a potential threat to individuals with hypertension and coronary atherosclerosis. Both of these health problems have been on the rise in Pacific Islands populations, especially in urban areas (Baker et al. 1986; Patrick et al. 1983; Salmond et al. 1985), and both can only be worsened by marijuana use.

Marijuana smoke is unfiltered and contains about 50 percent more cancer-causing hydrocarbons than tobacco smoke (Maugh 1982). Recent research has shown that "marijuana delivers more particulate matter to the smoker than tobacco cigarettes and with a net four-times greater burden on the respiratory system" (Addiction Research Foundation 1989:3). This same work revealed significant structural changes in the lungs of marijuana smokers, with a higher rate among those who also smoked tobacco. These changes are associated with chronic obstructive lung disease and with lung cancer. Another study has found significant short-term memory impairment in cannabis-dependent individuals that lingers for at least six weeks after use of the drug is stopped (Schwartz et al. 1989). As was discussed above for tobacco, the limited amount of research that has been done shows respiratory illnesses to be major serious diseases in Oceania. Clearly, smoking marijuana will simply raise the incidence of health problems that were already significant in the Pacific Islands even before marijuana gained popularity.

In the Pacific Islands, as in the United States, marijuana growing is attractive because it yields a higher cash return per unit of time per unit of land than other agricultural crops. Even though marijuana is grown as a cash crop and often sold by the "joint," the plant is easy to grow, requires little attention, and thrives in most island environments. As a result, most marijuana consumed in the Pacific Islands, like betel and kava, is locally grown and not imported by drug cartels or multinationals. Even so, marijuana grown in the islands is sometimes exported to larger and more lucrative markets (Nero 1985). This has become the subject of major police concern in Papua New Guinea, where there are some indications that organized crime may be involved in the purchase of marijuana grown in the highlands to be sent overseas (for example, *Niugini Nius* 1990). It will be well nigh impossible to uproot marijuana from Oceania today, but much more could be done to educate islanders about the health risks associated with its use.

OTHER DRUGS

As of 1989, hard drugs such as cocaine and heroin have made little headway in Pacific Islands communities. The most dramatic example of a place where such penetration has begun is Palau, where heroin first showed up in the early 1970s (Nero 1985:20-23). By 1985, cocaine was being used in Palau as well, and, by then, a number of Palauan heroin addicts had been sent to Honolulu for detoxification and treatment (Polloi 1985).

Although the Palauan case is somewhat unusual for the Pacific Islands at present, there are increased reports of hard drugs being shipped *through* the islands from Asia for metropolitan markets in Australia, New Zealand, and North America. Clearly, given the ease of air travel and relatively lax security and customs checks, more hard drugs will appear in the islands in the coming years.

CONCLUSIONS

Oceania's traditional drugs—betel and kava—create few if any social problems and pose minimal health risks to users. Moreover, these drugs are locally produced, and even when they are sold in the market the profits remain in islanders' hands and enrich the local economy. From an economic perspective, the cropping and selling of marijuana in most of the Pacific Islands operates in much the same way: small growers cultivate the plant for their own use or to sell in local markets. The major differences between marijuana and betel and kava are that marijuana is illegal and that smoking marijuana poses significant health risks. Oceania's other two major drug substances are produced and distributed in a very different manner and pose much more serious social and public health problems.

Over the past decade, an accumulation of studies has shown that alcoholic beverage and tobacco multinational corporations have increasingly targeted developing countries as prime markets for their products (for example, Cavanaugh and Clairmonte 1985;

Muller 1978; Stebbins 1990; Wickström 1979). This marketing involves aggressive advertising, often aimed especially at young people and women. Frequently, it takes the form of joint ventures with host governments, on the grounds that large profits can be shared (which ignores the significant health and social costs involved). The multinationals also have become infamous for inducing governments (for example, the United States) to threaten trade embargoes against countries that balk at the unrestrained marketing of alcohol and tobacco products within their borders (*The Nation's Health* 1989).

The developing countries of Oceania have been subject to this "legal pushing" of harmful substances, even though their populations are small and transport poses certain logistical problems. Breweries, ultimately owned by huge overseas corporations, operate in French Polynesia, Western Samoa, Tonga, Fiji, Vanuatu, and Papua New Guinea, and there are distilled beverage producers in Fiji and Papua New Guinea.

For example, domestic production of hard liquor began in Papua New Guinea in 1985 by Fairdeal Liquors Pty. Ltd. Fairdeal imports raw materials (concentrates and ethanol) from its parent corporation based in Malaysia and from other overseas sources. The company then mixes and bottles both its own brands and selected internationally known brands on franchise (for example, Gilbey's gin, Jim Beam whiskey) in its factory in the Port Moresby suburb of Gordons. Initially, Fairdeal was able to market its own product ("Gold Cup") in small, clear plastic sachets for around 35 cents (U.S.) each. These were a marketing success but a social disaster because irresponsible storekeepers sold them to children as well as adults, and because many men drank them to excess. The ensuing public outcry led the Prime Minister to ask the company to withdraw the sachets from the market two months after they were introduced. Following the outcry from concerned citizens, especially in the highlands (*The Times of Papua New Guinea* 1986), Fairdeal briefly closed its Port Moresby factory in December 1986 because the national government also imposed a 1,200 percent increase in the import tax on the concentrate used to produce liquor (The Times of Papua New Guinea 1986). But even with this momentary setback, Fairdeal continues to market its own brands in bottles for half the price of comparable imports. This is possible because by bottling locally the company still avoids paying as much excise duty as that paid by importers of alcoholic beverages that are bottled abroad.

It was announced in mid-1989 that new breweries would be built in Papua New Guinea and Western Samoa (*Pacific Islands Monthly* 1989). The Papua New Guinea venture, which since has fallen through, was to be constructed at Kerowagi in Simbu Province, and represented a proposed joint venture among Danbrew Consult of Denmark and the five highlands provincial governments. At least two highlands provincial premiers had to be cajoled into committing their provinces to participation in this scheme, and the highly controversial project was opposed by women's organizations and church groups. Papua New Guinea's major brewery—South Pacific—itself a subsidiary of the Heineken Group, bought out its sole competitor (San Miguel, PNG) early in 1983. San Miguel (PNG) was a subsidiary of "the most successful conglomerate group in the Philippines," a group that held overseas interests in mining, brewing, fishing, finance, and development in nine different countries in Asia and Europe (Krinks 1987).

In 1978, War on Want published a slender volume entitled, *Tobacco and the Third World: Tomorrow's Epidemic?* Just over a decade later, the *question* in that book's title has been answered—a smoking epidemic has swept the Third World, and the Pacific

Islands have not been immune to this global trend. While cigarettes and stick tobacco are locally produced in Papua New Guinea and Fiji by subsidiaries of the giant British Tobacco Company, the overwhelming majority of tobacco products sold in Oceania today are commercial cigarettes imported from the developed countries, principally Australia, New Zealand, and the United States. Promotional campaigns continue to have few, if any, restrictions placed upon them, and the costs of sweepstakes and raffle giveaways is small compared to the substantial profits to be earned once new consumers are "hooked."

A haze hangs over the Pacific Islands today, a result of widespread alcohol and tobacco abuse and of the smokescreens put up by multinationals to buy off politicians under the guise that production and marketing of these legal drugs contributes to economic development. In fact, the public health costs of alcohol and tobacco use and the social disruption surrounding alcohol abuse *undermine* economic and social development over the long run. If Pacific Islands governments do not develop more effective systems to prevent and control the aggressive marketing of alcohol and tobacco by multinationals, then the haze in the air and the glazed looks on the faces of island citizens will increase. The resultant social and health costs can only weaken Oceanic communities and make more difficult their dream of building prosperous, healthy, modern societies.

Acknowledgment: I am grateful to Linda A. Bennett for useful comments on an earlier version of this chapter.

NOTES

1. This statement remains true for Pacific Islanders; however, Australian Aborigines, to whom kava was introduced in the 1980s, and who consume it in quantities far in excess of those taken by Pacific Islanders, have developed such clinical side effects as weight loss, liver and kidney dysfunction, blood abnormalities, and possible pulmonary hypertension (Mathews et al. 1988; Riley and Mathews 1989).

2. Recently, in Papua New Guinea, and possibly elsewhere in the Pacific Islands, lime manufactured by commercial chemical firms has been substituted for lime produced in the traditional manner from ground seashells or coral. There is some evidence to suggest that the industrially manufactured lime is much more caustic than that traditionally used by Pacific betel chewers, and that this may increase the risk of oral cancer. Although controlled studies to demonstrate this have yet to be done, the Papua New Guinea Department of Health has mounted an active public health campaign advising people that if they chew betel, they run a risk of developing oral cancer.

Religious Experience and Worldview

INTRODUCTION

In recent decades, religion has become a particularly dynamic, volatile, and fluid forum for social and political expression in Third World societies. This can be seen in the recent growth and spread of fundamentalist and other religious movements (for example, the Islamic fundamentalist movement). The religious sphere frequently offers the means—the ideology, leadership, and social consensus—for Third World peoples to confront their past domination by foreigners and initiate social change in line with their own vision of the future. In this way, religious activity (ritual, ceremonies, and so on) can become a major vehicle for sociopolitical activism. It can also provide an ideological framework for the construction of new worldviews and identities by peoples whose cultures have been shattered by foreign domination.

As in other parts of the Third World, religious dynamism is an important theme in the social life of many Pacific Islands societies. Because the vast majority of Pacific peoples are Christians, their religious innovations and activism take place within the integrated framework of their own syncretic interpretations (mixes of indigenous and Christian belief) of Christian ideology and practice. The chapters in this section of the volume illustrate some of the various forms Pacific Islands religious expression and activism take.

Kenelm Burridge (Chapter 18) discusses the emergence of cargo cult activity in Melanesia after the region's peoples were converted to Christianity and integrated into a cash economy. Although most characteristic of the early contact era, such cult activity continues today. Burridge describes the structure of these syncretic religious movements, proposing that the forms they take and their focus on material wealth reflect indigenous Melanesian worldview and values. However, he notes that all human societies have experienced and are susceptible to cult phenomena, particularly under conditions of intense social stress, economic deprivation, and domination by outsiders.

Paul Roscoe (Chapter 19) provides an intriguing account of recent millennial cult activities in Yangoru Boiken (Sepik Province, Papua New Guinea). There, a millennial movement spread rapidly under the auspices of Canadian missionaries from the New Apostolic Church. The ideology of the Canadian missionaries was surprisingly consistent with the Yangoru worldview and expectations embodied in what had been an earlier, indigenous religious movement. Roscoe describes how the leader of the local movement "used" the missionaries and their church to resurrect his following and gain substantial political power.

Laurence Carucci (Chapter 20) analyzes the four-month-long celebration of Christmas (*Kūrijmōj*) on Ujelang (Republic of the Marshall Islands). Focusing on how the extensive ritual, feasting, and games involved activate cultural symbols and meanings, Carucci proposes that the celebration is a dynamic "communicative mechanism" that serves several important ends in the community. First, it is the means through which islanders construct and express a sense of their own socially empowered identity, one that has been made problematic by centuries of foreign domination and chronic cultural disruption. The ritual also allows the Ujelangese to achieve a degree of power over the supernatural (which includes both the Christian god and ancient deities), convincing it to bless the community with abundance in the new year.

Karen Sinclair (Chapter 21) describes the Maori tradition of religious prophecy and how in contemporary times these prophets are the locus of increasing Maori political activism. Sinclair notes that Christian ideology has been adapted to Maori worldview and examines how this ideology is now nurturing not only a growing Maori political consciousness, but also a Maori cultural "renaissance." She goes on to describe how Maori prophets "give voice to the grievances of their people" against the whites who not only took their lands, but virtually brought them to the brink of extinction as a people. Part of this cultural renaissance is active resistance against white domination and political efforts to obtain the return of Maori lands.

18

Melanesian Cargo Cults

Kenelm Burridge
University of British Columbia

A constant theme in the relatively short recorded history of Melanesia is the occurrence of cargo cults. These are socio-magico-religious activities which, involving genuine sociopolitical and economic as well as spiritual aspirations, are usually triggered by a person with charismatic qualities commonly known in the literature as a "prophet," who articulates the promise of an early realization of certain hopes and yearnings. The latter, in almost all cases, are phrased in terms of an imminent access to, or the prompt delivery of, quantities of manufactured goods and prepared foodstuffs. Hence the name cargo (in Tok Pisin, *kago*), goods off-loaded from the ships or aircraft of industrialized countries.

While some cargo activities have occurred in other parts of Oceania, the vast majority have taken place in Melanesia where, so far as present knowledge goes, they have been taking place since the late 1850s (Steinbauer 1979:181) continuing into the present. Overt activities in one place tend to recur, (as shown in Chapter 19, by Paul Roscoe, in this volume) or give rise to others in the vicinity. As one cult or movement fades away or is expunged by administrative action, another emerges in a slightly different form somewhere else. During the decade following the end of World War II, the incidence of occurrences increased greatly. More recently, some movements that might have been cargo cults have developed into independent Christian churches.

Communications between neighbors among the many thousands of villages and hamlets of Melanesia are zealously maintained; news about important events disseminates rapidly. Thoughts about *kago* or cargo have become common knowledge, and information about a particular cult often gives rise to a desire to imitate. And this may partly account for the spread and number of occurrences. Assuming, because it seems more reasonable, that there is one phenomenon, *The* Cargo Cult, which appears in rather differing idioms in one location after another, a rough "guesstimate" of the number of recorded instances since the 1850s would be around four hundred or so. Those activities that have never developed into an organized cult or movement, or which have gone unnoticed or unrecorded, would inflate that number considerably.

Because cargo activities envisage both new spiritual values (a new heaven) and a renewed sociomoral, economic, and political order (a new earth), they may conveniently be called millenarian-type. That is, they seem to be a subset in a local idiom of all those movements of socioreligious reform, revival, and renewal which are and have been endemic to the Christian tradition under conditions of sociocultural change, where missionaries have been active, and where denominational interpretations and forms of morality and order seem inconsistent. Although there are some instances of similar kinds of activities outside areas of Christian influence (mainly within Buddhism and Islam), including one in Papua New Guinea (Berndt 1952), the vast bulk—perhaps 90 percent—of the recorded instances have occurred within ambiences of Christian activity. Perhaps simply an artifact of the European passion for recording, the statistic is nonetheless telling.

Within the Christian tradition, movements of the kind have been called, variously, millenarian, messianic, or enthusiastic activities. Besides using these terms, but looking for names less closely associated with a specific religious-cultural tradition, some writers have permuted and/or combined interpretive framework, cultural emphases, place, and historical period to coin alternatives. Thus *accommodative, acculturative, adaptive,* and *adjustive* interpret the activities as attempts to reconcile a native tradition with an intrusive and more powerful culture. The terms *crisis* and *disaster* assume and look for a prior cultural or natural traumatic event as efficient cause. *Nativistic, militant,* and *denunciatory* evoke rebellious responses to foreign rule and cultural ways, reaching back to supposed traditional glories, and blaming current frustrations on wrongful moral ways. *Dynamic* or *dynamistic, vitalization,* and *revitalization* emphasize indigenous cultural renewals in the face of what is seen as moral decadence and decay. *Charismatic* and *prophet* avoid particularizing, and *Holy Spirit* and *salvation,* recently on the increase, reflect a growing awareness of spiritual (largely Christian) influences and the development of independent churches. Finally, if distinctions between activity, movement, and cult may sometimes be useful, they tend to break down in the face of the activities themselves.

BACKGROUND

Many years ago an anthropologist, A.C. Haddon, made the following observations about cargo movements:

> An awakening of religious activity is a frequent characteristic of periods of social unrest. The weakening or disruption of the old social order may stimulate new and often bizarre ideals, and these may give rise to religious movements that strive to sanction social and political aspirations. Communities that feel themselves oppressed anticipate the emergence of a hero who will restore

their prosperity and prestige. And when the people are imbued with religious fervour the expected hero will be regarded as a Messiah. Phenomena of this kind are well known in history, and are not unknown at the present day among peoples in all stages of civilization. (Haddon 1917:455)

Note the way in which Haddon lifts "cargo cult" out of its ethnographic specificity as a curiosity into a more generally human proclivity: the use of "bizarre," used by many later authors to describe both activities and aspirations; "feel…oppressed," indicating the state as a mainly subjective experience; and "Messiah," which, specific to Judaeo-Christianity, has become an archaism yielding to the more common prophet or leader or charismatic figure.

In the Melanesian context, Haddon's "social unrest" alludes to the general conditions under which so many cargo activities have taken place: the ways in which relatively small nonliterate and subsistence hunting, horticultural, and fishing peoples have been affected by the advent of Europeans, colonial forms of order, the decimation of populations by infectious and contagious diseases, and the inroads of modern commerce and industry.

The introduction of money, plantations, taxation, and forms of contract or indentured labor gave an added scope to some, but also made life generally more complicated and unpredictable for most. Prospectors, traders, and labor recruiters tended to be rough and very ready in their methods. Christian missionaries of several denominations and nationalities with not wholly similar doctrines and habits of work alleviated some problems but caused others. Hopes for new prosperities from cash crops such as copra, rice, and coffee were (and continue to be) often dashed by slumps in world market conditions. Finally, two World Wars with their phases of defeat and reconquest, the passage of military forces and materiel, and the exchange briefly, or more permanently, of German, British or Australian, Japanese, and American masters, modes of government, and imported goods hardly conduced to a stable present and predictable future.

The history of Melanesia has surely been one of continuing but varying kinds of change. Melanesians have been ruled by foreigners and borne on events over which they themselves have had little control. Until recently, and in spite of missionary efforts, purposive and organized educational and technological programs were severely restricted. And such conditions might indeed be thought to give rise to "social unrest." But it would be a mistake to make too much of them. Social unrest is easily assumed but analytically elusive. Melanesians are notoriously pragmatic and phlegmatic, greeting the strange and extraordinary with the same self-assurance as they do the everyday. While recent decades have seen small colonial townships grow into modern cities and towns, most Melanesians still lead simple subsistence lives varied by cash cropping and work on plantations or other kinds of wage labor. If Euro-Americans tend to think of social unrest as in some sense abnormal and temporary, activities very similar to cargo cults continually take place in what are thought of as normal and, indeed, well-ordered and prosperous circumstances of material plenty. In California, for example, movements much like cargo cults (for example, the Jonestown cult; see Krause 1978) have become expectable events. Those who take part in them may be wealthy or poor, prosperous or in straits, women or men. The leaders often are or become very wealthy, and if their followers otherwise "feel oppressed," it is surely a highly subjective feeling.

In spite of the several national independences achieved by Melanesians over the last decade or so, in spite of freedom from foreign rule and an albeit limited capacity to order their own lives in an economic sense, cargo activities still take place. Although (as suggested above) they are becoming less overtly materialistic and more explicitly religious, this in itself suggests that they reflect something more like anomie—social uncertainty, aimlessness, the absence of a structured social system providing defined, attainable and worthwhile goals and statuses—rather than a generalized "social unrest."

GENERAL COURSE

The general form of a cargo movement may be described quite briefly. Assuming a context of problems or anxieties in relation to sociocultural life, these concerns are discussed within the context of a past with its supposed securities and satisfactions, present discontents, and what seem to be viable solutions for the future. In Melanesia, the most common and persistent theme found in the difficulties that people experience at the village level is access to cargo—goods that arrive from across the sea, which white folk have in plenty without, so it would seem, actually working, but which Melanesians themselves lack. Why, they ask, do they not have a similar access? What kinds of action might remedy the matter and give Melanesians an equivalent access to all those goods and foodstuffs?

In the course of time, and as people talk over their problems, the talking begins to take a predictable route, the problems become more or less defined and familiar to those engaged in the conversation, and so become the basis for future discussion. One author (Burridge 1960:147–245) has called the familiar contents of such ongoing debates a myth-dream. The term is used advisedly because, while much the same process seems to take place in literate cultures, the results of debate and discussion become concrete in pamphlets and books and so become a defined ideology. A myth-dream, on the other hand, not necessarily absent from literate cultures, but much looser and more ambiguous than an ideology, may at the same time be more powerful. When joined to a traditional myth it has all the authority and magical or religious force that myths normally have in nonliterate cultures: sources of knowledge whose parts may be variously and inclusively interpreted as action imperatives, history, or as ambiguously instructional.

What distinguishes a myth-dream, roughly equivalent to what has become known as cargo ideology, from an ideology in the more usually accepted sense, is that while the latter is normally explicit and written down, the former depends upon memory and the spoken word. Unlike an ideology, which may be addressed soberly and objectively, a myth-dream gathers the emotions, desires, and frustrations to create an environment of eager expectation within which is hidden a "secret" that will one day be revealed. For Melanesians, this "secret" is why, how, or what it is Europeans possess that enables them to have and dispose of all those goods known as cargo.

In the cargo situation, the discussions that go on about the past, the present, what the "secret" might be, and a possible future is as much an activity as anything else. This indeed is what goes on most of the time—although seldom noticed by foreigners who cannot speak or understand the vernacular. Often enough things never get beyond this stage. Only when, within the context of the myth-dream, and after someone has had some kind of extraordinary experience—a dream or vision or encounter with a traditional spirit entity or Christian representation such as the Virgin Mary, the Holy Spirit, or the Archangel Gabriel—does anything further occur. Then, providing that the experience, the person who had it—who now becomes a prophet or charismatic or cult leader—and the action program put forward are acceptable and persuasive, cult activities proper begin to take place.

The operative terms are "persuasive" and "acceptable," weasel words that only define themselves after the event. For, while there have been many men and a few women who have aspired to the role of prophet or leader, most are rejected as mildly insane, not worth notice. This last, in spite of the fact that what the would-be leader has to say might, it is thought, be a divinely inspired rather than human instruction. Every so often, however, the message of a possible prophet fires a spark. This engages the serious attentions of a few, often men and women of relatively high status, who become close followers and committed to the activities outlined by the prophet or leader. They set about persuading kinsfolk, friends, neighbors, and doubters to join them in pursuing the program of activities recommended.

Precisely what differentiates a rejected would-be prophet from an acceptable one is rarely clear. Nor can we say why the spark should ignite in one place and not in a similar situation elsewhere. If it seems more reasonable to accept the leadership of one who has proved him/herself in ordinary life and who, moreover, has had a significant experience of the white people's world, this is certainly not always the case. Sometimes, to a European eye, a cult leader seems clearly deranged and, in hindsight, participants in a cult will often agree that he or she was *longlong*, "a little mad." Or again, if the visionary experience of an old woman or child is found acceptable at first, subsequent failures in leadership will throw doubt on the authenticity of the revelation.

Sometimes, fearful of the dire retributive disasters promised by the prophet or leader for noncompliance with the action program advocated—all millenarian-type activities are imbued with this kind of authoritarian black or white ethic—people may simply decide to play it safe. But accepting that a prophet is, as is claimed or thought to be the case, the vehicle of divine instructions, how Melanesians (or anyone else) can distinguish a false prophet with a delusory message from one whose revelation seems truly divinely inspired, is impossible to say. Although one may assume prophet and message have some sort of catalytic effect in relation to the "secret" of the cargo, the how and the why of it are not well understood, and the rationalizations produced after a failed event are not always to be trusted.

Finally, since there are many more negative instances than positive ones—instances of activities where, in what seem to be closely similar circumstances, no leader emerges and no definite cult or movement takes shape—the conditions in which a cult actually occurs cannot of themselves go all the way to explaining why in fact a cult or movement does take place. For this the negative instance also has to be accounted for, which we cannot do. That cargo cults are neither predictable nor, in hindsight, wholly explicable in social or cultural terms, places them in a universal context of dilemma relating to those kinds of ambiguous behavior which, seemingly demented or insane to some, are or may be to others truly divinely inspired, requiring one to act.

On the surface, many features of the message and action program announced by a charismatic leader do seem to merit the description "bizarre." On the other hand, on the symbolic level everything begins to make good sense. Thus, in earlier cults the destruction of gardens and crops—generally construed by Europeans as an act of faith in the cult leader's message, failing which no cargo will arrive and disasters such as floods, earthquakes, or fiery holocausts will certainly follow—can at the symbolic level be seen as the rejection of a way of life based on horticulture. And, it may also be appreciated as the prerequisite to rebirth into a mode of life based on commerce and industry, the way to gaining access to cargo. Indeed, since administrations, colonial or otherwise, generally prefer not to have starving populations on their hands, and set about shipping in emergency food supplies of flour, rice, and canned meat, fish, and vegetables, goods which make up much of the expected cargo, the cult may be said to have "worked" in some sense.

Most of the action programs begin to fall into place when seen as symbolic rituals of rebirth that find expression in a variety of idioms. Prescribed orgiastic dances, for example, in which all clothing is discarded to culminate in generalized sexual promiscuity, enact mythical times when there were no rules of sexual access, no rules of incest, no rules of marriage. Following the pattern of ritual rebirths everywhere (old rules—no rules—new rules, or, old order—no order/disorder—new order), after the rites, new rules of sexual access, supposedly adapted to or predicating an altered or new mode of life, come into force with stringent sanctions. Or again, forms of baptism are invented so that, collectively performed, the past may be washed away and, as in Christianity, the new man (who will have access to, and be able to manipulate, the cargo) brought into being. That is, the rites seem designed to transform ordinary but presently disabled or disadvantaged villagers into enlightened individuals able to play full and responsible parts in the new world of money, commerce, and cargo.

Building a large warehouse to receive the expected cargo, or leveling a tract of ground into an airstrip, or going off to a headland on the coast at dawn on the third day after a prescribed ritual to greet the ships approaching with cargo may be seen as practical measures of foresight permeated with both magical and religious faith. On the other hand, making a radio of palm wood and connecting it to a tall mast and aerial of forest vines in order to signal for cargo, while not without magical overtones, is also a symbolic enactment of the way of life being sought. Parading across village clearings in military fashion, giving staccato orders, and marching and wheeling with shouldered wooden guns; or putting flowers into vases to decorate their houses as Europeans do can easily seem naively imitative. But they can also be read as tests for the supposed "secret." Perhaps it lies dormant in European modes of inculcating a discipline and practicing an aesthetic…. And then, reflexively, since local administrations are aware that drilling or adorning houses with flowers may herald some kind of cargo activity, they tend to overreact and take the perpetrators to task. This encourages villagers to think they may be on the right track, getting close. As with shipping in emergency food supplies when a community destroys its crops, official reactions to cargo activities and suspicions of them cannot but be grist to the mill of cargo ideology.

Scribbling on a piece of paper and handing it in to a trade store in the hope of receiving a case of canned goods in exchange may seem silly to outsiders, a copying of European ways without understanding them. To the traditional villager with a limited experience of European ways, however, the question is why a villager's piece of paper is not effective, while a white man's is. Surface elements of racism and envy may be there, but at a deeper and symbolic level, the act in itself reveals a desire for literacy, clearly an important key—perhaps the "secret"—to understanding how the new world of commerce and access to cargo works. What is also clear is a groping toward knowing how to manage money, fairly obviously a primary measure of relative status in that social world from which Melanesians have been largely excluded because, it would seem, of the color of their skins and their subsistence mode of life.

The large variety of seemingly bizarre activities included in cargo cults in their initial stages fill out the bulk of the many accounts of the movements as wholes. The everpresent theme of rebirth points to a (desired) movement from a subsistence economy based upon the production and exchange of foodstuffs and valuables but without money (regarded as a general but factorial measure of value and status) to that modern mode of life made possible by money. Few cargo prophets do not allude to money in some way as the secret of gaining access to cargo. And, of course, they are right. Moreover, the notion of rebirth is not a matter of choice for this or that individual. It refers to a totality of the new and different: a new mode of life, new kinds of social relations, new ways of asserting status and, most importantly, equivalences of status in relation to whites. Even where there is a looking back to a past of supposed traditional prosperities and a meaningful and worthwhile life over which the ancestors presided, the themes of access to money, literacy, all the goods subsumed in *kago*, and equivalences of status recur. But now, instead of Melanesians attempting on their own to unravel a "secret" that whites seem unwilling to share, the ancestors are urged to persuade them to reveal it or, alternatively, provide the cargo directly.

Traditional distinctions in the roles of men and women are generally repeated in cargo movements. Adult men are usually the initiators and held responsible for their own acts and those of their wives and children. Men generally organize cult activities while women accompany them, reiterating traditional necessary complementarities. Although there are one or two reports of female dreamers or visionaries whose action programs have been carried out by men, no woman seems to have become an effective prophet on her own. Sometimes, in order to demonstrate his power, a cargo leader may demand what outside the cult context would earn him his quietus: the sexual services of his followers' wives and other women (see below concerning Yali). Whether or not women influence their husbands in the cult situation as they often significantly do in ordinary life is difficult to say. The evidence is lacking. The fact that girls and young women are noticeably present in mission schools and services (while their brothers tend to be elsewhere) is echoed today in the many international and regional conferences held in Oceania, which women dominate. But such women are not usually found among the participants of a cargo movement.

Mostly, cargo activities do not develop much further than their initial symbolic enactments. This is mainly because in the interests of what are seen as public safety, law, and good order—and most cargo cults do entail a deal of disorderliness in the initial stages—administrations move in rapidly to extirpate the activities as soon as it is known they have started. But it is also because, in most cases, Melanesian religious, political or socioeconomic leaders who might have been able to channel the energies of the cult into more acceptably productive activities have been lacking.

When a cult has been stopped or seems otherwise not to have been successful, life resumes on the surface its normal rhythms of hunting or fishing, farming, nurturing children, making exchanges or preparing feasts, and asserting relative status. Behind the facade of normalcy, however, the problems of making a significant and meaningful entry into the cash economy and creating a new sociopolitical order remain. While participants in a failed or aborted cult may be shamefaced at what seems to them in hindsight foolish, discussions regarding access to cargo resume. The local myth-dream is gone over and qualified, failure explained, the "secret" vaguely redefined, new possible solutions kicked around, the ambience made ready for a further outburst.

Nevertheless, no cargo cult is completely a failure. Being involved in the activities is a learning experience. With each set of activities, real access to cargo comes nearer. The symbolic values become more and more explicit, more readily translatable into pragmatic means-to-ends relations. If the last two decades have seen a development of religious elements resulting in the emergence of independent churches, they have also seen the growth of entrepreneurial businesses, trade unions, local councils, and other political institutions. Sometimes, in the past, a leader with unusual politico-economic skills and acumen has arisen and been able to maintain a position of influence despite an official ban on cultic activities. Or, unwilling to see their efforts end so fruitlessly, participants may sometimes insist on carrying on with the "work" (in Tok Pisin, *wok*), as the activities are called, in a less outwardly challenging way.

ETHNOGRAPHIC EXAMPLES

Paliau, who started and continued a movement on Manus in the Admiralty Islands (Schwartz 1962), is an example of an inspired and insightful leader who, despite much in his demeanor that a European might describe as not altogether normal, had effective political skills. Another cargo leader, Yali, active along the Rai coast in Papua New Guinea during the 1950s, was an able man who had been explicitly selected by the administration for a future leadership role. After valuable experience of European ways in the police force, he had been decorated for war service and taken to Australia to see how cargo was made (Lawrence 1964). Nevertheless, Yali began to adopt a cargoist mind-set. Persuaded and supported by very able aides, he came close to forging into a loose political entity the scattered villages of much of the Madang District. But since the activities of Yali and his aides were accompanied by allegedly forced sexual liaisons with the wives and sisters of others, and the illegal collection of a so-called tax from villagers, despite its past sponsorship of him the administration had to intervene. So Yali was (plausibly) imprisoned for rape and his aides dispersed. Bereft of leaders, the movement dissolved. Still, for many years thereafter, Yali lived on in many peoples' minds as a culture-hero who would one day return and make cargo available.

The John Frum movement on Tanna in Vanuatu (formerly the New Hebrides) is an example of a people carrying on with their "work" despite efforts to stop it (Guiart 1962). Starting shortly after the end of the Pacific war among a partly missionized people on a lonely, lightly administrated island, the myth-dream involved an expectation of cargo being spewed out of the crater of the active volcano there. Although the movement might have simply faded away, it has continued to this day as a stabilized and ordered community with Christian elements: a new and exclusive society invented by the people for themselves and remaining adamantly opposed to any interference from outsiders. One day, they say, the cargo will come. In the meantime they can manage their own lives in ways they think fit.

Finally, The Christian Fellowship Church of New Georgia in the Western Province, Solomon Islands, is an example of what might have been simply another failed cargo cult becoming, through the zeal and spiritual determination of its founder, Samuel Eto, an independent church. Starting as a burst of enthusiasm within a missionary enclave—fairly common in missionary contexts—which the white missionaries involved could not accommodate, Eto took control. Trained as a teacher and pastor, and convinced from his own experience that there had been a genuine infilling of the Holy Spirit, Eto and others seceded from the mission and founded their own organization (see Barr and Trompf 1983).

INTERPRETATIONS

Unlike the same kinds of cults or movements in Europe, the Americas, Africa, and Asia, Melanesian cargo cults have received what might seem a disproportionate amount of attention. Social scientists of all stripes and administrative officers as well as missionaries and sojourners have all put pen to paper. And, on the whole, each has tried to go further than what is implicit in a supposedly plain description and title to account for the activities. The frequency of cult occurrences, together with the large number of amateur as well as professional social scientists working in the area, has possibly had something to do this. Perhaps the overtly strange or bizarre nature of the activities and trying to decode them has been an irresistible challenge. Or, maybe it is the idea of cargo—the products of work in an industrialized society—being made to appear by magic, without work—despite the fact that Melanesians regard the activities as proper work or *wok*— that engages one's interest.

Going beyond these more or less plausible reasons, however, cargo cults seem to be a variant of a universal human proclivity: putting into a symbolic framework those very radical and deeply felt desires for sociocultural changes that will give renewed meaning to a life which seems presently to be without point or purpose, and for which the existing order provides few other alternatives (see Wilson 1973). And, explaining or accounting for this proclivity constitutes a critical test of theory in social science.

As we have seen above, Haddon (1917) explicitly located cargo cults or movements in a historical and universal context. But he wrote some years before history as such was virtually anathematized and considered outside the purview of social science, then defined by varieties of functionalism. Even when "social change" was substituted for history, researchers were crippled. There was little for it but to resort to homespun psychologies. Thus F.E. Williams (1923, 1934), a brilliant field anthropologist with rich material, more or less had to resort to the mass hysteria, dancing, and whirling that was immediately observable as an explanatory concept: a psychological proclivity so to do.

Many years later, using Williams's data as his ethnographic base but now freed from methodological objections to history, Cochrane (1970) was able to show convincingly that the complex of events reported by Williams was related to attempts to reform traditional ways of gaining status in light of Christian teaching and within the constraints associated with a cash economy and colonial rule. Williams's hysteria and whirlings, real enough, could now be seen as symbolic enactments of an impasse in peoples' desires and aspirations. Most of the events could be read as experiments in modifying a traditional system of gaining and asserting status, perceived now as no longer worthwhile or meaningful, so that a new system, in tune with and geared to existing conditions, might be brought into being.

Forty years separate Williams and Cochrane, however, and between the two World Wars little of the literature on cargo activities did much more than describe a set of events, treat them as kinds of psychosocial illness, and go on to prescribe remedial action: mainly education, particularly in Western technology and science. This was, of course, sound motherhood social engineering, or welfare advice. Education seemed to be the key to understanding a strange sociocultural environment and so being able to make sensible use of it. Despite Haddon's essay on the topic, cargo activities were still described as the bizarre goings-on of the ignorant, other, and crazed. The similar kinds of activities in history among both the educated and uneducated in North America and Europe were not appreciated as such. The cargo idiom tended to mislead, distract, and make peculiar. Thus, it was not until some years after the end of World War II, in the 1950s when history was readmitted to the discourse, that a few anthropologists began to seek a deeper understanding of what might be taking place in cargo activities.

Social historians such as Fulop-Muller (1935), Knox (1950), and Cohn (1957) began to exert an influence. The first of these, in a wide survey of millenarian-type movements in history that were, as Haddon had realized, similar to cargo cults, emphasized the role of the leaders or prophets in relation to collective hopes and aspirations. Knox, using a sociotheological framework, placed the enthusiastic or "divinely inspired" movements of Euro-America in a context of antinomianism (disregard of orthodoxies of order) and those changing social conditions which, continuing from the early beginnings of the industrial revolution, the mainline churches either ignored or seemed powerless to deal with. And Cohn's study of medieval millenarian movements, based in psychology, showed there were good reasons, seated in the sociopolitical conditions, why millenarists might be described as paranoid.

Besides the three authors mentioned above, major social historians and theorists such as Tawney (1926) and Weber (1947), long neglected by ahistorical anthropology, began to have an impact on anthropologists interested in cargo cults. These scholars sought to show how religions were correlated with social forms and how religious and/or political movements and the formation of new sects, denominations and polities were triggered by charismatic (Weber's coinage) leaders and altered social conditions, particularly the change from an agrarian to an industrial economy. Further, the works of Marx and Engels began to be appreciated by more and more social scientists as sociologies of history rather than as socialist political action programs.

Thus, Worsley (1957), an anthropologist working on Melanesian documentary materials, gave his study of cargo cults a generally Marxist interpretation. Very briefly, Melanesians were seen as a disenfranchised proletariat whose means of protest could not be other than in terms of the mindset they possessed: a syncretic mixture of the new ways being taught by Christian missionaries (not always well understood) and their own traditional magical or religious modes. No matter how sympathetic white administrators or plantation and other managers might think themselves, their real interests were in cheap labor and in keeping things that way. Melanesian aspirations in educational, technological, and social development were thwarted. Since there were no other channels through which Melanesians might voice their discontents and take positive action, magico-religious techniques, thought by most to be causative and integral to an efficient means-to-ends relationship, was all they had at their disposal. As time passed and Melanesians developed in awareness, Worsley thought, the aspirations contained in cargo activity would be translated into more considered and instrumental politico-economic action.

The impact of Worsley's work was decisive. It was no longer possible to think seriously of cargo cults as simply kinds of psychological derangement about which few could do much. They were embedded in the colonial system, in the forms of social order. The onus of responsible and effective action shifted to metropolitan governments and their dependent colonial and commercial systems. Educational and agricultural budgets expanded greatly, and efforts were made to familiarize villagers with modern political and economic processes through the formation of experimental political and economic institutions.

Belshaw (1950, 1954), Burridge (1960, 1969), Lawrence (1954, 1964), and Schwartz (1962) were among the first anthropologists who with field experience of cargo cults and activities, sought to unravel the meanings and relevances of the supposedly bizarre activities. To do this, they had to study the total sociocultural ambience of the peoples among whom they worked: their historical experiences with labor recruiters, plantation managers, traders, missionaries and administrative officers; how they regarded and treated money; the work they did for cash; their mythology and magical practices; and their spirit entities, economy, and status systems. In going thus to sociocultural conditions, they had to emphasize history, socioeconomic and political aspects, and the impact of Christian missionaries.

There have been, of course, many other anthropologists besides the four mentioned above who have published the results of their field experience with cargo cults. But the general interpretive tone had been set, and sealed by Fuchs (1965) and Lanternari (1965). The work of both these scholars on cargo cults and similar movements in Europe, Asia, Africa, and the Americas bedded the activities in conditions of radical sociocultural change with the emphasis on disenfranchisement, but credit was also given to the charismatic leaders and prophets. While homespun psychologies were bound to enter the work of most social scientists, Wallace (1956), professionally qualified, provided a psychological interpretation that complemented the work being done on cultural aspects.

Despite the wide variety in nomenclature of genre or type of cult or movement (above; also see La Barre 1971), and a sharpening of detail in identifying the issues involved (for example, Aberle 1962), there is today general agreement that cargo and similar movements are probably rooted in social and cultural conditions, chiefly in the disharmonies of opportunity, status, and political and socioeconomic satisfactions generated when a traditional economy is faced with modernization and the urgencies of money, commerce, and industry. Disagreements that continue to be debated go mainly to the relative importance of the particular issues that different interpretations emphasize. Thus, for example, while attitudes of racial inferiority/superiority, desire for status enhancement, psychological and/or politico-economic frustrations, and political disenfrachisement go together, distinguishing between them in mutual satisfaction tends to be difficult. Again, general economic disadvantages, relative (socioeconomic) deprivation, and being unfamiliar with modern finance and the ways in which money behaves evoke successive refinements whose relative significances must entail disagreement and debate. Replacing cultural disaster or loss by attempting to recreate a past that has forever gone instead of moving on to technological training and education stirs passions on both sides. Finally, there will always be arguments about the weight to be given to the prophet or leader in relation to those elements of millennial expectation (the myth-dream) in the total semantic environment of participants—particularly how the prophet or leader makes use of these elements.

There is, in addition today, the issue of why the numbers of cargo cults should be so very much less in the Highlands of Papua New Guinea than in the coastal areas. Part of the more general problem concerning the differences between Highlands and coastal peoples in Papua New Guinea, especially in relation to religious life, the question is only partially answered by the relatively late arrival of whites there in the 1930s compared to the period at least fifty years earlier along on the coasts. Those who came to the Highlands to explore, administrate, start plantations, and trade, certainly knew more about Melanesians and their ways than their predecessors on the coast. They were much more permissive and generous in their regard for Melanesian abilities, and they were subject to stricter laws and regulatory procedures than had been the case in earlier years in the coastal areas. Still, these features cannot wholly account for the relatively low incidence of cults in either the Highlands or, indeed, in Polynesia and Micronesia. One has to look elsewhere.

Apart from their cargo activities, the coastal peoples do not seem to be in any way less pragmatic and addicted to the niceties of material exchange than do the Highlands peoples. Nor have they been found to be in any real or intelligible sense more mystical or prone to unreason. While coastal peoples became as quickly accustomed to aircraft and traveling in them with as much aplomb as did Highlanders, the latter neither saw nor could be impressed by those great ships which came from beyond the horizon to unload their cargos. Nevertheless, coastal cultures and social orders were ravaged in ways Highlands cultures were not. In particular, Highlands cultures and political entities were and remain (as in Polynesia and Micronesia) much larger, more resilient, and less susceptible to breakdown than those on the coast.

Highlands peoples did not suffer depletions of population from epidemic diseases. The first World War did not touch them; the second brought them new sights and adventures without much risk to life or limb, and tangible prosperities. It did not bring new masters, new laws and curfews enforced at rifle point, food shortages, and suffering. Highlands cultural artifacts have not been virtually drained away by collectors; their systems of aesthetics, their painting, carvings, sculptures, dances and music, have not been allowed to decay or, as in instances in the coastal areas, quite deliberately destroyed. They have not been subjected to schemes of indentured and contract labor, which usually entailed going elsewhere and often overseas for long periods to work for the cash to buy valuable tools and goods to take home to the family. On the contrary, in the Highlands, many could walk to their work on plantations from their homes and buy a larger variety of goods from better-stocked stores not so much as a day's walk away.

Although, then, the kinds of relations that Highlanders have had with Europeans, and the conditions of their exposure to an industrial-commercial economy have been quite different, the question remains whether these features of themselves can explain or account for the relative presence or absence of millennial expectations. Perhaps such millenial expectations, at least in some of their antinomian aspects, have been absorbed into the gang strife and extortionist activities so often found in sprawling modern cities (as Port Moresby has become), and at which Highlanders are said to excel.

Nevertheless, the magico-religious elements in cargo cults should not be forgotten. The negative instances, where in the same sort of sociocultural conditions as elsewhere the talking and discussion do not develop into a cult or movement, are at least partially explained by the absence of a revelatory message. That is, without a revelatory message that is believed to have some sort of divine or transcendental origin, and without someone to voice it, no definite cult or movement occurs. The millennial expectations that might have informed such discussions about current affairs that may have taken place did not cohere. They remained unfocused. Thus the presence or absence of a prophet or leader able to strike the spark and give a persuasive voice to such millennial expectations as might be present appears to be critical to the emergence of a coherent cult. As to how that spark is struck, however, one is, in the end, despite a plethora of different idioms, as much in the dark as ever.

Given, therefore, an emphasis on the emergence of a prophet or leader, one may note that as part of their larger and more firmly structured political groupings, *authority* in leadership was very much more certainly fixed and acknowledged in the Highlands (and in Polynesia and Micronesia) than it is, was, or indeed could be in virtue of decimation by disease, in the coastal areas of Melanesia. That is, accepting that a state of anomie may—and is likely to—generate a desire for firm leadership and surer structuring of the social order, this is precisely what cargo leaders have tried to provide.

There is, too, a further issue, itself related to a sure and stable polity with acknowledged positions of leadership and authority. As has been noted above, the Tok Pisin word *wok* "work" is generally used to refer to the activities, the rites, that will give access to the cargo or *kago*. The same word, *wok*, is used for those activities which, outside the cargo situation, should result in an enhanced status. That is, while there is no doubt *kago* refers to prepared or manufactured goods, goods that Melanesians want, having the goods would yield, most importantly, equality of status and opportunity with Europeans. Moreover, there are further connotations in the usage and contexts of *kago* that reveal a meaning that can only be called transcendental. When Melanesians are asked about *kago* and pressed as to what they would do with the goods if in fact they arrived as a result of cultic activities, magically or from the ancestors of gods or God or from wherever, they begin to falter. Consume the food and use the artifacts obviously—but then what? A permanent and free supply of cargo?

At this point, as they start to ponder the implications, it becomes evident that the meaning of *kago* stretches out beyond its ordinary and everyday reference to manufactured material goods. It begins to mean something very like a religious or spiritual redemption; release from the obligations of sociocultural life, relief from the anxieties that attend asserting and maintaining status, and freedom from the burdens of moral doubt and choice (endemic to leadership in the coastal areas but much assuaged in the Highlands, Polynesia, and Micronesia where authority is better defined and fixed). In short, *kago* evokes a situation in which either all desires are satisfied, or there is no such thing as desire, only bliss. That is, *kago* refers in at least one aspect not to anything known on this earth but to a state of being which approximates roughly to what Christians call heaven, or "saved" and others call by other names.

Appreciate these aspects of cargo movements and it becomes clearer that they are, as Haddon pointed out, variants of a human proclivity with universal relevance. Anomie, an indeterminate and infirm structuring of society or community where moral authority and leadership are inconsistent and dispersed in a variety of ill-defined locations, may be seen as a sufficient cause. But seating the activities wholly in the prevailing sociocultural conditions is still open to question. If all Melanesians had as much access to manufactured goods as, say, North Americans or Europeans, would there still be *cargo* cults? One is safe in presuming not.

Would there be movements *like* cargo cults—variants that were closely similar to, say, Californian cults or movements? With this we cannot be so certain and cannot rule out the possibility. Anomie may be objectively determined. But it may also have a significant subjective or spiritual dimension which only reveals itself when least expected.

CONCLUSION

Over the space of, say, a half-century in relation to the Highlands of Papua New Guinea, and an added century for most of the peoples in coastal areas, Melanesians have moved from a stone-age technology rich in symbolism—where every quality of character, eye-glance, shift in the weather, shade of leaf or slope of hill and use of soil was charged with meaning—into an age where bureaucracy, technology, science, and reason are paramount, qualities are discounted in favor of quantity, and symbolisms are derided as primitive superstition. In such a world, cargo cults as such belong mostly to history. Although they still occur in places where access to money and the goods it can buy is difficult, in fringe areas of hesitation that modernization has not yet wholly penetrated, for most Melanesians, they have become an anachronism. Shift the idiom from its emphasis on material goods into the religious or transcendental aspects, however, and we find moral innovation and religious reform, reflected in the recent founding of independent churches, a feature that will probably continue for many years to come.

For social scientists, on the other hand, cargo activities will continue to pose problems which are not only intellectually and philosophically challenging, but vital to the development of the disciplines themselves. Slowly, cargo movements are beginning to be unravelled in all their complex variety of cultural activity and symbolism. But the major question of just why they should occur in one situation and not in another that is similar has yet to be answered. As social science advances in sophistication and Melanesian scholars start to study cargo movements, further nuances will surely come to light. Still, whether Melanesian scholars will do any better in relation to the cargo activities in their own history than Europeans and their descendants have done for the same kinds of movements in theirs remains to be seen.

19

The Brokers of the Lord:
The Ministration
of a Christian Faith
in the Sepik Basin
of Papua New Guinea

Paul B. Roscoe
University of Maine

> Any history of the wisdom of the Melanesians must record cargo beliefs as its first genuine philosophy which grapples with the uninvited imposition of the West. (Narakobi 1974)

For the Yangoru Boiken[1] of the East Sepik Province, Papua New Guinea (PNG), Sunday, February 15, 1981, was no ordinary day. That morning, contrary to routine, no one departed for the gardens or the sago groves, and, quite uncharacteristically, nobody seemed to have pressing business at Yangoru Government Station. By their thousands, people remained instead close to their home hamlets, the main exceptions being several hundred village officials and associates of the New Apostolic Church (NAC), a Christian faith currently headquartered in Zurich, Switzerland, who converged during the morning on the high foothill village of Ambukanja.

Beyond the fact that something of great moment was to take place in Ambukanja, few villagers knew precisely what to expect of the next few hours, an uncertainty that lent a strange, doleful suspense to the day. Nevertheless, there was a widespread rumor that Matius Yaliwan, Yangoru's most prominent spiritual leader, was to be crucified that afternoon in Ambukanja, thereby precipitating the millennium. In Sima village, adjacent to Ambukanja, speculation held that the earth would tremble, hurricane-force winds would rise, torrents of rain would pour down, the mountains above Yangoru would flash with lightning and reverberate with thunder, and a dense fog would close in over the earth. When the clouds lifted, Yaliwan would appear resurrected as the black counterpart of the white Jesus. Between them, the two Jesuses then would judge the living and the dead through a "glass," dividing them into three groups: white people (Christians by village definition), black followers of the New Apostolic Church, and all other blacks. The two divinities would return the latter group to the ways of New Guinea's ancestors, laboring in their gardens with stone tools. The whites and the black members of the NAC, however, they would usher into the *Kingdom bilong Malolo* (in Pidgin English "Kingdom of Rest"), an earthly paradise of cars, refrigerators, aeroplane travel, tinned foods, and other European-style material wealth. In this *Kingdom bilong Malolo*, it was said, black and white finally would live together in emancipated and harmonious perpetuity, sharing meals, talk, and siblings in marriage.

By 1981, Matius Yaliwan was no stranger to crucifixion and millenarianism. Ten years earlier, he had gained national prominence as the spiritual head of the Peli Association, a millenarian organization that had attracted one hundred thousand to two hundred thousand followers in a campaign to remove three cement trigonometric markers buried in the summit of Mt. Hurun, the 4,000 foot peak that dominates the Yangoru skyline. Following the removal of these markers, it was believed, Yaliwan would be crucified on the mountain top, precipitating the millennium. Although two of the markers eventually were removed, Yaliwan was not crucified, being dissuaded from the act apparently by a prominent Catholic missionary. Following the collapse of the movement under the subsequent weight of failed millenarian expectations, little then was heard about Yaliwan until the late 1970s when the arrival of the New Apostolic Church (NAC) prompted the resurrection of the Peli Association and renewed talk of his crucifixion as a precursor to the millennium.

The history of the NAC's entanglement with Yaliwan and Yangoru forms the descriptive and analytical focus of this chapter, which begins with a caveat. Anthropologists have long been accustomed to portraying their indigenous subjects with sober respect, and on this account it will be taken for granted that there is intended no mockery of the Yangoru Boiken people in what follows. Unfortunately, anthropological neutrality has not always been sustained in portraying missionary experience: in fact, as Taylor Huber (1988) has noted in her insightful historical ethnography of the Catholic Church in the Sepik, missiological anthropology is seldom slow in resorting to irony—to depicting, that is, how reality "reduces grand attitudes and large hopes to self mockery" (Geertz 1968:147). Since the Canadian missionaries of the NAC hardly could have intended their efforts to culminate in the crucifixion of Matius Yaliwan, the task this chapter sets itself necessarily risks irony. Lest my purpose be misconstrued, therefore, let me make clear at the outset that while the NAC may be criticized on many grounds, not least their disinterest in, and disregard for, the cultural context in which they operated, it is the poorest form of conceit to treat sardonically the collapsed hopes of people who sacrificed their time, labor, and expense in the hope, as they perceived it, of bettering the lot of their fellow humans.

In any case, if my intention in this chapter were merely to trace the ironic potential in culture contact, the chapter hardly would be worth the writing, for such ironies have been documented a thousand times before. Instead, my reason for examining the NAC's history in Yangoru is the light it sheds on the processes whereby ideology-based social movements are generated and sustained. It reveals that the movement the NAC precipitated was the product of both ideological and political factors. On the one hand, interest in the NAC was assured by several serendipitous, ideological congruences between their theology and Yangoru Boiken traditional and millenarian attitudes and beliefs. On the other, the scale of the resulting movement can be traced to the nature of the political relationships that were established between the visiting missionaries and a handful of Peli Association officials who succeeded in monopolizing their cause. Differentiated by their beliefs and goals, these two culturally distinct groups were paradoxically united by a common strategy of brokering divinity. The missionaries of the NAC believed themselves agents of the Lord, spreading His work and advancing the millennium, while the officials of the Peli organization successfully brokered the brokers, translating a crucial position as middlemen between missionary and villager into a huge political following and a handsome economic reward.

THE HISTORY OF CHRISTIANITY AMONG THE YANGORU BOIKEN

The Boiken people of Papua New Guinea (PNG) occupy one of the most extensive and ecologically diverse territories in the entire Sepik Basin. Their boundaries embrace the offshore islands of Walis, Tarawai, and Muschu, cross the coastal Prince Alexander mountains, descend through sharply dissected foothills, and then reach deep into the rolling grass plains north of the Sepik River. In 1980, these lands were claimed as home by some forty thousand people, divided into seven linguistically and culturally distinct subgroups.

Because of their coastal frontage, the Boiken were among the first people in the Sepik to be exposed to Christianity. Their experience began with the Catholic Church, which has been active in the region since the establishment, in 1896, of St. Joseph's Mission on Tumleo Island, off Aitape. From this literal beachhead, the influence of the cloth was born rapidly along the coast to islands and shorelines within reach of the mission's cutter, and, by the turn of the century, the Boiken coast had fallen within the bounds of this extended parish. In 1908, the Church established a permanent mission at the coastal village of Boiken, a circumstance that later furnished the modern day Boiken with their name, and from this base Frs. Eberhard Limbrock and Francis Kirschbaum set out on October 1, 1912, to penetrate the Prince Alexander Mountains behind the mission (Limbrock 1912). After three days of exhausting travel, they descended into the southern foothills of the range, becoming the first Europeans to enter the territory of the western-most Boiken dialect group, the Yangoru Boiken.

Numbering some thirteen thousand in 1980, the Yangoru Boiken are slash-and-burn cultivators of the foothill slopes around Yangoru Government Station. Their subsistence is based on yam and taro, supplemented with pigs, banana, a variety of bush (and now trade store) foods, and a feast-or-famine dependence on sago. The nuclei of their social life are patrilineage-like groups united into quasi-clan units, and their political life swirls around the activities of big men, whose prestige derives primarily from performance in ceremonial pig exchanges (see Gesch 1985; Roscoe 1983).

Although much of Yangoru Boiken life remains as it was when Limbrock and Kirschbaum appeared that October day eighty years ago, subsequent contact with the European world has brought significant changes, not the least of which have been the decline of warfare, spirit houses, and initiation practices. In part, these changes were hastened by the Catholic priests who followed in Limbrock's and Kirschbaum's footsteps. Shortly after his initial visit, Limbrock purchased land for a small bush-material church in the high foothill village of Ambukanja, and this modest pied à terre became an important node in the Church's back-country itineraries over the next twenty years. Around the mid-1930s, the Church then moved to consolidate its influence with permanent missions in Sassoya, to the east of Yangoru, and Ulupu and Maprik to the west. Its designs on Yangoru, however, were interrupted by World War II; consequently, it was 1948, once the disruptions of war had ebbed, before a permanent Catholic presence was established among the Yangoru Boiken, in the village of Negrie. Six years later, the mission moved to Yangoru Government Station, and in the same year, after four years of evangelizing patrols from their Hayfield base 25 kilometers to the east, the Assemblies of God established a rival Christian presence just down the hill. Seven or eight years later, the Seventh Day Adventists appeared in the village of Baimaru, whence they expanded to Nimbohu. And, around 1970, the Jehovah's Witnesses arrived in Kininyan (see Gesch 1985:26).

THE NEW APOSTOLIC CHURCH IN YANGORU

The rapid proliferation of missions in postwar Yangoru, each denouncing the other with varying degrees of civility, created considerable confusion in Yangoru's villages. With their restricted understanding of the world beyond the visible horizon, people interpreted missionary differences in diachronic rather than synchronic terms: instead of perceiving the proliferation of creeds as evidence of religious diversity in the world beyond, they concluded that, like waves, a succession of faiths had arisen and beached themselves in Yangoru, each displacing the one before. Thus, when the New Apostolic Church appeared in the late 1970s preaching of imminent apocalypse, it quickly was dubbed the "last mission"—the "last," that is, before the millennium.

The New Apostolic Church is itself a millennial faith, founded on a belief in the imminence of Christ's second coming. According to NAC theology, this "First Resurrection" will be heralded by a series of physical catastrophes in which a third of humanity will perish. Then will follow a blissful thousand year "Kingdom of Peace" in which the living and the dead will rise, the earth will be filled with the magnified brilliance of the solar bodies, nature again will become paradisical as once it was in Eden, and, with Satan bound, enmity and exploitation will be no more. As elysian as this Kingdom of Peace will seem, however, it will not be the true millennium but rather a period during which humanity will be offered an opportunity to become citizens of a yet more glorious "new heaven and new earth." A legion of 144,000 "firstlings," referred to also as "Kings and Priests," will offer the gospel to those who rejected it during their time on the profane earth. Those who then accept will escape the Day of Judgment and be admitted into the true millennium; those who again refuse will be doomed to appear before the Judgment Seat.

Such, according to the NAC, is the future of humanity. But the second coming of Christ will not occur until the Lord's apostles have "sealed" the number of followers that God deems sufficient to provide His army of "firstlings" in the Kingdom of Peace. In NAC belief, the task of "sealing" was begun by the apostles of biblical times, who possessed the divinity of the Lord and thus the power to remit sins. They traveled the world preaching of the First Resurrection and the New Creation to follow, and they gathered together the first Apostolic Church, people who accepted the gospel and through the apostles' divinity were reborn in Christ, their sins redeemed, as the first of the "firstlings." Before the apostles could finish this task, however, they were persecuted and martyred. Then began the "Dark Middle Ages," an era that only drew to a close around 1830, when an eclectic group of Roman Catholic, Greek Orthodox, and High Anglican adherents in Scotland and England became convinced from scriptural study of the need to re-establish the apostolate and complete its mission of recruiting the "firstlings."

To this end, small prayer groups gathered to pray for an apostolic return, and, in 1832, their prayers supposedly were answered with the establishment of the Catholic Apostolic Congregations. Under a newly appointed, twelve-fold apostolate, these Congregations set about "sealing" 144,000 "firstlings" before the end of the world, an event predicted several times before it was established as the day when the last of the twelve living apostles should die. In 1906, however, before this too could come to pass, a splinter faction established the New Apostolic Church (NAC) in Germany and appointed a set of new apostles.

To the faithful, the NAC is not an imitation of the biblical apostolic church but rather its direct continuation. Ordained, commissioned, and authorized by their Chief Apostle in Zurich, the modern apostles have the power, like their scriptural counterparts, to offer humankind salvation and redemption. Those who avail themselves of this ministry are "sealed" with the "Mark of the Lamb": the hands of an apostle are laid upon their forehead, and by this agency they receive the "Holy Spirit in the rebirth," are forgiven their sins, and are eligible to become one of the "Kings and Priests" who will present the gospel to their fellows in the "Kingdom of Peace." It is in seeking "the number [of 'sealed' followers] for which God longs" that the living apostles of the Church today travel

> to every possible country in the world and to the islands in the Atlantic, Pacific and Indian Oceans…No island is too remote for this living altar to be established among its inhabitants. (Kraus 1978:27–28)

It was in this quest for the "last lamb," who would set in motion the machinery of the millennium, that Canadian representatives of the NAC came to Yangoru. Although the mission's early history in PNG is unclear, their personnel were first reported in the Sepik in late 1977. Apparently, they toured the Sassoya region some 20 kilometers to the east of Yangoru and proposed construction of a church at Sembo, although after a public meeting the offer was declined (Gesch 1985:107).

Missionary visits by the NAC necessarily are limited to a few weeks every six months or so. The missionaries themselves must support their religious work through secular employment back home, and their PNG tourist visas permit no permanent residence. Consequently, it was not until May 1978 that they returned to the Sepik. During their absence, however, indigenous church workers in the provincial capital of Wewak had succeeded in establishing contacts along the coast and in the hinterlands, and the Canadians' reception on this second visit therefore was very different from their first. They traveled east and west along the coastal road to enthusiastic receptions in Suain and Turubu, and visited the inland village of Roma, deep in the grasslands south of the coastal ranges. But it was in the Yangoru village of Marambanja that they received the first inklings of their mission's rapidly waxing popularity. News of their earlier visit to Sembo had reached the ears of Daniel Hawina, a prominent leader of the 1971 Peli Movement, who promptly made contact with their indigenous representatives in Wewak, inviting the missionaries to visit Peli headquarters, in his home village of Marambanja, on their next trip.[2] The Canadians duly arrived in Marambanja to find a large crowd awaiting them, and their sermon—translated into Pidgin English—received an enthusiastic reception; that afternoon, a congregation of between one hundred to five hundred were baptized into the faith in the nearby headwaters of the Trubum River (Gesch 1985:107).

The events in Marambanja were a harbinger of what, to the missionaries, must have seemed the ultimate validation of their faith. Although no precise data are available, it is clear that their influence spread rapidly. In January 1979, on their next visit to Papua New Guinea, they reported "5,000 souls sealed"; six months later, during a three-day visit to the Sepik, another 3,918 were added to the lists (Anon. 1979:28). When I arrived in the field in September 1979, almost 99 percent of the residents in Sima village professed allegiance to the Church, a fraction that seemed fairly typical for the whole of Yangoru. Indeed, when the missionaries again returned to the Sepik in the middle of 1980, their following had expanded to the limits of their ability to minister it. As Father Fritz Marti (1980:47) reported to his District Apostle:

> As many as 5 services were held in a day and it was no surprise that we all were exhausted at the end of the day. However, the happiness over the harvest that could be brought in invigorated each one of us.
>
> In the four weeks 49 services were conducted, 10,667 souls sealed, 171 Administration Brothers ordained or promoted and 5 churches dedicated.

Aware that competing missions in Papua New Guinea were voicing open scepticism about the validity of these mass conversions, Marti (1980:47) continued:

> Dear District Apostle, this may seem to many a well orchestrated mass rallying of souls as we sometimes hear of other organizations, but we can assure you that all of these souls have tried the testimony they have received and have recognized and accepted the Apostles' doctrine as the true word of God.

The NAC's belief that the word of the Lord had fallen on fertile ground was understandable. In Yangoru, for example, for more than a year, substantial congregations of men, women, and children dutifully had gathered two or three times a month for Sunday masses served by indigenous, NAC-ordained priests and deacons. Before makeshift altars in bush-material churches, or beneath the coconut palms of a hamlet piazza, they had participated earnestly in the free-form prayers of their village clergy, calling on God to "make Papua New Guinea strong" and on the people of the world to join the NAC. They had listened politely to readings from the Pidgin New Testament, and they had hearkened attentively to sermons attributing their current lowly state to their ancestors' failure to follow the "Law of God."

Had the NAC missionaries spent more than a few days in Yangoru, however, they might have become aware that, behind this facade of orthodoxy, their doctrine had been received in a decidedly heterodox light. The first irregularity occurred in June 1978, just one month after the NAC's triumphant appearance at the Peli headquarters in Marambanja, when representatives of the *Organisasi Papua Merdeka* (OPM)—the rebel movement to wrest Irian Jaya from Indonesian domination—visited Peli headquarters to raise money for their cause. Quite what the OPM told people is now unclear, but it seems they promised commemorative badges in return for contributions to their cause. Many among their audience, however, interpreted the badges as a prerequisite for entry into the NAC's "Kingdom of Peace," and thousands of people each handed over K10 (about U.S.$15) to the Peli organization, some ordering two or even three.[3] How much of this money went to the OPM and where the rest ended up is unknown, but it is doubtful that it went to the NAC in Canada as most villagers believed. Whatever the case, within three months, the Peli leaders again were collecting money, this time selling membership "tickets" to the millennium at K0.70 (about US $1) each.

In January 1979, the NAC missionaries again visited Yangoru, but without notable consequence. By the middle of the year, however, as another visit approached, eschatological expectations began to mount, and reports circulated that Matius Yaliwan had summoned the people of the world to gather in Yangoru in preparation for his ritual execution on the summit of Mt. Hurun. In the Negrie region, it was said, his throat was to be cut, the blood allowed to fall on the ground, and the millennium then would commence. Western goods would materialize magically from the bloodied site of his execution, Russian soldiers would appear on the mountain top, and the skins of black people would turn white and vice-versa (Camp n.d.:9). The Peli Association again began to sell "tickets" for K0.70 each, entitling the bearer to become one of the 144,000 "Kings and Priests" in the imminent "Kingdom of Peace," but this time the sales had a novel twist. Taking their lead from NAC teaching that the dead can be "sealed" through a living descendant, Peli's leaders encouraged people to purchase "tickets" not only for themselves but also for their deceased relatives (see also Gesch 1985:110).[4]

The July visit of the Canadian missionaries passed without incident, however, and within days, new rumors were abroad that Yaliwan would be executed in September. In anticipation, the NAC's village priests and deacons conducted regular masses, but September brought only the arrival of a European anthropologist and his wife in Sima village, sparking a short-lived belief that, in answer to Yaliwan's summons issued two months earlier, the Europeans had begun to arrive in Yangoru.

Around this time, Yaliwan announced that he was going to stand for the Yangoru Saussia seat in the East Sepik Provincial Assembly: "If I win this election for the Provincial Government," his electoral poster stated, "I will be the leader of this country." In the expectation that his election would precipitate the "good times" (that is, the millennium), the frequency of village NAC services increased, with many a prayer offered for his victory. In December, he was successfully elected to the Assembly, but, as Gesch reports:

> …he was just as successfully blocked out of it. The first meeting…was taken up with business continuing over from the interim Assembly, and in the grinding details of allocations for sports in the budget, there was little place given for the proclamation of national salvation. (Gesch 1985:93)

With Yaliwan apparently meeting poor fortune in advancing the millennium by political means, the first four months of 1980 were comparatively uneventful. But, as May approached and news spread that the Canadian missionaries were expected in July, eschatological hopes stirred anew. In April, stories circulated that Yaliwan had paid a subterranean visit to the Papua New Guinea—Irian Jaya border and had uprooted the cement blocks marking the boundary. In an echo of the earlier Peli Movement, he reportedly urged his followers to remove every cement block that Europeans had set into the PNG earth, whereupon the "Kingdom of Peace" would be ushered in: the dead would rise, food, cars, ships, and planes would appear spontaneously, and everyone would have the easy office jobs enjoyed by whites, never again toiling in the fields.

In May 1980, excitement reached a crescendo with news that a day later in the month had been set for everyone to gather at Peli headquarters in Marambanja in preparation for the millennium. At NAC services in Sima village, the congregation was urged to raise K100 (about U.S.$150) to help Yaliwan arrange Army planes to take 100,000 paid-up NAC members on a tour of Canada, England, and Holland. Subsequently, it was announced that an OPM supporter was returning to Yangoru, and people were told to rally at Peli headquarters in Marambanja and prepare to "march like an army"—a proclamation probably linked to the OPM custom of drill marching their supporters using wooden rifles (Gesch 1985:108). Rumors also spread that an NAC missionary was expected, but the most dramatic news was that Yaliwan would be crucified, and everyone would die and be resurrected into a world of inverted power relations: "We will win, and Australia will lose and become 'rubbish men'."

Between May 14 and 17, therefore, people from throughout Yangoru gathered daily in Marambanja. To their disappointment, however, no "marching" took place. Indeed, the only significant event occurred on May 16, when a man from the coastal village of Suwain, apparently an OPM supporter, arrived and delivered a fiery antiwhite speech, claiming that American power was based on an "important thing" stolen from PNG earlier in the century and now hidden in the United States. He then shook hands with everyone and allegedly set a day in June for the beginning of the millennium. Meanwhile, Peli Association leaders busied themselves collecting K3 (U.S.$ 4.50) "tax" from each head of household present.

For the next month, village services were held on a regular basis, climaxing in the Yangoru visit of two NAC missionaries, who toured the villages in the last week of July on a hectic schedule of services, baptisms, "sealings," and ordainments. But with the millennium yet again failing to transpire, serious disillusionment set in, and despite a brief appearance of the missionaries in October, denouncing their flock's waywardness, Yangoru's excitement waned for the rest of the year.[5]

Up to this point, and despite the misgivings of at least one of their university-educated indigenous workers, the NAC's Canadian missionaries had seemed disinclined to believe that the success of their mission was anything but a manifestation of the Lord's work. By the latter part of the year, however, they too had come to recognize a problem and, in an interview on Radio Wewak, denounced cargo cults and all who participated in them. In Yangoru, however, the broadcast had the curious effect of only confirming the legitimacy of the millenarian activities conducted in the NAC's name. Since villagers had no reason to doubt they were following NAC teachings, they understood the denunciations to be directed at everyone who had failed to join the mission. Thus, followers of other missions were involved in "cargo cults," but the efforts to crucify Matius Yaliwan were part of "the work of God."

With the New Year, interest in the NAC picked up again on renewed news that Yaliwan was to be crucified, heralding his resurrection as the Black Jesus. And, at this less-than-auspicious juncture, the Reverend Arthur Blessitt of California chose to appear in Yangoru. Pursuing a personal crusade to awaken the more remote corners of the world to the message of the gospel, Blessitt had walked the length of the Sepik Highway dressed as Jesus, dragging behind him a large cross on wheels. His arrival in Yangoru on February 4 sent apprehensive spasms through the countryside, with some people fearing that Jesus had come to judge them for their sins, others believing the first of the resurrected ancestral spirits had returned.

But Blessitt passed on down the East Sepik Highway without event, and Yangoru moved on to political action. NAC services now became the venue for calls to resist Yangoru Council taxation. On February 8 in Sima village, for example, an ex-councillor decried the fact that despite the taxes paid year-in and year-out, the Council had failed to bring about "development" and "true independence," by which he meant the millennium; when the Council came to demand the yearly tax, he advised everyone, they should announce that the Old Jesus was dead and that they were awaiting the New Jesus, Matius Yaliwan, and his work.

On the same day, indigenous NAC officials instructed congregations throughout northern Yangoru to gather in their hamlets at week's end to perform *tuaxring xieri* ("group conciliation") ceremonies. On the appointed day, clans and subclans by the score laid out bags of rice and tins of mackerel on feasting mats to be blessed by a group of indigenous NAC priests. Following the blessings, the approbation of the ancestral spirits was secured with the ritual smashing of a coconut, and the food was then distributed among the participants. Similar ceremonies had been held in the Negrie area in late January, where Gesch (1985:110) described them as "congregational meals" with dead relatives. But, in northern Yangoru, as the little ceremonies were conducted in the conviction that Yaliwan's crucifixion and resurrection as the Black Jesus was imminent, they appeared more an indigenous adaptation of the Last Supper.

Sunday, February 15, brings us back to the events with which we started, with village officials of the NAC gathering in Ambukanja village for Yaliwan's crucifixion. Seated by huge piles of firewood or large quantities of cooked food to see them through the predicted apocalypse, the people of Sima passed the day in a subdued mood. Then, as dusk fell, Sima's NAC priest returned bearing the anticlimactic news that Yaliwan had postponed the event because of a stomachache. Three days later, soldiers from the PNG Defense Force appeared in the Yangoru countryside on a suspiciously well-timed training exercise and, amid rumors they had come to spy on Yaliwan or even arrest him, the movement died and had yet to reappear by the time my field work ended in April 1981.

THE BROKERS OF THE LORD

In the name of the NAC, the Peli Association created a movement out of all proportion to the scale of Yangoru's secular political followings. Although precise figures probably never will be known, Peli's supporters certainly exceeded ten thousand at times, and, by astute manipulation, its leadership extracted enormous sums of money from them:

between May 1978 and April 1981, a minimum of K20,000 (about U.S.$30,000) must have flowed through Peli coffers at a time when the mandated minimum rural daily wage was only K2.70 (about U.S.$4); a more probable figure easily could be K40,000.

There has been a longstanding interest in anthropology in the precipitants of millenarian organizations such as this—an interest that recently has broadened into the more general question of why ideology sometimes can be used so successfully to forge sociopolitical integration (for example, Keatinge 1981; Knauft 1985; Lindstrom 1984; Roscoe 1988). In the case of Peli and the NAC, there is no single answer to this question; rather, the explanation lies in a confluence of ideological and political factors.

To begin with, traditional Yangoru belief furnishes a context highly conducive to millenarian exploitation. Millenarian movements typically promise their followers economic prosperity and political independence, desiderata that the Yangoru Boiken believe are governed by *kamba*, the spirits of the dead, and *kworbo*, magical forces and spells. Thus, by implicating the spirits of the dead in the millennium and prescribing magical-like actions such as prayer, NAC theology—like several faiths before it—was assured a sympathetic ear in Yangoru.

A second factor favoring the NAC's reception was Yangoru's grand tradition of stripping the Christian message of exegetical qualifications and interpreting it in terms much more literal than intended. In his little bush church in Ambukanja village, for example, Limbrock probably sermonized about the importance Christian behavior would assume on the Day of Judgment, when the dead would rise and, with the living, face God the Father; probably, too, he spoke of the importance of prayer and church attendance if villagers were to become Christians like the white-skinned newcomers to their world. But, according to modern testimony, the congregations listening to these homilies attached an immediacy and a mechanicalism to them that Limbrock hardly could have meant. People flocked to his church and dutifully prayed beneath its eaves not from any interest in an afterlife but in the expectation that these magiclike actions would induce "God the Father" to come down to Yangoru, the spirits of the dead to return, and villagers to become white-skins with access to European property and power. Likewise, in response to missionary perorations against warfare, sorcery, and initiation as inimical to Christian faith, a movement spread through northern Yangoru in the late 1920s or early 1930s advocating the abandonment of all three in the belief that thereby villagers would "find God"—in a literal sense—become whiteskins and gain unfettered access to Western goods.

Later still, around 1960, the Yangoru Catholic mission became embroiled in millenarianism after encouraging intensive church prayer and ceremonial renunciations of sorcery and polygyny as a prerequisite for "the good times." Throughout northern Yangoru, sorcery was symbolically renounced with the burial of shell rings, second wives were put aside, and mass conversions to the faith followed, all in the expectation that these magiclike actions would effect the return of Jesus and the advent of the millennium (see Gesch 1985:122–126). In the late 1970s, therefore, when the NAC arrived with its quite literal pronouncements of an imminent millennium, it hardly is surprising that its creed sparked excitement in a population culturally vulnerable to millenarianism.

There were several aspects of NAC teaching, however, that lent it an appeal possessed by no other Christian faith. The most important, perhaps, was the mission's teachings about the precipitants of the millennium. In the original teaching of the apostolic churches, the "Kingdom of Heaven" would be ushered in once 144,000 souls had been "sealed" to act as the era's "Kings and Priests." By 1980, however, this doctrine had undergone a subtle change, presumably because membership long ago had exceeded 144,000 without producing the millenium. (In 1979 alone, the church "sealed" 190,369 members, claiming a total membership of 646,531 at the end of the year.) Today, the NAC refers merely to "the number God longs for" and claims only that a "sealed" follower has an *opportunity* to become one of the 144,000 "firstlings"—the implication being that not all who are "sealed" will become "firstlings" (Kraus 1978:18).

Unfortunately, these doctrinal modifications were lost on Yangoru, which understood only that the millennium would be triggered once 144,000 followers had been "sealed." Thus, villagers believed they were being offered an opportunity they had longed for—to become powerful officials ("Kings and Priests") like the Europeans they believed still dominated them—a prospect that certainly heightened the allure of the NAC's message. But the more potent element in the message as Yangoru understood it was its specification of a contingency that would bring about this desirable estate. Where other Yangoru missions had placed the day of glory beyond human action, conditional on God's will, the NAC stated quite explicitly that the power to precipitate it lay in human hands. As the mission explained on cards distributed to baptized villagers:

> The New Apostolic Church is seeking the last lamb in the present day (the midnight hours) so that the true way be shortened for Christ's return. It could be that perhaps you are that last lamb which the Lord's Emissaries are seeking to incorporate into God's own family. (cited in Camp n.d.:7)

By thus specifying a program of action to bring about the millennium—the "sealing" of the number of "Kings and Priests" God desires—the NAC unwittingly appealed to the essence of Yangoru's understanding of the universe: specific ritual acts can bring about specific consequences.

The second important aspect of the NAC's message was the nature of the action specified to precipitate the millennium. By stressing that the Lord desired a certain number of adherents, all with their hearts and minds dedicated to the NAC mission, the Church unwittingly evoked the Yangoru ritual of *tuaxring xieri*, a ritual that must be performed before any important group action can proceed. In its essence, the ceremony involves the smashing of a coconut and the sharing of food to signify to the participants and their ancestral shades accord upon a particular course of action, be it a pig-trapping expedition, a pig-exchange festival, or the sale of clan land. Indeed, it was just such a ritual that Yangoru villagers had practiced in February 1981, in apparent simulation of a Last Supper which, according to informants, was meant "to ensure that everyone was of one accord that Yaliwan's work must now proceed. The *kamba* must allow his work to go forward without interrupting it." The NAC's belief that a large number of people had to be brought into one faith (that is, one accord) before the millennium could occur thus made perfect cultural sense in Yangoru.

The third appeal of the NAC message was the urgency with which it was delivered. By 1980, the NAC's success in recruiting converts in many Third World countries had left them confident that they were close to recruiting the number of followers God desired for the millennium to proceed. Thus, when the Canadian visitors talked of an imminent millennium, they differed from other missionaries by speaking with the conviction that it might occur tomorrow, a point they reiterated in their sermons and their actions. As one of the Canadian apostles turned to leave his congregation in Sima village, for example, he called back that he hoped to return in two months but if he did not meet them again on this earth, he would meet them in heaven.

Finally, the NAC's focus on the work of apostles also may have had some appeal. In the Peli Movement's earlier attempt to secure the millennium by removing several cement trigonometric markers from the summit of Mt. Hurun, Matius Yaliwan and his co-leader, Daniel Hawina, had each been accompanied up the mountain by twelve "apostles" (Hwekmarin et al. 1971:16).

THE NAC'S SUCCESS IN YANGORU

Although these features of NAC philosophy seem necessary components for understanding the mission's rapid acceptance in Yangoru, its broad appeal, and the millenarian hue cast upon its activities, they do not constitute a sufficient explanation. Since the symbolic culture of many other societies, both in the Sepik and elsewhere in New Guinea, does not seem qualitatively different from Yangoru's, we might expect the NAC's creed also to have had equal appeal elsewhere. In fact, however, Yangoru was the NAC's most fertile ground. Of forty-three NAC churches listed in Papua New Guinea in 1981, the bulk were located in the Sepik (Gesch 1985:113), and it is estimated that Yangoru boasted at least half of the number by the end of 1980. (Many of the rest were located in former Sepik strongholds of the Peli Association.)

The other important factor in the NAC's Yangoru success lies in the political mechanics by which ideology-based movements like cargo cults are constructed. The traditional anthropological stereotype of Melanesian political action revolves around the "big man," a political entrepreneur who creates a following through the production and manipulation of tangible commodities such as pigs and shell wealth. Recently, however, there has been a growing awareness that, in some areas of New Guinea, political followings are created by the production and manipulation not so much of material goods as of knowledge and ideas:

> Those men who command attractive explanatory systems gather followers or, according to the stereotypic Melanesian model, exchange partners who become indebted in a commerce of ideas. (Lindstrom 1984:294)

In terms of numbers, in fact, ideology-based movements such as cargo cults seem to have been the more successful. But the production and manipulation of knowledge poses a problem not encountered by those who deal in material goods. Attractive explanatory schemes or ideas can be produced by almost anyone with a flair for semantic creativity, and leaders therefore must concern themselves not only with the production of knowledge but also with its legitimation. To attract a following, they must present themselves as particularly privileged sources of knowledge while seeking to undermine the validity and legitimacy of others. The more successful they are in thus legitimizing their schemes, the larger the following they will create.

The explanatory schemes with which Peli Association leaders attracted followers were, as we have seen, a series of eschatologically pregnant scenarios variously involving Irian Jaya rebel forces, military-style marching, the election of Yaliwan to the Provincial Assembly, and his crucifixion and resurrection as the Black Jesus. The agents that conferred legitimacy on these purportedly NAC-inspired schemes were the Canadian missionaries themselves, and, in particular, their mode of extemporaneous sermonizing. Because the NAC believes that the act of "sealing" confers divine enlightenment, its preachers assume their congregations have an intimate knowledge of NAC theology, terminology, and metaphor. The most striking aspect of their sermons, therefore, is how difficult they are to understand, even in the original English; by the time their message has been ground through a Pidgin translation, it has lost almost all intelligibility for a village audience. But, at times, elements of meaning with distinct millenarian overtones do filter through. For example, when the Canadian missionaries told Sima village of God's intentions for the world, the pidgin translation left the unmistakable impression that they had recently spoken with the Lord upon the matter. When they talked of "the keys to Heaven," and added metaphorically "we have those keys," Sima was left with the understanding that the keys to the pearly gates were hanging on a hook somewhere back in Canada. The result was a sermon mystifying to all but a cognoscente, yet studded with evident clues to its millenarian significance—in other words, a discourse conforming to the classic mold of all important Yangoru Boiken oratory. The sermons thus conferred validity on the pronouncements that Peli leaders, who claimed to be cognoscenti, were making in the NAC's name, while simultaneously allowing them wide latitude to interpret the NAC message and make pronouncements under its aegis.

The means by which the Peli leaders appropriated this legitimizing mantle was by the masterfully simple stratagem of monopolizing all access to the Canadian missionaries, effectively cutting out of the loop any pretender who might claim to represent the NAC in their stead. Their advantage was the organizational base they had instituted during the Peli Movement of the early 1970s. Indeed, it was through the old network of *komiti* members formed during the earlier movement that Peli first heard of the NAC, following the Canadians' 1977 visit to the Sembo region (Gesch 1985:107). Then, on their second visit, Peli's leaders acted swiftly to divert the missionaries to cult headquarters at Marambanja, offering Peli's organizational resources for their evangelizing activities in Yangoru. Subsequently, the infrequency and brevity of the Canadians' visits, and their inability to speak the lingua franca, allowed Peli a virtual monopoly over their contacts with Yangoru. Thus, when the missionaries visited Yangoru, it was with Peli headquarters as their base. When they began to appoint field organizers and ordain village priests, Peli's leaders were the first to be elevated. And when the missionaries sent messages from Canada concerning their itineraries and intentions in Yangoru, it was Peli who broadcast them to the region. In consequence, Yaliwan was able without fear of challenge to claim the NAC had come in response to his dreams (see Gesch 1985:94); others in the Peli leadership could claim the missionaries were returned spirits of the dead; and the Peli organization was able to organize a brisk sale of "tickets" and insignia to the millennium, claiming the money raised would go to the NAC in Canada.

Had Peli been unable to monopolize access to the NAC missionaries, it seems probable they never could have established the millenarian following that they did. Others with equal access would have been able to set up rival movements based on the legitimacy thereby conferred, thus cutting into Peli's hegemony and splintering the size of its following. As it was, the Peli leaders were able to place themselves in the classic position of brokers (Cohen 1975:80), presenting themselves to the missionaries as an indispensable channel to the people of Yangoru, and presenting themselves to Yangoru as the indispensable means of procuring the services of missionaries who would bring about the millennium.

EPILOGUE

I left Yangoru in April 1981, and information that can be presented here on what subsequently transpired is, therefore, fragmentary. According to Gesch (1985:113–114), the tax revolt of February 1981 prompted government action against the NAC: by the end of the month, two Canadians had been expelled from the country as "undesirable aliens...responsible for the reactivation of a cargo cult movement in Turubu/Yangoru area of the East Sepik Province, disrupting normal village life and upsetting authorities" (*Niugini News* 1981). Nonetheless, one of them was back on a tourist visa within a few weeks, denouncing Matius Yaliwan. Later in the year, the Provincial Assembly banned the mission entirely from the East Sepik Province, but the Premier later decreed it could return once properly incorporated with the authorities in Port Moresby. And so the missionaries continued to visit their Peli-ministered following in Yangoru, again becoming embroiled in politics in 1982 when the Melanesian Alliance Party briefly flirted with their Peli following.

When I returned to Sima in May 1987, the NAC's influence on Yangoru was in deep decline. Its village officials were still holding occasional services, but they were very poorly attended. The rest of the village had converted to the Assembly of God Mission—conversions, it should be added, with no detectable millenarian overtones—and most of the revivalist excitement was confined to the village's adolescents, who spent many evenings in a newly built church, energetically dancing in the light of hurricane lamps and singing pidgin gospel songs to the accompaniment of a small string band.

To the extent that millenarian hopes had survived in Yangoru, they were now caught up in the political vortices surrounding the upcoming national elections for the Yangoru-Sausia constituency. The hustings had split the area's villages along fairly traditional factional lines, the large number of candidates standing allowing each kin-group alliance in a village to champion its own candidate—almost as though politicians were totems rather than democratic vehicles. Patterns of support were determined primarily by relationship, locality, and election promises. In Sima, two factions voiced support for candidates to whom they could trace extended, ancestral kinship relations. Another candidate found favor because, like his supporters, his ancestral roots were in a village "up here, beneath Mt. Hurun." And every aspirant attracted backing for one or another improbable election promise: one pledged to build bridges and roads and raise the price paid for coffee and cacao beans; another undertook to supply roofing iron and other luxury items gratis; yet another vowed to bring rising trade-store prices under control.

Beneath this veneer of mundane expectations, however, was a base of fervent millenarian rumor. One story, for example, claimed that Michael Somare, then leader of the opposition, possessed "black power"—several black, magical stones kept in a small netbag—with which he had banished Julius Chan from the office of Prime Minister. The main expectation, however, focused on a new Papua New Guinean independence. Echoing the status of the NAC as the "last" mission, the upcoming poll was described as the "last" election. The current incumbents, it was said, were only "eating" people's tax money, talking and not getting on with the real job of instituting "Fritan Independens" (Freedom Independence). "Fritan Independens" was seen as the historical period that would succeed the current era of "Wok Independens" (Work Independence), the latter an era of false independence in which black people still had to work for a living. In the new, "Fritan Independens" era, however, the black and white peoples of the world finally would settle down together in equal communion, and the former would be admitted to the material estate and supposedly work-free life of the latter.

For his part, Yaliwan was still making headlines. A month earlier, in great secrecy, a young, educated woman from the Wosera Abelam area had been executed in Ambukanja. With his encouragement, allegedly, she had volunteered for sacrifice in the belief that three days later she would rise again as the Black Virgin Mary. After a week had passed with no resurrection, her father approached the authorities. The body was exhumed by a forensic expert, the episode was pieced together by the police, and Yaliwan was taken away to jail to await trial on charges of manslaughter.

NOTES

1. The data on which this chapter is based were gathered during 1979–1981 and 1987 in field trips sponsored by the Department of Community Medicine at the University of Papua New Guinea and funded by the Emslie Horniman Scholarship Fund, the Ford Foundation, the University of Rochester, and the Faculty Research Committee of the University of Maine. The assistance of these persons and institutions is very gratefully acknowledged, as is the extraordinary kindness, hospitality, and assistance of the people of Sima village.

2. With some of the very substantial funds raised in the 1971 movement, the Peli Association had built a large, permanent materials hall, with attached "offices," that still stands at the foot of a ridge spur in Marambanja.

3. The badges in question were not delivered until April 1980. They were cardboard shields, about 3" x 2", covered with red linen broken by a silver stripe.

4. The "tickets" I saw were ordinary trade-store receipts made out with the individual's name, his or her village, the words "7 Association" (one of the names by which the Peli Association is known), the initials "C.D.P." (Christian Democratic Party, another of Peli's aliases), "M.Y." (Matius Yaliwan), and "D.H." (Daniel Hawina), and a note of the sum paid.

5. Around this time, as Yangoru's interest in the NAC waned, the mission was reported to be gaining strong support in other parts of the Sepik, especially among the neighboring Abelam and along the coast.

20

Christmas on Ujelang: The Politics of Continuity in the Context of Change

Laurence M. Carucci
Montana State University

The celebration of Christmas on Ujelang Atoll is an all-encompassing event. For four months of each year the residents of this isolated atoll, over six hundred miles from the governmental center of the Republic of the Marshall Islands, dedicate all of their efforts to singing, dancing, and feasting. Their day-to-day patterns of interaction are modified as newly fashioned singing groups (*jepta*) structure the ways in which goods are collected and exchanged, and song fest competitions (*kamolu*) and other games establish the rules of interaction among the *jepta*. As we might expect, *Kūrijmōj*, "Christmas, Marshall Islands style," is a complex, syncretic event that blends aspects of Christianity and a diverse colonial past with indigenous religious belief. It is also a lengthy liminal period when the rules of daily existence are inverted in a classic calendric rite of passage (van Gennep 1960; Turner 1969).

Noting the syncretic character of *Kūrijmōj* and classifying it as a calendrical rite only allows the reader to begin to situate the overall character of this celebration. It leaves the most important questions unanswered. What does this lengthy celebration mean, and how does it accomplish its intent? These are particularly difficult questions since the meanings of *Kūrijmōj* are many-layered. If we begin by asking "what it is that *Kūrijmōj* accomplishes" and, "why it is so important to accomplish these things," the pragmatic meanings of this ritual are more easily brought to light.

A goal of this analysis is that readers may reconsider anthropological concepts like syncretism and social or cultural change and rid these concepts of their Western teleology and ethnocentric bias. In particular, this chapter examines how the celebration uses a series of culturally evocative symbols to construct and project a vital sense of community identity. The "New Pacific" is not somehow less than the old. It is not watered-down culture that naively mixes its own notions, and compromises them, as those of foreign powers are imposed. Instead, it is an ongoing, vital series of ideas and practices that are constantly being constructed to provide continuity with, and contrast to, a fully indigenous view of the past. At the same time, islanders fashion their current consciousness by comparing themselves to others who are judged to be "like" or "unlike" them. While these portrayals of person are fluid, they are necessarily rooted in the historical continuities each person and each community imposes on their own past identities. While this chapter reviews the major elements of the celebration that make this constantly changing order apparent, many of the details can be found in other places (Carucci 1980; 1983; n.d.).

For purposes of clarity and expediency, I shall describe *Kūrijmōj* on Ujelang as a series of increasingly active ritual phases all oriented toward a common goal. That goal is to secure prosperity and good fortune for the coming year. To ensure its accomplishment, Ujelang residents draw on their images of the past to project a desirable image of life's continuity into the future, while simultaneously overthrowing the past with its degenerated potency to cause the new year to come into being. The ritual actions of *Kūrijmōj* give humans access to the power necessary to try to bring this new state into being.

Obtaining access to ritual power is particularly important on Ujelang since it provides atoll residents with feelings of security that derive from a sense of control over a very unpredictable environment. The same ritual power also allows Ujelang people to construct an empowered image of themselves, since this group of islanders were considered by many to be the most backward and disadvantaged atoll community in the area. Their very cultural identity must be fashioned from within and constantly reinforced, for they have found themselves dominated by various colonial powers, exiled from their homeland and, most recently, caught between new Pacific Islands nations. Ujelang and nearby Enewetak atolls are separated from the westernmost of the Marshall Islands by nearly two hundred miles of ocean and are nearly as far from the Eastern Caroline Islands to the south and west. Their isolation is cultural and linguistic as well as geographic. Ujelang dialect, like that of Enewetak, differentiated them from other Marshallese (indeed, Ujelang and Enewetak people still tell stories that oppose themselves to Marshall Islanders and, in many contexts, speak of "the people of the Marshalls" as different from "the people of Ujelang" or "Enewetak folks").

Historical forces play at least as large a part as does cultural and geographic isolation in creating the necessity for an internally strong cultural identity. Only a handful of Ujelang people survived a typhoon in the late 1860s, and all of them left their homeland when copra traders transformed it into a copra plantation during the German administration of the late nineteenth century. Some of these exiles settled on Jaluij Atoll in the Marshall Islands, others traveled to Enewetak and married into that community, and some are said to have relocated as far away as Fiji. During the time that Japan administered Micronesia, between World War I and World War II, Ujelang and Enewetak were part of Pohnpei district, but, after the war, they were administered from the Marshall Islands as they had been during the earlier German colonial era.

This sense of uncertainty and homelessness continued during the American administration of Micronesia after World War II. Enewetak residents (along with the original Ujelang people who had married into their community) were exiled to Ujelang Atoll for

Fishing with a throw net for goat fish on the lagoon side of Enewetak islet. (Photo by L.M.Carucci)

over thirty years while their home atoll was used by the Americans for nuclear testing and other military experiments. During that time, Enewetak people began to think of themselves as "the people of Ujelang."

The community suffered many hardships while living in isolation on Ujelang. Sometimes they had to wait as long as eight months before a government supply boat would arrive to purchase copra (dried coconut) in exchange for desperately needed supplies. In these times of food shortage, much of the coconut had to be consumed as drinks and staples to complement the seafoods that were gathered each day. Ujelang people continued to support the two chiefs under whose reign they had lived on Enewetak and, if anything, became a more cohesive and unified community in order to deal with the hardships. While people on the atoll are divided into clans whose memberships are traced through female lines for purposes of marriage, they are also united into a large community through linkages of large bilateral extended families that cross-cut clan lines. Often, on Ujelang, people would say that everyone was "really a part of just one family" as a way to express their solidarity.

On Ujelang, the islanders prayed for an improved future, particularly at *Kūrijmōj* when good fortune for the coming year was determined. Finally, in 1980, Ujelang people were allowed to return to Enewetak Atoll. Since their return, they have been faced with adjusting to a homeland radically different from the hospitable atoll they remembered prior to the war.

Even more difficult has been the reformulation of a community identity suited to the "new Enewetak," a place and a people set in contrast to the remembered past. The fragmented past as Enewetak people and Ujelang people, as Marshall Islanders and Caroline Islanders, as colonized people of Spain, Germany, Japan, the United States, and the Republic of the Marshall Islands, has not only tested the community's cohesiveness, it has made the building of strong, yet malleable, cultural identities imperative. The celebration of Christmas, Ujelang style, provides one setting in which positive images of persons, of the community, and of the region, are fashioned with fervor.

THE "MAJOR MOTIONS" OF *KŪRIJMŌJ*

The First Phase: Preparations

During the first phase of *Kūrijmōj*, which begins by mid-October of each year, Ujelang people divide their small community (about three hundred and fifty residents in 1976) into song fest groups. One may choose to affiliate with any of the *jepta* on the atoll, but most people make their choice based on residence. On Ujelang, there were three song fest groups along with a women's church group and a children's group. With the rapid population increase that accompanied repatriation, the number of song fest groups had expanded to six (plus the women's and children's group) by 1990.

Even though islanders continue their normal subsistence activities—men fish and collect coconuts, and women gather pandanus, process breadfruit, and prepare these foods for consumption—as soon as the celebration begins, their day-to-day interactions are refocused primarily on the song fest groups. Foods are prepared specifically for the *jepta* instead of being readied as usual for church organizations, clans, or extended families. The foods become one of the group's "weapons" in ongoing "battles" with other *jepta* during *Kūrijmōj*. These battles take place at *kamolu*, "song fest competitions," when one group brings its repertoire of well-rehearsed songs and bundles of prepared foods to the practice house of another *jepta*.

The men from Yeolab *jepta* fish using the surround technique. (Photo by L.M.Carucci)

Song fest competitions start in November, after each group has had an opportunity to write a number of songs and begin to memorize them. Even during these initial days of *Kūrijmōj*, however, the schedules of daily life are inverted. Practices take place at night, normally a dangerous time when ancestor spirits, foreign spirits from other lands, and even stronger supernatural beings from the past are present on the islet in abundance, and people stay inside their houses and sleep. *Kūrijmōj* transforms this routine, and by the twenty-fifth of December, people stay up all night to perfect their songs and dances and to prepare foods for the largest feast of the season. In this inversion of the daily routine, the space between one day and the next is bridged, an act that is particularly significant on the twenty-fifth of December and on New Year's Eve when the continuity of one year is extended into the next.

The Second Phase: Song Fest Competitions

When the song fest competitions begin, the second phase of *Kūrijmōj* is under way. On Ujelang, unlike any of the other atolls in the Marshall Islands, and unlike the islands of the Federated States of Micronesia to the south and west, two games supplement the song fest competitions. The first is known as *karate*, metaphoric of the Japanese mode of self-defense, and the second as *kalabūuj*, from the Spanish word for "jail." One often-stated intent of the celebrations is to promote happiness, and *karate* and *kalabūuj* are games that assist in this aim. They are complex ritual forms, however, that create humor by manipulating critical social forms.

In *karate*, the women from one song fest group go into the bush lands or out in the ocean to capture the fish or birds that the men of another group are bringing home to contribute to a song fest feast for their own group. With yelps of "*karate*," the women strip the men of their uncooked foods and then treat the anglers to a feast of cooked foods. These activities are interspersed with suggestive sexual jokes and often with women and men romping in the sea, splashing water, and dunking one another in the shallows of the lagoon. Again, inversion dominates many parts of this encounter, with women entering the male domain (the bush lands and sea), taking the initiative in suggesting sexual encounters, and winning at *karate*, a modern representation of the warrior activities associated with "real men" of the past. Interestingly, however, the typical male role as the provider of raw, highly valued complements to a meal is not disrupted. Similarly, the standard definitions of the female as the one who transforms raw foods into a cooked meal are not altered either.

While not played as frequently as *karate*, *kalabūuj* is a game that gives men an opportunity to manipulate relationships within the female domain. In this encounter, women are taken captive when they wander through the village space of another group. If they have collected pandanus fronds or another item to prepare for *Kūrijmōj*, the men who capture them abscond with their goods. They take their prisoners into a house where they are feasted lavishly and prompted with jokes that suggest that the visiting women are being fully cared for sexually. Some days or perhaps a week later the women are returned to their home group dressed as men. The other song fest group is feasted and, again, jokes are made that note how comfortable and satisfied the women are with the other *jepta*.

As with *karate*, *kalabūuj* fashions itself around a series of inversions that focus on the domestic unit: men dominate the female space and provide cooked foods and sexual satiety for the women within the house. Also like *karate*, one dimension of the domestic relationship remains unchanged. Women, who represent the links of continuity within Ujelang matriclans, continue to control the reproductive force that determines core aspects of human existence for coming generations. In everyday life, central features of a person's being, including the basic character or personality, are transmitted from a female to her offspring along the "path" of a clan. In reproduction, a man only shapes the external features of his child. All core elements emanate from a woman who derives these from the clan substance she transmits. Like births within families, *Kūrijmōj* also attempts to provide continuity by bridging the boundary between one year and the next. The game of *kalabūuj* contributes to the aim of human reproductive success through analogy with the domestic group: it combines the women of one song fest group with the men of another and gives the men's group access to the reproductive force that women control.

The Third Phase: Feasting and Exchange

The third phase of *Kūrijmōj* occupies most of December, the time of Advent. On each Sabbath day preceding the twenty-fifth, one of the three Ujelang song fest groups presents its songs for the rest of the community, prepares a large feast for all who attend, and gives large baskets of food accompanied by monetary gifts to the minister, a Marshallese pastor affiliated with the United Church of Christ (UCC).

Prior to the 1960s, Marshallese Protestants were Congregationalists, direct disciples of the missionaries who traveled to Hawaii in 1820 and on to the Marshall Islands in 1857. It was another seventy-five years before mission-trained teachers reached Enewetak. The shift from the Congregational Church to UCC affiliation has had little effect on outer islanders, but has been the cause of factional disputes in the government center. While not all Ujelang residents are church members, every able-bodied member of the community participates in *Kūrijmōj*. Thus, even though this third phase of *Kūrijmōj* focuses more narrowly on activities within the church, the celebration as a whole is neither solely a "Christian" event nor, in its entirety, even a "religious" event.

During this period, the pace of *karate* and *kalabūuj* increases, and practice sessions and song fest competitions last nearly the entire night. Finally, on the twenty-fourth, the whole community puts forth its best efforts to ready itself for the twenty-fifth. Every inch of each home and houseplot must be cleaned, the community grounds must be spotless, specially fashioned clothes must be completed (or, in times of hardship, one's best clothes must be meticulously cleaned), and each person thoroughly washes to make the entirety of one's external form irresistibly attractive. The body is covered with oil and scented, and one's skin and hair are given a highly desirable sheen.

All of the twenty-fourth and Christmas eve night are dedicated to food preparation and to collecting the "gifts for God" that will go to the minister. Then, following a short church service on the twenty-fifth, the entire community gathers to exchange foods. These foods may be prepared by song fest groups, by groups selected to assist established church members, or by households.

Processing arrowroot, a traditional staple presented to the minister during *Kūrijmōj* (Ujelang). (Photo by L. M. Carucci)

At this point in the celebration, the communicative intent is transformed, and the food exchanges mark this shift. While the competition among song fest groups continues, one critical aim—to engage the deities in an ongoing exchange with mortal beings—becomes a dominant theme. God, "the highest of high chiefs," is the most important of these deities, although other indigenous deities and even ancestor spirits form part of the Ujelang pantheon. In this exchange between mortals and gods, it is crucial that all foods be displayed on the central church grounds, combined, and blessed before they are distributed. The largest and best portions are reserved for religious specialists, the minister, the assistant minister, the elders and deacons, and for the two atoll chiefs (the most highly ranked living beings on Ujelang).

The leader of the children's group explains the significance of their "tree" in the palm-frond decorated sanctuary (Ujelang). (Photo by L.M.Carucci)

During the remainder of the day and on into the night, each song fest group presents its entire repertoire of songs, accompanied by entry and exit marches, and dances. A skit is part of each performance and, at its culmination, each group's *wijke* "tree" is exploded. "Christmas trees" are piñata-like constructions in the shape of missiles, bombs, airplanes, or sailing craft. Once they are magically exploded, the tree's inner "branches" are revealed, heavily laden with money. Each group gives the riches in the tree to the minister, though in the past these monies were divided among the other song fest groups.

Each group's total performance will be judged by the minister according to the quality of the singing and dancing, the success of the "tree," the group's ability to capture the "hearts" (literally "throat") of the members of the audience through an irresistible appeal to the onlookers' emotions, and the value of the gifts presented. Each group tries to "exhaust its ability" in its performance, and at the end of the frenzied activities of the twenty-fifth day, the community retires, exhausted from its extended efforts.

The Final Phase: "Neu Yia" (New Year)

In the final phase of *Kūrijmōj*, the community waits apprehensively as the week between the twenty-fifth day and *Neu Yia* (January 1) passes. There is a fear that something will go wrong during this time, that the festivities up through the twenty-fifth day were not adequate, or that some misbehavior on the part of a community member will bring disaster. On New Year's Eve the foreboding ends, and the entire night is filled with cries of "*Appi Neu Yia*" (Happy New Year) as children rush from house to house and sing songs in exchange for treats and the applause of the residents of each dwelling. The night itself is transformed into day as the light of lanterns pushes the fringes of darkness into the peripheral spaces at the edge of the village.

On New Year's Day, foods are again displayed, blessed, and exchanged, and each song fest group engages in softball games with the other groups (recently supplemented by young women's volleyball games). Then, on New Year's Sunday, the performances of each *jepta* are repeated, on a smaller scale, and feast foods are prepared and exchanged for a final time.

Maan yia, "the front of the year," begins with a church service at the dawn of each day for the first week of the new year. People maintain their concern with proper behavior during this time, but once the week has ended, the celebration is allowed to meld itself into more typical routines of daily life without closure. In so doing, it creates a continuity between the past and the future at the juncture of each yearly cycle.

THE EMPOWERING POTENTIAL OF RITUAL FORMS

Ordinary Marshallese do not view themselves as empowered beings. Unlike chiefs, they do not have genealogical ties to deified lines that are imbued with sacred force. Marshall Islanders' views of personhood are group-oriented, and while individuals are occasionally separated out as actors in everyday discourse, they are not the focus of rights and abilities in the same sense that American "individuals" are possessed with these properties (see Lutz 1989). These Ujelang views are evident in the practices and utterances of their daily lives. For example, as a young student of Marshallese culture several years ago, I was struck by the hesitancy with which Ujelang people treated departures. Americans proclaim all-knowingly, "I'll see you tomorrow," but Ujelang people are not so presumptive. They would say, "If life is good, we will see one another again tomorrow," or "If it is God's will, we will see each other again." Similarly, Ujelang people do not believe that humans alone can cause the reproduction of life on earth, the proliferation of fish and plants, or the sun's northward movement after the winter solstice. Ritual actions, however, give Ujelang people a source of power, a "way of moving" or "a tool"—in analytic terms, a methodology—that allows them to intervene with the supernatural collectively as a group and to cause these essential life events to occur.

Of course, ritual action does not guarantee that the new year will be productive and plentiful. Indeed, the apprehensiveness with which people live through the week between December 25 and New Year's Day is evidence of their uncertainty. But each ritual communication increases the chances of success, and this is precisely why they exist. Indeed, one-third of the year would not be dedicated to a festive event like *Kūrijmōj* if it served no purpose.

It is inappropriate, however, to argue that the celebration of *Kūrijmōj* serves simple utilitarian purposes, such as directly increasing food production on the atoll. Copra production drops significantly during this time, although food production does increase. A functionalist might argue, that this increased production helps people get through the winter months when foods are less abundant. Unfortunately, this does not occur. During the ritual, people produce foods for others, not for their own consumption, and many people complain about all of the food that goes to the minister and is never redistributed. Nevertheless, islanders continue to produce foods for others in overabundance. As a result, severe shortages commonly occur in the first months of the new year, since the atoll has been stripped of many of its resources during *Kūrijmōj*.

Instead, *Kūrijmōj* gives people a ritual mechanism to tap the ultimate sources of production and reproduction. It does so by initiating an exchange between the community, God and the ancient deities that will force these entities to reciprocate. Minimally, these empowered beings will at least hear about their needs and, "if life is good," they will attend to them. The ritual forms are the communicative mechanisms which, in their very practice, enact critical fragments of that which they seek to attain. J. L. Austin says that in their very utterance, certain words cause states of being to come into existence—as when an official of the church or state says "I now pronounce you husband and wife" (Austin 1962). Such is the case with the ritual performances of *Kūrijmōj*. The trajectory of this communication will be briefly outlined, since some of the themes are necessary to show how core elements of identity are fashioned and expressed in the ritual.

COMMUNICATION WITH SACRED BEINGS AND THE RENEWAL OF THE SOCIAL ORDER

The battles among *jepta* recast community members into a set of groups who are not only opposed in the wars of *Kūrijmōj*, but interact as marriage partners. The larger aim is to get the deities to lend their sacred powers to the reproduction of humankind and the regeneration of nature, an end that is pursued by reproducing marriage arrangements and sexual relationships in their simplest forms—precisely the forms that gave living human groups their original potency. The only way to reinvigorate the degenerate social relationships of the past year is to tap their original source of force, a task that is accomplished with games between groups that are analogues of those initial marriage and sexual alignments.

Forces of attraction, both personal and sexual, are used to draw the song fest groups together, and exchanges instantiate their interdependence. Attractiveness derives not only from the performance which includes songs and dances, humorous routines, jokes, and well-phrased speeches that "grab one's heart (throat)," but from the participants who enhance their external appearance with oils, scents, flowers, and white powder. The exchange of foods between groups links them together, since the foods prepared by a song fest group are always consumed by the members of other groups.

Forms of attraction are also present in the games of *karate* and *kalabūuj*, events that explicitly depict the uniting of males and females in domestic arrangements. In both *karate* and *kalabūuj*, women and men take the initiative in domains which they typically neither control nor desire to enter. Through the use of humorous and creative inversions, women actively play the part of men and *karate* the men of another *jepta*, while the men in *kalabūuj* take the wandering women of other groups captive in the domestic spaces of the town and household. Nevertheless, men still provide uncooked foods in *karate* and women are the source of reproductive power in *kalabūuj*. Both games thus use parody and inversion to recreate pivotal reproductive and social relationships between men and women that have become worn out in the passing year. In so doing, they bridge the space between the past and the future. By reconstructing these relationships on the collective plane, they are renewed and projected as a template for regeneration in the coming year.

The regeneration of humankind and nature draws its power from a primordial source, and the rituals are designed to seek renewal by tapping that undiluted source. By re-enacting their role as providers, men replicate primordial qualities of Jebero, the ruling chief of the Marshallese heavens. In their reproductive role, women transmit primordial clan substance through females, ensuring the replication and transformation of society.

The Jebero tale is an ideal example of the ways in which *Kūrijmōj* refashions recollections of the old (in this case, people's thoughts about an "ancient" solstice celebration) into a new and vital form. The tale has a number of affinities with the story of Lono in Hawaii and solstice celebrations in other parts of the Pacific, but it also possesses facets that are uniquely Marshallese and Ujelangese. Fragments of regional and local identity are thus simultaneously fashioned and reflected in these explanatory stories.

In brief, the Jebero story sketches how the chiefly rule of the Marshallese universe was established, at the same time setting the boundaries for proper and improper action. Ideally, by the rule of primogeniture, the oldest male member of the ruling matriline should inherit the chieftainship, but chiefly rule not only conveys rights, it connotes responsibilities. In the Jebero tale, the primordial female chiefess of Ailiñlablab, chiefly atoll of the Marshall Islands, decides that the chiefly seat will be decided by the outcome of a canoe race among her sons. After announcing the race to her offspring, each begins to prepare his outrigger canoe. In accord with the rule of primogeniture, she first approaches Tumur, the oldest and most physically mature, to ask if he will allow her to board his boat on the day of the race to sail to the windward tip of the atoll. He refuses her and suggests she ask his younger sibling. The second oldest also refuses, and recommends she speak with the third. This pattern continues until she reaches Jebero, the youngest. He hears his mother's pleas and is saddened, since he knows that if she boards his canoe he will certainly lose the race, but he goes along with her request and she brings her things to load on his canoe.

As the race begins, Tumur, the oldest, takes the lead and Jebero, the youngest, burdened with his mother and her goods, is last. As Tumur's canoe begins to disappear in the distance, and Jebero faces certain defeat, his mother opens her parcels and reveals the makings of a sail. She then instructs him in its use and, once assembled, the canoe "flies." Jebero and his mother overtake Tumur as they approach the main islet on Ailiñlablab. As they land, the brothers are struck by a typhoon and cast into the open sea. After the people have feasted and celebrated with Jebero to witness his assumption of the chieftainship, he sends a fleet to rescue his siblings. He agrees to allow Tumur, his oldest sibling, to rule with him, and this is how it has remained.

Preparing to sail to the outer islets for fish and birds, Ujelang. (Photo by L.M.Carucci)

In Ujelangese cosmology, the critical elements of the Jebero tale are visible in the constellations. Jebero, represented by the stars of the Greek constellation Pleiades, rises as Tumur, denoted by a portion of the constellation Antares, sets. Jebero rules the heavens in the winter months (from October to March) while Tumur rules the skies during the summer. Jebero and his mother, represented by part of Orion, are linked together by the sail that allowed him to win the canoe race. The sail is the V-shaped group of five stars half-way between Pleiades and Orion visible in the winter sky.

In this tale, the expected outcome of the race—with Tumur, the oldest (and he who would rule by primogeniture) winning—is overturned because he fails to care for his mother. Indeed, "caring for," a property associated with women, is the focus of this tale and the reason that Jebero, the youngest, becomes the ruling chief. On Ujelang, this theme is particularly critical. Thus, Jebero agrees to share the rule with Tumur, something that does not occur in other Marshall Islands versions of the tale (for example, Rynkiewich 1972).

Jebero's links with regeneration are not limited to the coincidence of his rule (October through March) with the celebration of *Kūrijmōj*; he is also the source of the vitality of fish upon which the community relies for sustenance. In Marshallese cosmogeny, the earth is dome-shaped, like the back of a turtle. As Jebero sets, he travels a path along the bottom of the sea to return to the eastern horizon where he will reappear at the beginning of the following winter. During this time, Jebero's back is in contact with the bottom of the sea and as he defecates during the plentiful months of summer, fish consume his wastes and become vitalized and "greasy" (*iuei*).

The yearly cycle of chiefly and cosmological relationships is complemented by an epic story that constructs and represents the proper relationships of chiefs and commoners. In this story, the great frigate (*ak*: chiefly bird of the Marshall Islands), feeds off the products of smaller birds who represent common human beings (*kajur*: literally "the strength"). In one version:

> They say that all of us should look to the heavens and observe the approach of the bird that is the highest in the Marshalls, the frigate. The bird of chiefs, the bird of the skies. Well, all birds they look upward and see this bird, the highest of all birds. Now this bird will stay way up there on high and watch all the other birds feed upon the sea and make food for themselves. Onward and onward it goes, until they are full and they fly upward to a region in the middle of the skies and the frigate flies downward to scream out "AAK." As the (frigate) screams and slaps them, all of the birds vomit, and the frigate eats (these regurgitated bits) solely from the air. Now this is true of our chiefs as well. Nonetheless, the frigate must watch over the "strength" (the commoners)—and the (common) birds must also care for the frigate. The chiefs also watch their commoners and the commoners must watch out for their chief. But if the chief does not still care for commoners, well, that is in error.

The interdependence of chiefs and commoners maintains the well-being of the whole, but the original source of productive force, the primordial ruling chief Jebero, must keep the cycle vital. Jebero is obligated to participate in this process as well, since the very source of his power rests in the symbolic qualities of "kindness" and "caring for." Any other indigenous logic would have given the rule to Tumur, the oldest sibling. In the story of Jebero and the tale of the frigate, unconstrained rank is seen as dangerous and bad. It is the offspring who "follows the thoughts of his mother" who is given the chiefly title. These thoughts include "kindness," "watching over," and "caring for"—concepts associated with the bilateral extended families that Ujelang women give birth to and head (Carucci 1980).

In the householding game of *karate*, these familial and reproductive values are graphically depicted. Like Jebero, the men are the providers, and when they give up their foods freely, demonstrating their "kindness" and abilities to "care for," they are honored. In return, they receive promises of sexual favors and cooked foods, the products of women's labor within the household. Men depend upon the meals women provide and must have "food" of a sexual sort as well. This interdependence, the metaphoric parallel of that between chiefs and commoners, is necessary for both men and women, and society, to exist. Women require raw foods, particularly highly valued dietary complements, that are provided by men, and men derive sustenance from the meals women prepare. Unlike women, men also require sexual release that can only properly come from women. This obligates men to participate in domestic arrangements, not just "walk around from place to place" as dictated by their culturally proscribed "natural" propensities.

Karate stresses reproductive themes as well, with jokes about sexual unions and water splashing and romping in the sea. Because the sexual jokes are instigated by women (an inversion of day-to-day practice) and emphasize male sexual power, they highlight the inseminational force of Jebero, and of the men in *karate*.

Similarly, *kalabūuj* stresses the differential sexual characteristics of men and women, but it concentrates on the reproductive capacity women control. Not only do men actively capture women in *kalabūuj* and take the lead in suggesting they are sexually satisfied, they do so entirely within the women's domain, the village and household. The unique cultural characteristics of men and women also dictates that the end of *kalabūūj* is very different from *karate*. Men inherently "travel around" but women "stay put." If a woman were returned to her own group (her clan, family or, in this case, her song fest group), it would connote dissatisfaction or disruption in the domestic sphere. By returning as "males," the symbolic "marriage" exchange between the two groups is perpetuated, and peaceful relations are properly portrayed in the ritually constructed "domestic group."

In both *karate* and *kalabūūj*, critical social relationships are symbolically represented in a simplified form. Relationships between the primordial clans that first occupied Enewetak and Ujelang Atolls are recreated in symbolic battles when song fest groups compete with one another. Domestic arrangements, where oppositions of clan and gender are transformed into a necessary, if tenuous, unity are similarly depicted. And finally, hierarchical relationships between chiefs and commoners are also ritually enacted, and these become even more critical in the final phase of the celebration.

In each sabbath feast leading up to the twenty-fifth day, and equally on the twenty-fifth and on New Year's Sunday, foods are prepared for display in front of the church. The competition among song fest groups continues with all of the mechanisms of attraction and irresistibility—the songs, speeches, dances, personal appearance and scent—stressed to their limits. The direction of the exchanges has now shifted, and God (and the ancient deities) are part of the new audience that will witness the performance.

It is critical for God to watch over the celebration for, in the Ujelang view, it is the belief in God that separates the contemporary era, "the time of light," from the ancient past, "the era of darkness." But, at the same time, beliefs concerning Jebero and the other ancient deities are critical to an understanding of this renewal celebration. Moreover, the Ujelang view of God and the relationship of God and Christ (the "Son of God") are patterned on the characteristics and social relationships of the ancient deities. God, "the highest of chiefs," like the mother of Jebero, is inherently empowered with a *mana*-like force not shared by ordinary humans, and commoners are protected from this sacred force by a series of interdictions or tabus. In addition, the message of love and generosity Ujelang people associate with Christ is also analogous to the kindness and consideration of Jebero. Thus, a series of syncretic parallels unite the same sacred beings that, for historic purposes, are separated.

During the celebration, it is said that all preparatory work that contributes to the feasts is "God's work" and all of the gifts that go to the minister on the twenty-fifth day are "gifts for God." Certainly, many of the feast foods will be consumed by members of other song fest groups, but not before they have first been displayed and blessed on church lands. Many gifts also go directly to the minister, the earthly representative of God. Even though people complain about the minister's failure to redistribute (just as there are veiled complaints about "bad" chiefs in the story of the frigate), no one would fail to give these gifts.

The "Christmas trees," filled with gifts for God, epitomize the intangible deified force that is needed to realign the universe. Not only does the form of the trees (missiles, bombs, and so on) reproduce the most potent vessels of destruction known to humankind (the detonation of nuclear devices which Ujelang people witnessed during tests on their home atoll in the 1950s), these trees must be exploded "magically"—that is, from a distance, and seemingly without human interference. Only the potency of this force can rescue the sun on its ever southward tending course, can realign the stars, and can transform one year into the next (Makemson 1941). The gifts inside the tree must exhaust all of a group's resources. These gifts, which go to the minister, are intended for God, and their quality and quantity along with the songs, dances, and feast foods contribute to the success of the ongoing exchange with the chiefs and sacred empowering deities who first caused the earth to come into existence. In the Marshallese understanding, the sacred chiefs and God both possess vitalizing spiritual force (*menmen*) and are considered to be one and the same type of entity (*iroij lablab*).

Indeed, islanders' extreme caution, their concern with proper action, and their fear that something may go wrong between the twenty-fifth day and New Year's Day confirm the presence of the sacred deities at this time. Once these sacred spirits are swept from the village by the cries and songs of children on New Year's Eve, people's fears subside. Ordinary humans are no longer in danger of coming into contact with the sacred force deities possess. The night is entirely eliminated with light and the noise of the living, and the youngest members of the community, appropriately and irreversibly, bridge the boundary between the old year and the new.

THE FASHIONING OF UJELANG *KŪRIJMŌJ*

With this brief ritual outline in mind we can turn our attention to questions of identity and the way it is constructed by people from bits of their own envisioned past. The past provides community members with the building blocks for a more empowered image of their current condition, a condition they must measure vis-à-vis their contemporaries. At the same time, the past places conceptual constraints on the community's view of its own future. It causes dreams to be fashioned from realistic images of lived experience.

To outsiders, *Kūrijmōj* appears to be a collage of cultural forms from the atolls' recent and more distant past. Bits and pieces from ancient lore, from Spanish, German, and mission times, from the Japanese and American administrative eras, and from the war and the nuclear testing era appear to be intertwined in a hodge-podge syncretic form. But such a view casts events in a Western historical time frame, as though they were products of eras gone by in an ordered sequence of historical relevance. While there is some validity to this perspective, it nevertheless obscures the indigenous values and meanings of the symbols in question. In other words, it replaces issues of local significance (like the construction of empowered song fest groups and island identities) with outside concerns.

As has been suggested, the stories of Jebero and of the frigate bird provide important information about *Kūrijmōj*, details that clarify a Marshallese understanding of the yearly cycle. But these are not ancient tales. They are fully modern stories, ones that people use to construct and understand images of their own past. At the same moment that Ujelang people fashion images of their past, they establish continuities between their contemporary community and their culturally constructed past. They do this in order to gain access to the primordial sources of sacred force that originally allowed humans to reproduce themselves and caused nature to be plentiful. In its very fashioning, the past is critical because it contains all of the sources of power relied upon by the first Marshallese, the clearly successful forebears of contemporary generations. Living humans are less empowered, not only because their "success" is still to be determined, but also because they are further from the sources of sacred force than were their ancient forebears. Therefore, these "original" sources (though fully modern cultural products) must be tapped to reinvigorate the universe and cause the old year to be replaced with the new.

Quite antithetical to this indigenous view of history is a very different view that islanders hold contemporaneously. This second view distances current-day Marshall Islanders from their own ancient, "heathen" past and sets them apart from other peoples (including other Pacific Islanders') who do not exhibit proper "Christian" demeanor. In the celebration of *Kūrijmōj*, the movement from the ancient past to the "new" Christian era is filled with denials about the past and fears of reprisal for non-Christian beliefs. On Ujelang, the denials and fears derive from the warnings of missionary teachers prior to World War II who discussed the punishments for a wide array of sins, including the belief in local spirits and false gods (known as "demons" in missionary-scripted Marshallese).

Nonetheless, the symbolic shift from Jebero to Christ is surprisingly simple, since both are associated with "love," "kindness," and "caring for." Indeed, the first time that the Enewetak people heard about Christianity, a Marshallese chiefess aboard a war canoe told the warriors of Enewetak and those from her own atoll to "put down their weapons and fight one another only with love." Fighting with love is precisely the theme of *Kūrijmōj*, where the songs and foods are the objects with which song fest groups do battle with one another. Thus, Ujelang people portray themselves as fully modern and civilized in the way they fashion their ritual forms. This includes their attire which follows mission-inspired rules of dress. In contrast, Micronesian attire, such as that worn by Yapese, is associated in the minds of many Marshallese with the heathen ways of the past.

As with all elements of *Kūrijmōj,* however, clothing has not maintained the complex of meanings and intents the missionaries may have had in mind. It takes on new significance as part of the contemporary construction of meanings and identities. In the game of *kalabūuj*, clothing marks the distinctions between males and females, and is used to manipulate those identities for ritual ends. When money and supplies of cloth are plentiful, the common uniforms of song fest group members also provide a measure of group solidarity and an element of contrast with the members of other groups. Moreover, the irresistibility of an individual dancer is commemorated during the performances of *Kūrijmōj* when an opposite-sexed member of another song fest group "tugs on" a piece of the dancer's clothing in a game known as *ṭōbṭōb*. After the performance, the dancer gives the dress or skirt to the person who has tugged it. Ritual friendships are publicly confirmed and the identities of highly skilled dancers and their successful ritual suitors are both recognized in the exchange.

Tōbṭōb honors the skill of a sophisticated dancer by noting parallels with dancers of the past who are said to have performed during evening ceremonial and religious services known as *kiye*. The most talented of those dancers sacrificed all of their clothing to members of the audience who paid them honor by pulling the clothing from their bodies.

Tōbṭōb, karate, and *kalabūuj* are all ritual aspects of *Kūrijmōj* unique to Ujelang. In their very enactment, they set Ujelang apart from other parts of the Marshall Islands where *Kūrijmōj* is also an important event. Ujelang people see their own celebration as better than that of other Marshall Islanders, and they say that their Marshall Islands friends and relatives look forward to celebrating *Kūrijmōj* on Ujelang. Since the return of Ujelang residents to Enewetak in 1980, air service has allowed an increasing number of islanders from other atolls to experience the unique elements of *Kūrijmōj* with the Ujelang/Enewetak community. Ujelang people indicate that other Marshall Islanders think *Kūrijmōj* on Enewetak is the very best.

Indeed, while *Kūrijmōj* throughout the Marshall Islands is a major ritual event (see Pollock 1969), on Ujelang it is a core part of life which consumes a substantial part of the year. It is a focus of pride and a source of renown for the community. Ujelang has long been thought of by Marshall Islanders as the most "backwards" of outer islands, and only recently, as a result of the the sizable trust funds given to compensate the Ujelang/Enewetak residents for nuclear-related damages, have Marshall Islanders begun to treat Ujelang people with greater respect. In their low-status position, *Kūrijmōj* has served as a major source of pride for Ujelang residents. It has also provided an avenue for them to tap important sources of supernatural power in their self-envisioned past and use this power to face an unknown future. By giving the relatively powerless access to a source of power, *Kūrijmōj* allows them to fashion identities of significance out of their own history, and histories of significance out of their own positive identities.

Acknowledgment: This chapter is based on research conducted in the Marshall Islands in 1976–1978, 1982–1983, and 1990–1991. Funding was provided by the National Science Foundation and the National Endowment for the Humanities. All interpretations and conclusions are those of the author and do not necessarily represent the perspectives of the granting agencies.

21

The Maori Tradition of Prophecy: Religion, History, and Politics in New Zealand

Karen P. Sinclair
Eastern Michigan University

Religious innovation in the Pacific Islands is often understood most dramatically in terms of Melanesian movements (see, for example, Chapter 18, by Kenelm Burridge and Chapter 19, by Paul Roscoe, in this volume). However, the eastern part of the Pacific has also witnessed significant activity in this arena. In Polynesia, the nature and form of contemporary religious experimentation are closely linked to the region's colonial history. This is especially true of New Zealand, where the British colonial presence was most pronounced and where the effects of colonialism were devastatingly apparent. For Maoris, the indigenous Polynesian population of New Zealand (who number today about three hundred thousand), Christianity and colonialism have come to be understood in terms of one another. Yet, while British settlement has raised clear and distinct problems for the Maori, Christianity in its various forms has been posited as a solution to these colonial conundrums.

The Maori have been a minority in New Zealand since the mid-nineteenth century, when the New Zealand Company offered large shares of land to eager British immigrants (the white population numbers today about 2.6 million). As the colonial ground has shifted over two hundred years, there has been a commensurate alteration in the focus and emphasis of Maori religious activity. Throughout the nineteenth and twentieth centuries, many men and women have stepped forward to offer new, more favorable interpretations of the Christian theology of the intruders. The nineteenth century produced fearless leaders who employed a spiritual idiom to give voice to the social and political desolation of their people. Such movements held out the promise of redemption and salvation. This tradition of prophecy has provided both continuity and a means through which Maoris could attempt to reclaim their history. That these movements have persisted into the twentieth century reflects more than anything else the enduring Maori sense of grievance and injustice against the colonial interlopers. Even now, religious revelation and inspiration continue to be hallmarks of significant Maori political action.

Differences between Maori and the white colonizers, whom the Maori call *Pakehas*, are nowhere more visible than in the context of such Maori prophetic movements. For Maori, the revelation bestowed upon their prophets offers a glimpse of salvation and equality in the face of Pakeha claims to religious and temporal supremacy.

For Pakehas, however, such divine disclosures are understood not as religious assertions, but as Maori political declarations. In the often volatile New Zealand social climate, messianic claims have been interpreted by Europeans as political challenges. In this they are not far wrong for, in the Maori order, religion and politics were not traditionally, and are not today, separate spheres. It is hardly surprising that Maori persist in seeing the political implications of religious actions. In a like manner, the seemingly theological idiom of revelation has proven to be an effective vehicle for more farreaching secular, political statements. This chapter analyzes one important contemporary movement, *Maramatanga*. This movement, which began in the 1930s and has continued to grow in influence and prestige since that time, illustrates this conjunction of religion and politics.

BACKGROUND: EARLY COLONIAL AND MISSIONARY INFLUENCES

The Maori had been in New Zealand for eight hundred years before the arrival of Captain Cook in 1769. During this time they adapted Polynesian culture to New Zealand's more temperate climate. Indeed, it was the very temperateness of the climate that proved so alluring to British colonists. Initially, Maori were not especially hospitable to the foreigners in whatever shape they appeared—as missionaries, seamen, or settlers. Nevertheless, colonists and missionaries were not to be deterred, despite the inauspiciousness of early encounters. By the second decade of the nineteenth century, the British presence became undeniably established. Several denominations of missionaries introduced their own versions of Christianity in their attempts to Christianize and civilize what to their European sensibilities appeared to be "story book savages" (Wright 1959:38). At the same time, British settlers were increasingly intent on annexing land that had been under Maori control. Inevitably, many Maori traditions yielded to the newcomers' social innovations.

Throughout the nineteenth century, tribal stability continued to be undermined by Maori participation in the new market economy (Metge 1976). In the same vein, tribal leaders and religious specialists of the old order yielded to individuals equipped with the new prerogatives of power: literacy introduced by the missionaries; control of European technology; and an opportunistic or entrepreneurial bent that allowed the ambitious to capitalize on new situations. From the Maori point of view, the grandiose promise of spiritual salvation held out by early Christian missionaries produced instead warfare, disease, confusion, and demoralization.

Christianity did not, however, have a uniform impact on all areas of New Zealand (Howe 1984). On the contrary, there was much regional variation, which was compounded by the competitive strategies of Anglicans, Methodists, Catholics, and Mormons. For most contemporary Maori, the choice of Christian affiliation has been a matter of historical accident; conversions and loyalties often depended on the success of one denomination over the others in staking out particular territories. Even within a single denomination, success varied across regions and over time.

In 1840, the Treaty of Waitangi (so called because of the site chosen at the northern end of the North Island) was signed, ostensibly ceding New Zealand to the British Crown. It is now clearly known that there were two versions of the Treaty. The English version, always the working version in New Zealand courts, would indeed appear to have ceded Maori lands to the Crown. But the Maori version (the version signed by Maori chiefs), far from granting land rights to the British, actually guaranteed continuing Maori possession of land and protection of their autonomy. These differences are attributable to the fact that critical words like "sovereignty" and "autonomy" were translated in ways that circumvented understandings implicit in the Maori lexicon. New Zealand's two populations therefore brought to the Treaty two virtually irreconcilable interpretations of the Treaty's meaning and intent.

Linguistic differences, however, are only partially responsible for the difference in perspective that emerges when European and Maori accounts of the Treaty are placed side by side. Analyses of the late nineteenth and early twentieth centuries (Belich 1986; Binney and Chaplin 1986; Binney 1987) have forcefully demonstrated that a countervailing Maori perspective did (and does) indeed exist. When these studies are placed alongside conventional histories, a formidable challenge to the European domination of the New Zealand historical record is mounted.

These are more than academic quibbles. At present, the issue of Maori land, always a critical component of Maori identity, has moved into the forefront of New Zealand's political consciousness. The Waitangi Tribunal (discussed in greater detail below), constituted in 1975, is now renegotiating the Treaty and may reallocate critical land resources.

By the 1860s, land pressures were so intense that differences between Maori and settlers were arbitrated on the battlefield. The general impression, perpetuated for over one hundred years in New Zealand and British history books, is that the Maori, outnumbered and outmaneuvered by the technologically superior settlers, retreated in despair to the remaining marginal areas of the New Zealand hinterland. But recently, Belich (1986) has reanalyzed many of these battles and concluded that the land wars have been seriously misrepresented. By re-examining contemporary accounts of particular battles, Belich provides evidence of often-startling misreporting and distortions. Minor British successes became, in the telling, indisputable strategic victories, while major defeats were too frequently depicted as mere gentlemanly skirmishes. Victorian racial ideology was the prism through which these battles were filtered; through these lenses Maori inferiority was axiomatic. Similarly, studies of two East Coast Maori prophets have documented the discrepancies between the written records of British settlers and the oral traditions of Maori participants (Binney 1987; Binney and Chaplin 1986).

While differences in perspective can be anticipated as a matter of course, it is the view of the colonizer, the Pakeha, rather than that of the colonized, the Maori, which has dominated New Zealand historical chronicles. But the words of Maori leaders, especially their religious leaders, has struck a cautionary note: the historical record is provisional rather than absolute. It is this very provisionality of history that has captured the minds of Maori prophets for almost two hundred years and has reinforced their determination to have their voices heard.

NINTEENTH-CENTURY PROPHETS

Finding political solutions elusive and inadequate, Maori prophets have instead employed a religious idiom to express and encapsulate Maori experience. In the nineteenth century, Old Testament imagery, summoning forth a vision of a dispossessed but chosen people, proved to be especially apt. Implicit in the moving words of these prophets was a political message. To their dismay, the missionaries saw their newly introduced religion transformed into a vehicle for dissent and resistance.[1]

By adapting Christianity into an existing framework, Maori were able to assert their autonomy and put some spiritual distance between themselves and their Pakeha pastors. This remolding of Christianity to suit an essentially Maori epistemology has been maintained into the twentieth century (see Chapter 19, by Paul Roscoe, in this volume, for another similar case), often alarming Europeans, who have had difficulty defining exactly what it is about the new religions that has proved so troubling.

In most accounts, Maori religious innovation is linked to the land wars. However, Maoris were willing to interpret scriptures in ways that were disquieting to the missionaries well before land became an explicit issue (Binney 1966). The loss of land and missionary complicity in New Zealand's colonization galvanized Maori prophets, who sought to emphasize the inconsistencies in missionary doctrine. In fact, they were insisting on their own interpretation of events.[2]

The most famous of the nineteenth-century Maori prophets, and the first to gain a national reputation, if not a national following, was Te Ua Haumene from the west coast of the North Island. In the midst of the land wars, he urged his followers to command Jehovah to come to the assistance of the Maori. They danced around a pole erected for this purpose. To outsiders, this blend of borrowed militarism and millenarianism attested to the inadequacy of the Maori mind. But to insiders, a plea to the God of the Old Testament, a deity who, it seemed, had deserted the Maori, had an almost irresistible logic.

Te Ua Haumene achieved legendary status, which still exists today, among both Maori and Pakehas as the founder of the *Pai Marire* religion. For the Maori, he is a hero, a voice of Maori discontent and disaffection; while for the Pakehas, he represents the atavistic underside of a group that remains fundamentally untrustworthy. Te Ua Haumene relied on the Angel Gabriel for inspiration. Other Maori leaders also depended on spiritual guidance; power was often validated through revelation. But Gabriel had been introduced by the missionaries, and their astonishment must have been great when they realized that their own teachings had been incorporated into an ideology of resistance.

Indeed, the land wars forced much reconsideration and redefinition. It was cause for some disillusionment, for example, to see the missionaries, men of peace, take up arms against the natives. Too, the sanctity of Sunday as a day of rest and prayer did not deter the fierce activity of government guns. The extreme paradox, of course, was that here was a case of white Christians fighting Maori Christians. The knowledge that both sides were seeking similar divine protection must have been hard for Maori to bear once they began to suffer serious defeat. It seemed logical, therefore, that Maori communication with the Christian deity had to be reformulated. Increasingly, as the nineteenth century wore on, missionary Christianity was modified to accommodate elements of the Old Testament and the reintroduction of a specifically Maori ideology.

These new movements were not only anti-European, they were anti-mission. Prominent features of mission Christianity were rejected and reinterpreted. This reinterpretation of scripture into a Maori context—in particular, the perceived parallel between Maoris and Old Testament tribal Jews expelled by the infidel from their Promised Land—injected meaning into an otherwise alien context.

In the more than a century that has elapsed since Te Ua's death, five prophets have achieved national preeminence, while dozens of other visionaries have proliferated with more local followings. Some advocated accommodation to the European, while others attempted to establish self-sufficient communities that would be free of dependence on the Pakeha (see Scott 1981; Binney, Chaplin, and Wallace 1979; Binney and Chaplin 1986; Webster 1979). In attempts to prevent further settlement, Te Whiti, a Taranaki prophet, instructed his followers in techniques of passive resistance. However, Maori pacifism was almost always countered with Pakeha violence. Such high-handed tactics left a residue of bitterness and distrust that has lingered for most of the twentieth century.

From most published accounts, it is evident that there are striking similarities in the experience of Maori prophets: all have received divine inspiration, all have championed those aspects of Maoriness felt to be under attack (for example, language), and, perhaps most crucially, all have framed the political problems of the Maori in religious terms. It seems clear that the emergence of land as an issue in these movements is more than an economic consideration; the loss of their land symbolizes Maori feelings of disenfranchisement from their heritage (Sinclair 1977).

TWENTIETH-CENTURY PROPHETS

In the early twentieth century, the Maori population stabilized and increased while several Maori distinguished themselves in the national arena. A Maori renaissance was heralded. But the effects of this were largely lost in the influenza epidemic of 1918, which registered a disproportionately high Maori mortality rate, and in the world-wide economic depression, during which Maoris suffered more devastating dislocation than did New Zealanders of European ancestry. During this time, under the leadership of such prominent individuals as Sir Apirana Ngata, Princess Te Puea, and Te Rangi Hiroa (Sir Peter Buck), Maori health became a national priority, land schemes were organized to achieve economic prosperity for rural Maoris, and traditional art forms were resurrected and redefined. Maori dances were merged with European music to produce the action songs still heard today, old chants were organized and preserved, schoolchildren were taught *haka* (war chants), and Maori youths were once again taught their genealogy.

Twentieth-century prophets also recast their message. No longer referring to themselves and their followers as Jews, they turned instead to New Testament imagery. Maori selection, however, remained a critical component of their ideology. Each prophet consciously built upon the work of his or her predecessors, and, in so doing, generated significant links between the past and present. From a current vantage point, the prophetic tradition has left a legacy of enduring divine favor.

The beginning of twentieth-century religious activity took place on the banks of the Rangitikei river with an old prophetess named Mere Rikiriki. It was, according to followers of contemporary movements, her jumping into the river forty times to seek the Holy Spirit that brought Maori firmly into the New Testament. For most contemporary Maori, however, she is notable as the aunt of Wiremu Ratana, the most famous of Maori prophets.

Ratana started out as a faith healer, performing miraculous cures of the desperately ill and crippled. He received his message in the 1920s, an especially bad time for Maoris who had been decimated by the influenza epidemic and whose soldiers, returning from World War I, did not find equality in New Zealand society. Once again, Maoris were swayed by oratory that could not help but move the defeated and the dispossessed. Ratana's followers, who included individuals with tribal affiliations from all over New Zealand, were called the *morehu*, the "survivors," and he was known as the *mangai*, the "mouthpiece." The Ratana pantheon included a number of ministering angels who shared characteristics with traditional Maori and Christian mediators. By advocating the abandonment of *tohungaism* (adherence to non-Christian, traditional religious leaders) and sorcery, Ratana reflected the preoccupations of Maori national leaders. In many ways, he prepared Maoris to enter the Pakeha world, albeit on their own terms. In the 1930s, he focused on practical concerns, including Maori political representation in Parliament. In 1943, all four of the Maori seats in the New Zealand Parliament were held by members of the Ratana Church. The church still has an active membership today, with a hierarchical clergy recruited from all over New Zealand.

Throughout New Zealand today, local prophets continue to have followings. Their gifts are varied: some are faith healers; others are seers; while others maintain contact with areas of Maori culture not respected by the Pakeha majority. While the Maori renaissance has flourished, there has been a resurgence of interest in traditional Maori religion and in Maori versions or understandings of Christianity. These movements have existed for centuries and are only now gaining the recognition by the Pakeha that they have always had from the Maori.

The Social Context of Contemporary Maori Activism

Maori activism, which is reflected in the activities of *Maramatanga*, is much more pronounced today than it has been in the past. This is, in part, related to the growing social marginalization of the Maori population in New Zealand society.

Since shortly after World War II, many Maori have abandoned their traditional rural homes and emigrated to New Zealand's cities. Increasingly, unskilled and semi-skilled jobs have fallen to Maori and to other Polynesian migrants (see Chapter 10, "The Samoan Exodus," by Paul Shankman, in this volume). Pacific Islanders and Maori have, as a result of this process, formed an underclass with distinct characteristics. Pearson (1984:211) writes:

Over the past forty years the rapid process of Maori urbanization, and the recruitment of migrant labour from the Pacific Islands, has followed a familiar pattern that marks the movement of migrant replacement forces from peripheral areas of low economic growth to expanding metropolitan core areas. Polynesian labour, almost exclusively unskilled and semiskilled, and suffering the opprobrium and consequent discriminatory repercussions of a covert but widespread racism in the labour and property markets, rapidly formed a culturally and phenotypically distinctive subordinate fraction of the working class.

During these years, the Maori population has grown. In the early 1970s, Maoris were 8 percent of the population; in the 1986 census, they represented over 12 percent. The fertility rate of the Maori population remains significantly higher than that of non-Maoris and projections for the period 1981–2011 suggest that the Maori population may rise at over five times the rate of the Pakeha population (The New Zealand Population 1986:44).[3] Moreover, when compared to Pakehas, there is a much higher percentage of Maoris under age twenty-five.

Maori continue to have lower levels of educational attainment, higher school drop-out rates, and higher crime rates than their Pakeha counterparts. A young, unskilled Maori population raises troubling possibilities for both the Maori and for New Zealand. This cohort of young adult Maoris is unlikely to find anything other than unskilled or semiskilled employment. High levels of unemployment and a high incidence of teenage pregnancy suggests that this cohort will also face housing problems (New Zealand Planning Council 1986:57). Urban areas with heavy Maori concentrations will be most severely affected, as will rural areas which, traditionally low in employment opportunities, must now accommodate Maori youth returning from the city.

It is in this context that the Maori renaissance has stressed a revival of Maori arts and language, with preschool Maori language schools proliferating around the country and a vigorous re-examination of traditional Maori land rights. Land has become a critical link between the past and the future (Greenland 1984:86). Contemporary Maori activists assert that the process of New Zealand's colonization has deprived the Maori of both their land and their culture. In the continuing debate, Maori spiritual links to the land are contrasted to the Pakeha's purely economic interest. More to the point, the Maori lay their contemporary problems, including their status as an underclass, at the feet of a white society they contend is based on materialism and nonhumanistic values (see Greenland 1984; Hohepa 1978).

THE MARAMATANGA MOVEMENT

The *Maramatanga* movement originated in the 1930s, a time when Maori prophets identified themselves with the New Testament. It has remained active for sixty years. Over time, its focus has changed as the historical landscape has shifted. In the Maori renaissance of the 1980s and 1990s, there has been an increasing concern with land, autonomy, and cultural self-determination. Significantly, the idioms of inspiration and revelation, the mainstays of Maramatanga and, indeed, of Maori prophecy, have been readily placed in the service of more involved Maori activism.

Maramatanga means "light," "enlightenment," or "knowledge." The term derives further significance from its association with Mere Rikiriki. Like other movements,

Maramatanga self-consciously builds on affinities with other prophetic leaders. And, like other movements, *Maramatanga* subjects the recent past to scrutiny. By uncovering the essential correctness of the ancestral order, members of *Maramatanga* assert their own positive evaluation of the past and simultaneously, if implicitly, refute the Pakeha interpretation. Through rituals, inspirations, missions, and pilgrimages, the members of *Maramatanga* seek a Maori re-enactment and reinterpretation of history.

Mareikura, the major prophet of *Maramatanga*, was an itinerant preacher from the west-central portion of the North Island, an area hard hit by the depression of the 1930s. The individuals who joined his movement in the 1930s had all had experiences with other Maori prophets. They were conversant with the idiom of revelation and with the use of spiritual assistance in mundane affairs. Many of them had traveled all over the country to hear first-hand the wisdom of such leaders. Mareikura's message thus struck a responsive chord in an already receptive audience. His message elaborated upon, but did not depart from, the essentials of the prophetic tradition.

Although it was later experiences that would come to distinguish him, Mareikura's path to prophecy seemed to have been ordained from the very beginning of his life. Christened Hori Enoka, he was also given the name Mareikura—"heavenly messenger"— because the arrangement of the stars carried special meaning on the night of his birth.

Always involved with Maori iconoclasm, Mareikura often visited the *marae* of Mere Rikiriki in Parewanui, an area which had long been a gathering place for rituals associated with Maori prophets. Mareikura took her *ra* (special commemorative day), the twenty-seventh of July, as a particularly momentous occasion, organizing a celebration for members of his family and following on that date. Today, his descendants continue to celebrate this *ra* annually. They hold it in high regard, seeing in it their links to an illustrious legacy.

When Ratana turned to politics in the 1930s, followers of *Maramatanga* felt that it was Mareikura's responsibility to fill the spiritual void. His deferential demeanor and modesty was (and is today) often contrasted favorably with the ostentation seen as typical of Ratana. A gentle and kind man, Mareikura preferred to work behind the scenes, promoting his message through persuasion rather than rhetorical flourishes.

An Anglican by birth, Mareikura pursued the teachings of Christianity by attending a variety of churches. The Christian teachings that he absorbed in this manner were complements to the traditional Maori religion that he devoted hours to mastering, and which he worked hard to instill in his children.

Despite his erudition, nothing particularly distinguished him from other individuals with religious inclinations until the death of his beloved granddaughter, Liina. As her grieving relatives gathered around her coffin, Liina's spirit came back. However, the child's bereft mother, Mareikura's daughter, Anaera, was not comforted by the spiritual return of her lost child. On the contrary, she was terrified by it. Nevertheless, she was convinced, gently by her father and more forcefully by others, to allow the child's spirit, *wairua*, to speak through her. Anaera received songs in her sleep which she would wonderingly reproduce upon awakening. She continued, until her death in 1948, to be the somewhat reluctant human voice through which her daughter, Liina, spoke. Today Liina is referred to as *te karere o te aroha* or the "messenger of love." Her spirit has continued to provide inspiration and guidance for over five decades by sending dreams and songs to the movement's members.

While Anaera died years before I arrived, there is no doubt that her reluctance and awe were genuine. She was recruited into this role; she did not seek it. Guided by her daughter's messages, she fasted for a period of time to assure spiritual blessings and direction for subsequent generations. This was a momentous occasion, an event that led to what the members continue to refer to as "the opening of the channels." Essentially, this means that the spirits of the dead—the *wairua*—are able to communicate with any and all members of the movement without the assistance of a human intercessor. Many spirits have returned and are consulted before any major undertaking. They appear in dreams and thoughts, helping to keep movement members on track.

Thus, with the help of the *karere*, Mareikura and his daughter had made it possible for everyone to have access to the spiritual world; a leader would no longer be necessary. Mareikura became enshrined as the "last of the prophets," and his daughter, Anaera, was credited as the individual who "opened the channels." Together, they had given the followers of Maramatanga entrance to a realm hitherto accessible only to a religious elite.

The notion of a leaderless congregation suggested a new view of social relations. Traditional Maori society had been stratified according to principles of rank, gender, and seniority. Maramatanga's presumption of equality obliterated such distinctions. More-over, such a stance had important implications for the ways in which Maori-Pakeha relations could be envisioned. The new egalitarianism was extended to become a divinely sanctioned assertion of equality between New Zealands's two major ethnic groups.

For fifty years, the *wairua* ("spirits of the dead") have communicated with Mareikura's followers and their descendants. The members take their position seriously, referring to themselves as the "workers," the *kaimahi*, "the chosen few," the *hungaruarua*. Moreover, their work is referred to as the *tikanga*, the correct way.[4]

In addition to its egalitarian ethic, the *Maramatanga* movement stands out for its Catholic underpinnings. The Catholicism of the movement was virtually an historical accident. Mareikura's wife, who exerted an important influence upon him, was Catholic. Her donation of land gave a home to the fledgling movement. Catholicism therefore gained an edge over other denominations.

For most of the members of *Maramatanga*, however, their links to the prophetic tradition, especially at that time, overruled their loyalties to any particular missionary perspective. This attitude is typical of the ecumenical stance that most Maori adopted, and continue to adopt, toward Christianity. Indeed, while most members of *Maramatanga* are today Catholic, there is a willingness to accept individuals of other denominations. However, the influence of Catholicism is readily seen in the archangels and the Virgin Mary as accessible sources of revelation.

Contemporary Maramatanga *Ideology and Practice*

In traditional chants and songs, on movement flags, and in the selection of names given to buildings and to individuals, the Maori prophetic tradition is invoked and summoned into the present. To the members of *Maramatanga*, it is possible to posit this continuity because of the existence of a body of knowledge that links prophets to one another in an inclusive order, while at the same time, that same body of knowledge excludes Pakehas.

Indeed, as noted earlier, *maramatanga* means "knowledge," "enlightenment." The power that knowledge had in the past is clearly present in contemporary formulations. Seen in the context of Maori prophecy and European domination, knowledge is critical for Maori survival. Salmond (1982:82) writes:

> The Maori metaphor of knowledge (*maatauranga* or *waananga*) on the other hand draws upon notions of *oranga* (necessity of life) and *taonga* (cultural wealth), and here knowledge is depicted as above all exhaustible and destructible, a scarce resource conserved within the group, guarded by chosen individuals and never to be squandered.

Contact with spirits and with other divine forces has given followers of prophetic movements access to a system of knowledge that stands apart from European epistemology. Because it is divinely inspired, it possesses the power and authority necessary to challenge Pakeha conventions (see Binney 1984).

For their part, the spirits are seen as messengers and guardians; they both inform and protect their relations on earth. Wairua communicate through traditional Maori means; that is, they use songs, chants, and dreams to contact the living. Since the message is designated for the entire congregation (although infrequently, a more personal interpretation is put forth), much time is spent dissecting and analyzing messages for all possible implications.

While, on occasion, the spirits may divulge information of cosmic significance, they are just as likely to comment on the domestic affairs of their relations. The majority of these spirits are deceased kinspeople who in life were fairly intimate with the present participants in the movement and thus would be expected to approach the world in much the same manner. Consequently, their motives are seldom suspect and their messages generally have a reasonable amount of credibility and authority.

Kinship ties and individual commitments are activated throughout the year in a series of celebrations (*ra*) that commemorate events in the spiritual history of the movement. At such times, members convene to discuss spiritual matters and to enjoy an occasion that celebrates Maori hospitality. Commensality and solidarity are often explicit themes; traditional inequalities based on rank, genealogy, and gender are deemed insignificant. In the sacred, highly charged atmosphere of the *ra*, unity and harmony are emphasized.

For most members, the *ra* provide an opportunity to increase their spirituality. Such occasions are seen as refuges from a world that is dominated by Europeans. They are viewed as a time for replenishing the resources of the individual and of the group. It is almost with relief that people turn to the spirits and to one another to affirm the value of being Maori. Through songs and dreams, the spiritual world lends support to this contention. On the days set aside for the celebration of the spiritual, the members are confident that they are working under the auspices of the *wairua* in a world temporarily untainted by the Pakeha. This round of spiritual commemorations organizes the year for members of *Maramatanga* and remains an intensely satisfying experience.

Participation in the movement demands a reasonable fluency in the Maori language, a knowledge of Maori art forms such as action songs, and an appreciation of the subtleties of Maori oratory, characterized as it is by metaphor and complex imagery. Since virtually all important matters are discussed in Maori and since standing up in public to speak demands rudimentary knowledge of Maori etiquette, participation, rather than observation, requires at least minimal competence in a specifically Maori arena. More importantly, the boundaries of this domain preclude, by their definition, Pakeha involvement or intervention. The ideology and rituals of the movement thus generate a universe that is governed by Maori conventions.

In the early 1970s, several movement members, then in their thirties and forties, attended *whare wananga*, the traditional school of learning. In this school, sacred knowledge is passed down by a religious adept to select members of the group. The *whare wananga*, an ancient institution, was believed to have been replaced by introduced educational methods. It was an unlikely candidate for the contemporary world because of its reliance on Maori language. Most significantly, these institutions were reported by nineteenth-century ethnographers as exclusively the province of males. In fact, women had always participated and would continue to be participants in the contemporary school of learning. This misrepresentation is exemplary of the limitations of Pakeha understanding of the Maori world. Despite the views of Pakeha ethnographers, whose ideas have been adopted by the academic establishment, enclaves of individuals, such as the members of *Maramatanga*, have been sustaining and perpetuating their traditions despite official claims of cultural demise. By coming under the tutelage of learned men, the members of *Maramatanga* became very well-versed in esoteric aspects of Maoridom. In fact, one member is today a prominent ritual leader.

WAITANGI

Over time, *Maramatanga* followers have undertaken numerous missions to purify sacred areas and to appease the spirits of mountains and rivers. Starting in the late 1960s, there were a number of visions that specifically directed *Maramatanga's* members to Waitangi, the site of the original treaty signing that ceded New Zealand to the British in 1840.

The visions revealed a new interpretation of the events of 1840. According to these visions, at the time of the signing the chiefs who represented all tribal areas of New Zealand converged on Waitangi and argued forcefully among themselves about the wisdom of signing the Treaty.[5] Longstanding intertribal rivalries inevitably surfaced in a gathering of such powerful chiefs. A local *tohunga* (religious leader) grew concerned that such conflicts, and the uncontained expression of the chiefs' *mana* it invoked, could do harm to them all and suggested that the chiefs bury their *mana* in the ground. This would enable them to dispense with their rivalries and turn their attentions to the Treaty. Following the burial, the *tohunga* planted a *karaka* tree on top of this sacred spot. Here it would remain until claimed by a future generation. The tree, taking root in the sacred *mana* of the Maori people, would inevitably be *tapu* (ritually charged, sacrosanct), awaiting its destined conjuncture with a new generation.

For the members of *Maramatanga*, that future arrived in 1970, when the members journeyed to Waitangi, fulfilling their visions, and made peace with the tree. According to one woman, the tree shook her hand, signifying that a rapprochement between the past and the present had been reached. The intention of this first mission to Waitangi was literally to reclaim the *mana* of Maori ancestors and to restore the *mauri* (the "life force") to the people.

On this, as well as on later missions to Waitangi, members were accompanied by the *wairua* and by the Virgin Mary, who not only appears frequently but who is also embodied in a picture, "Our Lady of Perpetual Succor," which is always carried along on such sacred journeys. While a Christian icon may well be used to purify a Maori sacred site, it is the potency of the Maori past that is being asserted. That past's continuing power, while understood as problematic, is nevertheless axiomatic.

Throughout the 1970s, members of *Maramatanga* continued to go to Waitangi on annual pilgrimages to accomplish various goals (see Turner and Turner 1978 for a general analysis of pilgrimage). It would seem easy enough to argue that this was a group of pilgrims far removed from the general concerns of other Maori or of other New Zealanders. But, their trips to Waitangi proved prescient. Indeed, they anticipated the major events of the 1980s, particularly the Maori renaissance and renewed Maori activism. This anticipation permitted the members of *Maramatanga* to define themselves at the heart of everything significant in contemporary New Zealand politics. Although some of their younger children were involved in activist policies in the 1970s, for the most part, *Maramatanga* members remained uninvolved in larger national issues. Nevertheless, their actions presaged national concerns. By establishing links to the Maori tradition of prophecy, members of *Maramatanga* articulated many of the major concerns of the Maori as New Zealand's indigenous population.

These concerns, particularly the question of land and resource ownership and management, have come to national prominence in the Waitangi Tribunal. Under the Treaty of Waitangi Act (1975) and through its amendment in 1985, the Tribunal, which has been hearing claims involving rights to fishing grounds and control of resources, has restructured Maori-Pakeha relations. Anthropologists and historians (see Levine 1987; Sorrenson 1987) have suggested that the Treaty is being reinterpreted and Maori perspectives are, for the first time, being given a fair hearing. Inevitably, both Maori and Pakeha perceptions of the past must change as the Tribunal introduces a Maori view of history into New Zealand discourse.

The absence of a Maori perspective has only recently commanded scholarly attention. Claudia Orange writes:

> There was, then, no major study of the making of the Treaty and its role in the country's history through to the 1980s. Moreover, it seemed that historians (and other researchers) had not looked at Maori sources; and in the 1970s Maori voices—articulate and often strident—were more insistent about the need for New Zealanders to take cognisance of Maori viewpoints on the Treaty. That those viewpoints were substantially different from Pakeha perceptions was increasingly evident by the end of the 1970s. The land march, Bastion Point, and protest at the annual Waitangi Day "celebrations," each carried the message that the Maori and Pakeha had inherited different historical traditions. Those traditions derived from the viewpoints of the 1840 Treaty and of earlier events, in particular the 1935 Declaration of Independence.

The members of *Maramatanga*, while modest about their accomplishments, nevertheless believe that their revelation and their actions initiated a new era in Maori-Pakeha relations.

DISCUSSION

A turn toward the prophetic tradition and toward the wisdom obtained through revelation is an assertion of the importance of a Maori perspective. The prophetic tradition and the epistemological system that it embodies yields a view of the last two hundred years that emphasizes continuity rather than disjuncture in Maori experience. The past has not become calcified; rather it assumes a relevance today that matches its traditional importance. By looking back to both ancestors and past prophets, members of *Maramatanga* sustain "the continuing dialogue between the past and the present" that has always characterized Maori thinking.[6]

Knowledge is now derived from two traditions. The Christian pantheon, shaped and molded to accommodate its place in the Maori cosmos, has become a complement to more conventional sources of inspiration. Armed with spiritual reinforcement from two intellectual traditions, followers of Maori prophets have confronted the political dilemma posed by the European presence. Indeed, inspiration is a powerful weapon in the colonial world, as their trips to Waitangi and the continuing furor over the Treaty demonstrate.

Prophetic movements like *Maramatanga* have endured in New Zealand despite a constantly changing political climate. It is reasonable to question why these movements continue to be effective today. Far less dramatic than demonstrations and marches, they nevertheless remain faithful to Maori traditions. More specifically, they retain their fidelity to the fusion of religion and politics. This is perhaps nowhere more poignantly demonstrated than in the continued pilgrimages to Waitangi to reclaim land lost a century and a half ago. That the followers of Mareikura should feel vindicated is hardly surprising; in a world that is filled with surprises and nuances, they have a road map to negotiate their future. Anger and protest may appear less awesome when expressed in a theological idiom, but the message is clear to all who are listening. The cosmic and universal language so befitting revelation gives apt expression to defeat and dispossession. In the hands of Maori prophets, Christianity has proven itself a powerful instrument of resistance and disaffection.

From a European point of view, there are clear political consequences to denying the coherence of the Maori prophetic tradition. If Maori history can be seen to be ruptured, if Maori ties to their past can be demonstrably spurious, their present will then be more readily accessible to external (that is, Pakeha) definition. Europeans have viewed individual Maori prophets as isolated aberrations, as lunatics, whose followers demonstrate the unfortunate Maori vulnerability to superstition and deception. The political intent of such movements could thus be denied, while Pakehas would be free to dismiss Maori outrage and indignation.

Contemporary movements such as *Maramatanga* emphasize the Maori commitment to their past. But this does not mean that Maoris invent tradition. Rather, history is recast in a manner that emphasizes a Maori perspective. At worst, such recasting reflects the bias of the participant; at best, it is a healthy corrective to the Eurocentric domination of New Zealand history.

To assert that there is consistency in Maori experience, however, is not to argue that Maori culture is changeless or immutable. In fact, Maori knowledge is very much a process, continually being reinterpreted to lend meaning to the present (Borofsky 1987). Nor is it merely that Maoris de-emphasize certain changes and integrate them into existing cultural traditions. Instead, they have posited a new history, one that may present a powerful challenge to European chronicles. For, in both Maori and Pakeha traditions, knowledge is power. For the moment, Maoris and Pakehas have reached the juncture where history becomes contestable, where the past suddenly appears open to negotiation, and where the legacies and traditions of each are at stake.

Acknowledgments: Research was assisted in 1972–1974 by a Fulbright Full Grant, an NSF Research Traineeship, and a Brown University Graduate School Grant. In 1982, my field work was supported by a Sabbatical Leave from Eastern Michigan University. In 1987, my work was supported by an Eastern Michigan University Faculty Research Grant, an NEH Travel to Collection Grant (FE21005), and a Josephine Nevins Keal Foundation Grant. I also received assistance in the form of a Spring-Summer Research Grant to write this chapter and another Eastern Michigan University Faculty Research Grant to continue writing. Field work in 1990 was funded by an NEH Fellowship for College Teachers (FB 27099) and an Eastern Michigan University Sabbatical Leave.

NOTES

1. The imagery here was especially apt; leaders were seen as prophets leading their people to Canaan, while settlers were seen as Egyptians, banishing forever the chosen people from the chosen land. Witi Ihimaera, a notable Maori writer, invokes precisely this imagery in *The Matriarch*, a novel about the East Coast of the North Island in the nineteenth and twentieth centuries.

2. Recently, anthropologists have rethought the notion of cargo cults and similar movements. They are now seen as "rituals of resistance" to domination (See Kelly and Kaplan 1990).

3. According to 1981 census information, Maori women at age sixty had given birth on average to 6.11 children, while Pakeha women of the same age had given birth to 2.76 children. However, between 1962–1982, the Maori total fertility rate fell by 63 percent, a substantial narrowing of the gap between Maori and non-Maori (Population of New Zealand, 1986, vol. 1).

4. Sahlins (1985:58–59) characterizes *tikanga* as follows:

    > The Maori world unfolds as one eternal return, the recurrent manifestation of the same experiences. The collapse of time and happening is mediated for Maoris by a third term: *tikanga:* the distinctive action of beings/things that come out of their particular nature.

5. According to Maori traditions, seven canoes set off from Hawai'iki (the original homeland) and landed in New Zealand. These canoes are believed to have contained the ancestors of the current population, with each tribal group ultimately tracing its links to one of the seven canoes (see Simmons 1976 and Hanson 1989 for discussions of this tradition).

6. Traditionally, all knowledge derived from ancestors, while history, was seen to be an "unfolding of generational stages" (Kernot 1983:192). Maori orators face the past, for it is the past that lies before an individual—*ngaa raa o mua* "the days in front"—while the future remains unseen and unseeable to all but a chosen few (Kernot 1983; Binney 1984; Sahlins 1985).

References

Aberle, David F.
> 1962 A Note on Relative Deprivation Theory as Applied to Millenarian and Other Cult Movements. *In* Millennial Dreams in Action. Syliva Thrupp, ed. Pp. 209–214. The Hague: Mouton.

Addiction Research Foundation
> 1989 Marijuana Smokers' Lungs Show Structural Changes. The Journal 18(1):3.

Aikman, C.C.
> 1982 Constitutional Development in the Cook Islands. *In* Pacific Constitutions. Peter Sack, ed. Pp. 87–96. Canberra: Australian National University.

Aitken, Robert
> 1930 Ethnology of Tubuai. Bernice P. Bishop Bulletin No. 40. Honolulu: Bernice P. Bishop Museum.

Aldrich, R., and J. Connell
> 1988 France in World Politics. London: Routledge.

Allen, M.
> 1969 Report on Aoba: Incidental Papers on Nduidui District, Aoba Island. C. Leaney, ed. Port Vila. (Mimeograph).

Alley, Roderick
> 1986 The Emergence of Party Politics. *In* Politics in Fiji: Studies in Contemporary History. B. Lal, ed. Pp. 28–51. Hawaii: The Institute for Polynesian Studies, Brigham Young University.

Amarshi, Azeem, Kenneth Good, and Rex Mortimer
> 1979 Development and Dependency, The Political Economy of Papua New Guinea. Melbourne: Oxford University Press.

Anderson, Benedict
> 1983 Imagined Communities: Reflections on the Origins and Spread of Nationalism. London: Verso.

Andrews, Edmund L.
  1990   Tiny Tonga Seeks Satellite Empire in Space. New York Times, August 28, 1990:1.
Anggo, David
  1975   Kafaina: Group Action by Women in Chuave. Yagl-Ambu 2(3):207–223.
Anonymous
  1979   Report of Visit to Papua New Guinea by District Apostle Kraus and Apostle Wagner,
          July. 1979.   Canada District News 1:28–30.
Asia Yearbook
  1984   Far Eastern Economic Review: Special Issue.
Austin, John L.
  1962   How To Do Things with Words. J. O. Urmson, ed. New York: Oxford University Press.
Azarya, V., and N. Chazan
  1987   Disengagement from the State in Africa: Reflections on the Experience of Ghana and
          Guinea. Comparative Studies in Society and History 29:106–131.
Back, Susan M., Robin D. Post, and Genet Darcy
  1982   A Study of Battered Women in a Psychiatric Setting. Women and Therapy 1:13–26.
Baker, Paul T., Joel M. Hanna, and Thelma S. Baker, eds.
  1986   The Changing Samoans: Behavior and Health in Transition. New York: Oxford University Press.
Ball, E.
  1982   Long Island, Papua New Guinea—European Exploration and Recorded Contacts to the
          End of The Pacific War. Records of the Australian Museum 34(10):447–461.
Barr, John, and Garry Trompf
  1983   Independent Churches and Recent Ecstatic Phenomena in Melanesia: A Survey of Materials.
          Oceania 14(1&2):51–72, 109–132.
Bascom, William
  1948   Ponapean Prestige Economy. Southwestern Journal of Anthropology 4:211–221.
Bateson, Gregory
  1958   Naven. Stanford: Stanford University Press.
Bedford, R.D., and G. Lloyd
  1982   Migration Between Polynesia and New Zealand 1971–1981: Who Are the Migrants? New
          Zealand Population Review 8(1):35–43.
Beil, Barry
  1977   Personal Communication to Lorraine Sexton.
Belich, James
  1986   The New Zealand Wars. Auckland: University of Auckland Press.
Bellam, M.
  1982   The Ebbing Tide: The Impact of Migration on Pacific Island Societies. Wellington: New
          Zealand Coalition for Trade and Development.
Bellwood, Peter
  1987   The Polynesians: Prehistory of an Island People. (rev. edition). New York: Thames and Hudson.
Belshaw, C.S.
  1950   The Significance of Modern Cults in Melanesian Development. The Australian Outlook 4:116–25.
  1954   Changing Melanesia. Melbourne: Oxford University Press.
Bergin, A.
  1983   Fisheries in the South Pacific. Asia Pacific Quarterly 22:20–32.

Bergmann, H.F.W.

    1955   Annual Report, Ega Lutheran Circuit. Kundiawa, Papua New Guinea: Evangelical Lutheran Church of New Guinea Office. (Mimeograph).

Berndt, R.M.

    1952   A Cargo Movement in the Central Highlands of New Guinea. Oceania 23:40–65, 137–158.

Bernstein, Richard

    1990   Review of The Duel, by Francois Billacois. The New York Times, 18 September.

Bertram, I.G.

    1986   'Sustainable Development' in Pacific Micro-Economies. World Development 14(7):809–822.

Bertram, I.G., and R.F. Watters

    1985   The MIRAB Economy of the South Pacific Microstates. Pacific Viewpoint 26:497–519.

Binney, Judith

    1966   Papahurihia: Some Thoughts on Interpretation. Journal of the Polynesian Society 75:321–331.

    1984   Myth and Explanation in the Ringatu Tradition. Journal of the Polynesian Society 93:345–398.

    1987   Maori Oral Narratives, Pakeha Written Texts: Two Forms of Telling History. New Zealand Journal of History 21:18–28.

Binney, Judith, and Gillian Chaplin

    1986   Nga Morehu. Wellington: Oxford University Press.

Binney, Judith, Gillian Chaplin, and Craig Wallace

    1979   Mihaia. Wellington: Oxford University Press.

Bollard, Alan E.

    1974   The Impact of Monetization in Tonga. Master's thesis, University of Auckland.

    1978   Grower Response to Commercial Cash Crop Production: A Theoretical Approach with Practical Policy Implications. In The Adaptation of Traditional Agriculture. Development Studies Centre Monograph No. 11. E.K. Fisk, ed. Pp. 324–342. Canberra: Australian National University.

Borofsky, Robert

    1987   Making History: Pukapukan and Anthropological Constructions of Knowledge. New York: Cambridge University Press.

Bradley, Christine

    (In press)   Should Human Rights Apply to Wives? Wife-beating and the Work of the Papua New Guinea Law Reform Commission. In Modern PNG Society. Laura Zimmer, ed. Bathurst, Australia: Crawford House Press.

    1989   Personal communication to Dorothy Counts.

Breeze, R.

    1981   The Thorn in France's Rose. Far Eastern Economic Review 113:30–33.

Bromby, Robin

    1990   Then There Is Light: The Hope After Bougainville. Pacific Islands Monthly 60(3):23–26.

Brookes, J.I.

    1969   International Rivalry in the Pacific Islands 1800–1875. New York: Russell and Russell.

Brookfield, H.C., with D. Hart

    1971   Melanesia: A Geographical Interpretation of an Island World. London: Methuen.

Brouard, F., and R. Grandperrin

    1985   Deep-Bottom Fishes of the Outer Reef Slope in Vanuatu. Port Vila: ORSTOM.

Buenaventura-Posso, Elisa, and Susan Brown

1980   Forced Transition from Egalitarianism to Male Dominance. *In* Women and Colonization. Mona Etienne and Eleanor Leacock, eds. Pp. 109–133. South Hadley: J.F. Bergin.

Bureau of Statistics

1979   Social Indicators for Fiji. Issue No. 4. Suva: Bureau of Statistics.

Burridge, Kenelm

1960   Mambu. London: Methuen.

1969   New Heaven, New Earth. Oxford: Basil Blackwell.

Burton-Bradley, Burton G.

1966   Papua and New Guinea Transcultural Psychiatry: Some Implications of Betel Chewing. The Medical Journal of Australia 2(15 October):744–746.

1980   Psychosomatics of Arecaidinism. Papua New Guinea Medical Journal 23(1):3–7.

Calkins, F.

1962   My Samoan Chief. Honolulu: University of Hawaii Press.

Cameron, John

1987   Fiji: the Political Economy of Recent Events. Capitol and Class 33:29–45.

Camp, Cheryl

(n.d.)   The Mt. Hurun Movement: The Peli Association and the New Apostolic Church. (Unpublished manuscript).

Campbell, I.C.

1989   A History of the Pacific Islands. Berkeley: University of California Press.

Carrier, J.G.

1981   Labour Migration and Labour Export on Ponam Island. Oceania 51(4):237–255.

Carrier, J.G., and A.H. Carrier

1989   Wage, Trade, and Exchange in Melanesia: A Manus Society in the Modern State. Berkeley: University of California Press.

Carucci, Laurence

1980   The Renewal of Life: A Ritual Encounter in the Marshall Islands. Doctoral Dissertation, The University of Chicago.

1983   Sly Moves: A Semiotic Analysis of Movement in Marshallese Culture. *In* Semiotics 1981. John N. Deely and Margot D. Lenhart, eds. pp. 139–151. New York: Plenum Press. [An expanded version appears in Semiotica 62(1–2):165–177.]

(n.d.)   Ritual Renewals: Negotiations of Power in an Island World. (Unpublished manuscript).

Cavanaugh, John, and Frederick F. Clairmonte

1985   Alcoholic Beverages: Dimensions of Corporate Power. New York: St. Martin's Press.

Chesneaux, Jean

1986   France in the Pacific: Global Approach or Respect for Regional Agendas? Bulletin of Concerned Asian Scholars 18:73–80.

Chowning, Ann

1985   Kove Women and Violence: The Context of Wife-beating in a West New Britain Society. *In* Domestic Violence in Papua New Guinea. Boroko: Law Reform Commission of Papua New Guinea Monograph No. 3. Susan Toft, ed. Pp. 14–31. Boroko.

Clastres, Pierre

1977   Society Against the State. New York: Urizen.

Cochrane, Glynne

1970   Big Men and Cargo Cults. Oxford: Clarendon Press.

Codrington, R.H.
    1891   The Melanesians: Studies in Their Anthropology and Folklore. Oxford: Clarendon Press.
Cohen, Anthony P.
    1975   The Management of Myths: The Politics of Legitimation in a Newfoundland Community. Manchester: Manchester University Press.
Cohn, Norman
    1957   The Pursuit of the Millennium. London: Secker & Warburg.
Connell, John
    1979   The Emergence of a Peasantry in Papua New Guinea. Peasant Studies 8:103–137.
    1980   Remittances and Rural Development: Migration, Dependency, and Inequality in the South Pacific. Development Studies Centre Occasional Paper No. 22. Canberra: Australian National University.
    1981   Remittances and Rural Development: Migration, Dependency and Inequity in the South Pacific. *In* Population Mobility and Development: Southeast Asia and the Pacific. Development Studies Centre Monograph No. 27. G.W. Jones and H.V. Richter, eds. Pp. 229–255. Canberra.
    1983   Migration, Employment, and Development in the South Pacific.Country Report No. 22, Western Samoa. Noumea: South Pacific Commission.
    1985   Migration, Employment, and Development in the South Pacific. Country Report No. 5, French Polynesia. International Labour Organization, South Pacific Commission. Suva, Fiji: South Pacific Commission.
    1990   Modernity and Its Discontents. *In* Migration and Development in the South Pacific. Pacific Research Monograph No. 24. John Connell, ed. Pp. 1–28. Canberra.
Conroy, J.D.
    1970   The Private Demand for Education in New Guinea: Consumption or Investment? Economic Record 46:497–516.
Cook, Jon
    1976   Subsistence Farmers and Fishermen of Tubuai. Doctoral Dissertation, University of Kansas.
Corris, P.
    1970   Pacific Island Labour Migrants in Queensland. Journal of Pacific History 5:43–64.
Counts, Dorothy Ayers
    1980   Fighting Back Is Not the Way: Suicide and the Women of Kaliai. American Ethnologist 7:332–351.
    1984   Revenge Suicide by Lusi Women: An Expression of Power. *In* Rethinking Women's Roles: Perspectives from the Pacific. Denise O'Brien and Sharon Tiffany, eds. Pp. 71–93. Berkeley: University of California Press.
    1987   Female Suicide and Wife Abuse in Cross Cultural Perspective. Suicide and Life Threatening Behavior 17(3):194–204.
    1988   Ambiguity in the Interpretation of Suicide—Female Death in Papua New Guinea. *In* Why Women Kill Themselves. David Lester, ed. Pp. 87–110. Springfield, Ill: Charles C. Thomas.
    1990a   Beaten Wife, Suicidal Woman: Domestic Violence in Kaliai, West New Britain. *In* Domestic Violence in Oceania. D. Counts, ed. (Special Issue) Pacific Studies 13(3):151–170.
    1990b   Domestic Violence in Oceania. D. Counts, ed. (Special Issue) Pacific Studies 13(3).
Crocombe, Ron
    1987   The South Pacific: An Introduction. New Zealand: Longman Paul Limited.
Crowe, Peter
    1986   Personal communication to W. Rodman.

Curtain, Richard
 1980   The Structure of Internal Migration in Papua New Guinea. Pacific Viewpoint 21:42–61.
Danielsson, Bengt
 1955   Raroia: Happy Island of the South Seas. Chicago: Rand McNally.
 1983   French Polynesia: Nuclear Colony. *In* Politics in Polynesia. A. Ali and R. Crocombe, eds.
        Pp. 192–226. Suva, Fiji: Institute of Pacific Studies.
David, G.
 1985   La Pêche Villageoise à Vanuatu: Rencensement 1—Moyens de Production et Production
        Globale. Notes et documents d'Océanographie No. 12. Port Vila: Mission ORSTOM.
Division of Economic Planning, Pohnpei
 1986   Economic and Social Statistics of Pohnpei State. Pohnpei: Department of Conservation Resources.
Douglas, E.M.K.
 1977   Sojourner or Settler? Population Movements Between Some Pacific Island States and New
        Zealand. *In* Migration and Health in New Zealand and the Pacific. J. Stanhope, ed. Pp.
        143–159. Wellington: Wellington Hospital Epidemiological Unit.
 1986   New Polynesian Voyagers: Visitors, Workers, and Migrants in New Zealand. *In* Circulation in the
        Third World. M. Chapman and R. Mansell Prothero, eds. Pp. 415–434. New York: Longman Paul.
Dower, John
 1986   War Without Mercy: Race and Power in the Pacific War. New York: Pantheon.
Downs, Ian
 1953   Annual Report, Eastern Highlands District. Goroka, Papua New Guinea: Goroka District
        Office. (Mimeograph.)
Errington, Frederick, and Deborah Gewertz
 1987a Cultural Alternatives and a Feminist Anthropology. Cambridge: Cambridge University Press.
 1987b The Remarriage of Yebiwali: A Study of Dominance and False Consciousness in a
        Non-Western Society. *In* Dealing with Inequality. Marilyn Strathern, ed. Pp. 63–88. Cam-
        bridge: Cambridge University Press.
Europa World Yearbook
 1985   French Overseas Territories: French Polynesia. In Vol. 2: 1666–1669. London: Europa
        Publications.
Fairbairn, T.I.J.
 1985   Island Economies: Studies from the South Pacific. Suva: Institute for Pacific Studies.
Fairbairn-Dunlop, P.
 1984   Aspects of Samoan Personality. Pacific Perspective 12(2):24–29.
FAO
 1982   FAO Commodity Review and Outlook 1981–82. Economic and Social Development
        Series No. 22. Rome: FAO.
 1983   FAO Commodity Review and Outlook 1982–83. Economic and Social Development
        Series No. 25. Rome: FAO.
Farrell, Bryan H., and Roger Ward
 1962   The Village and Its Agriculture. *In* Western Samoa: Land, Life and Agriculture in Tropical
        Polynesia. J.W. Fox and K.B. Cumberland, eds. Pp. 177–238. Christchurch: Whitcombe and
        Tombs, Ltd.
Feil, Daryl
 1984   Ways of Exchange. St. Lucia: University of Queensland.

Fiji Constitution

  1970   The Constitution of Fiji. *In* Extraordinary Fiji Royal Gazette Supplement. No.40. October, 1970 Pp. 362–450. Suva: Government Printing Office.

Fiji National Youth Council

  1977   Alcohol Problems with the Young People of Fiji. Fiji National Youth Council Seminar Report, June 17, 1977. Suva: Youth Development Resource Centre.

Fiji Times

  1987   September 5 Issue. Suva, Fiji.

Finney, Ben

  1973a   Big-Men and Business: Entrepreneurship and Economic Growth in the New Guinea Highlands. Honolulu: University Press of Hawaii.

  1973b   Polynesian Peasants and Proletarians. Cambridge, Mass.: Schenkman.

  1987   Business Development in the Highlands of Papua New Guinea. Pacific Islands Development Program Research Report No. 6. Honolulu: East-West Center.

Finney, Ben, and Karen Watson, eds.

  1977   A New Kind of Sugar: Tourism in the Pacific (2nd edition). Santa Cruz, Calif.: Center for South Pacific Studies.

Firth, Stewart

  1989   Sovereignty and Independence in the Contemporary Pacific. The Contemporary Pacific: A Journal of Island Affairs 1(1&2):75–96.

Fischer, John L.

  1974   The Role of the Traditional Chiefs on Ponape in the American Period. *In* Political Development in Micronesia. D. Hughes and S. Lingenfelter, eds. Pp. 167–177. Columbus: Ohio State University Press.

Fitzpatrick, Peter

  1980   Law and State in Papua New Guinea. London: Academic Press.

Fitzpatrick, Peter, and Lorraine Blaxter

  1976   The Law and Urbanisation. *In* An Introduction to the Urban Geography of Papua New Guinea. R. Jackson, ed. Pp. 71–87. Port Moresby: University of Papua New Guinea, Department of Geography.

Flack, Barry

  1979   Self-Help Housing: Papua New Guinea Case Study, Horsecamp Settlement Port Moresby. Bachelor's thesis (architecture), University of New South Wales.

Fox, Richard

  1989   Gandhian Utopia: Experiments with Culture. Berkeley: University of California Press.

France, Peter

  1969   The Charter of the Land. Melbourne: Oxford University Press.

Franco, R.W.

  1987   Samoans in Hawaii: A Demographic Profile. Honolulu: East-West Center, East-West Population Institute.

Franz, Marion J.

  1983   Diabetes Mellitus: Considerations in the Development of Guidelines for the Occasional Use of Alcohol. Journal of the American Dietetic Association 83(2):147–152.

Frazer, Helen

  1989   Niue Looks to Constitutional Separation from New Zealand. Pacific Report 2(11):3.

Fuchs, Stephen
   1965   Rebellious Prophets: A Study of Messianic Movements. New York: Asia Publishing House.
Fulop-Muller (sometimes Miller), Rene
   1935   Leaders, Dreamers and Rebels. London: Harrap.
Garnaut, Ross, Michael Wright, and Richard Curtain
   1977   Employment, Incomes and Migration in Papua New Guinea Towns. Institute of Applied
          Social and Economic Research Monograph 6. Boroko: IASER.
Geertz, Clifford
   1968   Thinking as a Moral Act: Ethical Dimensions of Anthropological Fieldwork in the New
          States. The Antioch Review 28:139–158.
Gerritson, Rolf
   1979   Groups, Classes and Peasant Politics in Ghana and Papua New Guinea. Doctoral Disser-
          tation, Australian National University.
Gesch, Patrick F.
   1985   Initiative and Initiation: A Cargo Cult-Type Movement in the Sepik Against Its Back-
          ground in Traditional Village Religion. St. Augustin: Anthropos-Institut.
Gewertz, Deborah
   1984   The Chambri View of Persons: A Critique of Individualism in the Works of Mead and
          Chodorow. American Anthropologist 86:615–629.
Ghai, Y.
   1985   Vanuatu. In Decentralisation in the South Pacific. P. Larmour and R. Qalo, eds. Pp. 42–73.
          Suva: University of the South Pacific.
Gibson, K.
   1983   Political Economy and Labour Migration: The Case of Polynesians in New Zealand. New
          Zealand Geographer 39(1):29–42.
Gilbert, Richard
   1986   Arecoline: Popular but Unknown. The Journal 15(7):7.
Gillion, K.L.
   1977   The Fiji Indians: Challenge to European Dominance 1920–1946. Canberra: Australian
          National University Press.
Goldhart, the Reverend
   1947, 1951–1953 Annual Reports: Asoroka Lutheran Mission. Lae, Papua New Guinea: Evan-
          gelical Lutheran Church of New Guinea Headquarters.
Good, Kenneth, and Mike Donaldson
   (In press)   The Development of Rural Capitalism in PNG: Coffee Production in the Eastern
          Highlands. History of Agriculture Discussion Paper No. 29, University of Papua New Guinea
          and the Department of Primary Industry, Port Moresby.
Goodman, Grant, and Felix Moos, eds.
   1981   The United States and Japan in the Western Pacific: Micronesia and Papua New Guinea.
          Boulder, Colo.: Westview Press.
Gordon, Sir Arthur
   1879   Letters and Notes Written During the Disturbances in the Highlands [...] of Viti Levu, Fiji.
          Edinburgh: privately Printed by R. and R. Clark. [Ayer Collection, Newberry Library, Chicago].
Government of Western Samoa
   1976   The Migration Report. Apia: Department of Statistics.

Greenhouse, C.
    1985   Mediation: A Comparative Approach. Man (N.S.) 20:90–114.
Greenland, Hauraki
    1984   Ethnicity as Ideology. *In* Tauiwi. Paul Spoonley, et al., eds. Pp. 86–102. Palmerston North: Dunmore Press.
Gregory, Christopher
    1982   Gifts and Commodities. New York: Academic Press.
Guha, R.
    1983   Elementary Forms of Peasant Insurgency in Colonial India. New Delhi: Oxford University Press.
Guiart, Jean
    1962   Les Réligions de l'Océanie. Paris: Presses Univérsitaires de France.
Gupta, Prakash C., Jens J. Pindborg, and Fali S. Mehta
    1982   Comparison of Carcinogenicity of Betel Quid with and without Tobacco: An Epidemiological Review. Ecology of Disease 1:213–219.
Habu, Bosanu
    1981   Personal communication to Lorraine Sexton.
Haddon, A.C.
    1917   Five New Religious Cults in British New Guinea. E.W.P. Chinnery and A.C. Haddon, co-authors. The Hibbert Journal 15(3):448–453.
Hanson, Alan
    1973   Political Change in Tahiti and Samoa: An Exercise in Experimental Anthropology. Ethnology 12(1):1–13.
    1989   The Making of the Maori: Culture Invention and Its Logic. American Anthropologist 91:890–902.
Harding, T.G.
    1967   Voyagers of the Vitiaz Strait: A Study of a New Guinea Trade System. Seattle: University of Washington.
Harrison, G.E.
    1974   The Availability of Foodstuffs and the Effects of Shortages on the Continued Development of Western Samoa. (Unpublished manuscript).
Hauser-Schaublin, Brigitta
    1977   Frauen in Kararau. Basel: Ethnologisches Seminar der Universität und Museum für Völkerkunde.
Hay, D.R., and F.H. Foster
    1981   The Influence of Race, Religion, Occupation and Other Social Factors on Cigarette Smoking in New Zealand. International Journal of Epidemiology 10(1):41–43.
Healey, Christopher
    1979   Women and Suicide in New Guinea. Social Analysis 2:89–106.
Heine, Carl
    1974   Micronesia at the Crossroads. Honolulu: University of Hawaii Press.
Heise, Lori
    1989   Violence Against Women. The Spectator, 26 April, p. A7. Hamilton, Ontario.
Hocart, A.M.
    1929   Kingship. Oxford: Oxford University Press.

Hofmann, Reverend Georg
1937–1938 Annual Reports: Asaroka Lutheran Mission. Lae, Papua New Guinea: Evangelical Lutheran Church of New Guinea Headquarters. (Mimeographs.)

Hohepa, P.
1978 Maori and Pakeha: The One People Myth. *In* Tihe Mauri Ora. M. King, ed. Pp. 98–111. Wellington: Methuen.

Honolulu Star-Bulletin & Advertiser
1990 Security Council Ends Most Isle Trusteeships. 23 December.

Hooper, A., and J. Huntsman
1973 A Demographic History of the Tokelau Islands. Journal of the Polynesian Society 82(4):366–411.

Hoskin, John O., Michael I. Friedman, and John E. Cawte
1969 A High Incidence of Suicide in a Preliterate-Primitive Society. Psychiatry 32:200–210.

Howe, K.R.
1984 Where the Waves Fall. Honolulu: University of Hawaii Press.

Howlett, Diana R.
1962 A Decade of Change in the Goroka Valley, New Guinea: Land Use and Development in the 1950s. Doctoral dissertation, Australian National University.
1973 Terminal Development: From Tribalism to Peasantry. *In* The Pacific in Transition: Geographical Perspectives on Adaptation and Change. Harold C. Brookfield, ed. Pp. 249–273. New York: St. Martin's Press.

Huber, Mary Taylor
1988 The Bishop's Progress: A Historical Ethnography of Catholic Missionary Experience on the Sepik Frontier. Washington and London: Smithsonian Institution Press.

Hughes, Ian
1973 Stone-Age Trade in the New Guinea Inland: Historical Geography without History. *In* The Pacific in Transition: Geographical Perspectives on Adaptation and Change. Harold C. Brookfield, ed. Pp. 97–126. New York: St. Martin's Press.

Hwekmarin, L., J. Jamenan, D. Lea, A. Ningiga, and M. Wangu
1971 Yangoru Cargo Cult, 1971. Journal of the Papua New Guinea Society 5:3–27.

Hyden, Goran
1980 Beyond Ujamaa in Tanzania: Underdevelopment and an Uncaptured Peasantry. London: Heinemann.

Iamo, Wari
1987 One of the Things That Brings Good Name Is Betel: A Keakalo Conception of Betel Use. *In* Drugs in Western Pacific Societies: Relations of Substance. ASAO Monograph No. 11. Lamont Lindstrom, ed. Pp. 135–148. Lanham, Md.: University Press of America.

Jacobson, Gerald, and S. H. Portuges
1978 Relation of Marital Separation and Divorce to Suicide: A Report. Suicide and Life Threatening Behavior 8:217–224.

Janes, C.
1990 Migration, Social Change, and Health: A Samoan Community in Urban California. Stanford: Stanford University Press.

JK Report on Micronesia
1989 Audit of Public Projects Makes Shocking Disclosures. February 1–3. Pohnpei.

Johnson, Giff
  1990   Micronesia in Review: Issues and Events, 1 July 1988 to 30 June 1989, Marshall Islands.
    The Contemporary Pacific: A Journal of Island Affairs 2(1):157–159.
Johnson, Patricia Lyons
  1981   When Dying Is Better Than Living: Female Suicide Among the Gainj of Papua New
    Guinea. Ethnology 20:325–334.
Joralemon (Lockwood), Victoria
  1983a   Agricultural Development and Socioeconomic Change on Tubuai, French Polynesia.
    Doctoral dissertation, University of California, Los Angeles.
  1983b   Collective Land Tenure and Agricultural Development: A Polynesian Case. Human
    Organization 42(2):95–105.
  1986   Development and Inequity: The Case of Tubuai, A Welfare Economy in Rural French
    Polynesia. Human Organization 45(4):283–295.
Josephides, Lisette
  1985   The Production of Inequality. London: Tavistock.
Jupp, J.
  1982   Custom, Tradition, and Reform in Vanuatu Politics. *In* Proceedings of the 1982 Politics
    Conference: Evolving Political Cultures in the Pacific Islands. Pp. 143–158. Laie, Hi.:
    Institute for Polynesian Studies.
Kamm, Henry
  1988   Fijians Fretting Under One-Man Rule. The New York Times, 22 July:2.
Kaplan, Martha
  1988a   Land and Sea and the New White Men: A Reconsideration of the Fijian *Tuka* Movement.
    Doctoral dissertation, University of Chicago.
  1988b   The Coups in Fiji: Colonial Contradictions and the Post-Colonial Crisis. Critique of
    Anthropology 8(3):93–116.
  1990   Meaning, Agency and Colonial History: Navosavakadua and the Tuka Movement in Fiji.
    American Ethnologist 17(1):3–22.
Keatinge, Richard W.
  1981   The Nature and Role of Religious Diffusion in the Early Stages of State Formation: An
    Example from Peruvian Prehistory. *In* The Transition to Statehood in the New World. Grant
    D. Jones and Robert R. Kautz eds. Pp.172–187. Cambridge: Cambridge University Press.
Keesing, Felix
  1941   The South Seas in the Modern World. New York: John Day.
Keesing, Roger
  1978   Politico-Religious Movements and Anticolonialism on Malaita: Maasina Rule in Histor-
    ical Perspective. Oceania 48:242–261; 49:46–73.
  1980   Antecedents of Maasina Rule: Some Further Notes. Journal of Pacific History
    15:102–107.
  1982   Kastom and Anticolonialism on Malaita: "Culture" as a Political Symbol. *In* Reinventing
    Traditional Culture: The Politics of Kastom in Island Melanesia. R. Keesing and R. Tonkinson,
    eds. (Special Issue) Mankind 13:357–373.
Kelly, John
  1988a   Bhakti and the Spirit of Capitalism in Fiji: The Ontology of the Fiji Indians. Doctoral
    dissertation, University of Chicago.

1988b   Fiji Indians and Political Discourse in Fiji: From the Pacific Romance to the Coups. Journal of Historical Sociology 1(4):399–422.

1989   Fear of Culture: British Regulation of Indian Marriage in Post-Indenture Fiji. Ethnohistory 36(4):372–391.

(1991)   A Politics of Virtue: Hinduism, Sexuality and Counter-Colonial Discourse in Fiji. Chicago: University of Chicago Press.

Kelly, John, and Martha Kaplan

1990   History, Structure and Ritual. Annual Review of Anthropology 19:119–150.

Kernot, B.J.

1983   The Meeting House in Contemporary New Zealand. *In* Art and Artists in Oceania. S. Mead and B. Kernot, eds. Pp. 181–197. California: Ethnographic Arts Publications.

Kilby, Peter

1969   Entrepreneurship and Economic Development. New York: Free Press.

King, Hilary, Paul Zimmet, L. Robin Raper, and Beverley Balkau

1984   Risk Factors for Diabetes in Three Pacific Populations. American Journal of Epidemiology 119(3):396–409.

Kiste, Robert C.

1974   The Bikinians: A Study in Forced Migration. Menlo Park, California: Cummings Publishing.

1976   The People of Enewetak Atoll Versus the U.S. Department of Defense. *In* Ethics and Anthropology. Michael Rynkwich and James Spradley, eds. Pp. 61–80. New York: John Wiley.

1983   The Fine Print of the Compacts. Pacific Islands Monthly 54(11):22–23.

1986   Termination of the U.S. Trusteeship in Micronesia. The Journal of Pacific History 21(3):127–138.

1989   The Pacific Islands, A Contemporary Overview. *In* Strategic Cooperation and Competition. Pp. 44–79. Washington, D.C.: National Defense University.

Knauft, Bruce M.

1985   Ritual Form and Permutation in New Guinea: Implications of Symbolic Process for Socio-Political Evolution. American Ethnologist 12:321–340.

1987   Managing Sex and Anger: Tobacco and Kava Use Among the Gebusi of Papua New Guinea. *In* Drugs in Western Pacific Societies: Relations of Substance. ASAO Monograph No. 11. Lamont Lindstrom, ed. Pp. 73–98. Lanham, Md.: University Press of America.

Knox, R.A.

1950   Enthusiasm. Oxford: Clarendon Press.

Kraus, M.

1978   Completion Work in the New Apostolic Church. Waterloo, Canada: New Apostolic Church.

Krause, Charles A.

1978   Guyana Massacre. New York: Berkley Publishing.

Krinks, Peter

1987   Embattled Brewers: The Continuing Struggle for San Miguel. Australian Geographer 18(2):165–170.

La Barre, Weston

1971   Materials for a History of Studies of Crisis Cults: A Bibliographic Essay. Current Anthropology 12(1):3–44.

Lal, Brij V.

1983 Girmityas: The Origins of the Fiji Indians. Canberra: The Journal of Pacific History.

1986 Politics in Fiji: Studies in Contemporary History. Honolulu: The Institute for Polynesian Studies, Brigham Young University.

1988 Power and Prejudice: The Making of the Fiji Crisis. Wellington: New Zealand Institute of International Affairs.

1990 As the Dust Settles: Impact and Implications of the Fiji Coups. (Special Issue) The Contemporary Pacific: A Journal of Island Affairs 2:1.

Lancy, D.F.

1978 Cognitive Testing in the Indigenous Mathematics Project. *In* The Indigenous Mathematics Project. D.F. Lancy, ed. (Special Issue) Papua New Guinea Journal of Education 14:114–142.

1979a Education Research 1976–1979: Reports and Essays. Port Moresby, Papua New Guinea: UNESCO/Education.

1979b Introduction. *In* The Community School. D.F. Lancy, ed. (Special Issue) Papua New Guinea Journal of Education 15:1–7.

1983 Cross-cultural Studies in Cognition and Mathematics. New York: Academic Press.

Land and Titles Court Records

(In press) Mulinuu and Tuasivi, Western Samoa.

Langmore, Diane

1974 Tamate—A King. Melbourne: Melbourne University Press.

Lanternari, V.

1965 [1960] The Religions of the Oppressed. New York: Mentor.

Lateef, Shireen

1986 Because They Have Nice Uniforms: The Career Aspirations of Schoolgirls in Suva, Fiji. *In* Development in the Pacific—What People Say. Pp. 45–57. Melbourne: Australian Council for Overseas Aid.

1990 Rule by the Dandas: Domestic Violence Among Indo-Fijians. *In* Domestic Violence in Oceania. D. Counts, ed. (Special Issue) Pacific Studies 13(3):43–62.

Law Reform Commission of Papua New Guinea.

1986 Marriage in Papua New Guinea. Boroko.

Lawrence, Peter

1954 Cargo Cults and Religious Beliefs Among the Garia. International Archives of Anthropology 47:1–20.

1964 Road Bilong Cargo. London: Manchester University Press.

Leahy, Michael J., and Maurice Crain

1937 The Land That Time Forgot: Adventures and Discoveries in New Guinea. New York: Funk and Wagnalls Co.

Lederman, Rena

1986 What Gifts Engender. Cambridge: Cambridge University Press.

Legislative Council of Fiji

1946 Extracts from Debates of July 1946. Suva: Government Press.

Lemert, Edwin M.

1967 The Secular Use of Kava—With Special Reference to Tonga. *In* Human Deviance, Social Problems, and Social Control. Edwin M. Lemert, ed. Pp. 234–245. Englewood Cliffs, N.J.: Prentice-Hall.

Lepowsky, Maria

    1982   A Comparison of Alcohol and Betelnut Use on Vanatinai (Sudest Island). *In* Through a Glass Darkly: Beer and Modernization in Papua New Guinea. Institute of Applied Social and Economic Research Monograph No. 18. Mac Marshall, ed. Pp. 325–342. Boroko, Papua New Guinea: IASER.

Levine, H.B.

    1987   The Cultural Politic of Maori Fishing: An Anthropological Perspective on the First Three Significant Waitangi Tribunal Hearings. Journal of the Polynesian Society 89:421–433.

LeVine, Robert A.

    1966   Dreams and Deeds: Achievement Motivation in Nigeria. Chicago: University of Chicago Press.

Lewthwaite, G.R., C. Mainzer, and P.J. Holland

    1973   From Polynesia to California: Samoan Migration and Its Sequelae. Journal of Pacific History 8:133–157.

Limbrock, Eberhard

    1912   Buschreise ins Hinterland von Buckin. Steyler Missionsbote 40:126–127,142–143.

Lindstrom, Lamont

    1984   Doctor, Lawyer, Wiseman, Priest: Big-men and Knowledge in Melanesia. Man (NS) 19:291–309.

    1987   Drunkenness and Gender on Tanna, Vanuatu. *In* Drugs in Western Pacific Societies: Relations of Substance. ASAO Monograph No. 11. Lamont Lindstrom, ed. Pp. 99–118. Lanham, Md.: University Press of America.

Lingenfelter, Sherwood

    1977   Socioeconomic Change in Oceania. Oceania 48(2):102–120.

Lockwood, Victoria

    1988   Development, French Neocolonialism, and the Structure of the Tubuai Economy. Oceania 58(3):176–192.

    1990   Development and Return Migration to Rural French Polynesia. International Migration Review 24(2):347–371.

Lutz, Catherine

    1989   Unnatural Emotions: Everyday Sentiments on a Micronesian Atoll and Their Challenge to a Western Theory. Chicago: University of Chicago Press.

MacClancy, J.

    1981   To Kill a Bird with Two Stones: A Short History of Vanuatu. Port Vila: Vanuatu Cultural Centre.

Macdonald, B.

    1986   The Lesa Case, and the Citizenship (Western Samoa) Act, 1982. *In* New Zealand and International Migration. A. Trlin and P. Spoonley, eds. Palmerston North: Massey University.

MacLennan, Robert, Darius Paissat, Anne Ring, and Steve Thomas

    1985   Possible Aetiology of Oral Cancer in Papua New Guinea. Papua New Guinea Medical Journal 28:3–8.

Macnaught, Timothy

    1982   The Fijian Colonial Experience: A Study of the Neotraditional Order Under British Colonial Rule Prior to World War II. Pacific Research Monograph No. 7. Canberra: Australian National University.

Macpherson, C.

1976   Polynesians in New Zealand: An Emerging Eth-class? *In* Social Class in New Zealand. D. Pitt, ed. Pp. 99–112. Auckland: Longman Paul.

1981   Guest-Worker Movements and Their Consequences for Donor and Recipient Countries: A Case Study. *In* Population Mobility and Development: Southeast Asia and the Pacific. Development Studies Centre Monograph No. 27. G.W. Jones and H.V. Richter, eds. Pp. 257–277. Canberra.

1985   Public and Private Views of Home: Will Western Samoan Migrants Return? Pacific Viewpoint 26(1):242–262.

Macpherson, C., and L. Macpherson

1987   Towards an Explanation of Recent Trends in Suicide in Western Samoa. Man 22:305–327.

Madsen, William

1974   The American Alcoholic: The Nature-Nurture Controversy in Alcoholic Research and Therapy. Springfield, Ill.: Charles C. Thomas.

Makemson, Maude W.

1941   The Morning Star Rises: An Account of Polynesian Astronomy. New Haven: Yale University Press.

Mamak, Alex

1978   Colour, Culture and Conflict. Sydney: Pergamon Press.

Marcus, George E.

1974   A Hidden Dimension of Family Development in the Modern Kingdom of Tonga. Journal of Comparative Family Studies 5:87–102.

1978   Land Tenure and Elite Formation in the Neotraditional Monarchies of Tonga and Buganda. American Ethnologist 5(3):509–534.

1980   The Nobility and the Chiefly Tradition in the Modern Kingdom of Tonga. The Polynesian Society Memoir No. 42. Wellington: The Polynesian Society.

Marshall, Donald

1961   Ra'ivavae: An Expedition to the Most Fascinating and Mysterious Island in Polynesia. New York: Doubleday.

Marshall, Mac

1979   Weekend Warriors: Alcohol in a Micronesian Culture. Palo Alto, Calif.: Mayfield Publishing.

1987a   An Overview of Drugs in Oceania. *In* Drugs in Western Pacific Societies: Relations of Substance. ASAO Monograph No. 11. Lamont Lindstrom, ed. Pp. 13–49. Lanham, Md.: University Press of America.

1987b   'Young Men's Work': Alcohol Use in the Contemporary Pacific. *In* Contemporary Issues in Mental Health Research in the Pacific Islands. Albert B. Robillard and Anthony J. Marsella, eds. Pp. 72–93. Honolulu: Social Science Research Institute, University of Hawaii.

1988   Alcohol Consumption as a Public Health Problem in Papua New Guinea. International Journal of the Addictions 23(6):573–589.

(n.d.)   The Second Fatal Impact: Cigarette Smoking, Chronic Disease, and the Epidemiological Transition in Oceania. Social Science and Medicine.

Marshall, Mac, and Leslie B. Marshall

1976   Holy and Unholy Spirits: The Effects of Missionization on Alcohol Use in Eastern Micronesia. Journal of Pacific History 11(3):135–166.

1990   Silent Voices Speak: Women and Prohibition in Truk. Belmont, Calif.: Wadsworth Publishing.

Marti, Fritz
1980   Report of Trip to Papua New Guinea (South Pacific Ocean) by Apostles Wagner and Woll and Priests Klebe and Marti, June 1980. Canada District News 2(3):47–49.

Matane, P.
1986   A Philosophy of Education for Papua New Guinea. Ministerial Committee Report, November 1986. Boroko: National Catholic Education Secretariate.

Mathews, John D., et al.
1988   Effects of the Heavy Usage of Kava on Physical Health: Summary of a Pilot Survey in an Aboriginal Community. The Medical Journal of Australia 148:548–555.

Mathie, Alison, and Elizabeth Cox
1987   New Directions for Women in Non-Formal Education. Waigani, Papua New Guinea: Office of Women's Affairs.

Maugh, Thomas H. II
1982   Marijuana 'Justifies Serious Concern'. Science 215:1488–1489.

May, R.J.
1982   The View from Hurun: The Peli Association. *In* Micronationalist Movements in Papua New Guinea. R.J. May, ed. Pp.32–62. Canberra: Australian National University.

McClelland, David C.
1961   The Achieving Society. Princeton: Van Nostrand.

McHenry, Donald F.
1975   Micronesia: Trust Betrayed. New York and Washington: Carnegie Endowment for International Peace.

McKinnon, K.R.
1968   Education in Papua and New Guinea: Current Directions and Future Challenges. Australian Journal of Education 12(1):102–105.

McSwain, Romola
1977   The Past and Future People. Melbourne: Oxford University Press.

Mead, Margaret
1933   Unpublished Field Notes. Washington, D.C.: Library of Congress.
1935   Sex and Temperment in Three Primitive Societies. New York: William Morrow.

Meggitt, Mervyn J.
1971   From Tribesmen to Peasants: The Case of the Mae Enga of New Guinea. *In* Anthropology in Oceania: Essays Presented to Ian Hogbin. L.R. Hiatt and Chandra Jayawardena, eds. Pp. 191–209. San Francisco: Chandler Publishing Co.

Metge, Joan
1976   The Maoris of New Zealand. London: Routledge and Kegan Paul.

Mishra, Vijay
1979   Rama's Banishment: A Centenary Tribute to the Fiji Indians, 1879–1979. London: Heinemann Educational Books.

Moore, S. F.
1978   Law and Social Change: The Semi-Autonomous Social Field as an Appropriate Subject of Study. *In* Law as Process: An Anthropological Approach. S.F. Moore, ed. Pp. 54–81. London: Routledge and Kegan Paul.

Morauta, Louise

 1985   Urban Movement and Rural Identity: A Papua New Guinea Example. Pacific Viewpoint 26:221–241.

 1986   Law and Order in Papua New Guinea. *In* Law and Order in a Changing Society. Louise Morauta, ed. Pp. 7–19. Canberra: Australian National University Press.

Morauta, Louise, and Dawn Ryan

 1982   From Temporary to Permanent Townsmen: Migrants From the Malalaua District, Papua New Guinea. Oceania 53:39–55.

Moynagh, Michael

 1981   Brown or White? A History of the Fiji Sugar Industry, 1873–1973. Pacific Research Monograph No. 5. Canberra: Australian National University.

Mulderink, A.

 1980   Aibale Timotheus: One of Papua New Guinea's Remarkable Men. Northeast New Guinea 1(2):13–19.

Muller, Mike

 1978   Tobacco and the Third World: Tomorrow's Epidemic? London: War on Want.

Murphy, H.B.M.

 1983   Assignment Report: Promotion of Community Psychiatry. Manila: World Health Organization, Regional Office for the Western Pacific.

Narakobi, Bernard

 1974   Who Will Take Up Peli's Challenge? Point 1:93–104.

Nations Health

 1989   July, p. 6.

Nero, Karen L.

 1985   The Roots of Identity: Gender and Alcohol/Drug Use in Palau. Paper presented at 84th Annual Meeting of the American Anthropological Association, Washington, D.C.

 1990 The Hidden Pain: Drunkenness and Domestic Violence in Palau. *In* Domestic Violence in Oceania. D. Counts, ed. (Special Issue) Pacific Studies 13(3):63–92.

New Zealand

 1986   New Zealand Census 1986. *In* Population of New Zealand, Vol. 1. Auckland.

New Zealand Planning Council

 1986   The New Zealand Population: Change, Composition and Policy Implications. Auckland.

Newbury, Colin

 1980   Tahiti Nui: Change and Survival in French Polynesia 1767–1945. Honolulu: University of Hawaii Press.

Newman, Philip L.

 1965   Knowing the Gururumba. New York: Holt, Rinehart and Winston.

 1979   Personal communication to Lorraine Sexton.

Newsweek

 1989   May 8, p. 13.

Niuginis Nius

 1990   March 8, Pp. 1–2.

 1981   March 4.

Norton, Robert
    1977   Race and Politics in Fiji. New York: St. Martin's Press.

O'Collins, Maev, ed.
    1986   Youth and Society: Perspectives from Papua New Guinea. Canberra: Australian National University Press.

O'Connell, D.P.
    1969   The Condominium of the New Hebrides. British Yearbook of International Law 43:71–145.

O'Grady, J.
    1961   No Kava for Johnny. Auckland: Ure Smith.

Oliver, Douglas
    1981   Two Tahitian Villages: A Study in Comparison. Honolulu: The Institute for Polynesian Studies.
    1989a   The Pacific Islands (3rd. ed.). Honolulu: University of Hawaii Press.
    1989b   Oceania: The Native Cultures of Australia and the Pacific Islands. (2 vols.) Honolulu: University of Hawaii Press.

O'Meara, Tim
    1987   Samoa: Customary Individualism. *In* Land Tenure in the Pacific (3rd ed). R. G. Crocombe, ed. Pp. 74–113. Suva: University of the South Pacific Press.
    1990   Samoan Planters: Tradition and Economic Development in Polynesia. New York: Holt, Rhinehart & Winston.

Oram, N.D.
    1970   Indigenous Housing in Port Moresby. *In* Port Moresby Urban Development. New Guinea Research Bulletin 37:45–89.
    1974   Urban Expansion and Customary Land. *In* Problems of Choice Land in Papua New Guinea's Future. Peter G. Sack, ed. Pp. 170–180. Canberra: Australian National University Press.
    1976   Colonial Town to Melanesian City: Port Moresby 1884–1974. Canberra: Australian National University Press.

Orange, Claudia
    1987   The Treaty of Waitangi. Wellington: Allen and Unwin.

Overseas Fiji Times
    1988   November 11 Issue. San Jose, Calif.

Pacific Islands Monthly
    1980   Independence Not On. Vol. 51 (July-December):23.
    1986   Move to Outlaw Cigarette Ads. Vol. 57(11):6.
    1989   Brewing on the Rise. Vol. 59(17):30–31.

Pagelow, Mildred Daley
    1984   Family Violence. New York: Praeger.

Pataki-Schweizer, K.J.
    1985   Suicide in Contemporary Papua New Guinea: An Attempt at an Overview. *In* Culture, Youth and Suicide in the Pacific. F.X. Hezel, Donald Rubinstein, and Geoffrey White, eds. Pp. 139–151. Honolulu: Pacific Islands Studies Program.

Patrick, R.C., I.A.M. Prior, J.C. Smith, and A.H. Smith
    1983   Relationship Between Blood Pressure and Modernity Among Ponapeans. International Journal of Epidemiology 12(1):36–44.

Patrol Reports, Various (Finschafen)

(n.d.)   National Archives, Port Moresby, Papua New Guinea.

Pearson, David

1984   Two Paths of Colonialism. *In* Tauiwi. Paul Spoonley, et al., eds. Pp. 203–222. Palmerston North: Dunmore Press.

Peoples, James

1985   Island in Trust: Culture Change and Dependence in a Micronesian Economy. Boulder, Colo.: Westview.

Petersen, Glenn

1979   Breadfruit or Rice?: The Political Economics of a Vote in Micronesia. Science & Society 43:472–485.

1982   Ponapean Matriliny. American Ethnologist 9:129–144.

1985   A Cultural Analysis of the Ponapean Independence Vote in the 1983 Plebiscite. Pacific Studies 9:13–52.

1987   Redistribution in a Micronesian Commercial Economy. Oceania 57:83–98.

1990a   Some Overlooked Complexities of Pohnpei Social Complexity. Micronesica. *In press*.

1990b   Free Labour in Colonial Pohnpei. *In* Labour in the South Pacific. C. Moore and J. Leckey, eds. Townsville: James Cook University Press.

Philpott, Malcolm

1972   Economic Development in the Sepik River Basin. Port Moresby, Papua New Guinea: Department of Transport.

Pitt, D., and C. Macpherson

1974   Emerging Pluralism. New York: Longman Paul.

Pollock, Nancy

1969   A Pragmatic View of Marshallese Christmas Ritual. University of Hawaii Library Prize Paper for Pacific Research, University of Hawaii. Hamilton Library. (Unpublished manuscript).

1978   Takapoto: La Prosperité, retour aux îles. Journal de la Société des Océanistes 60(34):133–135.

Polloi, Tony

1985   Personal communication to Mac Marshall.

Pomponio, Alice

1983   Namor's Odyssey: Education and Development on Mandok Island, Papua New Guinea. Doctoral dissertation, Bryn Mawr College.

1985   The Teacher as a Key Symbol. Papua New Guinea Journal of Education 21(2):237–252.

1990a   Seagulls Don't Fly Into the Bush: Cultural Identity and Development on Mandok. *In* Cultural Identity and Ethnicity in the Pacific. Jocelyn Linnekin and Lin Poyer, eds. Pp. 43–79. Honolulu: University of Hawaii.

1990b   What Did the Earthquake Mean? *In* The Humbled Anthropologist: Tales From the Pacific. Philip R. DeVita, ed. Pp. 35–45. Belmont, Calif.: Wadsworth.

1992   Seagulls Don't Fly Into the Bush: Cultural Identity and Development in Melanesia. Belmont, Calif.: Wadsworth.

Pomponio, Alice, and D. Lancy

1986   A Pen or a Bushknife? School, Work and "Personal Investment" in Papua New Guinea. Anthropology and Education Quarterly 17(1):40–61.

Posposil, L.

1958   Kapauka Papuans and Their Law. Yale University Publications in Anthropology No. 54. New Haven: Department of Anthropology, Yale University.

1969   Structural Change and Primitive Law: Consequences of a Papuan Legal Case. *In* Law in Culture and Society. L. Nader, ed. Pp. 208–229. Chicago: Aldine.

1978   The Ethnology of Law. Menlo Park, Calif.: Cummings Publishing.

Pournelle, Jerry

1977   High Justice. New York: Pocket Books.

Premdas, R.

1985   Rebellion, Decentralization, and the State in the Southwest Pacific: The Case of Vanuatu. Kabar Sebarang 19:1–23.

1986   Melanesian Socialism: Vanuatu's Quest for Self-Definition. Pacific Islands Group, Centre for Developing Nations Monograph No. 1. McGill University.

1987a   Melanesian Socialism: Vanuatu's Quest for Self-Definition. The Journal of Commonwealth and Comparative Politics 25:141–160.

1987b   Melanesian Socialism: Vanuatu's Quest for Self-Definition and Problems of Implementation. Pacific Studies 11:107–129.

Ranney, Austin, and Howard R. Penniman

1985   Democracy in the Islands: The Micronesian Plebiscites of 1983. Washington, D.C.: American Enterprise Institute for Public Policy Research.

Read, Kenneth E.

1952   Nama Cult of the Central Highlands, New Guinea. Oceania 23:1–25.

1959   Leadership and Consensus in a New Guinean Society. American Anthropologist 64:425–436.

1965   The High Valley. New York: Charles Scribner's Sons.

Reay, Marie

1975   Politics, Development, and Women in the Rural Highlands. Administration for Development 5:4–12.

1980   Personal communication to Lorraine Sexton.

1987   Laying Down the Law in Their Own Fashion. *In* Anthropology in the High Valleys: Essays on the New Guinea Highlands in Honor of Kenneth E. Read. L.L. Langness and Terence E. Hays, eds. Pp. 73–108. Novato, Calif.: Chandler & Sharp Publishers, Inc.

Redmond, R.

1989   Torn Between Two Cultures: Samoans Struggle to Adapt. Seattle Post-Intelligencer, 30 August:A1–A5.

Republic of Vanuatu

1982   The First National Development Plan 1982–1986. Port Vila: National Planning and Statistics Office.

1983   Report on the Census of Population 1979. Vol. 1: Basic Tables. Vila, Vanuatu: National Planning and Statistics Office.

1984   The Mid-Term Review of Vanuatu's First National Development Plan. Port Vila: National Planning and Statistics Office.

Richards, Dorothy E.

1957   United States Naval Administration of the Pacific Islands (3 vols.) Washington, D.C.: U.S. Government Printing Office.

Ridings, P.J.

  1983   Resource Use Arrangements in Southwest Pacific Fisheries. Honolulu: East-West Center.

Riesenberg, Saul

  1968   The Native Polity of Ponape. Washington: Smithsonian Institution.

Riley, Malcolm, and John Mathews

  1989   Heavy Kava Use by Aboriginal Australians. *In* Kava: Use and Abuse in Australia and the South Pacific. John Prescott and Grant McCall, eds. pp.26–28. Kensington, NSW: National Drug & Alcohol Research Centre, University of New South Wales.

Rodman, Margaret

  1983   Following Peace: Indigenous Pacification of a Northern New Hebridean Society. *In* The Pacification of Melanesia. ASAO Monograph No. 7. M. Rodman and M. Cooper, eds. Pp. 141–160. Lanham, Md.: University Press of America.

  1986   Remre Fishing Association: A Socio-Economic Evaluation. Report Prepared for CUSO. Vanuatu. (Unpublished manuscript).

  1987a   Constraining Capitalism? Contradictions of Self-Reliance in Vanuatu Fisheries Development. American Ethnologist 14(4):108–122.

  1987b   Masters of Tradition: Consequences of Customary Land Tenure in Longana, Vanuatu. Vancouver: UBC Press.

  1989   Deep Water: Development and Change in Pacific Village Fisheries. Boulder, Colo.: Westview.

Rodman, William

  1985   'A Law Unto Themselves': Legal Innovation in Ambae, Vanuatu. American Ethnologist 12:603–624.

Rodman, William, and Margaret Rodman

  1985   Rethinking Kastom: On the Politics of Place Naming in Vanuatu. Oceania 56:242–251.

Rogers, Robert F.

  1988   Guam's Commonwealth Effort 1987–1988. Guam: Micronesian Area Research Center, University of Guam.

Roscoe, Paul B.

  1983   People and Planning in the Yangoru Subdistrict, East Sepik Province, Papua New Guinea. Doctoral dissertation, University of Rochester.

  1988   The Far Side of Hurun: The Management of Melanesian Millenarian Movements. American Ethnologist 15:515–529.

Rubinstein, R.

  1981   Knowledge and Political Process on Malo. *In* Vanuatu: Politics, Economics and Ritual in Island Melanesia. M. Allen, ed. Pp. 135–172. Sydney: Academic Press.

Ryan, Dawn

  1977   Toaripi in Port Moresby and Lae. *In* Change and Movement. R.J. May ed. Pp. 147–154. Canberra: Papua New Guinea Institute of Applied Social and Economic Research and Australian National University Press.

  1985   Bilocality and Movement Between Village and Town: Toaripi, Papua New Guinea. *In* Circulation in Population Movement. Murray Chapman and R. Mansell Prothero, eds. Pp. 251–268. London: Routledge and Kegan Paul.

Rynkiewich, Michael

  1972   Land Tenure Among Arno Marshallese. Doctoral Dissertation, University of Minnesota.

Sacerdoti, Guy
1982   Cracks in the Coconut Shell. Far Eastern Economic Review 8(January):45.
Sahlins, Marshall
1958   Social Stratification in Polynesia. Seattle: University of Washington Press.
1972   Stone Age Economics. Chicago: Aldine-Atherton.
1985   Islands of History. Chicago: University of Chicago Press.
Salisbury, Richard F.
1956   Asymmetrical Marriage Systems. American Anthropologist 58:639–655.
1962a   From Stone to Steel: Economic Consequences of a Technological Change in New Guinea. Victoria: Melbourne University Press, for The Australian National University.
1962b   Early Stages of Economic Development in New Guinea. Journal of the Polynesian Society 71:328–339.
Salisbury, Richard, and Elizabeth Tooker, eds.
1985   Affluence and Cultural Survival. Washington: American Ethnological Society.
Salmond, Ann
1982   Theoretical Landscape on a Cross Cultural Conception of Knowledge. *In* Semantic Anthropology. ASAO Monograph 22. David Parkin, ed. Pp. 65–88. London: Academic Press.
Salmond, Clare E., Jill G. Joseph, Ian A.M. Prior, Don G. Stanley, and Albert F. Wessen
1985   Longitudinal Analysis of the Relationship Between Blood Pressure and Migration: The Tokelau Island Migrant Study. American Journal of Epidemiology 122(2):291–301.
Samoa Times
1977   January 28.
Sanadhya, Totaram, and Benarsidas Chaturvedi
(n.d.)   My Twenty-One Years in the Fiji Islands. John D. Kelly and Uttra Singh, transls. Suva: The Fiji Museum.
Scaglion, Richard
1990a   Legal Adaptation in a Papua New Guinea Village Court. Ethnology 29:17–33.
1990b   Spare the Rod and Spoil the Woman? Family Violence in Abelam Society. *In* Domestic Violence in Oceania. D. Counts, ed. (Special Issue) Pacific Studies 13(3):189–204.
Scarr, Derryck
1967   Recruits and Recruiters. Journal of Pacific History 2:15–24.
1980   Viceroy of the Pacific, A Life of Sir John Bates Thurston. Pacific Research Monograph No. 4. Canberra: The Australian National University.
1984   Fiji: A Short History. Sydney: George Allen and Unwin Australia.
Schwartz, T.
1962   The Paliau Movement in the Admiralty Islands 1946–1954. Anthropological Papers of the American Museum of Natural History 49(2). New York.
Schwartz, Richard H., Paul J. Gruenewald, Michael Klitzner, and Paul Fedio
1989   Short-Term Memory Impairment in Cannabis-Dependent Adolescents. American Journal of Diseases of Children 143:1214–1219.
Scott, Dick
1981   Ask That Mountain. Auckland: Heinemann.
Scott, J.
1985   Weapons of the Weak: Everyday Forms of Peasant Resistance. New Haven: Yale University Press.

1986   Resistance Without Protest and Without Organization: Peasant Opposition to the Islamic *Zakat* and the Christian Tithe. Comparative Studies in Society and History 29:417–452.

Sevele, F.V.

1973   Regional Inequalities in Socio-Economic Development in Tonga: A Preliminary Study. Doctoral Dissertation, University of Canterbury, New Zealand.

Sexton, Lorraine

1986   Mothers of Money, Daughters of Coffee. Ann Arbor: UMI Research Press.

Shankman, P.

1976   Migration and Underdevelopment: The Case of Western Samoa. Boulder, Colo.: Westview Press.

Shineberg, D.

1967   They Came for Sandalwood: A Study of the Sandalwood Trade in the South West Pacific 1830–1865. Melbourne: Melbourne University Press.

Shore, Bradd

1982   Sala'ilua: A Samoan Mystery. New York: Columbia University Press.

Shutler, R., and M.E. Shutler

1975   Oceanic Prehistory. Menlo Park, Calif.: Cummings Publishing.

Simmons, D.R.

1976   The Great New Zealand Myth: A Study of the Discovery and Origin Traditions of the Maori. Wellington: Reed.

Sinclair, Douglas

1977   Land: Maori View and European Response. *In* Te Ao Hurihuri. M. King, ed. Pp. 107–128. New Zealand: Hicks Smith.

Smith, Carol A.

1976   Exchange Systems and the Spatial Distribution of Elites: The Organization of Stratification in Agrarian Societies. *In* Regional Analysis: Social Systems. Carol A. Smith, ed. Pp. 175–243. New York: Academic Press.

Smith, David

1983   An Anti-Smoking Movement for Papua New Guinea. Papua New Guinea Medical Journal 26(1):59–61.

Smith, Robert

1978   Personal communication to Lorraine Sexton.

Sorrenson, M.P.K.

1987   Towards a Radical Reinterpretation of New Zealand History: The Role of the Waitangi Tribunal. New Zealand Journal of History 21:173–188.

South Seas Digest

1986   Reagan Signs Micronesia Compacts. Vol. 5(21):1.

Stanhope, John M., and Ian A.M. Prior

1982   Alcohol, Smoking and Pregnancy Outcome Among New Zealand Maori. Australian Alcohol/Drug Review 1:74–76.

Stanley, D.

1986   South Pacific Handbook (3rd edition). Chico, Calif.: Moon Publications.

Stark, Evan, and Anne H. Flitcraft

1985   Spouse Abuse. Working paper solicited and edited by the Violence Epidemiology Branch, Center for Health Promotion and Education, Centers for Disease Control, Atlanta,

Georgia, as a background document for the Surgeon General's Workshop on Violence and Public Health. October. Leesburg, Virginia.

Starr, J., and J. Collier

1987   Historical Studies of Legal Change. Current Anthropology 28:367–372.

Stebbins, Kenyon R.

1990   Transnational Tobacco Companies and Health in Underdeveloped Countries: Recommendations for Avoiding a Smoking Epidemic. Social Science & Medicine 30:227–235.

Steinbauer, Friedrich

1979   Melanesian Cargo Cults. Max Wohlwill, trans. London: George Prior Publishers.

Stephens, B. Joyce

1985   Suicidal Women and Their Relationships with Husbands, Boyfriends, and Lovers. Suicide and Life Threatening Behavior 15:77–90.

Strathern, Marilyn

1988   The Gender of the Gift. Berkeley: University of California Press.

Sutter, F.K.

1989   The Samoans: A Global Family. Honolulu: University of Hawaii Press.

Swatridge, C.

1985   Delivering the Goods: Education as Cargo in Papua New Guinea. Melbourne: Melbourne University Press.

Tagupa, W.

1976   France, French Polynesia, and the South Pacific in the Nuclear Age. *In* Oceania and Beyond: Essays on the Pacific Since 1945. F. King, ed. Pp. 200–215. Westport, Conn.: Greenwood.

TamTam Government Newspaper of Vanuatu

1981   21 November:2

1982   20 February:1

Tawney, R.H.

1926   Religion and the Rise of Capitalism. New York: Harcourt, Brace and Company.

Tenorio, Froilan Cruz

1989   1988 Annual Report, Office of the Resident Representative to the United States of America for the Northern Mariana Islands. Washington, D.C.

Theile, Kenneth

1957   Annual Report, Kewamugl Bible School. Copy located at Nomane Lutheran Mission, Chimbu (Simbu Province). (Mimeograph).

Thomas, Nicolas

1989   The Force of Ethnology: Origins and Significance of the Melanesia/Polynesia Division. Current Anthropology 30(1):27–41.

Thompson, V., and R. Adloff

1971   The French Pacific Islands. Berkeley: University of California Press.

Times of Papua New Guinea

1986a   October 16, p. 5.

1986b   July 7, p. 5.

1986c   December 4, p. 1.

Tinker, Hugh

1974   A New System of Slavery: The Export of Indian Labour Overseas 1830–1920. London: Oxford University Press.

Toft, Susan, ed.

    1985   Domestic Violence in Papua New Guinea. Law Reform Commission of Papua New Guinea, Monograph No. 3. Boroko.

Tousignant, Michel, and Brian L. Mishara

    1981   Suicide and Culture: A Review of the Literature (1969–1980). Transcultural Psychiatric Research Review 18:5–32.

Turner, Victor

    1969   The Ritual Process: Structure and Anti-Structure. Chicago: Aldine Publishing Company.

Turner, Victor, and Edith Turner

    1978   Image and Pilgrimage in Christian Culture. New York: Columbia University Press.

U.S. Department of State

    1985   Trust Territory of the Pacific Islands. 38th Annual Report to the United Nations. Washington, D.C.: U.S. State Department.

Valjavec, F.

    1986   Anthropology in Vanuatu: A Selected Survey of Research. Anthropos 81:616–629.

van Gennep, Arnold

    1960   The Rites of Passage. Chicago: University of Chicago Press.

Vayda, Andrew

    1959   Native Traders in Two Polynesian Atolls. Cahiers de L'Institut de Science Économique Appliquée: Humanités, Série V, no.1:119–137.

Wade, R.

    1988   Village Republics: Economic Conditions for Collective Action in South India. Cambridge: Cambridge University Press.

Wallace, Anthony F.C.

    1956   Revitalization Movements. American Anthropologist 58:264–281.

Walsh, A.C.

    1982   Samoa: Migration, Urbanization and Development in South Pacific Countries. In United Nations Economic and Social Commission for Asia and the Pacific. Pp. 81–99. Bangkok, Thailand: United Nations.

Walsh, A., and A. Trlin

    1973   Niuean Migration: Niuean Socioeconomic Background, Characteristics of Migrants, and Their Settlement in Auckland. Journal of the Polynesian Society 82(1):47–85.

Ward, Martha

    1989   Nest in the Wind: Adventure in Anthropology on a Tropical Island. Prospect Heights, Ill.: Waveland.

Warry, Wayne

    1982   Bia and Bisnis: The Use of Beer in Chuave Ceremonies. In Through a Glass Darkly: Beer and Modernization in Papua New Guinea. IASER Monograph No. 18. Mac Marshall, ed. Pp. 83–103. Boroko: Papua New Guinea Institute of Applied Social & Economic Research.

Washington Pacific Report

    1986   Reagan Signs Compact into Law. Washington Pacific Report 4(8):1.

Watson, Pamela

    1987   Drugs in Trade. In Drugs in Western Pacific Societies: Relations of Substance. ASAO Monograph No. 11. Lamont Lindstrom, ed. Pp. 119–134. Lanham, Md.: University Press of America.

Weber, Max

    1947[1964]   The Theory of Social and Economic Organization. Talcott Parsons, ed. Glencoe: The Free Press.

Webster, Peter
    1979   Rua and the Maori Millenium. Wellington: Price Milburn.
Weeks S., and G. Guthrie
    1984   Papua New Guinea. *In* Schooling in the Pacific Islands: Colonies in Transition. R.M.
            Thomas and T.N. Postlewaite, eds. pp. 29–64. Oxford: Pergamon.
Weiner, Annette
    1976   Women of Value, Men of Renown: New Perspective in Trobriand Exchange. Austin:
            University of Texas Press.
Wendt, Albert
    1974a   Flying Fox in a Freedom Tree. New York: Longman Paul.
    1974b   Sons for the Return Home. Auckland: Longman Paul.
    1977   Pouliuli. Honolulu: University of Hawaii Press.
Westermark, George
    1985   Family Disputes and Village Courts in the Eastern Highlands. *In* Domestic Violence in
            Papua New Guinea. Law Reform Commission of Papua New Guinea Monograph No.3.
            Susan Toft, ed. Pp. 104–120. Boroko.
    1986   Court Is an Arrow: Legal Pluralism in Papua New Guinea. Ethnology 25:139–149.
Wickström, Bo
    1979   Cigarette Marketing in the Third World. Gothenburg: University of Gothenburg, Depart-
            ment of Business Administration, Marketing Section.
Williams, F.E.
    1923   The Vailala Madness and the Destruction of Native Ceremonies in the Gulf Division.
            Territory of Papua, Anthropology Report No. 4. Port Moresby.
    1934   The Vailala Madness in Retrospect. *In* Essays Presented to C.G. Seligman. E.E. Evans-
            Pritchard, et al., eds. Pp. 369–379. London: Kegan Paul, Trench, Trubner.
Wilson, Bryan
    1973   Magic and the Millennium. New York: Harper and Row.
Wilson, J.S.G.
    1966   Economic Survey of the New Hebrides. Ministry of Overseas Development. Overseas
            Research Publication No. 15. London: Her Majesty's Stationery Office.
Wolf, Eric
    1982   Europe and the People Without History. Berkeley: University of California Press.
World Bank (International Bank for Reconstruction and Development)
    1965   The Economic Development of the Territory of Papua and New Guinea. Baltimore: Johns
            Hopkins Press.
Worsley, Peter
    1957   The Trumpet Shall Sound. London: MacGibbon & Kee.
Wright, Harrison
    1959   New Zealand 1769–1840:The Early Years of Western Contact. Cambridge:Harvard University Press.
Wu, Chong-Tong, ed.
    1982   Tourism and Socio-economic Development: Asia and the Pacific. (Special Issue) Annals
            of Tourism Research 9:3.
Yupae, Naomi
    1986   The Social and Economic Status of the ARI Monitored Population. Unpublished manuscript
            on deposit in the Papua New Guinea Institute of Medical Research. Goroka, Papua New Guinea.

Contributors

Kenelm Burridge started anthropological studies at the University of Oxford after obtaining his M.A. in Jurisprudence. He was the first doctoral student at the Australian National University and has since held teaching or research posts at the Universities of Malaya, Baghdad, and Western Australia. He was appointed to the University of British Columbia and is now Professor Emeritus. He has conducted field research in Melanesia, Malaysia, and Australia. His major works are *Mambu: A Melanesian Millennium* (1961), *Tangu Traditions* (1969), *New Heaven, New Earth* (1969), *Encountering Aborigines* (1973), and *Someone, No One* (1979).

Laurence M. Carucci is an associate professor of anthropology at Montana State University. He received his doctorate from the University of Chicago and has spent over three-and-one-half years (1976–1978, 1982–1983, 1989, 1990–1991) living with the people of Ujelang and Enewetak Atolls in the Republic of the Marshall Islands. He has written numerous articles based on this research and is currently completing a book that provides an in-depth analysis of *Kūrijmōj*.

Dorothy Ayers Counts is Professor of Anthropology at the University of Waterloo, Waterloo, Ontario. She has conducted field research in West New Britain, Papua New Guinea on numerous occasions between 1966 and 1985. Her recent publications include: *Middlemen and Brokers in Oceania* (edited with William Rodman, 1982), *Aging and its Transformations: Moving Toward Death in Pacific Societies* (edited with David Counts, 1985), and "Sweeping Men and Harmless Women: Responsibility and

Gender Identity in Later Life," in *Aging in the Third World*, Part II (ed. Jay Sokolovsky, 1985).

Frederick Errington received his Ph.D. from Cornell and is presently Five College Professor of Anthropology at Mount Holyoke College. He has conducted field work among the Chambri, the Karavarans (Duke of York Islands, Papua New Guinea), the Minangkabau (West Sumatra), and the residents of Rock Creek, Montana. *Karavar: Masks and Power in a Melanesian Ritual* was published in 1974; *Manners and Meaning in West Sumatra* in 1984; and *Cultural Alternatives and a Feminist Anthropology: An Analysis of Culturally Constructed Gender Interests in Papua New Guinea* (with Deborah Gewertz) in 1987. He and Deborah Gewertz have most recently completed *Twisted Histories, Altered Contexts in a New Guinea Society: Representing the Chambri in a World System.*

Ben Finney is Professor of Anthropology at the University of Hawaii. He has conducted research in Papua New Guinea, French Polynesia, Hawaii, and at sea aboard the reconstructed Polynesian voyaging canoe *Hokule'a*. He is the author of *Big-Men and Business in the Highlands of Papua New Guinea* (1987), *Polynesian Peasants and Proletarians* (1973), and *Hokule'a: The Way to Tahiti* (1979).

Deborah Gewertz is Professor of Anthropology at Amherst College. She received her Ph.D. in Anthropology from The Graduate School of the City University of New York. Her publications include numerous articles about the Chambri, and she is the author of *Sepik River Societies: A Historical Ethnography of the Chambri and their Neighbors (1983) and of Cultural Alternatives and a Feminist Anthropology: An Analysis of Culturally Constructed Gender Interests in Papua New Guinea* (with Frederick Errington, 1987). She and Errington have most recently completed *Twisted Histories, Altered Contexts in a New Guinea Society: Representing the Chambri in a World System.*

Thomas G. Harding is Professor of Anthropology at the University of California, Santa Barbara and served as the Director of the University of California Education Abroad Program in Australia (1989–1991). His research has focused on the peoples of island Melanesia and New Guinea. His major publications include: *Cultures of the Pacific* (coedited with Ben Wallace, 1970), *Voyagers of the Vitiaz Strait* (1967), and *Kunai Men: Horticultural Systems of a Papua New Guinea Society* (1985). Most recently, he has conducted research in Appalachia and is presently completing a book on that research.

Martha Kaplan received her Ph.D. in Anthropology from the University of Chicago in 1988 and is presently a visiting professor at Vassar College. She has conducted research in Fiji (1982, 1984–1985, and 1986). Her recent research focuses on the *Tuka*, a Fijian political-religious movement. Her publications include "'Luve ni Wai' as the British Saw It: Constructions of Custom and Disorder in Colonial Fiji," *Ethnohistory* 36(4), and "Meaning, Agency and Colonial History: Navosavakadua and the Tuka Movement in Fiji" *American Ethnologist* 17(1). She is presently pursuing postdoctoral research on British colonial culture in Maharashtra, India.

Robert C. Kiste is Director of the Center for Pacific Islands Studies, University of Hawaii at Manoa. He conducted his doctoral fieldwork in 1963–1964 with the peoples of Bikini and Enewetak Atolls in the Marshall Islands. In subsequent years, he conducted further research there and has assisted their legal counselors in negotiations with the United States government (*The Bikinians: A Study of Forced Migration, 1974*). From 1967 to 1978, he was a member of the Department of Anthropology, University of Minnesota. His current interests focus on developing nations and regional affairs in the Pacific Islands.

Victoria S. Lockwood received her Ph.D. from the University of California, Los Angeles and is presently an assistant professor of anthropology at Southern Methodist University. She has conducted research on the French Polynesian island of Tubuai (1980–1981, 1985, 1987, and 1991). Her most recent publications include "Capitalist Development and the Socioeconomic Position of Tahitian Peasant Women" (*Journal of Anthropological Research*, 1988); "Development and Return Migration to Rural French Polynesia" (*International Migration Review*, 1990) and "Capitalism, Socio-economic Differentiation, and Development in Rural French Polynesia" (*Research in Economic Anthropology*, 1991).

George E. Marcus is Professor and Chair of the Department of Anthropology at Rice University. He was the inaugural editor of the journal, *Cultural Anthropology*. His major publications include: *Anthropology as Cultural Critique* (coauthored with Michael Fischer, 1986); *Writing Culture: Politics and Poetics of Ethnography* (coedited with James Clifford, 1986); *The Nobility and the Chiefly Tradition in the Modern Kingdom of Tonga* (1980); and various articles on contemporary society and culture in Tonga.

Mac Marshall is Professor of Anthropology at the University of Iowa. He has conducted research on Moen Island (Chuuk), Namoluk Atoll, and in Papua New Guinea. He is currently working on a project concerning Mothers Against Drunk Driving (MADD) in the U.S. His publications include: *Weekend Warriors: Alcohol in a Micronesian Culture* (1979), *Through a Glass Darkly: Beer and Modernization in Papua New Guinea* (1982), *Culture, Kin, and Cognition in Oceania: Essays in Honor or Ward H. Goodenough* (edited with J. L. Caughey, 1989), and *Silent Voices Speak: Women and Prohibition in Truk* (with Leslie Marshall, 1990).

Douglas L. Oliver has worked in the Pacific since 1942 and is acknowledged as one of the foremost scholars of Oceania. In 1978, he retired as Chair of Pacific Islands Anthropology at the University of Hawaii and is now Professor Emeritus. He is also Professor Emeritus at Harvard University, and is a member of the National Academy of Sciences and of the American Academy of Arts and Sciences. His numerous publications include *A Solomon Island Society* (1955), *Ancient Tahitian Society* (three volumes) (1974), *Two Tahitian Villages* (1981), and, most recently: *Oceania: The Native Cultures of Australia and the Pacific Islands* (two volumes) (1988), *Native Cultures of the Pacific Islands* (1989), *Return to Tahiti: Bligh's Second Breadfruit Voyage* (1989), and *The Pacific Islands* (3rd rev. ed.) (1989).

Tim O'Meara is an assistant professor of anthropology at the University of North Carolina at Wilmington. He has done research on agricultural and fisheries development in Samoa and in Micronesia, and on the revival of traditional culture and religion among California Indians. Recent publications include: "Modern Samoan Land Tenure: Customary Individualism" in *Land Tenure in the Pacific* (ed. R. Crocombe, 1987); "Anthropology as Empirical Science" *(American Anthropologist, 1989)*; and *Samoan Planters: Tradition and Economic Development in Polynesia* (1990).

Glenn Petersen teaches anthropology, geography, and international studies at the Graduate School and Baruch College in the City University of New York. He has been studying Micronesian political economy and social life since 1974. He is the author of *One Man Cannot Rule a Thousand* (1982), *Decentralisation and Micronesian Federalism* (1986), and *Lost in the Weeds* (1990).

Alice Pomponio received her doctorate in anthropology from Bryn Mawr College, and she is presently an associate professor of anthropology at St. Lawrence University. She has done research in the Siassi Islands of Papua New Guinea and in Siena, Italy. Her recent book, *Seagulls Don't Fly Into the Bush: Cultural Identity and Development in Melanesia* (1992) pursues the problem of cultural identity and the appropriateness of development projects on Mandok Island.

Margaret Critchlow Rodman is an associate professor in the Department of Social Anthropology at York University in Toronto, Ontario, Canada. She has conducted research in Vanuatu in 1978 and 1982, publishing *Masters of Tradition* in 1987. More recently, she studied village fisheries development in Vanuatu in preparation for writing *Deep Water* (1989). Since 1983, she has been the editor of the Association for Social Anthropology in Oceania Monograph Series. Her journal articles include "Moving Houses" (*American Anthropologist*, 1985) and "Constraining Capitalism" (*American Ethnologist*, 1987).

William L. Rodman is an associate professor of anthropology at McMaster University in Hamilton, Ontario, Canada. He has conducted research in Vanuatu since 1969, and, most recently, in 1985. His publications include "Big Men and Middlemen: The Politics of Law in Longana" (1977) and "'A Law Unto Themselves': Legal Innovation in Ambae, Vanuatu" (1985), both in *The American Ethnologist*, and an edited volume (with Dorothy Counts), *Middlemen and Brokers in Oceania* (1983).

Paul B. Roscoe is assistant professor of Anthropology at the University of Maine. He has conducted research in the Sepik Province of Papua New Guinea at various times since 1979. His recent publications include: "The Pig and the Long Yam: The Expansion of a Sepik Cultural Complex" (*Ethnology*, 1989), "The Far Side of Hurun: The Management of Melanesian Millenarian Movements" (*American Ethnologist*, 1988), and "From Big-men to the State: A Processual View of Circumscription Theory" (*American Behavioral Scientist*, 1988).

Dawn Ryan received her Ph.D. in anthropology from the University of Hawaii and is presently Senior Lecturer at Monash University, Victoria, Australia. Her field research among the Toaripi people began in 1959 and has been concerned principally with rural-urban migration, urbanization, and socioreligious movements. Recently, these interests have been broadened to encompass consideration of changing leadership patterns, the importance of Christianity as an integrating force in Papua New Guinea, and the historical links between Papua New Guinea and Australia.

Lorraine Dusak Sexton is Senior Project Director with The Vanderveer Group, Inc., a group of consultants who conduct primary research in the health care field. Her current research interest is the analysis of cognitive structures developed by American physicians. Before joining Vanderveer, she conducted anthropological field work in Oceania on topics related to socioeconomic development and gender roles. In addition to numerous articles, she has published a book on her Wok Meri research, *Mothers of Money, Daughters of Coffee* (1986) and coedited a special issue of the journal *Food and Foodways* (1988) about the implications of changing food habits in Pacific Island nations.

Paul Shankman is an associate professor of anthropology at the University of Colorado at Boulder. He has been doing field work in Western Samoa periodically since 1966. Among his publications are *Migration and Underdevelopment: The Case of Western Samoa* (1976), "The Samoan Conundrum," *Canberra Anthropology* (1984), and "Race, Class, and Ethnicity in Western Samoa" in *Ethnicity and Nation Building in the Pacific* (ed. M. Howard, 1989).

Karen P. Sinclair received her Ph.D. from Brown University and is Professor of Anthropology at Eastern Michigan University. She has been involved in research on the Maori for almost twenty years and has published numerous articles on various aspects of Maori culture. Most recently, she has received a National Endowment for the Humanitites Fellowship to complete a book on Maori religion and the cultural construction of history.

Ben J. Wallace is Chairman of the Department of Anthropology and Vice President of the Institute for the Study of Earth and Man at Southern Methodist University. He has conducted research in the Pacific, Southeast Asia, and South Asia. His major publications include: *Cultures of the Pacific* (coedited with Tom Harding, 1970), *Social Sciences and Farming Systems Research: Methodological Perpsectives on Agricultural Development* (coedited with Jeffrey Jones; 1986), and *The Invisible Resource: Women and Work in Rural Bangladesh* (1987, with R.M. Ahsan, S.H. Hussain, and E. Ahsan).

Index